KANT ON ABSOLUTE VALUE

KANT ON ABSOLUTE VALUE

A CRITICAL EXAMINATION OF CERTAIN KEY NOTIONS IN KANT'S *Groundwork of the Metaphysic of Morals* AND OF HIS ONTOLOGY OF PERSONAL VALUE

Aliquod potius bonum mansurum circumspice. Nullum autem est, nisi quod animus ex se sibi invenit. Sola virtus praestat gaudium perpetuum, securum; etiam si quid obstat, nubium modo intervenit, quae infra feruntur nec umquam diem vincunt.

Cast about rather for some good which will abide. But there can be no such good except as the soul discovers it for itself within itself. Virtue alone affords everlasting and peace-giving joy; even if some obstacle arise, it is but like an intervening cloud, which floats beneath the sun but never prevails against it.

Seneca *Epistle XXVII*

PATRICK Æ. HUTCHINGS

WAYNE STATE UNIVERSITY PRESS, DETROIT, 1972

First published in 1972

Library of Congress Catalog Card Number 75–174669
ISBN 0 8143 1459 7

Printed in Great Britain

FOR SUSAN

Neigung vepflichtet der Seele Kräfte—
Pflicht ist der Neigung schönste Kraft

CONTENTS

PART TWO

CONTENTS

A NOTE TO THE READER

The thesis of this essay is that Kant's notions of "absolute worth", the "unconditioned" and "unconditioned worth" are rationalistic and confused, and that they spoil his ontology of personal value and tend to subvert his splendid idea of the person as an End in himself.

The rationalistic doctrine which the present analysis discloses in Kant's *Groundwork of the Metaphysic of Morals* is one which may seem so odd to twentieth-century readers that they may be tempted to suppose, 'Nobody could mean *that*!'

For this reason the analysis is conducted, partly at least, in terms of a historical comparison, between Kant's *Groundwork* and a slightly earlier, relatively unimportant *Dialogue Concerning Happiness* by the English eighteenth-century writer James Harris. Harris is a minor figure. He makes dull reading, and his arguments are, perhaps, of no great philosophical interest in themselves. But a comparison between Harris and Kant is, if the reader will bear with it, highly instructive. In his account of the "Sovereign Good" Harris says, outright and clearly, things which Kant puts obliquely and much more obscurely in his talk of "unconditioned worth" and "absolute value". This abstract language of Kant's carries the metaphysics of the *Metaphysic of Morals*. Harris's more commonplace exposition shows us where, in principle, the metaphysic comes from: and what, in the end, it comes to.

Harris is to Kant as Plato's 'same notice set up elsewhere on a larger scale and in larger lettering':

> "Would it not be a godsend to be
> able to read the larger notice first,
> and then compare it with the smaller,
> to see if they are the same?"

Let us then 'suppose that we are short-sighted men' and profit from Harris's large, clear, naive hand.

The metaphysic which this essay finds in the *Groundwork* is not simply the official metaphysic of the three great *Critiques*, though it is related to, and may throw light on the larger system. What can be found is something more local, and more domestic to the *Groundwork*.

Since there can be detected a smaller metaphysic in the *Groundwork*, and one with its own internal economy, discussion has been kept, as far as possible, to the particular text. References to Kant's other works have been kept to a minimum.

The third chapter of the *Groundwork* has not been discussed at all. The first two chapters can be, and are often enough studied by students, as autonomous and self-contained expositions of Kant's moral philosophy: the third chapter presupposes some knowledge of, and some sympathy with, the grand 'official' metaphysic and with the distinction between phenomena and noumena which is central to it. This distinction is one which the author of this essay is unwilling—for reasons outside the scope of the present enquiry—to accept. However, in so far as the distinction is presupposed as a background to the doctrines of the *Groundwork*, it has been adverted to from time to time, mostly in footnotes. These footnotes can give no more than hints at the reasons which might, in the author's opinion, be brought up to justify profound unhappiness with the phenomenal-noumenal distinction itself, and with its consequences.

When Kant asks, "What kind of a Law can it be the thought of which even without regard to the results expected from it has to determine the will . . . ?" [*G*. p. 69: p. 21: A. pp. 17–18],[1] he is asking this against the background of a notion of a will determinable by *pure* reason, a will almost if not quite noumenal. This must be understood if we are to make full sense of Kant's question. However, in so far as Kant brings, in the *Groundwork*, certain moral intuitions to bear on the problems that he raises, one may match one's own intuitions with his, and seek to controvert him on grounds, simply, of moral philosophy.

How far a local and particular metaphysic can be shown to be developed in the *Groundwork*, and how far this differs from, coheres with, illuminates, or complicates the grand, and one is almost tempted to say *sublime*, metaphysic of the *Critiques*, the reader must decide for himself—if he has the patience to go through the arguments in the pages which follow.

[1] For abbreviations used, see SOURCES section following.

A NOTE TO THE READER

The reader, if there is any such, who is not already acquainted with the whole outline of Kant's philosophy, may take this present essay, as indeed he must take the first two-thirds of Kant's own *Groundwork*, simply as a set of arguments in moral philosophy.

SOURCES

The quotations from James Harris's Third Treatise, the *Dialogue Concerning Happiness*, come from the posthumous edition:

The Works of James Harris, Esq., with an Account of his Life and Character, by His Son, the Earl of Malmesbury, London, 1801.

The *Works* were issued in two volumes and no publisher's name appears on the title pages, only the words: "London/Printed by Luke Hansard/for F. Wingrave, Successor to/Mr Nourse in the Strand [Rule]. 1801.

Volume I, which contains the Three Treatises, has a frontispiece engraved by C. Bestland after a portrait of James Harris by Joseph Highmore.

Citations from the *Dialogue Concerning Happiness* are given as *D*. [Note: Harris's typography, punctuation and use of capitals and italics are highly idiosyncratic. No attempt has been made to normalize the text, but the rococo of the 1801 printing has not been reproduced exactly.]

The German text of Kant's *Grundlegung zur Metaphysik der Sitten* referred to is the Buchenau-Cassirer edition, being Volume IV of *Immanuel Kants Werke*, Berlin (Cassirer), 1922, pp. 242–324.

Citations from this edition are given as C[assirer].

The English translations quoted from are:

Professor H. J. Paton's *The Moral Law*. London (Hutchinson), 1947, and from the translation by Thomas Kingsmill Abbott, 1873, entitled, *Fundamental Principles of the Metaphysic of Ethics:* this translation, published by Longmans, is currently available as a single volume, or bound up with *Kant's Critique of Practical Reason, and other works on the theory of Ethics* (Sixth Edition, 1909/1967).

Page numbers after citations from the *Groundwork* are given (i) from Paton, (ii) from the Abbott single volume, (iii) from the *Critique of Practical Reason and Other works* . . . volume: e.g. *G.* p. 64: p. 14: A. p. 12.

Quotations from the *Critique of Practical Reason* are from the larger Abbott volume: e.g. *C.Pr.R.*, A. p. 238.

Quotations from the smaller works, *The Metaphysical Elements of Ethics* (Preface), etc., are from the larger Abbott volume also: e.g. A. p. 306.

Quotations from the *Critique of Pure Reason* are from the Kemp-Smith translation, published by Macmillan, e.g. *C.P.R.*, pp. 379–90.

Quotations from the *Critique of Judgement* are from James Creed Meredith's translation, 1928, published by the Oxford University

Press, 1952 edition, 1961 reprint: page references are also given to J. H. Bernard's translation, published by the Hafner Publishing Company, New York 1966. The numbering of §§ differs in these editions, and references are given to both systems, e.g. §14=75 M[eredith] p. 50: B[ernard] p. 245. Similarly, *C. Teleolog. J.* §6=67, M. pp. 27–8: B. p. 225 [The pagination of Part II of the *C.J.*, i.e. the *C. Teleolog. J.*, begins anew in M: it runs straight through in B].

Note on punctuation

Throughout this essay double inverted commas are used for exact and direct quotation: single inverted commas indicate a paraphrase, or indirect citation.

Double inverted commas are also used for hypothetical utterances, those ascribed to nobody in particular, and standing for 'What one might say': such utterances are, however, sometimes put in single inverted commas when they are in close proximity to exact quotations, and might be confused with these.

Inverted commas are also used to mark the use, mention distinction; and though one would avoid these entirely if one could, there are occasional quotation marks which make the *soi-disant* point against the expression which they enclose.

PART ONE

CHAPTER I

KANT, HARRIS AND THE ABSOLUTE VALUE

Everybody reads Kant's *Groundwork of the Metaphysic of Morals* at some time in his philosophical formation, and almost nobody reads James Harris's *Three Treatises: the First Concerning Art, the Second Concerning Music Painting and Poetry, the Third Concerning Happiness*. Harris is essentially a minor figure, and he has not been reprinted since his son's handsome, posthumous edition of the *Works* published in 1801. Nevertheless the almost total neglect of Harris's writings, though understandable enough, is to be regretted. There is one argument in the *Dialogue Concerning Happiness*, which throws considerable light on one of the most complex and intractable arguments in Kant's *Groundwork*.

Harris's central argument in the *Dialogue Concerning Happiness*, throws into sharp relief Kant's difficult, and often somewhat obscure thesis that reason's "true function" "must be to produce a will which is good not as a means to some further end, but in itself". This thesis of Kant's about "the true function" of reason and of will is extremely important, but its obscurity seems to have led to its being less often glossed than glossed over. The doctrine of the end of willing ought to be brought out as clearly as may be. And it must, indeed, be brought out if we are to understand the precise nature of Kant's moral theory as it appears at least in the *Groundwork*: a theory in which teleology of a rationalist kind colours the whole of the notion of morality. Harris supplies us with an illuminating parallel, a useful and systematic clarification of the crucial argument about reason's end.

Harris was a man of parts, but hardly an original mind: David Hume found him "a good Writer",[1] Doctor Johnson

[1] Hume refers to Harris in a letter to the Abbé le Blanc:

Mr Harris, about two years ago, publish'd a Book, which he calls Hermes

thought him "a coxcomb", and was short with Boswell for venturing the opinion that Harris was "a very learned man, and in particular, an eminent Grecian":

> *Johnson*: 'I am not sure of that. His friends give him out as such, but I know not who of his friends are able to judge of it.'[1]

Whichever may be the juster opinion of him, "coxcomb" or "good Writer", Harris remains a useful man, and the moderate glow of his talent happens to illuminate, very serviceably, the shadowy corners of another's genius. Whatever his merits as a Grecian, Harris interests us as a particular kind of rationalist.

James Harris was born in 1709, the eldest son of James Harris of The Close, Salisbury. His mother, his father's second wife, was Lady Elizabeth Ashley Cooper, daughter of the second, and sister of the third Lord Shaftesbury, the author of the *Characteristicks*. By no means as able or as celebrated as his uncle, Harris enjoyed a considerable reputation as a student of the classics, and, if Johnson had some reservations about his scholarship, Monboddo and his circle had not. Harris was an amateur of music, and a fairly successful man of affairs. Though his very handsome fortune appears to have relieved him of any necessity to 'get himself a place', he became, in 1761, M.P. for

or Universal Grammar. Notwithstanding his Affectation of Greek, & his Mimickry of Aristotle, he is a good Writer . . .

The Letters of David Hume, edited by J. Y. T. Grieg, Oxford (Clarendon Press), 1932, Letter 10, October 1754, Vol. I, p. 208. Hume does not seem to have read the *Dialogue Concerning Happiness* published ten years before: his comments would have been invaluable.

[1] *Boswell's Life of Johnson*, edited by G. Birkbeck Hill, Oxford (Clarendon Press), 1887, cf. Vol. V, p. 337, [Harris 'a coxcomb . . .'], and Vol. II, p. 225. Boswell has some misgivings, it would seem, about recounting the "coxcomb" remark, but his own letter to Temple quoted as a note to p. 225 of Vol. II shows that Boswell, too, could be provoked by Harris's "style" and "little peculiarities". Just, if always sentimental, Boswell gave Harris credit for his humanity (cf. Vol. II, p. 225), and for "that philanthropy and amiable disposition, which distinguished him as a man" (cf. Vol. V, p. 378). In the Highmore portrait Harris looks, indeed, amiable and philanthropic, and a little wooden. Has Highmore caught, by this device, the priggishness that Doctor Johnson found in Harris; or is it simply that the painter, hardly one of the first rank, has failed to animate the likeness?

Christchurch, a Lord of the Admiralty in 1763, and in the same year a Lord of the Treasury. In 1774 Harris became Secretary and Comptroller to the Queen, and, his son records, "In Her service he died".

As Leslie Stephen writes in his note on Harris in the *Dictionary of National Biography*, "His books are dry and technical, but have a certain interest from his adherence to Aristotelian principles during the period of Locke's supremacy". Harris's characteristic teleologism is more rationalistic however than it is Aristotelian, and it is this rationalistic strain in him which makes him so useful an example when we come to consider Kant's *Groundwork*, with its difficult, highly compressed, teleological arguments.

Harris lived, a gentleman amateur of philosophy, and he died a philosopher, collected and 'philanthropic' to the end. His son, the first Earl of Malmesbury, writes in his *Memoir*:

> Before [his] last volume was entirely concluded, my Father's health had evidently begun to be very much impaired. He never enjoyed a robust constitution; but for some time, towards the end of his life, the infirmities under which he laboured had gradually increased. His family at length became apprehensive of a decline, symptoms of which were very apparent, and by none more clearly perceived than by himself. This was evident from a variety of little circumstances, but by no means from any impatience of fretfulness, nor yet from any dejection of spirits, such as are frequently incident to extreme weakness of body, especially when it proves to be the forerunner of approaching dissolution. On the contrary, the same equable and placid temper which had distinguished him throughout his whole life, the same tender and affectionate attention to his surrounding family, which he had unceasingly manifested while in health, continued without the smallest change or abatement, to the very last; displaying a mind thoroughly at peace with itself, and able without disturbance or dismay to contemplate the awful prospect of futurity.
>
> After his strength had been quite exhausted by illness, he

> expired calmly on the 22d of December, 1780, in the 72d year of his age.[1]

Uncommonly fortunate in his life, the author of the *Dialogue Concerning Happiness* had enough philosophy to make a seemly and edifying end.

The *Three Treatises*, the last of which we shall be considering at length in the present essay, were published in 1744, when Harris was thirty-five and the young Kant, at the very beginning of his career, was twenty.

If two men of the same period and culture produce what is in effect the same argument it is, clearly, instructive to compare their versions of it. And if one of them puts the argument in a very complex way, in a difficult text which is concerned with a great deal else besides, while the other lays the pattern of ideas out very explicitly in an unbuttoned dialogue, with very little else of substance to distract the reader—in such a case it is very useful indeed to make a comparison The strange but rather flat things that Harris has to say about the Sovereign Good help us to unravel the highly complex remarks that Kant makes about "good will" and "unconditioned worth".

Harris has very little else to offer in his *Dialogue Concerning Happiness* besides his rationalistic argument from what he calls the "Accommodateness, Durability, Self-derivedness and Indeprivability" of Rectitude of Conduct to its simultaneous identification, *as* the Sovereign Good and *with* happiness.

Rectitude of Conduct or rational willing itself must be the Sovereign Good, since it is the only good that is unfailing. It is, in Harris's words, "Accommodate", "Durable" and "Indeprivable", which notoriously the objects of will are not.

The Sovereign Good, if it is to have these three characteristics of "Accommodateness" and the rest, must be a function of willing as such; the Sovereign Good cannot be any mere object of the will, since any such external object may, for all our best efforts, for ever elude our grasp.

Everything that Harris says is either working up to this conclusion or is written to recommend it. Kant has a great deal in the *Groundwork* besides the argument that the function and purpose of reason are, "to produce a will good not as a

[1] Harris's *Works*, pp. xix–xx.

means but in itself". And the importance of the other things is such that this particular doctrine tends to be overlooked. Nevertheless Kant's *Groundwork* is as it announces itself to be, a "groundwork of the *metaphysic* of morals". And it is precisely in the argument about will as 'a good in itself' that the larger part of Kant's metaphysic lies. If we are to take Kant's title to his own book seriously, then his rationalist philosophy of will warrants our attention, and the particular metaphysics of "the absolute worth of mere will" must be gone into.

Again, more of pure ethical import follows from Kant's metaphysic than is generally allowed. In the last resort the whole notion of personal value, which lies at the root of the formulation of the categorical imperative in terms of Ends-in-themselves, is conditioned by and in a sense depends upon the metaphysic of will. The third Part of the present essay examines the derivation of personal value from the value of good will: but it is only when we know, in some detail, what good will is, and what its absolute value comes to, that we can effectively challenge the curious metaphysic of the *Groundwork*. And when it is examined we see how curious it indeed is.

Kant's metaphysical deduction, which sets good will up as the absolute value and as reason's end, parallels Harris's argument about the Sovereign Good in a very striking way. Both men argue from the fact that something is always *available* to us, namely rational willing or Rectitude of Conduct, and that something else *ineluctably follows from this* (namely "the worth of a mere will" [Kant], or "Praise" [Harris]), to the conclusion that these things, or a composite of them, are the *end* for which our reason was intended. But the arguments are more than parallel, they meet. Harris's "Rectitude of Conduct" and Kant's "good will" are both chosen as final ends for the same reasons, and the difference in terminology between Harris and Kant dissolves in a virtual identity of argument and of conclusion.

The emphasis in Harris is placed on the "Availability" of Rectitude of Conduct, while in Kant the stress is on the ineluctability of the worth of such conduct. Even so, these differences are not great enough to obscure the fact that it is the same, central, rationalistic, consideration which weighs equally with each man when he selects his candidate for the title of "absolute worth" or "Sovereign Good".

The crucial thing about good will—in at least one of the senses that this expression has in Kant—is also the crucial thing about Rectitude of Conduct, namely: that it always lies within the agent's grasp, it is always his to control. However ill an action turns out, and however far it may fall short of success, at least the agent's own part in the matter, his willing, cannot be taken from him. Though Fortune is capricious, and spiteful Chance snatches away the hoped-for fruits, yet still the agent has acted as best he might, and this remains his portion. It remains, too, his "worth" and his "Praise".

The consideration: that for all one may have failed to achieve one's end, one has willed as one has willed and that well, becomes for Harris and for Kant a principle of the most crucial importance. The metaphysic of morals in the *Groundwork* grounds itself on this simple truth: willing, not the things willed, is all that we can command absolutely, and its own goodness is the only good which lies always within the power of the will.

1. "*Absolute Worth*"

Kant's *Groundwork* is studded with expressions like "absolute worth", "absolutely good", "unconditioned", "inner, unconditioned worth" and "pre-eminent good", phrases of Empsonian ambiguity which not only colour the exposition of the categorical imperative and the formula of the End-in-Itself, but which finally determine the tone of these very notions.

Kant's "Idea of the absolute value of a mere will" and his notion of the *unconditioned* are more like aesthetic ideas, in the sense which he himself defines in the *Critique of Judgment*, than pure philosophical ones, and we shall explore this point in Chapter IV below.

Kant's Idea of unconditioned-ness holds in suspension, as it were in a swirling, liquid medium, a number of things which would turn out to be of different colours and weights if once they were allowed to settle. "*The unconditioned*" in the *Groundwork* is a powerful but hardly explicit Idea which answers to, and keeps in a kind of intuitive synthesis, the disparate notions: (*a*) that good will is the condition of the right management of life; (*b*) that duty takes precedence over mere inclination; (*c*) that whatever the issue of an action, rectitude remains imputable to the will of the agent if he acted in accordance with a rational principle; (*d*) that the moral law is not derived from private, egotistical interest; (*e*) that duty is 'the Idea of a reason which determines the will by *a priori* grounds'; and (*f*) that men exist as Ends-in-Themselves.

The central core of Kant's notion of unconditionality and of the unconditioned, absolute worth of good will lies in the considerations which he raises in the third and fourth paragraphs of Chapter I of the *Groundwork*. The argument of these paragraphs, and of those immediately following, is parallel to the argument of Harris in the *Dialogue Concerning Happiness* where he concludes that the Sovereign Good is Rectitude of Conduct: the examination of this parallel will occupy a large part of the present essay.

Seeing what it is that Harris is recommending, and why, we can expand Kant's rather terse arguments, and lay out their implications. This done, we can then see how the doctrine of the end of reason is relevant to the rest of the *Groundwork*.

It is possible to illuminate the dense thicket of the *Groundwork* with the bland if not brilliant light of Harris's arguments: Part One of the present essay will be devoted explicitly to this task. Part Two will deal with a set of somewhat loosely related issues which arise out of the text of the *Groundwork*, and Harris will be of less use and interest to us in this Part. Part Three of the essay will deal with Kant's axiology and his ontology of personal value, and it is perhaps useful to say something of this at this point, since it is the clarification and rectification of Kant's axiology which provides the ultimate aim and the *raison d'être* of this essay itself.

2. *The Importance of the Enquiry: Good will's end and the Worth of Persons*

Perhaps the most important doctrine which the *Groundwork* offers modern readers is the one summed up in Kant's formula of the End-in-Itself. Rational nature, the person, is 'an end against which we should not act', and 'one which in all our willing we must not rate merely as a means, but always at the same time as an end'. This doctrine is of crucial importance to any humanist ethic, and Kant's enunciation of it might stand alongside Jefferson's thundering political formulation as we find it in the opening sentences of the Declaration of Independence, where the inalienability of personal rights is asserted as "self evident". However, Kant's formulation of the idea of the worth of the person seems to rely in the *Groundwork* less on a self-evidence which challenges denial, than on a deduction, and on a deduction which might very well invite contention. There is at least one passage in the *Groundwork* which quite explicitly grounds the value of persons on the value of will, and this derivation seems, even at a casual reading, to be altogether objectionable. But it is only after we have explored, in some detail, the workings of rationalism and of Stoicism in both Harris and Kant, that we are in a position to put our finger on the precise things that strike us as odd in Kant's axiology.

Kant's ontology of personal value is, indeed, flawed; and we must see not only that it is, but also why.

Kant's *Groundwork*, if indeed it attempts a Transcendental Deduction of human value, largely mismanages that deduction. When we have seen what is wrong with Kant's argument, we are left with having to begin all over again.[1]

3. *Parallel or Influence?*

Whether Harris influenced Kant, whether Kant ever read Harris, I am in no position to decide. Kant could have read Harris. The *Three Treatises* were first published in London in 1744, and this edition formed the basis of a German translation printed in Danzig in 1756. Kant's *Groundwork* was not published until 1786, so there was ample time for him to have read his English contemporary.

Harris enjoyed some celebrity in Germany in the 1770s; Herder draws on him in his *Kritische Wälder* of 1769, in which he criticizes Lessing's *Laokoön*. The importance of Lessing and of Herder, and the nature of the dispute about the aesthetic categories in which they were engaged, all point up the

[1] The point of these present remarks, if they have the point intended for them, may not become quite clear until Part III of the Essay: meanwhile, there is a partial specification of one crucial point in Part I, Chapter IV, Section A.1; q.v.; see also footnote 1 to this, pp. 87–88.

possibility of Kant's having looked into Harris. There are even some notably striking parallels between the *Groundwork* and the *Dialogue Concerning Happiness*—as well as some notable, but almost predictable, divergences—which one might sharpen a little and try to present as signs of Kant's having read Harris. However, in these matters a pinch of external evidence is worth a pound of internal, and if there is any external evidence available, then I am not aware of it.

Against the possibility of influence it can be argued that Herder refers in the *Kritische Wälder* to the two aesthetic dialogues and not to the third, *Concerning Happiness*, but a conscientious, not to say scrupulous, man such as Kant might, even so, have finished the book once he had opened it—if he did open it.

Central to the aesthetic dialogues is Harris's notion of an "Energy". This idea, which influenced Herder, recurs in a crucial section of the *Dialogue Concerning Happiness*, in the very passage in which Harris seeks to demonstrate his central doctrine that "The very Conduct is the End", a doctrine which parallels, strikingly, Kant's talk about "the absolute worth of mere will". If Kant did indeed pick up Harris's book, then there is one important notion that might have carried him from the aesthetic dialogues, through to the *Dialogue Concerning Happiness*.[1]

On the other hand, no direct influence need be postulated for the parallel between Harris's and Kant's account of

[1] The "Energy" passage of the *Dialogue Concerning Happiness* (ed. cit., p. 109) is discussed below in Part I Chapter V, "The New Strange Doctrine", Section A.2, pp. 139–40.

For a discussion of Herder's use of Harris's notion of an "Energy" see Robert T. Clark Jr., "Herder's Conception of 'Kraft' ", *P.M.L.A.*, Vol. LVII (1942).

For more general discussions of Harris's aesthetic ideas see also: William K. Wimsatt and Cleanth Brooks, *Literary Criticism: a Short History*, New York (Knopf), 1959, p. 373; and see E. H. Gombrich, "Moment and Movement in Art", *Journal of the Warburg and Courtauld Institutes*, Vol. 27 (1964).

Harris is still of some interest to students of language—see Noam Chomsky's *Cartesian Linguistics*, New York, Harper & Row, 1966, pp. 15–16. (The passages from Harris which Chomsky quotes bear on the important ethical issue of freedom. Harris believed in freedom as firmly as did Kant, but did not think of it as noumenal.)

"absolute worth" and the Sovereign Good. A general similarity of culture, a common reading of Seneca, Cicero and Epictetus, and a tinge of Leibnizian rationalism in both men would account well enough for the central and perhaps only genuinely significant fact: that they both hit on the same argument and on the same "Accommodate" good when they embark on their separate, but essentially parallel and equally rationalist quests for a *summum bonum*, an absolute worth, fit to be Reason's end.

It is the rationalism and not the Stoicism which is crucial both in Harris and in Kant. Anyone in the eighteenth century could, it seems, be a Stoic. Even Hume could take up the pose and hold it, at least for the length of one essay. Hume, however, did not surround his Stoicism with the rationalist arguments so dear to Harris, and so seductive to Kant, and he did not develop the idea of a rationalist Sovereign Good, so disastrous to both.

Hume's somewhat conventional exercise in Stoicism can be useful to us in two ways: it can remind us, very elegantly indeed, of the moves in the Stoic game as it was played in the eighteenth century; and it can raise for us, coolly and without much involvement, the very issues that are heightened and brought out with some intellectual passion by the rationalism of Harris and Kant. Before we come, at length, to consider what Harris and Kant made of certain commonplaces, it may be useful to pause and see them *as* commonplaces.

4. *David Hume: Stoicism without Rationalism*

Harris's Stoicism is compounded with a little metaphysics, Hume's is not. The essence of Hume's uncomplicated Stoic doctrine was indeed to be put, by another Scot, into a couplet:

> 'Tis the pursuit rewards the active mind,
> And what in rest we seek, in toil we find.[1]

The material content of Harris's doctrine, and of Kant's, is all to be found in antique writers, and so in any eighteenth-century gentleman's library. Hume, in his essay "The Stoic: Or the man of action and virtue",[2] assembles the materials for

[1] Henry Mackenzie, *The Pursuits of Happinesss* [1770], in *The Works of Henry Mackenzie Esq.*, Edinburgh (Ballantyne), 1808, Vol. VIII, p. 70.

[2] David Hume, *Essays, Moral, Political and Literary* Part I: Volume I of the edition of T. H. Green and T. H. Grose, London, 1882 [Vol. III

a view which could become remarkably like the one that Harris puts forward. Hume balances the principle that "the great end of all human industry is the attainment of happiness",[1] against the inevitable failure of this industry, and resorts, precisely as Harris does, to the equivocal eudaemonism of *the chase*. The rewards of action, like the rewards of the hunt, are to be found rather in the action itself than in its hoped-for fruits. This hunting parallel will do for some cases: but not for all. We may hunt for sheer sport, but sometimes we do it for more pressing reasons.

The image of the hunt is a last resort, however, and Hume's moral and eudaemonistic ideal is virtue, or a kind of sociable prudence, crowned with success; a success which both arises from virtue and graces it. Hume states the matter thus:

> Like many subordinate artists, employed to form the several wheels and springs of a machine, such are those who excel in all the particular arts of life. He is the *master* workman who puts those several parts together, moves them according to just harmony and proportion, *and produces true felicity as the result of their conspiring order*.[2]

But success and true felicity are not to be had at will, simply for the price of effort. Thus, happiness is less uncertain if we look for it rather in our labour itself than any possible fruits. The ideal of a 'true felicity of conspiring order' which Hume favours yields to harsh fact, and this ideal of felicity and order gives way to the useful image of the chase:

> While thou hast such an alluring object in view, shall that labour and attention, requisite to the attainment of thy end, ever seem burdensome and intolerable? *Know, that this labour itself is the chief ingredient of the felicity to which thou aspirest*, and that every enjoyment soon becomes insipid and distasteful, when not acquired by fatigue and industry. See the

of the Scientia Verlag Aalen facsimile 1964]: page references are to the Green and Grose [facsimile] edition.

There is a note on the sub-title page of Harris's *Treatise the Third: Concerning Happiness, A dialogue*, "*Finished Dec. 15. A.D. 1741*": this would make Harris's essay almost exactly contemporaneous with Hume's which was printed in 1742.

[1] Hume, p. 205.

[2] *Ibid.*, p. 205. (Italics mine, in the last phrase.)

hardy hunters rise from their downy couches, shake off the slumbers which still weigh down their heavy eyelids, and, ere *Aurora* has yet covered the heavens with her flaming mantle, hasten to the forest. They leave behind in their own houses, and in the neighbouring plains, animals of every kind, whose flesh furnishes the most delicious fare, and which offer themselves to the fatal stroke. *Laborious man disdains so easy a purchase*. He seeks for a prey, which hides itself from his search, or flies from his pursuit, or defends itself from his violence. Having exerted *in the chase* every passion of the mind, and every member of the body, he then finds the charms of repose, and with joy compares his pleasures to those of his engaging labours.[1]

Action for Hume, or for Hume as Stoic, is, and must be, its own reward, since happiness set in anything else is essentially vulnerable. The chase provides Hume, as it provides Harris, with a possible but precarious reconciliation between 'the great end . . . the attainment of happiness' and the inevitable failures of human action. Hume writes:

> I need not tell you, that, by this eager pursuit of pleasure, *you more and more expose yourself to fortune and accidents, and rivet your affections on external objects, which chance may, in a moment, ravish from you.*[2]

And Hume the Stoic cannot help moralizing, in the most edifying fashion, on the uncomfortable truth to which he has just drawn our attention:

> I shall suppose that your indulgent stars favour you still with the enjoyment of your riches and possessions. I prove to you, that, even in the midst of your luxurious pleasures, you are unhappy; and that, by too much indulgence, you are incapable of enjoying what prosperous fortune still allows you to possess.[3]

Even if our fortune does not fail us, then our own appetites will. One way or the other, we can neither hope to possess,

[1] Hume, pp. 205–6. (Italics mine.)
[2] *Ibid.*, p. 207. (Italics mine.)
[3] *Ibid.*, p. 207.

nor to enjoy if we possess; so the prudent man will set his happiness in the quest rather than in the quarry.

Action, like virtue, is its own reward, and Hume's eloquence when he writes of virtue very nearly matches the fervour of Kant's encomiums to "good will". But, more importantly, Hume produces from the common stock notions about the intrinsic worth of virtue which recall, if they by no means exactly parallel, Kant's talk of "absolute worth", and notions which recall, as well, Kant's endlessly disputed remarks about the need for disinterestedness in all moral situations.[1]

Hume would like to set up some distinction between virtue's intrinsic value and her extrinsic value, between the worth of virtue and the worth of whatever we can hope for as the recompense of virtue. His distinction is traditional enough: virtue's value is her "charm", and what we can hope to gain from the pursuit of virtue is "glory". One might say, a little cynically, that the very least we can hope to gain from virtue is glory.

The idea of "glory" suggests that something else besides virtue's sweet self may be gained. The endless dialectic recommences, stilled only for a moment by the conjunction of "charm" and "glory", placed as it were, back to back, and facing two ways like a Janus figure.

Hume begins his account of the matter by asking the most difficult question of all as a rhetorical one, thus suggesting that he already has the answer to it:

> *But where is the reward of virtue? And what recompense has Nature provided for such important sacrifices as those of life and fortune, which we must often make to it?* virtue's 'portion' Oh, sons of earth! Are ye ignorant of the *value* of this celestial mistress? And do ye meanly inquire for her *portion*, when ye observe her *genuine charms*? But know, that Nature has been indulgent to human weakness, and has not left this favourite child naked and unendowed. *She has provided virtue with the richest dowry*; but being careful lest the *allurements of interest* should engage such suitors as were insensible of the native worth of so divine a beauty, she has wisely provided, that this dowry can have no charms but in the eyes of those

[1] See Part II of the present essay.

> who are already transported with the love of virtue. *Glory is the portion of virtue*, the sweet reward of honourable toils, the triumphant crown which covers the thoughtful head of the disinterested patriot, or the dusty brow of the victorious warrior. Elevated by so sublime a prize, the man of virtue looks down with contempt on all the allurements of pleasure, and all the menaces of danger. Death itself loses its terrors, when he considers, that its dominion extends only over a part of him, and that, in spite of death and time, the rage of the elements, and the endless vicissitude of human affairs, he is assured of an immortal fame among all the sons of men.[1]

Virtue's *value* is her "*genuine charm*", and "*glory*" is her *dowry*. Kant's "absolute value of mere will" and Harris's "Praise" bracket these two ideas almost exactly, Kant's "absolute value" falling on the side of virtue's charm and value, and Harris's "Praise" on the side of her portion. Even Hume's pejorative reference to "interest" chimes in with certain phrases of Kant's.

Hume had all the Stoic materials to hand, and if only he had been more of a rationalist, he might have produced precisely the same doctrine of the end of practical reason as we find in Kant and Harris: but then Hume was no kind of rationalist at all.

The crucial difference between Hume on the one hand and Harris and Kant on the other, is that they believed implicitly, and he not at all, in a neat and tidy teleology, a system of final causes which would inevitably provide for the inexorable realization of all ends set within itself.

The possibility of ending up with a doctrine like Harris's or Kant's would not have attracted Hume in the slightest, and he might have replied to Harris's *Dialogue* in the spirit, and to Kant's speculations on the ends of nature[2] in the precise words, of his letter to Francis Hutcheson:

> I cannot agree to your Sense of *Natural. Tis founded on final Causes; which is a Consideration, that appears to me pretty uncertain & unphilosophical*. For pray, what is the End of Man? Is he

[1] Hume, p. 209. (Italics in the first sentence Hume's.)

[2] See *Groundwork*, Chapter I paragraphs 4–7: these are discussed at length below.

> created for Happiness or for Virtue? For this Life or for the next? For himself or for his Maker? Your Definition of *Natural* depends upon solving these Questions, which are endless, & quite wide of my Purpose.[1]

One may confidently suppose that Kant's talk, in the *Groundwork*, about our misunderstanding or understanding "*the purpose of nature* in attaching reason to our will as governor", and his examination of his own idea of absolute value "from this point of view", would have been met by Hume with a flat denial of the teleological principle itself. Granted some general teleological notions, then Kant's deduction of absolute value is still contestable: but one cannot see Hume making even the first concession to the teleology which Kant treats as axiomatic.

With the Stoic materials all to hand, and with finalism in the air, someone was bound to produce Harris's doctrine, and Kant's. But it was to be expected neither from Hume's temperament nor from his principles that he should set out to revise Seneca, and erect good will or Rectitude of Conduct as "the good which will abide": "*nullum autem est, nisi quod animus ex se sibi invenit*".

Indeed, in the letter to Hutcheson which we have already quoted, Hume renounces firmly, and no doubt easily, the sorts of temptations, if not the very ones, into which Harris and Kant fell. Hume writes:

> . . . I am persuaded, that a Metaphysician may be very helpful to a Moralist; though I cannot easily conceive these two characters united in the same Work.

Hume had the materials, but he was not by any means the man to produce the rationalism of Harris's *Dialogue* or to write Kant's *Groundwork of the Metaphysics of Morals*.

The present essay is concerned to examine just that union of the characters of the metaphysician and the moralist which Hume could not easily conceive.

[1] *The Letters of David Hume*, Grieg, Vol. I, p. 33, letter No. 13, July 1739 (Italics mine); also quoted by E. C. Mossner in *The Life of David Hume*, Edinburgh (Nelson), 1954, Ch. II, p. 134. In a postscript to this letter, Hume quotes Cicero against the Stoics, making against Hutcheson a point that T. H. Green was later to make against Kant (see below, Part I Chapter IV, and Appendix to Part I).

CHAPTER II

KANT, HARRIS AND THE ABSOLUTE OR SOVEREIGN GOOD

Celui qui ne craint pas fortune n'est pas bien sage.
Ludovico Sforza: Written on the wall of his dungeon in France.

The central concern[1] of the *Dialogue Concerning Happiness* is to establish the nature of "the Sovereign Good", and the argument falls into two broad sections: (1) setting up the "*Pre-conceptions*" of a Sovereign Good; and, (2) finding a candidate to match up to these. The present discussion will be found to fall into two parts, answering to these two sections of Harris's enquiry.

Harris's *Dialogue* itself is broken into two parts, corresponding to the two large sections of the argument, the setting up of the Pre-conceptions of the Sovereign Good, and the election of the candidate to match them. The first half of the *Dialogue* breaks off, with nice rhetorical effect, at the point where it seems that nothing can be found to match the Pre-conceptions of the Sovereign Good. Happiness is shown not to be that good, and no suitable alternative has been suggested. But we are left with an image which looks forward to the only possible alternative that could be identified with the Sovereign Good seen as Harris sees it. This alternative, then, is installed in its pre-ordained niche, in the second half of the argument.

A. THE PRECONCEPTIONS OF THE SOVEREIGN GOOD

Harris's son writes, in his prefatory memoir of his father, that:

Lord Monboddo, speaking of the Dialogue upon Art, praises

[1] The greater part of the *Dialogue Concerning Happiness* is taken up with the arguments for and about the Sovereign Good, but the last two §§9 and 10, pp. 127–41 of the edition cited, are given over to a dialogue within the *Dialogue*, where the Friend F.S. recounts the "Religious Theories" of yet another friend, Theophilus, who "retained in his Discourse . . . a large portion of that rapturous, anti-prosaic Stile in which [the Muses] usually choose to express themselves" (cf. *D.*, p. 128). The religious sentiments expressed combine deistic and conventional, sentimental piety in roughly equal proportions.

> it, as containing "The best specimen of the dividing, or diarethic manner, as the ancients called it, that is to be found in any modern book with which he is acquainted".[1]

The argument of the *Dialogue On Happiness*, too, is cast in this copious, diarethic form, and a great deal of it is as commonplace in content as it is tedious in style. Occasionally one may detect the influence of Shaftesbury, but the chief sources, meticulously documented by Harris himself, are Aristotle, Cicero, and, above all, Epictetus.[2] Harris is hardly original; but, for all his borrowing of other men's ideas and for all his tedium, he has the virtue of being extremely clear on the matter of his chief argument.

Our present purpose is to examine the central thesis of Harris's *Dialogue*: the argument, namely, that Rectitude of Conduct and the Sovereign Good must be one and the same. Harris's case is clear in its articulation and paradoxical in its conclusion; it exhibits, lucidly, a structure that we shall encounter again, less transparent and more dangerous, in Kant.

Our immediate concerns are (1) to see what Harris calls "the Pre-conceptions" of the Sovereign Good: and (2) to discover what was chosen for this role of chief good and why.

Since Harris's *Works* are not readily available it seems useful to give rather longer and more copious quotations from them

[1] "Some Account of the Author", pp. xii–iv of the edition of the *Works* cited. [Letters of Lord Monboddo and of James Harris are reprinted in William Knight's *Lord Monboddo and His Contemporaries*, London (John Murray), 1900, q.v.]

[2] Harris's most often quoted sources are Arrian's *Discourses* of Epictetus, and the works of Cicero, notably, and as one might expect, the *De finibus*. His notes are extensive, covering some fifty-nine pages of the posthumous edition.

It is curious that the only occasions in the *Dialogue on Happiness* on which Harris specifically quotes his uncle are to acknowledge Shaftesbury as the source, at a remove, of classical quotations: c.f. *Works*, Vol. I, p. 38 [Aristotle, *Poetics*, Chap. 7]; p. 174 [Horace, *Satires* book 2 of Satire 7]; and p. 187 [Arrian's *Epictetus*, book 3, chapter 13]. Perhaps even so congenial a "modern" thinker as his uncle was not to be countenanced by direct acknowledgement? Perhaps he was too close in time, if not in spirit, to Mr Locke? Certainly Harris was not without family feeling as well as family pride, and the *Three Treatises* are dedicated to, and have the form of a letter to, "The Right Honorable the Earl of Shaftesbury", the philosopher's son and heir.

than one would from a better known and more accessible writer.

Some of the eighteenth-century cultural commonplaces that Harris makes use of will be noted by the way, when they occur again in Kant or contrast with what he has to say, but the rest may be left to whoever wants to read Harris for himself.

The dialogue form very occasionally adds rhetorical force to the argument, but there is absolutely no conflict of ideas. Harris as Harris gives himself very dull lines, and rarely ventures beyond "It must be owned", "It appears probable", or the occasional rather banal question, whose sole purpose is to elicit a highly predictable reply. The dialogue element can, therefore, be edited out of most quotations without distortion, and this has been done, for the sake of brevity, in a few of the passages quoted below. Likewise, "Harris" will stand both for the author of the *Three Treatises* and for the Friend, where there seems no point in keeping the distinction up.

It is easy reading the *Dialogue* to see how Dr Johnson could call Harris "a prig", "a coxcomb", 'not as a man but as an authour' and be highly scornful of what Boswell called the "affectation of Mr Harris's writing, [and his] habit of clothing plain thoughts in analytick and categorical formality".[1]

Even so, one may admire the relentless way in which Harris pursues the thin line of his argument in the *Dialogue Concerning Happiness*. The argument is painfully slow, and the conclusion of it is at once odd and conventionally Stoic; but there is instruction to be had from it, and from its painful inexorability.

1. *The Problem out of which it all arises*

§§1–2 of the *Dialogue*

After a short introduction, and an apostrophic dedication to "F.S." in section one, the search for the Pre-conceptions of

[1] "Coxcomb", 'not as a man' (Boswell glosses), 'but as an author', *Life* Vol. V, pp. 337–8 cited above; "Harris . . . is a prig and a bad prig. I looked into his book [Hermes] and thought he did not understand his own system", *Life* Vol. III, p. 245, q.v. Dr Johnson's objection in this same passage to Franklin's definition of Man, 'a tool making animal', "But many a man never made a tool; or suppose a man without arms, he could not make a tool", shows the Doctor's mind at its most unphilosophical, if one excepts the notorious refutation of Bishop Berkeley.

Bearing this in mind we can perhaps discount the second of the snubs

the Sovereign Good and for the Sovereign Good itself begins. In the second section[1] of the *Dialogue* we find the scene set, and the crucial issue introduced somewhat flatly, but not without a degree of literary polish, appropriate to the putting of so venerable a question:

> It was at a time, when a certain Friend, whom I highly value, was my Guest. We had been sitting together, entertaining ourselves with Shakespear. Among many of his Characters, we had looked into that of Woolsey. How soon, says my Friend, does the Cardinal in Disgrace abjure that Happiness, which he was lately so fond of? Scarcely out of Office, but he begins to exclaim
>
> Vain Pomp and Glory of the World! I hate ye.
>
> So true is it, that our Sentiments ever vary with the Season; and that in Adversity we are of one mind, in Prosperity, of another. As for his mean Opinions said I, of Human Happiness, it is a Truth which small Reflection might have taught him long before. There seems little need of Distress to inform us of this . . . (*D.*, p. 65.)

The great issue of happiness and its fragility has become so banal that this way will do as well as any other to open it. But it remains a great issue, for all its banality.

Harris would be a eudaemonist if he could; unfortunately human happiness is uncertain, fickle and vain. Not Wolsey's happiness only, but any man's may fail. And the scandal of this sets Harris off in pursuit of the Sovereign Good which, like sovereign metal, is not to be corroded and dissolved by Fortune's acid. Whatever the Sovereign Good is to be, it must be something above the mutability of situation, time and chance.

The problem of the transience of human goods seen as Harris sees it, predetermines its own solution. The problem

that Johnson administered to Harris in the conversation of 1778, recounted in Vol. III, pp. 256–8, q.v. However ill an opinion Dr Johnson had of James Harris, Harris was magnanimous and just enough to regard Johnson's *Dictionary* very highly: see Vol. III, p. 115.

[1] Second Section: corresponding to the §§2–16 of Part One of the *Dialogue*, in the edition of Harris cited: pp. 65 ff.

can be solved, Harris thinks, only by his finding an *immutable* Sovereign Good, and there is a kind of paradox in his first two basic moves: (*a*) he begins by setting up this mutability-immutability problem; but (*b*) goes on at once to sketch the Sovereign Good in terms of Happiness, the very thing whose transience sets the problem. Of course Harris is aware that there is a paradox here, but his whole strategy lies in accepting a eudaemonistic starting-place, and using this as a base from which to press forward to a Stoic-rationalistic conclusion.

The whole structure of Harris's argument rests on the assumption that, when certain presuppositions inherent in practical eudaemonism itself are laid bare, then we shall see the limitations of our first unreflective concept of happiness, and reform this concept in accordance with our new insight. If it is less metaphysical than Kant's *Groundwork*, the *Dialogue* is, even so, revisionary. Harris constructs an argument out of our ordinary notions of happiness: and this is an argument which will force us to revise these very notions, and which will cause us to fix our happiness, "not in the casual Prosperity of Fortune . . . but in just complete Action throughout every part of Life, whatever be the Face of things".

2. *The Dialectic of Eudaemonism and Stoicism*

"The general idea" of the Sovereign Good says Harris, "is easy and plain, but the Details and Particulars perplexed and long" (*Dialogue*, p. 66). Harris states the "general idea" in straight eudaemonistic language:

> THE SOVEREIGN GOOD IS THAT, THE POSSESSION OF WHICH RENDERS US HAPPY (*D*., p. 67).[1]

[1] The dialectic between eudaemonism and fortune is of course formulated, classically, in the oppositions, and *ententes*, of Epicureanism and Stoicism. One finds in Harris, perhaps, that resolution of Epicureanism into Stoicism which Esther A. Tiffany argued—rather unconvincingly—can be found in his uncle Shaftesbury. Harris cites a very Stoical passage from Epicurus, "the Founder of a Philosophy, little savouring of *Enthusiasm*" in support of his own definition of the Sovereign Good as Rectitude of Conduct, see *Dialogue*, pp. 112–13, and 111. (The passage is cited below, Part I, Chapter V, Section B, pp. 153–4); see "Shaftesbury as Stoic", by Esther A. Tiffany, *P.M.L.A.*, Vol. XXXVIII (1923), pp. 642–84, and Benjamin A. Rand, *The Life, Unpublished Letters, and Philosophical Regimen of Anthony, Earl of Shaftesbury*, New York, 1900.

This, we all know; but it is not so easy to say *what* it is, "the possession of which renders us happy". Even the testimony of mankind of "the whole human race" seems unreliable on this point:

> Would you not think it something strange, to seek of *those* concerning GOOD, who pursue it a *thousand ways*, and many of them *contradictory*? (*D.*, p. 67).

Harris asks.

Nevertheless Harris thinks that there may be something in this possibility of a universal testimony:

> And yet . . . were there a Point, in which such *Dissentients* ever *agreed*, this *Agreement* would be no mean *Argument* in favour of its *Truth* and *Justness*. . . . What if it should appear, that these were certain ORIGINAL CHARACTERISTICS AND PRE-CONCEPTIONS OF GOOD which WERE NATURAL UNIFORM AND COMMON TO ALL MEN; WHICH ALL RECOGNISED IN THEIR VARIOUS PURSUITS; AND THAT THE DIFFERENCE LAY ONLY IN THE APPLYING THEM TO PARTICULARS? (*D.*, pp. 67–8.)

The strategy is set. We cannot pin the Sovereign Good down beyond a very general characterization, "it makes us happy"; but if we examine the various and particular things that men take to be good, then we can discover the unvoiced presuppositions of all goodness up to which the Sovereign Good would have to measure. These various things which men value are good because of some characteristic or other. Whatever else may be true of it, the Sovereign Good will at least have the general if not the specific characteristics of each and all of these particular goods.

3. *The Induction of the Pre-conceptions*

There is a slight and uninteresting argument in the *Dialogue* to prove the foregone commonplace that "one Pre-conception is discovered . . . common to Good in general . . . all Good is supposed something agreeable to Nature". And there is another, rather more curious argument, to show that the Sovereign Good "must be somewhat conducive to that which is superior to *mere Being* [that is] . . . conducive to *Well Being*" (*D.*, pp. 68–9), but this second argument is much less interesting than its conclusion.

As we read on, we find that Harris's notion of *well-being* is oddly exquisite and luxurious.

In the long run the notion of well-being which Harris adduces is utterly paradoxical, since for all the baroque splendour of his picture of the good life Harris is to end as a Stoic. Consider for the present, how exquisite, and how opulent his notion of well-being is:

> Is there a Man scarcely to be found of a Temper so truly mortified as to acquiesce in the *lowest* and *shortest Necessaries of Life*. Who aims not, if he be able, at something *farther*, something *better*? . . . Do not Multitudes pursue . . . *infinite* Objects of Desire, acknowledged every one of them, to be in no respects *Necessaries*? Exquisite Viands, delicious Wines, splendid Apparel, curious Gardens, magnificent Apartments adorned with Pictures and Sculpture; Music and Poetry, and the whole Tribe of *Elegant* Arts? (*D.*, p. 68.)

This is all very aristocratic—as Harris indeed was—not to say sybaritic, with its "curious gardens", and long-galleries of pictures; and the ultimate Stoic irony will be all the nicer for it. This irony begins to take shape, inexorably, in Harris's next paragraph:

> What labour, what expense, to procure those rarities, which our own poor country is unable to afford us? How is the world ransacked to its utmost Verges, and luxury and arts imported from every quarter?—Nay more—How do we baffle *Nature* herself; invert her Order; seek the Vegetables of Spring in the rigours of Winter, and Winter's Ice during the heats of Summer? I replied, We did. And what disappointment, what remorse, when Endeavours fail? It is true. If this then be evident, said he, it should seem that whatever we desire as our Chief and Sovereign Good, is something *which, as far as possible, we would accommodate to all Places and Times*. I answered, so it appeared. (*D.*, p. 69.)[1]

[1] The tone of the example points up very nicely the inner dialectic of Epicureanism and Stoicism: indeed the example is so luxuriously eudaemonistic that some moralists might find it objectionable, if it were not for

The notion that the Sovereign Good, whatever it may turn out to be, "is something which as far as possible *we would accommodate to all Places and Times*" is well, if oddly, launched by the examples of opulent well-being. How well, and how paradoxically, it is launched we shall see when we come to the second part of the argument (below Section B).

Two more acknowledged goods, *Wealth* and *Property*, are cited, (*a*) as falling under this general presupposition of *Accommodateness*; and (*b*) as extending it in the direction of a notion of *Self-Sufficiency* or *Self-derivedness*. Harris then continues:

> Is it not that *wealth* may *continually* procure us whatever we fancy *Good*; and make that *perpetual* which would otherwise be *transient* . . . Is it not farther desired as *supplying us from ourselves*; when without it, we must be beholden to the benevolence of *others*, and *depend on their caprice* for all that we enjoy. (*D*., p. 70.)

As with Wealth and Property, so with Power. Power is:

> contested for . . . to help us, like Wealth, to the Possession of what we desire . . . [and] further to *ascertain*, to *secure* our enjoyments . . . (*D*., p. 70.)

Likewise, the very prudence with which some men avoid the pursuit of wealth, power and property is made to serve Harris's argument:

> To invert the whole why are there, who seek recesses the most distant and retired? fly courts and power, and submit

the saving irony. See for instance the passages of C. S. Lewis in his moral fable *Perelandra* which might have been written to fit Harris's example. At one point of the novel Lewis's protagonist Ransom reflects:

> This itch to have things over again . . . was it possibly the root of all evil? No: of course the love of money was called that. But money itself—perhaps one valued it chiefly as a defence against chance, a security for being able to have a thing over again . . .

C. S. Lewis, *Perelandra*, London (Bodley Head), 1943, p. 53. See also pp. 52–5; retitled *A Voyage to Venus* for the Pan paperback edition, q.v. p. 40 and pp. 38–41.

Harris's rationalistic and Stoic conclusions are based on a convincing phenomenology of luxury, on an acute analysis of the concept of the delightfully-accommodate.

> to *Parcimony* and *Obscurity*. Why all this, but from the *same* intention? From an Opinion that *small* possessions used moderately, are *permanent* . . . (*D.*, p. 70.)

Adding the fruits of these quite empiric considerations to the two philosophical and conventional preconceptions of *naturalness* and *conduciveness to well-being*, Harris can now fix his definition of the Sovereign Good:

> The Sovereign Good . . . ought to be something—AGREEABLE TO OUR NATURE; CONDUCIVE TO WELL BEING; ACCOMMODATE TO ALL PLACES AND TIMES; DURABLE, SELF-DERIVED AND INDEPRIVABLE.

The whole metaphysic of the *Dialogue* is, in effect, spun out of these notions of "the *Accommodate*, the *Durable*, the *Self-Derived*, and the *Indeprivable*". These are the conditions of the Sovereign impassivity of the Sovereign Good.

Rationalistic notions of teleology graft themselves on to the stocks of accommodateness, self-derivedness, and indeprivability quickly and, in a sense, fruitfully, to produce the Stoic conclusion which we find in the second half of the argument.

Human consensus has established, if obliquely, these preconceptions of the Sovereign Good, accommodateness, durability, and self-derivedness and indeprivability. And this is enough:

> It matters little how they [men in general] *err* in the *Application* [of the notion of the Sovereign Good]—if they would have that as *Durable*, which is in itself most *Transient*—that as *Independent*, and their own, which is most precarious and *Servile*. It is enough for us, if we know their Aim—enough, if we can discover, what it is they propose—the *Means* and *Method* may be *absurd*, as it happens. (*D.*, p. 71.)

Once we know the aim, the score of hits and misses is not of any great moment. Harris, however, is to take us through a series of possible applications of method to aim, and he goes on to consider a set of typical Lives before he concludes that none of them can contain the Sovereign Good. This part of the *Dialogue* can be summarized without much loss, though it will be useful to take note of a few of the counters which Harris puts down.

4. *Attempts to Satisfy the Preconceptions of the Sovereign Good* (i): §§3–8 of the *Dialogue*

Four lives are distinguished under "the two grand *Genera*, the LIVES OF BUSINESS and of LEISURE" (*Dialogue*, p. 73). These are *Political* and *Lucrative* life on the one hand, and the *Contemplative* and the *Pleasurable* lives on the other. Each of these four lives is considered, and the good and happiness of each is found to be ". . . on this *sublunary*, this *turbulent* Spot" (*D*., p. 79), neither 'accommodate to all times and places', nor 'indeprivable':

> . . . *to such a Being as MAN, with such a Body, such Affections, such Senses, and such an Intellect—placed in such a WORLD, subject to such Incidents—not one of these LIVES is productive of that GOOD, which we find all men to recognize thro' the same uniform PRE-CONCEPTIONS; and which thro' one or other of these Lives they all of them pursue.* (*D*., p. 81.)

Extrapolating from common goods, Harris produces a set of preconceptions of the Sovereign Good up to which no typical Life can match. Nothing sublunary, nothing mutable, can be the Sovereign Good, since *immutability itself* is in a sense what we are really seeking in all common goods. Harris is more radical than Aristotle, and he fixes his Sovereign Good in something safer still than the eudaimonia of theoria. Harris fixes his ultimate good in something more accommodate and indeprivable, durable and self-derived, even than the pleasures of philosophy.

Aristotle can define the happy man: "he will have this required property of permanence, and all through life he will preserve his character; for he will be occupied continually, or with the least possible interruption, in excellent deeds and excellent speculations . . .". But to define such a man, and to find one so fortunate, are two different things. And Aristotle had his own misgivings; "*whatever his fortune be*, he will take it in the noblest fashion, and bear himself always, and in all things suitably, since he is truly good and 'foursquare without a flaw' ".[1] It is just these misgivings that drive Harris to the impregnable but rather uncomfortable 'eudaemonics' of Rectitude of Conduct. While he would obviously have liked to linger, with Aristotle and the poet Mackenzie, over the picture of the possible case where:

> "The springs of action move the wheels of bliss",[2]

Harris is haunted by the equally possible and vastly more probable case "where dark misfortune lowers". And so he must set his Sovereign Good above all possibility of failure: it is precisely its imperturbability which is to make his good Sovereign.

5. *Teleology: "... to what purpose Powers?"*

A point of particular note in this section of the *Dialogue* is a teleological argument which comes at the end of the discussion, and rejection, of the Life of Pleasure: a Life, 'dependent on Foreign External Causes' and 'not suitable to such a changeable, such a turbulent Spot as this'. This teleological argument does

[1] *Nichomachean Ethics,* Chapters 10 and 11. Aristotle does not underestimate Fate's malignancy; and he too can sound a Stoic note:

> But the dispensations of fortune are many, some great, some small. The small ones, whether good or evil, plainly are of no weight in the scale; but the great ones, when numerous, will make life happier if they be good; for they help to give a grace to life themselves, and their use is noble and good; but, if they be evil, will enfeeble and spoil happiness; for they bring pain, and often impede the exercise of our faculties.
>
> But nevertheless true worth shines out even here, in the calm endurance of many great misfortunes, not through insensibility, but through nobility and greatness of soul. And if it is what a man does that determines the character of his life, as we said, then no happy man will become miserable; for he will never do what is hateful and base. For we hold that the man who is truly good and wise will bear with dignity whatever fortune sends, and will always make the best of his circumstances, as a good general will turn the forces at his command to the best account, and a good shoemaker will make the best shoe that can be made out of a given piece of leather, and so on with all other crafts.
>
> If this be so, the happy man will never become miserable though he will not be truly happy if he meets with the fate of Priam.

N.E. Book I, Ch. 10, 12–14. Peters's translation, London (Kegan Paul), 1895, p. 26. The Sovereign Good of Aristotle is not proof against the fate of Priam; Harris's, Harris thinks, is.

[2] Mackenzie, *The Pursuits of Happiness* [1770].

two things: (i) it at once shows the direction of Harris's final solution; and (ii) it parallels both the major argument of the *Dialogue* itself, and Kant's argument in paragraphs 1 to 7 of the *Groundwork*, Chapter I. Harris's case against the candidature of Pleasure for the role of the Sovereign Good runs like this:

> Besides, if [Pleasure] be our Good, our Happiness, and our End; to what purpose *Powers*, which bear no *Relation* to it? Why *Memory*? Why *Reason*? *Mere Sensation* might have been as exquisite had we been *Flies* or *Earthworms* . . . no *Animal* . . . *possesses its faculties in vain*. And shall man derive no GOOD from his best, his most *eminent*? From that which is peculiar to himself? (*D.*, p. 78.)

Harris lists the intellectual powers which in his view appear to some degree irrelevant to a life of Pleasure, and he suggests the obvious consequence: "This seems no . . . mean Argument in favour of CONTEMPLATION" (*D.*, p. 79). But where Aristotle takes this prima facie case for a life of theoria to be provable,[1] Harris rejects it in the end—he would take the tag "call no man happy"[2] more seriously than Aristotle does—and the argument as an argument for theoria lapses, while remaining potentially an argument for something else again, neither Pleasure nor Praxis nor Theoria:

> . . . but here alas: on this *sublunary*, this *turbulent* Spot . . . how little is [Contemplation . . . without Trouble or Molestation] or anything like it *practicable*? Fogs arise which dim our Prospects—the *Cares of Life* perpetually molest us—*Is Contemplation suited to a Place, like this*? It must be owned, said I, not extremely. (*D.*, p. 79.)

If contemplation even, the most indeprivable as well as the purest of pleasures, is 'not extremely suited to a place like this', then something else must be. What else, and why, anyone can guess who is already familiar with Kant's parallel argument in the *Groundwork*, the argument which begins, "Suppose now that for a being possessed of reason and a will the real purpose of nature were his *preservation*, his *welfare*, in a word his *happiness* . . ." (*Groundwork*, pp. 62–3: 12: A. p. 11). It is

[1] *N.E.* cf. especially Book X, Ch. 7.
[2] *Ibid.*, Book I, Ch. 10.

clear that Harris's argument is pointing in the same direction as Kant's: the parallel will be examined, below.

Though Harris does not explicitly take up again in the *Dialogue* this argument about 'the purpose of powers such as Reason', his whole subsequent strategy is an implicit development of it. We need do no more at this stage than note the present form of the argument, since the implicit developments of it will occupy us at some length later on.

6. "*This is to live according to Nature, to follow Nature, and to own and obey Deity*"[1]

(ii): §10 of the *Dialogue*

Harris's discussion now takes a different tack, the specification of the Sovereign Good by Lives having come to nothing. The situation of, "Every Being on this our *Terrestrial Dwelling*" is now considered: "[Every Being] exists *encompassed with infinite Objects*"; and these Objects are seen to differ in their Effects and Consequences: "some . . . are *Apt*, *Congruous* and *Agreeable* to [a Being's] *Natural State* . . . others are *Inapt*, *Incongruous* and *Disagreeable*" (*D*., pp. 82–3). Everything can be seen as either '*Agreeable*, *Disagreeable* or *Indifferent*', to some beings, these relations themselves being determined from species to species. "*Every particular Species*" is "*itself to itself*, the Measure of *all things in the Universe* . . . as things vary their Relations to it, they vary too their Value . . ." (*D*., pp. 83–4.)

This is all common doctrine and Harris is doing no more than set his scene.

§§11–14 of the *Dialogue*

Further, every animal species has a *Sense* or *Feeling* of its *Natural State*, and is *well affected* to it, and so, "to all these *Externals* which appear *apt*, *congruous* and *agreeable* to it" (*D*., p. 84). Hence each species sees objects as worthy of *Pursuit* or *Avoidance* or as worthy of neither, and thus Harris comes to a division of things into the *Pleasurable*, *Avoidable* and *Indifferent*.

Things stand to man in these three relations. If we know man's "truly NATURAL CONSTITUTION", we can know which objects are really Pleasurable, Avoidable or Indifferent. A number of the most general Aristotelian and post-Aristotelian

[1] Shaftesbury, *Regimen*, p. 6.

notions of nature are rehearsed by Harris to the same purpose, the building up of yet another ethic of Nature.

Society is now introduced, as that "without which no man could have been born, or brought to maturity", and the various needs of man are cited to demonstrate the needfulness of "some Art, the Bakers, the Millers, etc."; Harris's catalogue ends up with "Twenty Arts", to which no one man "had he even Genius", would be quite equal (*D.*, p. 80). The principle of the division of labour is introduced next, since even the Genius who might just encompass all the Arts would not have the Leisure effectively to practise them all, and Harris works up by degrees to: "a fair *Community* rising". He sees in his mind's eye, "No longer Woods, no longer Solitude, but all is Social, Civil and Cultivated . . .". Now Harris can ask the expected rhetorical question: "Can we doubt any further, whether *Society* be *Natural*?" (*D.*, p. 89). All this and more rather dull matter leads to the re-enunciation of the Aristotelian commonplace that "MAN by Nature is truly a SOCIAL ANIMAL" (*D.*, p. 91).

More and equally tedious considerations lead Harris to the point where he feels justified in announcing that "MAN is by Nature a RATIONAL ANIMAL" (*D.*, p. 95); and there follows a longish, and not entirely satisfactory, discussion of Reason, which fortunately is not much to our present purpose and can be omitted.

The whole argument has been tending slowly to the point which is summed up, in §15, by the introduction of the notions of Justice and Prudence:

> If then, said he, we pursue our Disquisitions, agreeably to this Idea of Human Nature, it will follow that all Things will be *Pursuable, Avoidable and Indifferent to Man*, as they respect the Being and Welfare of such a *Social*, *Rational Animal* . . . I replied, They must.
>
> Nothing therefore in the first place, can be Pursuable, which is *destructive of Society*. It cannot. Acts therefore of Fraud, and Rapine, and all acquired by them, whether Wealth, Power, Pleasure or any thing, are evidently from their very Character not fit to be pursued. They are not. But it is

> impossible not to pursue many such things, unless we are furnished with some *Habit or Disposition* of Mind, by which we are induced *to render to all Men their own*, and to regard the Welfare, and Interest of Society. It is impossible. But the *Habit or Disposition of rendering to all their own*, and of regarding the Welfare and Interest of Society, is JUSTICE. (*D.*, p. 98.)

The calculations "regarding the Welfare and Interest of Society" are made by the "Habit or Faculty" of Prudence, on which a rational, non-egotistical, eudaemonistic conduct turns. There is a clear but altogether to be expected parallel here between Harris's *Prudence* and Kant's most primitive sense of "*good will*", a will which 'adjusts the whole principle of action to universal ends'. Both men use the same rather obvious notion in a very obvious but quite crucial way, and a parallel so nearly inevitable cannot by any means be thought significant. What is interesting, however, is that they both pass, as we shall see, from this notion to a less obvious one, and to the same less obvious one and for the same extremely rationalistic reasons.

Harris continues his exposition with a consideration of "the *Impulses of Appetite*, the *Impetuosities of Resentment* [and] the *Charms* and *Allurements* of a thousand flattering Objects" which "may tempt us, in spite of ourselves, to pursue what is both *Imprudent* and *Unjust*". All this leads Harris to the conclusion that "we should be furnished with some Habit which may *moderate* our Excesses; which may temper our Actions to the Standard of a *Social State*, and to the Interest and Welfare, not of a *Part*, but of the *Whole* Man" (*D.*, p. 99). This "Habit" is the one which we call Temperance.

Harris would seem, from all this, not to draw Kant's sharp distinction between "a good will" which adjusts to universal ends, and "that moderation in affections and passions" which—"though unconditionally commended by the ancients"—is nevertheless not, for Kant, "absolutely good". Harris sees Temperance as the habit, the psychological auxiliary of Prudence or good will, and he looks no deeper. Harris does not consider the possibility which Kant raises, that a man may be Temperate without Prudence, "without the principles of a good will", and so may be "a cool scoundrel and more abominable for his coolness" (cf. *Groundwork*, pp. 61–2: 11: A. p. 10). Like his more distinguished kinsman[1] Harris has no entry under "scoundrel" in his index. Under "self" he has "*vid. Interest, Happiness, Virtue*"; while under "Interest" Harris has among others, two entries altogether too bland and too optimistic: "Interest: all governed by . . . and Justly"; and: "Interest, Private and Public, *inseparable*". Harris's index almost matches, indeed, the urbanity of Shaftesbury's, which contains the quite splendid: "Selfishness . . . Destructive of Self Enjoyment . . . Folly of the Endeavour".

Harris is content to state his principle of action, then, in terms either of Prudence or of Temperance, since he takes these virtues to be if not virtually identical, at least clearly complementary. "Nothing can be Pursuable which is not correspondent to Prudence", and "Nothing can be Pursuable which is not either correspondent to Temperance, or at least not contrary" (*D.*, p. 99).

The only other virtue which remains to be introduced, is Fortitude, and this is brought in to make up the set. We are offered the principle: "Nothing is truly Pursuable to such an Animal as Man, except what is correspondent, or at least not contrary to JUSTICE, PRUDENCE, TEMPERANCE AND FORTITUDE . . . In tracing the source of Human Action we have established those FOUR GRAND VIRTUES which we esteemed for their Importance, the very HINGES OF ALL MORALITY" (*D.*, pp. 100–1).

This is all common doctrine for its day, and for the modern reader it will no doubt seem common to the point of utter banality. But the interest begins to quicken a little when we come to what looks to be Harris's doctrine of practical reason:

> . . . it should follow, that a *Life*, whose *Pursuings* and *Avoidings* are governed by these *Virtues*, is that *True and Rational Life*, which we have so long been seeking; that *Life*, where the *Value of all things is justly measured by those Relations*, *which*

[1] I have to hand only the 1732 edition of Shaftesbury's *Characteristicks* which though it lists "Sacrifice, human"; "savage, see Goth"; "Scandal" and "Sceptick" makes no mention at all of *Scoundrel*. Malmesbury's index to the 1801 edition of Harris is equally innocent.

> *they bear to the Natural Frame and real Constitution of Mankind*—in fewer Words, A LIFE OF VIRTUE appears to be THE LIFE ACCORDING TO NATURE . . .
>
> But in *such* a life every *Pursuit*, every *Avoiding* (to include all) every *Action* will of course admit of being *rationally justified*. It will. But *That, which being Done admits of a Rational Justification* is the Essence of genuine Character of an *Office*, or MORAL DUTY. For thus long ago it has been defined by the best Authorities. Admit it. If so, then a LIFE ACCORDING TO VIRTUE, IS A LIFE ACCORDING TO MORAL OFFICES OR DUTIES. It appears so. (*D.*, p. 101.)

This notion of *rational justification* may not perhaps be identical with Kant's "Idea of a reason which determines the will by *a priori* grounds" (*Groundwork*, p. 76: 29: A. pp. 24–5), but it certainly implies the idea of a will determined by reason, and the idea of a will which is, because reasonable then and therefore, the root and ground of the cardinal virtues.

Such a rational will might too, just possibly, be the ground of a life of Aristotelian, rational happiness. But of this, one can never have a firm assurance in this imperfect world.

Notice that for Harris there is no sign of that conflict which some people find in Kant[1] between *duty*—Moral Office, the rationally justifiable—and *interest* or happiness. For Harris a life of those things which, having been done admit of rational justification, might very well, in principle at least, be a life of happiness. If a life so rationally and so morally organized is not happy, then this is due not to what happiness is, but to what the world is not. Happiness is a rational end, but the world is not a eudaemonistic system. Harris sees no essential conflict between happiness and "Office", between eudaimonia and a Life of Rectitude, and where they run together, he rejoices at their harmony:

> As far as nothing is inconsistent with such a Life and such a

[1] Whether Kant's remarks, that only when an action is done, "not from inclination but from duty [then] for the first time [the agent's] conduct has a real moral worth" (*G.*, p. 67: 18: A. p. 16), and his passage about the amiable and benevolent man (*G.*, pp. 65–6: 15–16: A. p. 13) are hard sayings or simply difficult ones, is not part of our immediate purpose to decide: but see below Part II Chapter III, Section C, pp. 248 ff.

> Character, we may justly set Existence before Death; prefer Health to Sickness; Integrity of the Limbs, to being maimed and debilitated; Pleasure to Pain; Wealth to Poverty; Fame to Dishonour; Free Government to Slavery; Power and Magistracy to Subjection and a Private State—Universally, whatever tends either to *Being*, or to *Well-Being*, we may be justified, when we *prefer* to whatever appears the *contrary*. (*D*., p. 102.)

The sometimes real and always possible conflict between duty and happiness, does not trouble Harris at all here. What does concern him is something different, and no less real:

> And when our several Energies, exerted according to the Virtues just mentioned, have put us in Possession of all that we require: *when* we enjoy, *subjoined to a right and honest mind, both Health of Body, and Competence of Externals*: what can there be wanting to *complete our Happiness*; to render our State *perfectly consonant to Nature*; or to give us a more *Sovereign Good*, than that which we *now* enjoy? Nothing, replied I, that I can at present think of. (*D*., p. 102.)

But there *is* something, and "F.S." thinks of it at once: it is *absolutely secure possession of what we do enjoy*: Durability.

7. *Why Happiness is not the Sovereign Good*

It is not any conflict of principle between well-being and duty, but a defect, a flaw, in the human situation which forces Harris to decide that Happiness, in the ordinary sense, is not after all the Sovereign Good:

> There would be nothing indeed, [wanting to complete our Happiness] said he, were *our Energies never to fail*; were *all* our Endeavours to be ever crowned with due *Success*. But suppose the contrary—Suppose the *worst Success* to the *most upright Conduct*; to the wisest Rectitude of Energies and Actions. It is possible, nay Experience teaches us it is too often fact, that not only the Pursuers of what is *contrary to Nature*, but that those who pursue nothing but what is *strictly congruous to it*, may *miss of their Aims*, and be *frustrated in their Endeavours*. Inquisitors and Monks may detest them for their Virtue, and pursue them with all the Engines of

> Malice and Inhumanity. Without these, Pests may afflict their Bodies; Inundations o'erwhelm their Property; or what is worse than Inundations, either Tyrants, Pirates, Heroes or Banditti. They may see their Country fall, and with it their bravest Countrymen; themselves pillaged and reduced to Extremities, or perishing with the rest in the general Massacre.
>
> —cadit & Ripheus, justissimus unus
> Qui fuit in Teucris & servantissimus aequi.[1]
>
> It must be owned, said I, this has too often been the Case. Or grant, continued he, that these *greater* events never happen —that the Part allotted us, be not in the *Tragedy* of Life, but in the *Comedy*. Even the *Comic Distresses* are abundantly irksome—Domestic Jars, the Ill Offices of Neighbours—Suspicions, Jealousies, Schemes defeated—The Folly of Fools; the Knavery of Knaves; from which, as Members of Society, it is impossible to detach ourselves. (*D.*, pp. 102–3.)

This is all very material. Given the human situation, Happiness cannot measure up to the Pre-conceptions of the Sovereign Good, any more than can Pleasure or Contemplation. If we escape great ills, then we may have our happiness spoilt by little ones. Happiness does not endure, but for Harris the Sovereign Good *must* endure. In its endurance lies its claim to the title of Sovereign.

Since Happiness is not always *Accommodate*, or *Durable*, *Self-Derived* and *Indeprivable*, Harris cannot put it forward as his Sovereign Good. Out of this rejection of Happiness's claim to Sovereignty there arises an argument for another, and rather different pretender to the title.

This is the argument whose schema and conceptual germ we are to find again in Kant: Harris develops it thus:

> Where then shall we turn, or what have we to imagine? We have at length placed HAPPINESS, after much Inquiry, in

[1] *Æneid*, Book 2, verse 426:

Then Ripheus fell, he who of all the Trojans
Was most fair minded, the one who was most regardful of justice.

From the translation of C. Day Lewis, Oxford (O.U.P.), 1952.

> ATTAINING the *primary and just Requisities of our Nature, by a Conduct suitable to Virtue and Moral Office*. But as to *corresponding with our Preconceptions* (which we have made the Test) does this System correspond better than those *others*, which we have rejected? Has it not appeared from various Facts, too obvious to be disputed, that in many *Times* and *Places* it may be absolutely *unattainable*? That in many, where it exists, it may *in a moment be cancelled*, and put irretrievably *out of our Power*, by Events *not to be resisted*? If this be certain, and I fear it cannot be questioned, our specious long Inquiry, however accurate we may believe it, has not been able to shew us a *Good*, of that Character which we require; a Good *Durable, Indeprivable and Accommodate to every* Circumstance—Far from it—Our Speculations (I think) rather lead us to that *low Opinion* of Happiness, which you may remember you expressed, when we first began the subject. They rather help to prove to us, that instead of a *Sovereign Good*, it is the more probable sentiment, *there is no such Good at all*. I should indeed, said I, fear so. For where, continued he, lies the difference, whether we pursue what is *congruous* to Nature, or not *congruous*; if the *Acquisition* of *one* be as *difficult*, as of the other, and the *Possession* of *both* equally *doubtful and precarious*? If *Caesar* fall, in attempting his Country's Ruin; and *Brutus* fare no better, who only fought in its Defence? It must be owned, said I, these are melancholy Truths and the Instances, which you allege, too well confirm them. (*D*., pp. 103–4.)

The image of fallen Caesar and Brutus who fared no better, closes the first part of the *Dialogue*; and it suggests to the perceptive what indeed the Sovereign Good must be.

B. THE PRE-CONCEPTIONS OF THE SOVEREIGN GOOD SATISFIED

The essence of Harris's Stoicism is to be found in a passage of Epictetus which he prints in a note:

> Did I ever say to thee, that thou shouldst go and address, as tho' thou wert to SUCCEED; and not rather with this

> only view, that thou mightest DO THAT WHICH IS BECOMING TO THY CHARACTER?[1]

Harris's *Dialogue* takes a great deal of time and a great many words to say no more than Epictetus put into a sentence. The *Dialogue* resumes in Part the Second:[2]

> Brutus *perished untimely, and Caesar did no more*—These Words I was repeating the next Day to myself, when my Friend appeared and cheerfully bade me Good-Morrow. I could not return his Compliment with an equal Gaiety, being intent, somewhat more than usual, on what had passed the day before. Seeing this, he proposed a Walk in the Fields. The Face of Nature said he, will perhaps dispel these Glooms. No assistance on my part, shall be wanting, you may be assured. I accepted his Proposal; the Walk began; and our former Conversation insensibly renewed.
>
> Brutus, said he, *perished untimely, and Caesar did no more*—It was thus as I remember, not long since you were expressing yourself. And yet suppose their Fortunes to have been exactly parallel—Which would you have preferred? Would you have been *Caesar* or *Brutus*? *Brutus*, replied I, beyond all Controversy. He asked me, Why? Where was the Difference, when their Fortunes, as we now supposed them, were considered as the *same*? There seems, said I, abstract from their *Fortunes*, something, I know not what, *intrinsically preferable* in the Life and Character of *Brutus*. If that, said he, be true, then must we derive it, not from the Success of his Endeavours, but from their *Truth* and *Rectitude*. He had the Comfort to be conscious that his Cause was a just one. It was impossible the other should have any such Feeling. I believe, said I, you have explained it. (*D.*, pp. 105–6.)

Truth and Rectitude are two-faced notions here: Brutus, and our preference for his fall over Caesar's if we had to choose either for ourselves, determines our attitude to what Harris is

[1] Harris's own construe of a passage in Bk. III, c. 24 of Arrian's *Epictetus*: cf. Harris's note XXVII, p. 169 of the edition of the *Works* cited.

[2] There is no §1 to this Part: the division into §§ begins, on page 110 of the edition cited, with §2.

about. But something else, a notion of indeprivability and ineluctability, determines the design for Harris himself. The notion of the indeprivability of Rectitude weighs rather more with Harris here than does the "Comfort" that the consciousness of righteousness assuredly brings even to the unfortunate.

We would, if failure were inevitable anyhow, all prefer failure with honour to failure with dishonour. We would prefer the fate of Brutus to the fate of Caesar. Harris exploits our well-bred moral preferences nicely in getting us to accept Rectitude of Conduct as the Sovereign Good. But this is not all he does; and his next passage is absolutely crucial. The special argument from rationalism to Stoicism lies here:

> Suppose then, continued he, (it is but merely an Hypothesis) suppose, I say, we were to place the SOVEREIGN GOOD *in such a Rectitude of Conduct—in the CONDUCT merely, and not in the Event.* (*D.*, p. 106.)

This argument for Rectitude of Conduct as the Sovereign Good does not turn, as the Brutus-image and our acceptance of it do, on the *Rectitude* of righteous conduct, but *on its being something that is always open to us to attempt.* The whole point is that Conduct lies within our will and competence in a way in which the "Event", that is, success, does not. We can be deprived of success, the effort can fail; but we can always make the effort. The effort of a rational and so righteous will is always accommodate and self-derived: and our having tried is indeprivable.

In Rectitude of Conduct alone, in short, can we find something 'Accommodate to all times and places Self-Derived, and Indeprivable':

> Suppose we were to fix our HAPPINESS, *not in the actual Attainment* of that Health, that Perfection of a Social State, that fortunate Concurrence of Externals, which is congruous to our Nature, and which we have a Right to pursue; but solely fix it *in the mere DOING whatever is correspondent* to *such an End*, even tho' we *never* attain, or are near attaining it. (*D.*, p. 106.)

If the Sovereign Good is to be "Indeprivable", then we had

better fix our happiness in "*the mere Doing*", that is, accept as the Sovereign Good the very effort to do whatever can be 'rationally justified' in the circumstances in which we find ourselves.

As Harris asks, a few pages later in the *Dialogue*, "Can there be any *Good* so *Durable* as the power of always doing Right"? (*Dialogue*, p. 110).

"*Doing*" is all that we can command; and when success fails us, then at least our having tried cannot be taken away from us. Unlike the end we aim at, the "Doing" itself is quite independent of 'the fortunate Concurrence of Externals':

> In fewer words—what if we make our Natural State *the Standard only to determine our Conduct*; and place our Happiness *in the Rectitude of this Conduct alone*?—On such an Hypothesis (and we consider it as nothing further) we should not want a *Good* perhaps, *to correspond to our Pre-Conceptions*: for this, it is evident, would be correspondent to them *all*. Your Doctrine, replied I, is so new and strange, that though you have been copious in explaining, I can hardly yet comprehend you. (*D*., p. 106.)

"Your doctrine is so new and strange", this phrase is to be taken up again, if quite independently, in very similar words in Kant's remark about "the suspicion of some high-flown fantasticality", a suspicion which he seeks to disarm before he begins the exploration of his own notion of "the absolute value of mere will", in the first Chapter of the *Groundwork*, paragraph 4 (p. 62: 12: A10).

Harris the bland, not to say sybaritic, eudaemonist of the "delicious Wines, splendid Apparel, and curious Gardens" knows that he will have to do what he can to soften the paradoxes of his Stoicism and to bring us to accept the uncomfortable identification of the Sovereign Good, Happiness and Rectitude of Conduct each with the other.

The principle of Harris's Stoicism extrapolates, with quite devastating paradox, from that accommodateness which is what we seek in all luxuries; but this does nothing to soften the identification of Happiness with Rectitude of Conduct. For all that it may be absolutely and totally accommodate, righteous conduct may too, on occasion, be less than luxurious, and it may go quite contrary to eudaimonia conceived of in the everyday worldly sense.

The forms of Harris's argument, and his dilemma, are both obvious: only something which measures up to the *Preconceptions* can be the Sovereign Good. The one thing that does this is Rectitude of Conduct. So, righteous conduct must be the Sovereign Good. But as a conventional Aristotelian Harris has already characterized the Sovereign Good as "that the possession of which makes us happy" and since, if two things are identical with a third then they are identical with one another, Rectitude of Conduct and what-makes-us-happy each being equal to the Sovereign Good, must be identical with each other. We can follow this argument, but we may still find it difficult to believe in its conclusion.

The grounds of Harris's doctrine are rationalistic and metaphysical; we must fix our happiness in righteous effort, not piously because it is righteous, but *a priori* because it is self-derived, indeprivable and accommodate. The psychological implausibility of the Sovereign Good, 'that the possession of which makes us happy', turning out to be bare Rectitude of Conduct is something that we shall have to swallow, along with the curious fate of the argument from luxury and from utterly hedonic "Accommodateness" with which Harris begins. The best Harris can do for us is to dilute the paradox sufficiently for us to get it down.

It is not Harris's fault that the only durable, the only indeprivable, self-derived and accommodate thing should turn out to be Doing, or Rectitude of Conduct. This is just the human condition. We have, always, as Harris insists, 'the Right to pursue what is congruous to our nature', that is we have the right *to pursue what will procure our happiness in the ordinary sense*. But we cannot expect that we will always obtain what we pursue. Not success alas, but only righteousness remains always within our grasp,[1] and we had better fix our

[1] Unrighteousness too, of course, is always within our grasp. But it would be impossible, without being totally perverse, to construct a parallel argument for unrighteousness as the Sovereign Good/Bad. To do so, one would have to insert the diabolist's "evil be thou my good" as a principle. We know that wicked steps towards what we want may fail just as easily

happiness in what we can be sure of. Harris can argue, as he does later on, that this hard truth is neither as hard as it seems, nor as little acknowledged by the natural man in his ordinary notions about happiness as we might at first imagine. Even so, the best that Harris can hope to do, and the best that he claims to do in the end, is to mitigate a little the paradox of finding a Sovereign Good which identifies Happiness and bare Rectitude of Conduct with one another in itself.

1. *Conduct and Praise*

The Stoic end must lie in "Conduct", or in something as immanent: but if the immanent end is at least open to the outside world, so much the better. Harris's Stoic might say with Home's Douglas:

"Dead or alive, let me be renown'd!"

Reknown lies outside the agent, but its seeds are within him; so, cut off in the flower of his youth, Douglas can say:

"Some noble spirits, judging by themselves,
May yet conjecture what I might have prov'd,
And think life only wanting to my fame"[1]

as virtuous ones: but wickedness for its own sake, while attainable, is not the sort of thing that a rational agent would want to attain. Wickedness must succeed, or it loses its point. As Sydney Smith put it, "To do wrong and gain nothing by it, is surely to add folly to fault". "Gunpowder Plot Anniversary, Sermon to the Mayor and Corporation at Bristol, 1829", quoted by Hesketh Pearson, *The Smith of Smiths*, London (Right Book Club), n.d., Chapter IX, p. 193.

[1] *Douglas*, by John Home, Act V, Line 87, Douglas's soliloquy; and Act V, ll. 212 ff., his death speech. (The play was first acted in Edinburgh on the 14th December, 1756.) [Lord Monboddo wrote to Harris, in a letter of 28th September, 1769:

> And it is an ill sign of our taste in dramatic writing that so few discoveries are to be found in our English plays. There is however one in a late play, I mean the tragedy of *Douglas*, which I think is most happily executed, and exceeds anything of the kind I know, either ancient or modern, without excepting even the famous discovery in the *Oedipus Tyrannus* mentioned by Aristotle as a model of the kind . . . I do not know whether you have read the play, but if you have not, I desire you would.

Monboddo recommended *Douglas* for its dramatic structure: but he might have expected Harris to approve it for still other reasons, though Harris

Doing and Rectitude of Conduct are, in an odd sense, ineluctable as well as being accommodate and the rest. The act, as an act of will, is always imputable, and it remains imputable, even when it fails of its end. This ineluctable imputability is independent of the intended results of "Doing", which itself cannot fail, even when the "Doing" is otherwise sterile, to be imputable to the agent for good or ill. The act may fail to achieve its end, but there is another "end" again which is ineluctable. Doing cannot but redound to the credit or the discredit of the doer. Every moral action merits praise—or blame—and the notions of praise,[1] desert, credit, merit, are notions of something which, even in a sublunary situation, cannot be hindered from coming to be:

> It amounts all, said he, but to this—Place your *Happiness* where your Praise is. I asked, Where he supposed that? Not, replied he, in the Pleasures which you feel, more than your Disgrace lies in the Pain—not in the casual Prosperity of Fortune, more than your Disgrace in the casual Adversity—but in *just complete Action throughout every Part of Life, whatever be the Face of things, whether favourable or the contrary.* (*D.*, pp. 106–7.)

Your Praise lies *in your action*—not in the mouths of men—and your action lies, essentially, *within your will.* Will, action and

would have found the last line of Anna's speech, Act I, Lines 285–90, a very hard saying. See Knight, *Lord Monboddo and his Contemporaries*, pp. 63–4,
Hume, too, thought very highly of *Douglas*:

> When it shall be printed I am persuaded it will be esteem'd the best; & by French Critics, the only Tragedy of our Language.

Letter to Adam Smith, March 1757. *Greig*, Vol. I, p. 246. Home was of course a relative of Hume's, and we might suspect the author of the *Essay of the Standard of Taste* of partiality here, if there were not plenty of evidence of the satisfaction that *Douglas*, for all its frigidity, gave to contemporary audiences. It remains an important document, and offers us useful insights into the philosophic as well as the dramatic temper of the time.

[1] Harris is not alone in his ambiguous use of "praise". Many—if not all—Stoic writers fall at some time or other into the ambiguity praise/praiseworthiness. It may be as much a matter of fortune as anything else is, whether a man *gets* the praise he deserves. However a man cannot fail to have—and so in his heart "enjoy"—*praiseworthiness*. Whether you are *worth* praising or *worth* blaming lies with you: whether you *are* praised or *are* execrated is itself as uncertain as is anything.

praise are immanent, and so they are ineluctable and indeprivable. The rationalist preconceptions of Harris could not be satisfied any more fully than that!

The notion of indeprivability, and its role as a ground for the choice of "Doing" and of "Action" as the Sovereign Good, require no further illustration. The notion of ineluctability, here in germ in Harris's remark about "Praise", leads us at once to Kant's argument; it leads us to the pregnant third paragraph of the first section of the *Groundword*, a passage which parallels quite remarkably the arguments from Harris which we have been considering.

CHAPTER III

THE ARGUMENT IN KANT: I

L'habitude de la vertu est la seule que vous puissiez contracter sans craint pour l'avenir. Tôt ou tard les autres sont importunes.

Diderot (*Le Père de Famille*)

Kant argues through the fourth to the eighth paragraphs of Chapter I of the *Groundwork* that: "the purpose of Nature in attaching reason to our will as governor" (*G.*, p. 62: p. 12: A. pp. 10–11) is *that each reasonable agent may produce "a will good in itself"*. This is an important doctrine, though it is one often passed over by readers anxious to get on to what they take to be the real business of the *Groundwork*, the enunciation of the categorical imperative cast in terms of the question, "Can I will this maxim of action universally?"

The teaching about the end of will is important because both the formulation of the categorical imperative in terms of universalizability, and the "Formula of the End-in-itself" are themselves conditioned, in different ways, by certain notions of *absolute value* and by notions of *unconditionality* which arise out of this doctrine of will and its end.

Kant's idea of "the absolute value of mere will" must be understood if we are to see what he meant by the categorical imperative itself in at least two of its formulations—and in all of them if they all stand together.

A. THE IMPORTANCE OF THE DOCTRINE OF THE END OF WILLING

There are a number of important issues which depend wholly or in part on Kant's doctrine of the end of willing, and if they are to be profitably understood, so then must it be. It may be useful at this point to expand on the remarks already made in the General Introduction to this present essay, above, Chapter I, Section 2.

It would be to prejudge the whole question of what the *Groundwork* is about to suppose, as is sometimes nowadays done at any rate implicitly, that the logical formulation of the categorical imperative in terms of universalization and the test of contradiction is the real core of it. An equal, and better, case could be made for the formulation in terms of the person as End, since the person is *a*, if not indeed *the*, crucial factor in all live cases where we must decide whether or not maxim *m* can in fact be universally willed. "If I willed this universally, what then would happen, *and to whom*?" And "to whom" does not ask a question expecting any particular, favoured, proper name for an answer: any person's designation will count, morally. Whatever Kant himself may have thought about the matter, it is obvious to anyone who uses his ethical test: "Can I will this maxim universally?", that what counts against a bad maxim is not simply the "contradiction", or even the systematic confusion, that would follow from its universal adoption, *but this confusion seen as affecting persons*. We live as persons among persons: not simply as observers of, or ciphers in, some elegant formal system whose chief, if negative, aim, is to avoid all internal self-contradition. Nor, if one restated the aim of a pure system positively in terms not of avoiding contradiction but of achieving harmony, would the thing have any ethical point, or any bite on our conduct, unless it was made quite explicit that the harmony was to be valued as a harmony of and for *persons*.

Kant's own notion of a Kingdom of Ends is, or should be, more than the notion of a formal system of non-contradictory and mutually compatible maxims.

A Kingdom of Ends is a systematic set of relations between persons, and while the formulation of the categorical imperative in terms of the avoidance-of-contradiction-in-willing may answer to the element of *system*, the formula of the End-in-itself answers to the persons of whom, and for whom, the system *is*.

Furthermore, to take a wide cultural view, the formulation of the categorical imperative in terms of "the rational being who exists as an End in himself" (*Groundwork*, p. 95, etc.: p. 55, etc.: A. p. 46, etc.) is likely to seem more important to modern readers, brought up on existentialist ethics, than is the bare 'logical' formula of universalizability. And anyone who set out to recommend Kant to our contemporaries, and to represent him in the most favourable light, would be advised to stress the principle of the *End-in-itself*.

If, as we suggest, both the cases where we can find a neat systematic contradiction, and the ones where we cannot, depend finally on *our figuring to ourselves the maxim as universalized and so having consequences for persons*, then the modern predilection for *I* and *Thou* rather than I and Contradiction-Averted is not simply a matter of contingent cultural fashion, but answers to something in the nature of the case.

Not only are we all, in a sense, existentialists, people living according to situational and personalist ethics, but we all ought to be, too.

The "contradiction" of bad willing, if we must use this notion, lies oftener in *me, a person, willing to do to another what I would not tolerate in my own person*, than it lies in my willing to use a system, for example, the system of promising, in such a way as inevitably to undermine it, or, more bloodlessly, in such a way as to 'contradict my own will'.

What is any mere *system* to me that I cannot undermine it if it suits me? This question shocking perhaps to some, can be answered only in terms of the existence, and so the value, of any system, for example, the promise-system, as a social artefact. A social arrangement of this kind has a value for the persons who make use of it and therefore it is not within my competence, my moral competence, to disrupt it at will.

Promising and promise-keeping have value not because they constitute a system, but because the system is one of value to, and serving the value of, persons.

The "existential" formula cast in terms of the Ends-in-themselves, Beings-against-whom-we-must-never-act, is bound up in a special way with Kant's notions about absolute worth and (as we shall see in Part III of the present essay) the definitions of *absolute value* which Kant sets up in Chapter I are recalled, both specifically and by the symptomatic repetition of crucial phrases, when he comes to expound the doctrine of the absolute value of the person in his Second Chapter (*Groundwork*, pp. 95–6, 105: pp. 55–6, 65: A. pp. 46–7, 53). As we shall argue, it looks there as though Kant spoils, or comes close to spoiling, his doctrine of *absolute personal value* by grounding it in the altogether doubtful metaphysic of his doctrine of *absolute value*.

We may compare Kant in this matter, as we have already suggested, above Chapter I, Section 2, with another representative figure of the Enlightenment, the author of the most lucid and elegant perhaps of all the documents of the era, the Declaration of Independence. Jefferson's doctrine of personal value rests on its own self-evidence, quite without metaphysical embroilments. This, at least, is the way he presents it. He writes:

> We hold these truths to be self evident, that all men are created equal, that they are endowed by their Creator with inherent and unalienable rights, that among these are life, liberty, and the pursuit of Happiness.

Anyone who denies the evidence of these truths must deny *them*, if he can, as they stand compelling and obvious to every man of sense.

Kant's idea of the value of the person is not allowed to present itself simply as evident. It seems to rest on, and at all events is propounded in the *Groundwork* in the context of, a whole metaphysic of morals. The particular metaphysic must at least be noticed before we appropriate the notion of personal value for our own contemporary uses.

We cannot ignore the doctrine of the end of reason in favour of the 'logical' part of the *Groundwork*, because the formula of the End-in-itself is, in the end, more important than the 'logical' formulation of the categorical imperative, and the doctrine of the end of reason has an important bearing on the notion of Ends. The two ideas are, at times, in occult competition with each other, and as they scramble for priority, Kant comes down, it seems, for the wrong contender.

The doctrine of the end of reason is of the utmost importance to our understanding of the formula of the End-in-itself, since our philosophical task may be—and I shall maintain that it is—to disembroil the notion of the End-in-itself from just those metaphysical entanglements in which the doctrine of the end of reason involves it.

We may feel no particular need for a rationalistic metaphysic of morals to support our principle of personal value.

But what we need, and what Kant had and what he presumably thought he needed, are quite different things. The difference ought to be frankly acknowledged.

All these considerations aside, the notion that the *telos* of reason is good will is already perhaps sufficiently interesting on its own account, and its discussion needs no further justification.

B. THE DOCTRINE OF THE END OF REASON

1. *The Function of Reason*

The conclusion of Kant's argument in the seventh paragraph of Chapter I of the *Groundwork* is this:

> [Reason's] true function must be to produce a will which is *good* not as a *means* to some end, but in itself. (*G.*, p. 64: p. 14: A. p. 12.)

The argument itself has two elements (i) the presupposition of a teleological principle,[1] and (ii) the putting up of an apt candidate for the role of end of reason, where such a role is structured in advance by rationalist teleologism.[2]

[1] Hume thought reasoning from final causes "pretty uncertain & unphilosophical" (cf. above p. 30): Kant did not, as is evident from his *Critique of Teleological Judgement.* Whether the teleological argument in the *G.* is hedged sufficiently by Kant's own principle that "*The conception of an objective finality of nature is a critical principle of reason for the use of the reflective judgement*" [Headnote to §14=75 M. p. 50: §75 B. p. 245] is too large an issue to go into here. Kant's whole concept—his family of concepts—of *finality* would need to be thoroughly explored, along with his notion of ". . . the practical purposiveness which pure reason imposes on us". *C.P.R.* A. 817 B. 845, K.–S. edition, p. 643.

[2] The candidate for the end of reason which Kant puts up in the *Metaphysical Elements of Ethics* is essentially a rationalistic one: ". . . *fortitudo moralis* constitutes the greatest and only true martial glory of man; it is also called the true *wisdom*, namely the practical, because it makes the *ultimate end* [= final cause] of the existence of man on earth its own end. Its possession alone makes man free, healthy, rich, a king, &c., nor can either chance or fate deprive him of this, since he possesses himself, the virtuous cannot lose his virtue", A. p. 317. This must, of course, be set against Kant's more Christian and less purely Stoic notions on virtue and its consequences.

In Kant the teleological principle is explicit, he writes: "Nature in distributing her aptitudes has everywhere else gone to work in a purposeful manner" (*G.*, p. 64: p. 14: A. p. 12), and so she must therefore have a purpose here, in attaching reason to our will. In Harris as we have seen (Chapter II, Section A.5), the doctrine of the teleology of reason is explicit in one place only, that is in the rehearsal of the unsuccessful argument for the view that the Life of Contemplation is the Sovereign Good. This argument in favour of theoria is rejected, as the reader will recall, because even the life of contemplation can be destroyed by the cruel strokes of Fate, and were contemplation the end of life, the teleology would not seem inexorable enough. A less than inexorable teleology is none at all for Harris, and contemplation is rejected as an ultimate end, and the election to the throne of the Sovereign Good is made in favour of mere righteous willing as such. "*Conduct*" as Harris calls it is the Sovereign Good, since in "Conduct" alone have we something that is "Accommodate, Self-derived and Indeprivable".

When Harris says that the Sovereign Good is Rectitude of Conduct, and Kant that the purpose of reason is the production of *good will*, it may not be at once evident that they are both saying the same thing. However, if we look at the reasons which each adduces, and at the considerations which each brings forward to support his central notion, it is apparent that righteous conduct and good will are virtually identical for a good part of their connotations, and perhaps for all the part that is really significant.

The considerations which are brought forward to support the notions of the *Sovereign Good* and *good will* do more than simply support, they radically define these ideas. Two notions which have the same radical definitions must come to the same, however much their labels differ. The two contexts of definition, Harris's and Kant's, are siblings of the same union: by Stoicism out of rationalism.

Harris produces his argument largely by his induction of the "Pre-conceptions" of all acknowledged sorts of goodness: Kant produces his by staking everything on his teleological principle, but the difference between the two men is slighter than it might appear, and the argument is the same, for all that it has two presentations.

2. *Good will and, or as, the Ineluctable Good*

The *Groundwork* might very well have carried as its motto, these lines:

> "Dost thou love watchings, abstinence and toil,
> Laborious virtues all? Learn them from Cato:
> Success and fortune thou must learn from Caesar."[1]

The crux of Kant's argument for the conclusion that *the purpose of reason is the production of good will* lies in the passage which Professor Paton in his edition heads "The Good Will and its Results" (*G.*, p. 62), though this section might, with more justice, be titled, "The Good Will and the irrelevance of any results". Here is the crucial passage, dense and complex. It is a piece of philosophizing which ought to be read with great care, since it defines, effectively, that "good will" which is, according to Kant, reason's end:

> A good will is good not because of what it effects or accomplishes—because of its fitness* for attaining some proposed end: it is good through its willing alone—that is, good in itself . . .[2] Even if, by some special disfavour of destiny or by the niggardly endowment of step-motherly nature, *this will is entirely lacking in its power to carry out its intentions; if by its utmost efforts it accomplishes nothing*, and only good will is left (not, admittedly, as a mere wish, but as the straining of every means so far as they are in our control); even then

[1] Joseph Addison, *Cato*, Act II, Sc. I (Cato to Juba) [Published in 1713; in French, 1767; and in German in 1735].

[2] The sentence omitted from this passage raises special problems of its own which we consider below in Chapter IV, Section A. 8(i), pp. 102 ff.

One could query Kant's phrase in the first sentence quoted "not . . . because of its *fitness** for some proposed end". An effort must, surely, to be jewel-like, be *fit* in some general way for obtaining some end, even if it does not in fact attain it. To merit credit for trying to do *x* we must take the sort of steps that might reasonably be expected to produce *x*, whether in fact they do so or not on a particular occasion. See below Part II, Chapter III. "Fitness" is indeed, if not all, yet, still necessary: it is necessary even to "the absolute value of mere will"; see below *passim*, and see Appendix to Part I.

> it would still shine as a jewel for its own sake *as something which has its full value in itself* . . . (*G.*, p. 62: p. 11: A. p. 10; Italics mine.)

Now in fact "Step-motherly Nature" makes it quite certain that some at least of even our utmost efforts will fail. So it is safest, with Harris, to:

> . . . suppose the worst success to the most upright Conduct. (*D.*, p. 102.)

and:

> to place the SOVEREIGN GOOD in . . . *a Rectitude of Conduct—in the* CONDUCT merely, and not in the Event. (*D.*, p. 106.)

And this is precisely what Kant, too, is advising us to do.

Kant's paragraph defines, as we have said, a notion of "good will". The crucial consideration, the defining phrase, is the first of the two in italics. A good will, in the sense at issue here, is what *is* or *exists as soon as an effort has been made to realize* [*a good*][1] *intention*; "even if by its utmost efforts it accomplishes nothing", the will has "accomplished" its own goodness. Good will is what exists, then, independently of the success or failure of the act itself. Or, to use Harris's terms, good will lies in the "Conduct" and not in the "Event", and for this reason it must be the Sovereign Good. Conduct, the righteous 'straining of every means', unlike the Event, is always accommodate, self-derived and indeprivable. The *immanent good of the good will* is, *because immanent, always assured.*

Kant's specification of "good will" as "not a mere wish but the straining of every means" makes it neatly equivalent to Harris's Rectitude of Conduct. And the same considerations of final causality weigh with each man, to make one choose *Rectitude of Conduct* as his Sovereign Good, and the other choose *good will* as reason's end.

Both are rationalists, at least to the extent that they believe implicitly that the end or ultimate value of the rational, moral,

[1] Of course good will, in the sense of merit, supervenes only on a good intention. The precise force of this point will emerge in the course of our argument.

life must be something that cannot fail. The only thing which cannot fail is "good will" or "Conduct", seen not as an end-seeking function but rather as a pure immanent function of human rationality as such. Hence this "Conduct" must be, for Harris and Kant, the ultimate, pre-ordained good.

The virtual identity of the two men's notions is brought out a little further in a phrase of Harris's which follows shortly on the one about placing the Sovereign Good in the Conduct not in the Event:

> The Doctrine amounts all . . . but to this—place your *Happiness* where your Praise is. (*D.*, p. 106.)

We have already encountered this notion of Praise at the end of our last chapter, and we must now fit it formally into the Kantian context.

Harris's "placing" of Happiness has no analogue in the paragraph of Kant's which we are considering,[1] but the notion of Praise has an exact analogue. Harris's notion of *Praise* parallels the second of the phrases italicized in Kant, the last line of the paragraph quoted, where he says that good will is "something which has its full value in itself", and both "Praise" and "good will" can be brought together under the neutral and common idea of *ineluctability*.

Praise,[2] and Kant's 'jewel-like sheen', a value which is 'full in itself', are identical in that they are the *ineluctable* results of righteous action, or to be more precise, of righteous willing. Praise and the jewel-like sheen accrue whether or not the will flowers into the achievement of an external action. Whatever can be hindered from coming-to-be, praise, or to be exact, praiseworthiness and the jewel-like sheen of the righteous act itself, cannot. Not only are they ineluctable; they have a unique ontological status, because they are immanent in the will of the agent ("self-derived"), and do not depend on those

[1] There is however some parallel to Harris's "Placing" of our happiness in Righteous Conduct in one of Kant's later remarks; ". . . reason which recognizes its highest practical function the establishment of a good will, in attaining this end is capable only of its own *peculiar kind of contentment* . . ." (*G.*, p. 64: p. 14: A. p. 12).

[2] Or, to be precise, *Praiseworthiness*, since one can sometimes merit praise and not get it, except from oneself. The tension between "*Praise*" and *praiseworthiness* runs, of necessity it seems, through all Stoic systems.

outside circumstances which govern the possible coming-to-be or failure-to-be of an act's external consequences. Praiseworthiness is the only 'ontological necessity' that human agents can command, the only thing whose existence they can infallibly cause.

The notion of ineluctability is perhaps stronger and more sharply defined in Kant than it is in Harris, and it accounts, as we shall see in detail later, for Kant's splitting of the general notion of good will into two polarized senses, a fatal division which occurs in the early part of Chapter I of the *Groundwork*, and which carries through, with unfortunate consequences, to the accounts which he gives of the categorical imperative, and of the person as End.

Harris has the notion of ineluctability in the idea of "Praise", and of course, it is there potentially, in the notions which lead him to make his remark about Praise. Kant has the notion of ineluctability and stresses it.

We find the Kantian notion of ineluctability not only in the passage we are considering, but later in the *Groundwork* (paragraph 16; p. 62: 20: A. p. 17), in a very important phrase when he is talking about "*that pre-eminent good which we call moral*". There, in the later passage, Kant seems in danger of defining the *moral* goodness of that "pre-eminent good" just in terms of a notion of ineluctability. Moral good is, for Kant, "a good which is *already present in the person acting* . . . and has *not to be awaited merely from the result*". Kant throws the emphasis on the ineluctability of the value of moral action, and this fact is crucial to the whole understanding of what he has to say: this matter of the good which does not need to be awaited, and Kant's use of the idea of it in paragraph sixteen will be referred to a number of times in the course of the essay: see Table I at the end of Part I, Chapter IV.

Ineluctability is a presiding idea both in the *Dialogue* and in the early paragraphs of the *Groundwork*: what Harris is after is precisely this thing which he and Kant find: something which can *be*, and can *come-to-be*, as an immanent result of human action, despite the chances and ill-success to which the external results of action are for ever liable. That this thing is moral is, in the last resort, less central to its election as the Sovereign Good than is the fact that it is ineluctable.

In a sense Harris and Kant are simply writing variations on Cicero's theme, "*virtue is its own reward: officii fructus sit ipsum officium*",[1] but they are very rationalistic, philosophical variations. Harris begins with classical, world-weary reflections on the mutability of the human condition, but he glides insensibly into a teleologism quite as definite if not quite as explicitly stated as Kant's, and ends up in a universe of absolutes. The idea of a finality in nature is uppermost, and sad reflections on the caprices of fortune serve only to bring out the rationalist presupposition, that if not a man's fortune then something else of his must be immutable and ineluctable. What else could this be but rational action itself, and the virtue or merit which is engendered by the mere attempt at rational action?

This "good" is a matter of rational action persevered with, indeed, as far as human powers will go; but it is not a matter of such action carried to the point of success. We can command, not the ends that we will, but only our willing itself. Our Higher End lies therefore in willing, strenuous if need be, but in willing itself, and not in the will's uncertain objects.

3. *Happiness and the Ineluctable*

In a sense, perhaps, Harris and Kant do nothing more, as metaphysicians, than over-interpret Seneca:

> We have reached the heights if we know what it is that we find joy in and if we have not placed our happiness in the control of externals.[2]

Instead of sighing for something that is indeed 'a happiness beyond the control of externals', Harris and Kant cling steadfastly to the only thing that is internal and immanent, "good will" and its "absolute worth": "Conduct" and its "Rectitude".

Rational action itself, Conduct seen as itself valuable and shining jewel-like, is the rationalists' Sovereign Good: *quod animus ex se sibi invenit.*

If one is a doctrinaire enough rationalist, then whatever is valuable in this ineluctable way is, by that token, the only possible locus of happiness. To take the teleological principle a

[1] Cicero, *De Finibus*, Book III, Section 73.

[2] Seneca, *Epistle XXIII*, trans. R. M. Gummere, London (Loeb/Heinemann), 1917/1953, Vol. I, p. 159.

step further, happiness for the rationalist must itself be made infrangible; and it must be identified with the only things that cannot be taken away from us: the possibility of rational action, and our having acted rationally. The argument is obvious in its predestination, and even in Kant who is less concerned in the *Groundwork* with Happiness than is the amiable Harris in his *Dialogue*, we can detect traces of an identification of happiness with the 'peculiar satisfactions' of good will.[1]

Whether or not we choose to fix our happiness in it, this ineluctable value, this immanent worth of a will willing, is the only sublunary ontological necessity, and the only thing that cannot fail us. This alone should make it impressive to the mind that will not have nature's or human nature's end thwarted.

Only its low eudaemonoligical tone makes us hesitate to identify "Conduct" or "good will" with that Sovereign Good the possession of which, as Harris says, "renders us happy". Harris does not hesitate, but he is at pains to justify his identification of these two things, and to smooth as best he can the inevitable discomforts of the identification.

Kant simply elevates immanent, indeprivable, ineluctable worth to first place on his teleological scale, and to first place on his axiological scale as well, without any apology; and he notices the claims of happiness just long enough to put them, firmly, in a very second second place.[2]

Harris and Kant are, of course, facing an issue which ancient philosophers had already grappled with, the eudaemonists more despairingly even than the Stoics. Aristotle writes, at the beginning of Book seven, chapter eleven of the *Nicomachean Ethics*, a passage whose substance seems central to Harris's preoccupations:

> What is the nature of pleasure and pain? The problem is one which must be studied by the political philosopher, whose

[1] *G.*, p. 64: p. 14: A. p. 12. But see *C.Pr.R.*, A. p. 131: A. pp. 255–6.

[2] Happiness is of course given a higher place in Kant's scheme of things in the *C.Pr.R.* God is brought in by Kant, as by many other moralists, as a *deus ex machina*. And when Kant writes 'the concept of God is one that belongs . . . not to speculative reason, but to morals' the dilemma of virtue unrewarded and un-eudaemonic is—at least partly—what prompts him: *C.Pr.R*, Sc. VIII, A. p. 238. See too ". . . the *hope* of happiness first begins with religion only . . ." A. p. 227.

> business it is as the master-craftsman to set up an end, this end being the standard by reference to which we are enabled to say whether anything is absolutely good or bad. Such a study is equally essential in ethics, for we settled that virtue and vice are concerned with pains and pleasures, *while most people maintain that happiness—the summum bonum—must be accompanied by pleasure.*[1]

And it is clear that Aristotle is usually prepared to fall in with 'what most people maintain', but it is one thing to acknowledge that pleasure must accompany the *summum bonum*, and quite another to find some unfailing thing, some unfailing good, which has indeed the required hedonic tone. We may agree with Aristotle that moral virtue has to do with pains and pleasures,[2] but this will not prevent our finding that virtue itself is as often painful as it is pleasant. Virtue is far less often rewarded than we feel she should be; "If only the world were a *fair* place!"

Aristotle's eudaemonism may be more congenial than Kant's and Harris's Stoicism, but it must seem, to a rationalist, more wishful than frank. The best that Aristotle can offer us in the way of pleasant Sovereign Good is a theoria which indeed is 'self sufficient to an exceptional degree',[3] but even theoria is not quite above the reach of a destructive Fortune. The wise man may be "the most self-sufficing of men"[4] but even he can be brought down, as Aristotle himself acknowledges.

Aristotle and our eighteenth-century rationalist are sharply opposed here on the answers that they give to the unanswerable conundrum of happiness and permanence. Aristotle is determined that happiness, as it is commonly understood at least among the better sort of men, must be part of the Sovereign Good, or it is no Sovereign Good. Harris preaches a Senecan "placing" of happiness which amounts, at least sometimes, to a

[1] *Nicomachean Ethics*, Book VII, Ch. 11 (1152*b*). The quotation is from J. A. K. Thomson's translation (Penguin Books), p. 217; the language of this translation brings out more sharply, even, than does Peters's (q.v., p. 239), the close resemblance between Aristotle's conception of the problem and Harris's.

[2] *Ibid.*, Book II, Chapter 3, ed. cit., p. 59 (Peters, p. 39).

[3] *Ibid.*, Book 10, Chapter 7, ed. cit., p. 303 (Peters, p. 338).

[4] *Ibid.*, ed. cit., p. 304 (Peters, p. 339).

renunciation of it. And Kant comes close to denigrating the whole idea of happiness.

What must serve as an *end* of reason is something irrefrangible, something beyond the control of externals; this is the systematic demand of rationalism What is to be called "The Sovereign Good" must be desirable in and for itself; this is the inevitable demand of ordinary rational eudaemonism. And there is, existentially, a cramp situation: nothing seems quite to satisfy both demands.

Perhaps Aristotle's life of theoria comes nearest of all candidates to meeting both demands, but near enough is not good enough here. When Aristotle says that, "the life of the intellect is the best and pleasantest for man, because the intellect more than anything else *is* the man"[1] he provides an essential rationale for his contemplative eudaimonia as eudaimonia: but nothing can make the self-sufficiency of theoria more than relative. 'The man' is as vulnerable as his function, even when this function is pure intellectual contemplation: and external forces can make even so internal and so pure a pleasure as contemplation impossible.

When he stresses the relative self-sufficiency of theoria, Aristotle finds himself in an honourable and already old tradition:

> I loved her above health and beauty, and choose to have her instead of light, *for the light that cometh from her never goeth out.*
>
> (*Wisdom* 7. 10.)

Even so, *Wisdom* is not a eudaemonistic book in the way in which the *Nichomachean Ethics* is: nor could it be. The *Ethics* sees the human situation as a problem: *Wisdom* sees it as a mystery. Both are, in their own way, right. They are right as long as one does not suppose that to see something as merely problematic is thereby to guarantee a solution to the problem: and as long as one does not think that the mysterious view is essentially empty and evasive, or does not allow it to become so.

Perhaps the choice is between rationalism, and eudaemonism. Or, if they are to be reconciled, perhaps the reconciliation can only be Augustinian?

To put it a different way again, is rationalism in metaphy-

[1] *N.E.* ed. cit., p. 305 (Peters, p. 341).

sical ethics itself no more than the intellectual analogue of those other, simpler, more immediate pangs that we feel in a world where we cannot have what we would have, or keep what we may have? Is it the case that the desire for absolute happiness sublimates itself, so to speak, into a quest for philosophical absolutes such as the Sovereign Good and Kant's good will? If this is indeed the case, then sublimation is less creative here than it is elsewhere in man's affairs.

C. THE TWO NOTIONS OF GOOD WILL

Whatever may be the ultimate roots of the rationalists' absolutes, we have seen how Harris and Kant define theirs, and we have seen how conduct and good will partake of the same ineluctability and the same immunity from chance and fortune.

We must now consider, specifically, the way in which Kant's rationalistic notion of good will relates to and depends upon, the other simpler and more primitive notion of good will, that is on good will as reason.

Good will may be for Kant—and this for teleological reasons—absolute: but though absolute, good will taken in this sense is not primitive. Kant starts his argument in the *Groundwork* with a simpler notion of good will, the one for which we have reserved the label "good will 1". This simpler notion is the ground of the axiologically absolute notion which Kant goes on to develop: the 'absolute' notion can be—and will henceforth be—labelled "good will 2".

Kant defines the primitive notion of *good will* as "good will 1" in the first two paragraphs of the *Groundwork*, and then he goes on, in the third paragraph which we have just examined, to define his second, consequent, and almost but never quite separate, notion of "good will 2", the notion of good will as an absolute. We must now examine his definition of the first notion, and consider in some detail the splitting off of the second notion from it.

Ineluctable worth can be generated only by the willing of a will which is already in some sense righteous. Kant defines a sense of righteous or reasonable willing not unlike that of

Harris—and not unlike the sense used by most moral philosophers. We must consider this definition and see, as Kant himself probably did not, how he then further defines an almost separate notion of good will on the basis of the first notion, using the consideration of ineluctability to shift the emphasis from *rational action as such* to *rational action as inevitably-praiseworthy*.

Harris just manages to keep the two ideas together: Kant contrives if not to separate, at least to polarize them; in Kant the implicit splitting becomes very nearly explicit. But both men begin with the same basic notion of reason as the guide to human action.

1. *The Primitive Notion of Good Will*

We must turn now to the notion of good will, or of reason, or of reason as the regulator of conduct, which we have so far taken for granted. This is the idea with which Kant begins his argument in the first paragraph of the *Groundwork*: "good will" as the ineluctable good is an idiosyncratic notion, but Kant does not begin eccentrically. His first moves are as commonplace as anyone's. Before he begins to expound his own rather particular doctrine Kant makes his *devoirs* to the ordinary moral notions of the Enlightenment.

Harris's notions of *Prudence*, *Moral Office*, *Moral Duty*, *Rational Justification* and *Rectitude of Conduct* are all introduced so loosely, so conversationally, that it would be pedantic to criticize him for his lack of rigour: he might reply to us that we know well enough what he means by such notions, and well enough was all that he aimed at. He is reminding us of what we already know, not instructing us.

Kant is another man again: his book is dense, severe and far from conversational, and every expression has its weight and place. But the difficulty with him is to determine these weights, and to map the topography of these close-knit arguments, arguments which profess, too, to *extend* our ordinary rational knowledge of morality.

There are two related questions which we must set ourselves as we read the first two paragraphs of the *Groundwork*: (i) what is the meaning of "good will"? (ii) what is good will's function, what does good will do? The answers to these two questions will be interdependent: *good will* is defined to some extent by its function, and its function is defined by it.

Question One: What is the meaning of "good will"? There are ten occurrences of the expression "good will" in the first eight paragraphs of the *Groundwork* (pp. 61–5 of Paton's edition: pp. 10–15 & 9–13 of Abbott's). There are, as well, instances of such intractable expressions as "inner and unconditioned worth" (p. 61: p. 11, Abbott, "Intrinsic unconditional value"); "absolutely good" (p. 61: p. 11: A. p. 9); "absolute value of a mere will" (p. 62: p. 12: A. p. 10), "absolute value of the mere will"; and "will . . . good . . . in itself" (p. 64: p. 14: A. p. 12). If we were to examine Kant's text as rigorously as perhaps we ought, then each of these occurrences, and each of these expressions, would merit a particular analysis.

The notion of good will with which Kant begins, commonplace, important, and one about which he and his readers could hardly be thought to differ, leads us insensibly into the celebrated, and as we have said, idiosyncratic notion; and it leads us into the argument about the supposed "purpose of nature in attaching reason to our will as governor" which we have examined above: Section B, 1 and 2, pp. 63–69 (*G.*, pp. 62–3: pp. 12–13: A. pp. 10–11). But if we are to understand fully both the grounds and the upshot of this argument itself we must see how Kant develops it from the first line of the *Groundwork* where he begins with a remark about good will.

The senses of "good will" shift with the shifts of the argument.

Question Two: What is "good will", and what does it do? There is a sentence of Charlotte Brontë's, written, of course, in English, and written moreover forty years after Kant's death, which provides, even so, an excellent introduction to the first paragraph of the *Groundwork*. The date and the place and the language may be wrong, but the tone of the passage is exactly right:

> There is a great deal of *sense* in your last letter. Be thankful that God gave you *sense*, for what are beauty, wealth or even health without it?[1]

[1] Letter to Miss Ellen Nussey, March 11, 1848, quoted by Clement K. Shorter in *Charlotte Brontë and Her Circle*, London (Hodder & Stoughton), 1896, p. 227. (Italics mine.)

The robust, rather eighteenth-century notion of *sense* is as close as may be to Kant's first, primitive, notion of good will, good will 1. And the very cadence even of Charlotte Brontë's sentence recalls the rhythm of the opening passage of the *Groundwork*. Nothing, says Kant, can be conceived of as good without qualification except a good will; and good will is the qualification of of every other good, of "power, wealth, honour, even health". Ordinary goods are not always good at all, "but they can also be extraordinarily bad or hurtful when the *will* is not *good* which has to make use of these gifts of nature" (*G.*, p. 61 : p. 10: A. p. 9).

The notion of *good will* as *the qualification of other goods* is a great deal easier to grasp indeed, than is the idea of *good will* itself being conceivable as a '*good without qualification*'.

To call good will the qualification of other goods is already to specify a notion of it: and what Kant means by "good will" in paragraphs one and two of the *Groundwork* comes out clearly in the famous passage:

> Power, wealth, honour, even health and that complete well-being and contentment with one's own state which goes by the name of 'happiness', produce boldness, and as a consequence often over-boldness as well, unless a *good will* is present by which their influence on the mind—and so too the whole principle of action—*may be corrected and adjusted to universal ends* . . . (*G.*, p. 16: p. 10: A. p. 9 Italics mine.) [Abbott's " . . . and adapt it to its end", here is an unsatisfactory translation of '*allgemein-zweckmässig mache*'.]

"Good will" here is practical reason which adjusts our actions to social-universal-ends, it is in effect Charlotte Brontë's, or even Jane Austen's, "sense" and is certainly Harris's "Prudence".

It is the business of good will to 'correct and adjust' the whole principle of action and make it *allgemein-zweckmässig*, that is, to make the principle one which *tends to everyone's ends*, and not the agent's alone.

Even if Kant himself uses the word "prudence" in a sense[1]

[1] Kant uses "prudence" pejoratively, as in the distinction: "whether it is *prudent* or whether it is *right*, to make a false promise" (*G.*, p. 70: p. 22: A. p. 19), and he uses it somewhat ambiguously in the occurrences in Chapter II (see especially the footnote to *G.*, p. 83: p. 39: A. p. 33).

Kant's chief objection to prudence lies, of course, in that fact that its

quite different from Harris's, he could, at least on the first page of the *Groundwork*, meet in doctrinal if not verbal concord both with Harris, and with that other Englishman, John Armstrong, who held, very much in accord with the spirit of the age, that

"Virtue and Sense are one."[1]

A prosaic doctrine, but one that it would be difficult to reject out of hand.

Armstrong's use of "*sense*" runs through English at least from Dryden on, persisting well into the nineteenth century. And this expression "sense" could be used properly enough as a synonym for "good will" in the two opening paragraphs of Kant's *Groundwork* since, on the face of it, these paragraphs present no doctrinal, but only verbal eccentricities. Indeed it is the apparent lack of doctrinal oddity in Kant's initial paragraphs which makes the doctrine of the end of reason (*Groundwork*, paragraphs 4–7) all the more curious by contrast.

There is a danger that the very blandness and ordinariness of Kant's opening remarks may disarm the reader, and that he may miss entirely the contrast between Kant's first moves and his quickly developed doctrine: for example, Professor J. W. Scott in his *Kant on the Moral Life* did not find it necessary, though his book is a detailed commentary on the *Groundwork*, to distinguish between the sense of "good will" in paragraphs 1 and 2, and the sense of "good will" in paragraph 3 and those which follow. Professor Scott passes over both the extraordinary rationalism of paragraph 3, and the sudden transition from the commonplace to the idiosyncratic notion of good will, with peaceable words:

> Elucidation is hardly needed of an ethical view so unmistakable as this. Kant is interrogating the moral consciousness,

end is happiness, and 'happiness is no determinate concept' (cf. *G.*, p. 85: 41: A. p. 35). The desire to have the will determined by an *a priori* principle, which leads Kant to evict Prudence from the Temple of the Virtues, is not identical with, though it has the same 'feel' as his determination to find in *good will* an *absolute value*: and behind the similarity of feel there lies, if not an identity, at least a strong analogy of argument. The contingent and the doubtful must give place to the *a priori*, the absolute, the ineluctable and the immanent.

[1] John Armstrong, *The Art of Preserving Health* [1744], Book IV line 265. Harris's son, in his *Memoir*, p. xxv, uses the phrase, "to justice, to good-nature and to good sense" [1801].

> and this is his first finding from the moral stand point, he says, *a will is good because of what it inwardly is: not because of what it is able for.*[1]

Indeed? What Professor Scott has Kant say is so, in a sense; but in another sense it most decidedly is not so. What makes the will good, in the most general sense, *is* just what it is able for: the *good*, that is the *point*, of practical reason or the rational will is that it may 'bring out', so to speak, the goodness of other goods. Kant himself makes this clear, quite explicitly, in his first two paragraphs. There, the will's function is to adjust to universal ends,[2] and in this its own 'unconditioned' goodness lies.

Likewise, at the level of specific actions, what makes the will good is precisely what it is apt for. Whether the will attains what it is apt for (out for, would attain), is, again from a certain point of view, irrelevant, but the will must be *apt* for a good end before *it itself* is good. To put it very baldly: the will must be apt for an end before it can properly be called 'will'; and it must be apt for a good end—or one judged good—before it can be called 'good will'. Professor Scott's contrast between what a will "inwardly is" and what it is "apt for" is an absurd one. Even if the "inward" goodness of a will is independent of the will's attaining the outward end willed, it is still determined by some 'outward' good which must be given as a precondition of willing, and of willing-a-good. Mistaken though he may be, Professor Scott is hardly going beyond the general sense of Kant's own text, and to this extent he is a faithful, if altogether too uncritical, commentator.

That the will is good because of what it is apt for is an important doctrine, and one which Kant states, implicitly, in his first two paragraphs: but it is one which he apparently

[1] J. W. Scott, *Kant on the Moral Life, an exposition of Kant's "Grundlegung"*, London (A. C. Black), 1924, p. 44. (Italics mine.)

[2] Universal ends, for Kant, set up some more determinate concept of themselves than does happiness. Universal ends are ends that can be "universally willed", that is, "willed without contradiction": it is this ability-to-be-willed without contradiction that provides the cash value, such as it is, of the determinateness of the concepts of universal ends. See below, Part II, Chapter I, Section A.3, and Part II, Chapter III, Sections B and C.

forgot in his subsequent pages. Professor Scott merely passes over that very transition of senses and uses of "good will" which lies at the root of so many misunderstandings of Kant, and at the root of Kant's own possible misunderstanding of his own ideas. But, so did Kant.

For all the authority of its author, one finds Professor Paton's exposition of the early paragraphs of the *Groundwork* less satisfactory than it might have been. Paton, like Scott, writes words of peace. Though he is clearly conscious of the objections that have been levelled at what is, or seems at least to be, Kant's doctrine of the irrelevance of the ends of the will, Paton rests his case on a simple denial: Kant was not saying the things which he is accused of saying.

What is interesting about accusations that Kant does scant justice to the idea of the will as determinable-by-ends is, indeed, that such allegations should have been made at all; and this is precisely what we must go into, the apparent, the *prima facie* oddity of what Kant says.

The key to the criticisms of Kant which Coleridge made and which T. H. Green rediscovered for himself, criticisms namely that Kant is too cavalier in his treatment of the role of specific ends as determining the will and its goodness or badness, lies precisely in the curious transition, inevitably seeming to be passed over by commentators, which Kant effects from the conventional commonplaces of paragraphs 1 and 2 of the *Groundwork*, to the hermetic rationalism of paragraph 3 ff. At the risk of tedium excessive even in a philosophical essay, we shall endeavour to tease out a few strands of the tangled skein of considerations which Kant, his friends, and even some of his critics have ravelled together over the last two hundred years. (For the relevant passages from S. T. Coleridge and T. H. Green, see below, Appendix to Part I.)

We must both notice the transition from paragraphs 1 and 2 to paragraph 3 and spell out in detail its full significance. We must ask ourselves, (i) what is the point of *good will* thought of as practical reason, as Charlotte Brontë's *sense*? (ii) what is the point of good will thought of as absolutely good because prescinding quite from the success of action? (iii) what differences and similarities are there between the views of *good will* that one gets from these two different standpoints?

2. *Good will 1: 'Sense', and the Harmonizing of Ends: Good Will 1 as the Qualifier of Other Goods*

There is, as we have already suggested, not much to choose between Kant's first notions of *good will* as they occur on page 1 of the *Groundwork* and Harris's "Prudence". Paton's translation of Kant's, "*auch das ganz Prinzip zu handeln berichtige und allgemein-zweckmässig mache*" as "good will by which . . . the whole principle of action may be corrected and adjusted to *universal ends*" looks forward to the principle of universalizability a shade more explicitly perhaps than the original text does, introducing the ultimate theory-impregnation sooner, but it hardly affects either the extremely traditional look or the highly conventional substance of the argument which Kant is putting forward.

Kant's notion here of making the maxim conform to 'universal' ends matches neither Seneca's "universal principles"[1] nor, as yet, his own 'logical' formulation of the law in the first formulation of the categorical imperative. It reflects, or would reflect were we to cut it off quite from the rest of the book, nothing more than that loose, eighteenth-century utilitarianism which Bentham and Mill's more uncompromising doctrines of ultilty tend to obscure for us in our backward glances down the perspective of history.

The notion itself of "adjustment to universal ends/to everyone's ends" need go no further than Hume's utilitarianism; Hume writes: ". . . everything which *contributes to the happiness of society* recommends itself directly to our approbation and good will".[2] What are everybody's ends, but everybody's happiness, and what is it to make a principle *allgemein-zweckmässig* if not to make it conduce to everybody's well-being? Happiness is, as Harris's index has it, an "*Interest*", but "a social one": a Kingdom of Ends is nothing if not a society.

The notion of an eighteenth-century utilitarian *entente* between Kant's moral philosophy and Hume's cannot but strike

[1] "Do you ask what, then, the wise man has found out and what he has brought to light? . . . There is the law of life, *and life he has made to conform to universal principles.*" Seneca, *Epistle XC*, trans. R. M. Gummere, London (Loeb/Heinemann), 1917/1953, Vol. II, p. 421. (Italics mine.)

[2] Hume's *Enquiry*, Sc. V, Pt. II: Selby-Bigge edition, Oxford (O.U.P.), p. 219.

us at first sight as odd. But it does not follow that it is altogether absurd. If we were to substitute for the sentimental and always slightly ironical Hume the more sober and measured Burke, then a real *rapprochement* might be possible. Burke speaks very much with the voice of the eighteenth-century when he says:

> In reality there are two, and only two, foundations of law; and they are both of them conditions without which nothing can give it any force; I mean *equity* and *utility*. With respect to the former, it grows out of the great rule of equality, which is founded upon our common nature . . . the other foundation of law which is utility must be understood . . . [as] *general and public utility*, connected in the same manner with, and derived directly from, our rational nature. . . .[1]

Here we have all the counters, the minima of a moral system which Kant might accept: (1) here is equity, both (*a*) the essence of one strand of the notion of universalizability—"Can I will that *another* equally might . . . ?"—and (*b*) a safeguard against too crass a utilitarianism, "It is expedient for you that one man should die for the people", but it is not equitable. Here too is (2) public utility which, limited by equity, comes to a recognition of *universal* ends. General utility tends towards the good of a Kingdom of Ends.

And all this is rooted in our 'common, rational nature'; Burke as much as Kant contrives "to show the unity of practical and rational reason in a common principle";[2] he can claim to effect the very thing that Kant sets out in his own *Preface* to do.

Burke does not stress here the *reason* or *good will* which would adjust the maxims of action, but he lays out clearly to what

[1] Edmund Burke, "Tracts on the Popery Laws" [1765 (?), published posthumously]: see, *The Works and Correspondence of the Right Honourable Edmund Burke*, London (Rivington), 1852, Vol. II, p. 17. It is interesting to notice that Burke's like Mill's utilitarianism is set in a context of protest and arises out of criticism of certain social and political institutions. Burke here may be echoing, consciously or otherwise, an older doctrine of utility, cf. St Thomas Aquinas, "The immediate end of human law is man's own *utility*", *Summa Theologica*, Ia, 2æ, xcv, 3.

[2] Burke's principle is of course known by induction that is, here, by common sense; Kant's is given *a priori*. There is a distinction. But the question poses itself: is there really a difference? See below, Part II, Chapter III, Sections B and C.

maxims should be adjusted: public utility; and *how* they should be adjusted—equitably. This doctrine is hardly more, and certainly no less, than any man of sense would have to agree to.

What is adjusted to is public utility, and the adjustment is done equitably. And for Kant, and for Burke and for Harris, the adjustment is made by reason, or by "Prudence", whose function Harris says it is to "discern" what is to be pursued or avoided if we are to make actual those "best Dispositions to society", those "most upright Intentions" which he so amiably presumes us to have (*Dialogue*, II, p. 98). This is all very common doctrine for the Age of Reason, and we might very well expect to harmonize out in its concert the idiosyncratic notes sounded by our very different representative men, Hume, Harris, Burke and Kant.

At all events, we are not puzzled as we begin the *Groundwork* to put a sense to Kant's notion of good will as the *qualification* of the gifts of nature which "can . . . be extraordinarily bad and hurtful *when the will is not good* which has to make use of them".

The notion of good will's being itself something "which can be taken as *good without qualification*" (which notion is introduced mysteriously in the second paragraph of the *Groundwork*) is, however, more obscure. With this particular idea we seem to move from the realm of moral commonplace to the realm of rationalistic absolutes. Kant's quite ordinary doctrine of "sense" becomes quickly enough a rather less ordinary doctrine: and one in which "sense" plays a rather minor part.

3. *Good Will as itself Good without Qualification*

Kant's talk of a good will, whose use is "[der] Prinzip . . . *allgemein-zweckmässig mache*", tells us nothing about a will which could '*itself*' be "*good without qualification*", even though the notion of such an unqualifiedly good will is introduced in the first three lines of the first paragraph of the *Groundwork*. Nor does Kant's generally utilitarian talk tell us anything about a will which is "absolutely good" or which has "inner and unconditioned worth".

These last two phrases, which occur in the second paragraph of the *Groundwork*, must in the end be read in conjunction with, or at least be taken as foreshadowing, the difficult argument in the third paragraph: this is an argument about good will which, though the good will in question rests on and presupposes prudence, practical reason and "sense", goes, as we have seen, beyond such notions as we ordinarily think of them, and begins the process of setting up an *absolute value* of a metaphysical sort.

For Kant, absolute value itself is to be thought of not in terms of reason and its regulative function with regard to conduct, the notion on which indeed it ultimately depends, but in terms of the ineluctable merit which, succeed or fail, accrues to the pure immanent function of right willing as a pure function.

Kant's argument that good will is needful if the good of other things is to be realized, and his suggestion that it itself cannot be misused—a suggestion which must be distinguished from the remark that good will can itself be "good without qualification"—is a standard enough one in moral philosophy.

Kant's "good will" that cannot be misused has just the concept-loading that we find Aristotle's "virtue" displaying, in a passage which foreshadows quite remarkably the notions of the first two paragraphs of the *Groundwork*:

> It is argued that one who makes an unfair use of [the] faculty of speech may do great harm, *this objection applies to all good things except virtue*, and above all to those things which are most useful, such as strength, health, wealth, generalship; for as these rightly used may be of the greatest benefit, so, wrongly used they may do an equal amount of harm.[1]

Virtue and good will, or practical reason, have their eternal appointed task, which is to manage all other goods to best and to 'universal' advantage. We understand this well enough. Virtue cannot be misused, since such a use of reason would be neither 'virtuous' nor 'reasonable'. But what it would be for the will itself (and alone of all goods) to be able to be "taken as good without qualification" remains still obscure. To say that the will is the *qualification sine qua non* of the goodness of other things is not yet to explicate its own unqualified goodness. And, indeed, we shall have to devote our next chapter to an unravelling of this, and of other notions of unqualifiedness and unconditionedness.

[1] Aristotle, *Rhetoric*, *I.1.*13, trans. J. H. Freese, London (Loeb/Heinemann), 1926, p. 13. (Italics mine.)

4. *Good will* 1: *the Goodness of the Needful Will*

Before we go on, however, to unravel the perplexities of Kant's notion of the unconditioned, and of his idea of 'goodness without qualification', a task which will call upon everything we have so far said about his extreme rationalist argument, we may pause and look at one final commonplace which seems to be present in the first two paragraphs of the *Groundwork.* This is the commonplace that a capacity for the adapting of one's maxims to universal ends implies the obligation to cultivate a disposition to *do* this adjusting. This notion is implicit in the passage from Aristotle which we quoted in Section 3 immediately above, and it provides the substance of the tautology-rule that, "Virtue cannot be wilfully misused, since so *mis*-used is is not virtue".

Good will or virtue is practical reason understood as in and of itself implying a bias towards right action. There is no other way in which a moralist can understand practical reason.

The notion of practical reason with which we operate implies both that this reason must be used well (any other use is 'unreasonable') and that nobody can really be said to have practical reason, no matter how clever he may be, unless he is disposed to act well rather than badly, that is, to do acts which are right rather than acts which are wrong. This bias towards virtue which moralists build into the notion of practical reason is what enables them to use "practical reason", "good will" and "virtue" as synonyms. The bias towards virtue which reason contains, and the commitment to a moral disposition which it embodies, are obvious enough: if we were asked to justify either, what could we answer? We would be embarrassed not so much to find a reply as to understand the question.

Nevertheless, though there is no question here of the justification of a moral commonplace, it may be useful to examine Kant's remarks on the second of these notions: that to be reasonable—to have good will—commits one to some, at least minimal, moral disposition.

5. *Good will* 1.1: *Moral Reason Implies Moral Disposition*

Kant is less bland, or perhaps less sanguine than Harris, and he goes on in the second paragraph of the *Groundwork* to toughen up the "sense" notion of good will making, in a somewhat moralistic way, two points that might be worth separating. The points are: (i) that we are all *expected* in the sense of "required" to have just those good dispositions towards the welfare of society which Harris so casually allows us, and (ii) that if we do not have these and are happy, then any "rational and impartial spectator can never feel approval [moral? or rational? or both?] in contemplating [our] uninterrupted prosperity". "A touch" at least of *good will* as, in Kant's rather pious phrase, "pure and good will" seems to constitute the "indispensable condition of our very worthiness to be happy".

Whatever the precise meaning of the passage is, it is safe to say at least that Kant is insisting here on some element of good disposition as an essential part of that rational good will which does the universal adjusting. You have not got good will in the required sense if you *could* "adjust to universal ends" but are not disposed to do so. If you *can* test your maxims and 'universalize' then you *must:* or, to put it morally and proto-morally, you *ought to universalize* your maxims, and ought so to test them. This is the obligation of obligations, the form of obligation itself. Good will as rational will necessarily "includes" the acknowledgement of this particular ought. Kant's insistence on the obligations of good will, and his rejection of the rather easy and sentimental optimism which found expression in the writings of Shaftesbury and Rousseau, is notable and laudable: but beyond this particularly firm insistence on obligation there is nothing so far in his doctrine to distinguish Kant from the run of his contemporaries. For one paragraph at least of the *Groundwork*, Kant writes much like anyone else.

Read in a minimal way, Kant's definition of "good will" in the first paragraph of the *Groundwork* hardly goes beyond the commonplaces of his age, or of any reasonable moral philosophy. But in the second paragraph he introduces notions of *inner worth* and *absolute goodness* which suggest, if they do not yet cry out for, an analysis in terms of something more technical and specific than these commonplaces. These notions of inner worth and absolute goodness look a little like the ordinary counters of moral philosophy perhaps, and we may seek to exhaust their value simply in terms of the notions of good will 1 and 1.1; but equally they look forward to their own striking inflation into currency of the full metaphysic of morals. Here we return to consider again, from another perspective, the notion of good will 2; that is will, if righteous, then *eo ipso* ineluctably value-producing—the notion with which we began this chapter.

6. *Good will and Unconditioned Worth*

Kant himself begins the *Groundwork* with the mysterious suggestion that good will could be, besides being the condition of the the goodness of other things, 'itself good without qualification': and he uses the technical expression "unconditioned worth" and "inner worth" a dozen or so times later on. These are enigmatic suggestions, obscure clues laid down by our author, which it is our exegetical duty to follow up. What is unconditioned worth?

We began this present chapter by broaching the subject of Kant's doctrine of the end of reason, the doctrine that reason's end is to produce "a will which is good . . . in itself", but we have not by any means exhausted the notion of *worth* or the notion of *good will* which his rationalistic teleology sets up as reason's end.

The end of reason is the production of good will, or, as Kant says, of "the absolute worth of mere will": what can this mean? We shall see in our next chapter.

CHAPTER IV
THE ARGUMENT IN KANT: II

> In the works on transcendental philosophy which have been published of late years, we find the words *infinite*, *absolute*, *indeterminate*, *unconditioned*, frequently repeated, and made to play a very prominent part in the explanation of the most recondite secrets which can be presented to the consideration of man.
>
> James Balmes, *Fundamental Philosophy*

A. UNCONDITIONED, ABSOLUTE VALUE

The task which we set ourselves in this chapter is to unravel, as well as we may, Kant's notion of "the absolute worth of mere will". If the end of reason is the production of this worth, then we should know what it is that we are supposed, by Kant if not by Nature and Nature's God, to spend our lives generating.

1. *Good Will 2: Inner Unconditioned Worth: the Absolutely Good*

To say that certain qualities of character, circumstance and the like 'are not absolutely good' (cf. *Groundwork*, second paragraph), and that they lack 'inner and unconditioned worth' (loc. cit.), is to say something which can be understood easily enough. The saying can mean, in the first place, that good will or practical reason is necessary to adjust these qualities and circumstances to social and moral ends. And it can mean, in the second place, that a man's moral credit lies not in the happy chance of his natural endowments, but in his character and in his management of himself and his gifts. However, it is not absolutely clear that these two commonplaces quite exhaust Kant's intended meaning here in the first two paragraphs of the *Groundwork*.

To use a distinction which Kant himself makes in another context, we know what it would be to say that good will was *needful*, but not to say that it, or its value, was for that reason *necessary*,[1] or, to use the language of the *Groundwork* itself, "absolute".

[1] Immanuel Kant's *Critique of Pure Reason*, trans. N. Kemp-Smith, London (Macmillan), 1929/1950: A634, B662, p. 527. There is, indeed,

That is to say, if we know well enough what it is for certain qualities of character and circumstance *not* to be "absolutely good", we know a great deal less well what it would be for good will, or practical reason, to be *itself* "*good without qualification*"; and Kant's suggestion that it is good in this way (*Groundwork*, paragraph 1), remains obscure. If we are looking, in the *Groundwork*, for a transcendental deduction of moral or personal value, then we are not going to get it: not complete and rounded, anyhow. And what we do get is flawed, and it is flawed just by such obscure notions as this one, notions of 'goodness without qualification' and "absolute, unconditioned worth".

If it must be admitted that "all the goods in the world" are not good without good will to "make use of" and to "adjust" them, it can nevertheless be argued, equally well, that good will itself is not actually good, and not good for anything, unless it has something to adjust. Good will's own goodness seems to be qualified by the consideration that it itself must have something to qualify. In the sense of being a condition, good will is unqualified in its worth: in the sense that its own worth is conditional upon there being something to condition, the worth of good will is as conditional, as qualified in its own way, as is the worth of anything else.

Good will in Kant's first sense of it in paragraphs one and two of the *Groundwork* is concerned with action; and action is concerned with the making or unmaking of states of affairs in the light of both our moral and our non-moral value-judgments. If, *per impossible*, there were no states of affairs, or if we could do nothing to change the world in any way, what would be the good of will, or the good of good will?

a way in which the needful might be shown to be the necessary in ethics. The notion of man as an End in himself begins such a transcendental deduction. Kant's mistake is not to attempt such a useful deduction: it ies in his allowing himself to be side-tracked by the empty "absoluteness" of "good will" when this expression "good will" is taken in the second of the two senses which Kant defines, contextually, in the *Groundwork*. The useful elements of a transcendental deduction which the *Groundwork* contains, must be disengaged from the empty rationalism of the talk of "the absolute worth of mere will". But we begin, in this note, to trespass on the argument of the whole of the present essay.

Contemplative reason may always contemplate, but practical reason must seek to effect something, or at least to affect something. And though we may applaud Kant's ambition "to show the unity of practical and theoretical reason in a common principle" (*Groundwork*, Preface, p. xii: p. 8: A. p. 7), we may have the gravest misgivings about his tendency, or what at least seems to be his tendency, to obscure the essential difference between theoretical and practical reason. Theoretical reason is contemplative, and contemplation is an immanent act of the contemplating subject: practical reason is, as reason perhaps, equally immanent, but as practical it is essentially outward-directed and end-directed.

Kant seems on the whole, in the *Groundwork* at least, to obscure this difference between theoretical and practical reason by his over-emphasis of the point about the "value of mere will". Under the influence of the special—and perhaps valid but certainly misplaced—notion of the will as a faculty of immanent action, he seems to lose sight of the logical priority of, and the practical necessity of, goals as determining the will.

Willing may be in a sense complete and immanent, prescinding from whatever happens or fails to happen, but this is not the first or the last truth about the will. And it is by no means the most important truth about it.

The notion of an immanent practical will is ultimately absurd, unless it is frankly acknowledged that such a will is parasitic upon an end-directed and end-seeking practical reason.

In a world where we could *do* nothing, could practical reason pursue even pure righteousness? What would this come to? All acts of righteousness are first *acts* and then *acts of righteousness*. The good man relieves the widow and the orphan, he allows the interests of others precedence over his own; in short, he does things, or he refrains from things that he might do, in the light of reasonable and altruistic considerations. He 'adjusts to universal ends'. But one could do nothing righteously in a world where one could literally do nothing, except perhaps, and this itself can only just be conceived, conform one's will to the will of God, accepting what happened as His doing.

Even here, the sense of "will" in "conforming one's will to the will of God" is parasitic upon the active, manipulative end-seeking and world-changing sense of will which we already have.[1] If, *ex hypothesi*, we did not have this sense, it is not at all easy to see what one would be conforming to the (still active) will of God, or how one could conform it.

The first good of good will is precisely the good issue to which it can bring other goods, as Kant acknowledges in his first paragraph. When a man has done, or at least sincerely attempted, a righteous act (that is an act which is right and therefore righteous-when-willed), then and only then can he enjoy the consequent and second good of good will, good will 2, the ineluctable merit of righteous action, the inevitably supervening merit which inheres in righteous but ineffective willing. This good inheres in righteous willing as righteous, and in ineffective willing, despite its ineffectiveness. Merit is independent, certainly, of the attainment of the good end, but it depends essentially on the attempts to bring about that end and so, logically, upon there being that end to attempt.

There are two or three interrelated strands in Kant's thought about good will: (1) he seems to do less than justice to the fact that, logically, nothing could be rightly willed unless the will had objects, and unless some of them were worthy ones; nothing could be rightly and meritoriously willed, unless there were things fit to be willed; (2) he seems to overstate the value of good will, taken in the sense of good will 2, the sense of ineluctable merit due to righteous, if unsuccessful willing. And (3) he seems further to want to say that this value is, of itself, greater than any other value that could be produced in any action-situation.

These strands are almost inextricably bound together; common to all three strands, and rendering their mutual involvement a matter of principle and not of mere chance, is Kant's powerful, aesthetic, and intractable notion of "the unconditioned".

Reading the *Groundwork* one is inclined to feel the scepticism that Balmes felt—see the epigraph to the present chapter—about the explanatory power of the notions of the "*absolute*" and the "*unconditioned*". Not only does the idea of the unconditioned fail to bring enlightenment, it seems to wrap

[1] Kant accepts this point: see *C.Pr.R.*: ". . . in the notion of the will, the notion of causality is already contained". A. p. 145.

everything up in the profoundest obscurity: and Kant's notion of the "absolute" worth of mere will brings confusion rather than clarity into morals and into axiology. It spoils the *Groundwork*.

2. "*The Good Will and its Results*"

Professor Paton has in his edition of the *Groundwork* two paragraphs of exegesis on "the good will and its results". In the first, his précis of Kant is so elegant, and his use of the Kantian language so confident—"the *conditioned* good of its products cannot be the source of the *unconditioned* goodness which belongs to a good will alone"—that those of us who are puzzled by the author may be as mystified by the commentator.

It is only in the second paragraph of his exegesis that Paton says something that the very ordinary sort of reader can bite on: he says, apropos of Kant's third paragraph, that 'there is nothing in it to suggest that for Kant a good will does not aim at producing results'.

At best, however, this is mere reassurance, and we get no insight into the reasons why so many readers, from unsophisticated undergraduates to acute and sympathetic ones, should feel that Kant's doctrine of the will is one of a will independent of ends. The impression that Kant overlooks the importance of ends may be mistaken, but it would be interesting to see why it is ever taken at all: T. H. Green, for example, seems to have received it, and Coleridge certainly did.

The extraordinary emphasis which Kant puts upon the good but possibly unsuccessful will, the will barren of worldly results, and the constant reiteration of the gnomic notion of the unconditioned, have something to do with the misunderstandings to which Kant has been subject. In the end it is probable that the notion of the unconditional muddled not only his readers, but the philosopher himself. The worst suspicions of undergraduates and of transcendental philosophers, both, may be justified, at least in part, by the text of the *Groundwork*.

3. "*Unconditioned*"[1]

The first use of the expression "unconditioned" which we get is in paragraph two of the *Groundwork*, where certain qualities

[1] As was remarked in the Note to the Reader which prefaces this essay. the discussion of Kant's whole official metaphysic is beyond its scope. This

of character are said to lack "unconditioned worth": but the notion of unconditioned worth looks back, in a sense, to the gnomic suggestion, in the first three lines of paragraph one, that the good will can be conceived of as *good without qualification.*

The first use of the notion of the unconditioned which is specific enough to define it is, though the expression "unconditioned" does not occur there, in paragraphs four and five, that is in the paragraphs which develop paragraph three, and which mount the argument, so neatly paralleling Harris's, about the ineluctable and so unconditioned goodness of rational willing as willing.

The whole doctrine of the end of reason, the doctrine that reason's end is to produce good will, seems to be developed in terms of the notion of good will defined in paragraph three of the *Groundwork.* It seems to be developed, that is, in terms of the idea of the pure and unconditioned worth of good will 2. Practical reason, taken barely and by itself, is alluded to in the first three lines of paragraph one, but never explained; and the phrase "inner and unconditioned worth" is used in paragraph two, but hardly defined there. What takes over and dominates the argument here, and indeed throughout the rest of the *Groundwork,* seems to be the notion of good will 2, to whose goodness results, and the attainment of results, are irrelevant.

In paragraph three of the *Groundwork* we seem to have, if anywhere, the consideration which defines the domestic grammar of the mysterious expression "unconditioned", and which provides the core for the teleology of the fifth, sixth and seventh paragraphs of the first chapter of the book.

In this notion of the "unconditioned", and in Kant's insistence on the idea of an absolute good, namely, *merit, not*

being so, the richest sources of definitions of *the unconditioned* must be neglected: but see the index to Kemp-Smith's edition of the *C.P.R.* Note especially the *C.Pr.R.*, Of the Deduction of the Fundamental Principles of the Pure Practical Reason, A. p. 138: also *C.Pr.R.*, Ch. III, A. pp. 160–1, 166–7 and p. 206: see too A. p. 213. Note also the *C. Teleolog. J.* §6 = 67, M. pp. 27–8: B. p. 225; §16 = 76, M. p. 57: B. p. 250: §23 = 84, M. p. 100*n*; B. p. 286*n*. However, it is significant that, the official metaphysics apart, the notion of the unconditioned can be found to do so much work in *G.*—and so much metaphysical work, of an internally structured kind.

conditional upon the success of acts, lie the germs both of Kant's own more unfortunate remarks, and of the innumerable perplexities and misunderstandings which have afflicted readers and exegetes of the *Groundwork* for so long. Here too, in the notion of an "absolute" and "unconditioned" good, lies the fatal weakness of the *Groundwork*.

The notion of the unconditioned, and the suspicion that Kant underrates not only the value but the logical priority of ends over the willing of them, are things which we shall pursue through the present and subsequent chapters. Kant, if not eccentric on these topics, at least looks, and has notoriously looked, to be so. Before we consider these questions at length, however, it is convenient to deal with yet another closely related aspect of Kant: that is with the curious and patently eccentric, axiology which he erects upon the notion of the unconditioned—that is the ineluctable—worth of a good will.

Kant's axiology of good will is, or ought to be, a scandal to reverent and peaceable exegesis. Furthermore, it is not at all easy to see how the scandalized reader can be reassured here; taking the text as it stands one finds in it a very curious doctrine indeed.

4. *The Background to the Axiology of Absolute Worth*

The notion of ineluctable merit itself, good will 2, is commonplace enough, and nobody would want to disallow it.

What is neither commonplace, nor at all obviously allowable, is the theoretical superstructure which Kant seems so anxious to erect on this one relatively fragile foundation.

The point that we must allow is that there is merit due to willing a right act in righteousness, whatever the issue of it may be. And when Kant says in paragraph three of the *Groundwork* (p. 62: p. 11: A. p. 10), that this ineluctable good will "has its full value in itself", we might settle for a reverent interpretation, namely, "He means, 'there is here *a kind of value* which is "full in itself" regardless of success, though success would make the whole situation even more valuable again' ". However, Kant himself seems to cut this reverent reading off at once by writing: "Its usefulness and fruitfulness can neither add to nor subtract from this value."

Yet even this second saying might be reverently interpreted: " 'This value' means '*This* value'; that is: success in an action could not add to the *specific*, *immanent*, *value* of the conduct, which is independent of the actual success of the conduct, but only to the total value of the situation." Yet again the reverent interpretation seems to be blocked by Kant's: "Its usefulness would be merely as it were, the *setting* which enables us to handle it better in our ordinary dealings or to attract the attention of those not yet sufficiently expert, but not to commend it to experts or to determine its value." [. . . "or to attract to it the attention of those who are not yet connoisseurs, but not to recommend it to true connoisseurs, or to determine its value." Abbott]

Now it looks here as though Kant were doing less than justice to the value of what might be achieved by moral action, over and above the immanent merit accruing to the action as such, taken as an act of well-directed will: taken that is, as good will 1 producing good will 2. It is obvious that Kant wants to do justice—one might think more than justice—to this intrinsic, ineluctably-accruing value of moral action, "*das seinem vollen Wert in sich selbst hat*", but he seems to be overdoing it. Expertise and connoisseurship are taken to extremes if what is valued most is the righteousness of righteous effort, and not the possible good ends of the right action.

What *is* it that usefulness serves as a "setting" for? What *is* it that the expert can value quite apart from this apparently inessential "setting" of usefulness?

The notion of good will with which Kant opens the *Groundwork* has, unlike the notion in paragraph three, a great deal to do with usefulness: it has to do with the adjustment of maxims to universal ends and in a clear sense, to utilitarian ends. Nevertheless in paragraph three we are faced with a good will whose value is said to be such that mere usefulness is to it as the reliquary is to the relic. There is a double puzzle here: (*a*) how Kant can say, simply, that there *is* this good that is so much better than usefulness; and (*b*) how he can say it, beginning his talk as he does, within a context in which good will and usefulness of a 'universal' kind mutually define one another.

In the third and fourth paragraphs of Chapter I, early though they may be in the book, we are at one of the watersheds of the *Groundwork*. The first two paragraphs seem, as we have seen, to define a notion of "good will" in rather traditional social-cum-moral terms, in terms that is of the adjustment of principles to universal ends—and here, ends get their due place in the system. This being so, there are no insuperable difficulties in the way of our conceding Kant most of what he has to say in paragraphs one and two. Even if reason 'is and ought to be the slave of the passions', she is at least a pedagogue. Hume as much as Kant would want everything nicely adjusted to the easy functioning of society, or to the harmony of a Kingdom of Ends, and it is difficult to see how anyone could take exception to the various commonplaces of the first paragraph of the *Groundwork*.

Indeed it is difficult to see how one could fail to agree, in a general way at least, with Kant's doctrine in the first two paragraphs. The doctrine is all so ordinary that some version of it turns up in every moral system. The notion of practical reason, whether we call it "good will" or "sense" or "prudence"[1] or something else, is, it seems, central to moral systems as such. To call this essence of morality "good will" rather than "practical reason" is, perhaps, to go no further than, as we have already said in our discussion of good will 1.1, to stress the element of disposition towards rational action which lies implicit in the concept, and to develop the element of disposition towards more than purely egostical action which lies as close.

If one were to set oneself Kant's specific question: 'What is the purpose of our having reason attached to our will as governor?' one could answer it in terms of good will, taken in the commonplace sense of the first two paragraphs of the *Groundwork*: we have practical reason in order that we may act practically, and in order that we may act reasonably when we act practically.

What is the point of reason: to what purpose is it?

Ordinary moral consciousness sees the end of practical

[1] Though, as we have already noticed in Chapter III (footnote 1, p. 76) Kant himself uses the expression "prudence" in a sense closer to "cynical calculation" than to "practical reason".

reason as, despite everything immanentist that can be said, essentially external to the will itself and its functioning. The end of practical reason is the good ends which it may serve.

Kant's answer to his own question about the purpose of nature in assigning us reason seems to be different from the answer that ordinary common sense would give: he seems to want to say that we have practical reason, that is *good will 1 and 1.1*, for good will's own sake—that is, we have practical reason for the sake of *good will 2*.

Reason's "true function", he says, "must be to produce a will which is good not as a means, but in itself." This will, good in itself and not as a means, looks, on the face of it, suspiciously like the ineluctable, absolute good of good will 2. Further, as if to heighten our suspicions, Kant goes on to talk of the production of a good will good in itself as reason's "first and *unconditioned* purpose". This "unconditioned" is ominous.

There is a possible doctrine in all this, but a very odd one. A theist might, for example, take what we may characterize as the 'great examination' view of life. He might have God treat our good works as examiners treat examination scripts, pieces of paper to be read, and graded and to be burned after the long vacation. On such a view all that remains of a man's answers, and all that matters, is his passing or failing—and his class.

God might be thought to be conducting a cosmic pass and honours school, and we might envisage Him as noting and remarking only the merit due to our actions—or the merit due to our efforts, successful or unsuccessful—and letting the actions themselves drop into oblivion.

Theologically this may be neither a very sophisticated nor a very dignified view to take of God's concern with human action, but at least the model makes some sense. What happens, however, when we take God away, or at least fail, as Kant fails in the *Groundwork*, to mention Him? There remains of course the agent, and he can register his own inner worth in being conscious of his own rectitude. Or we can use impersonal devices like talk about "character" and talk of "worth of character" to register the worth-that-might-be-observed but is not observed by anyone in particular.

The trouble with this is, of course, that "worth" here, even, as elsewhere, tends to get a utilitarian overtone: a "worthy character" is—in colloquial speech—one who is disposed to act in accord with the principle of adjustment to universal ends. All worth talk, that is to say, both (*a*) supposes an observer; (*b*) tends to have him, at least minimally, utilitarian. The notion "worth" has these two dimensions, it records an observed utility, or a possibly observed, possible one.

It is difficult to separate "absolute" inner and unconditioned worth from the agent's consciousness of it as rectitude, and—a different thing again—from our judgment of it as socially useful. In so far as it is thought of as *absolute* and *inner*, Kant's "worth" tends to look like merit-in-the-eye-of-God, thought of when no positive allusion is being made to God.[1] Even the admissible absoluteness of "absolute" worth wears very thin.

What is skimmed off the good action, whether it fails or succeeds, is a merit; and there is always the uneasy feeling that we have when reading Kant that we want to, but must not, ask the question: "Merit, in whose eyes?"

5. *"Conduct" and "Good Will"*

In so far as he sets his end in "Praise" rather than in "the absolute worth of mere will" Harris is, to some degree, less immanentist than Kant, since praiseworthiness looks outward towards praise. But his *end* and his *Sovereign Good* remain effectively immanent as long as they are to be found in Rectitude of Conduct, and Harris's "Praise" is, perhaps no more than praiseworthiness looking outward in hope of some recognition. For him, the only assured end of Conduct lies in Conduct itself; it does not lie in any outward success, or even in any outward acclaim that such Conduct might achieve, seen as noble though fruitless.

[1] One is not, of course, saying that the postulation of God's existence is a presupposition of morality: that is quite a different issue. All that one wants to say here is that certain talk of merit and goodness looks like talk on a God's-eye model, but allows for no God to have an eye. Such a model is, then, very odd.

External ends are desirable: Praise is desirable: but since these may fail, the *end* is internal, and Rectitude of Conduct dwells apart with its own praiseworthiness. They dwell apart for Harris, however, not because of their own absoluteness, but because of Fortune's fickleness. Harris is always open to non-immanent ends—for all that he settles for immanent ones. It is by no means obvious that Kant is so open to non-absolute ends of will.

Kant goes further than Harris in the direction of an immanent Praise/praiseworthiness, and the primitive notion of good will 1 quite gives way in the *Groundwork* to the subsequent notion. That is to say good will 2, as ineluctable-praiseworthiness, takes over the role of end of reason. It is this good will, the immanent result of the exercise of practical reason which becomes, for Kant, reason's end. And it is the immanence that is, for Kant, of the essence of the end.

We might draw up a scale with Aristotle and Kant marking the extremes, and Harris in the middle. For Aristotle the end of practical reason is, unlike the end of contemplative reason, not internal but external, and the point of practical reason is what it might achieve by manipulation of the world. For Harris, the point of practical reason is not *always* what it might achieve, because sometimes it may achieve nothing, and so the pure unfailing function of choice or willing becomes for him the real end of reason. Though this function of choice is always tied to some attempt to manipulate the world, the attempt itself and not the success of it is the *telos* of reason simply because this is the only end which cannot fail. For Kant in his *Groundwork* phase the point of practical reason lies even more unequivocally in what reason can always achieve, namely in its immanent function, as generative of that kind of value which "is full in itself" and 'shines like a jewel' regardless of the external issue of the willing. For Kant the end of reason lies in something which we might mark by calling it *praise-worthiness*;[1] and to be inwardly praiseworthy, if not publicly

[1] As we have said before, actual praise may not be given: nor need the jewel-like sheen be seen by anybody:

Full many a gem of purest ray serene
The dark unfathomed caves of ocean bear.

Thomas Gray.

praised, is a *telos* to which we can always attain. Kant carries *à l'outrance* the immanentism of Harris, while doing less justice than his predecessor, at any rate as the words of his text stand, to the ends which must determine a will before the will can be even immanently righteous.

Kant wishes to keep not only the effort of the will immanent and self-contained, but the determination of it as well. The moral law issues in "an imperative which, without being based on, and conditioned by *any further purpose to be attained by a certain line of conduct*, enjoins this conduct immediately" (*Groundwork*, pp. 83–4: p. 39: A. p. 33). The full discussion of this level of Kant's immanentism, however, must be postponed until Part II, Chapter III of the present essay.

Both Harris and Kant make "good will" in some sense of that expression, the Sovereign Good. Harris wants us to fix our happiness in Rectitude of Conduct because it alone comes up to the Pre-conceptions; Kant wants us to see good will—and good will rather in the consequent than the primitive sense—as the end of reason, and as something absolutely valuable in itself. For Kant *good will 2* is the *absolute good.*

Kant seems to be saying that good will—that is good will 2—is the absolute good teleologically. He seems to be maintaining that the production of this particular good will is reason's end. And if he is not actually saying this as well as seeming to say it, then one is at a loss to know what the doctrine of the end of reason is about at all.

Kant says, quite clearly and without ambiguity, that good will is axiologically absolute: this axiological doctrine is no more evidently true than is the teleological one which marches with it. Some, at least, of the ends of good will are as valuable, or more valuable, than good will itself. We shall come to examples in Section A.8 below.

Common sense does not welcome either Kant's teleology or his axiology. One is loath to concede him either that good will 2 is reason's patent end, or that good will 2 is axiologically absolute. The absoluteness that good will 2 does have remains its simple portion; it gives it no real claim at all to these altogether grander and more exciting kinds of absoluteness.

6. "*The Absolute Worth of Mere Will*"

The expression "absolute worth" is one which we perhaps nowadays would avoid if we could, and even the early nineteenth-century scholastic Balmes found it very little to his taste. Kant however had none of our modern scruples. And when he talks about "the absolute worth of mere will", the "absolute" in this expression faces two ways: (i) towards an axiology and so towards a set of individual axiological comparisons between this absolute value and the value of the merely useful, and (ii) towards the considerations of ineluctability which define this use of the expression "absolute", considerations which we have already examined at length both in Harris and in Kant.

There is a progression in Kant, from (i) the commonplace sense of "good will" on the first page of the *Groundwork*, a sense for which one could substitute some expression like "practical reason", (see the first seven occurrences of the phrase, in the first two paragraphs, *G.*, pp. 61–2: pp. 10–11: A. pp. 9–10), to (ii) the subsequent sense, commonplace in essence but by no means commonplace as Kant uses it, which occurs and is developed in the third paragraph labelled by Paton, so ironically, "*The good will and its results*". Good will as will full of righteousness (will having generated ineluctable worth), that is, good will as good will 2, takes over from good will 1 (or good will as the power to act reasonably, the power to 'adjust one's principles to universal ends'), and this second notion of good will becomes at once not only Kant's candidate for the role of the end of reason, but, as well, the central notion in Kant's axiology.

7. *Good Will, a Divided Concept*

We said in Section A.4 on page 95 above that the third paragraph of the *Groundwork* is a watershed: now we can see how this metaphor applies. The first two paragraphs of the *Groundwork* are one side of the ridge, and in them we have good will as practical reason, good will 1. The third and subsequent paragraphs are the other side of the ridge, and here we have good will as the will full of ineluctable merit, good will 2: it is from this side that Kant is to fill his axiological reservoirs. From these reservoirs flow notions which determine his axiology and his ontology of value and which seep into Kant's treatment of the categorical imperative itself.

Kant's account of the categorical imperative, the imperative which might be termed 'The Form of the Category of Prudence', though essentially an account of good will in the primitive sense, is profoundly affected by the consequent sense of "good will" which takes over in his axiology, and which reinforces his predisposition to see the categorical imperative as essentially formal, and as unconditioned by any material considerations.

Harris is content to set up as his Sovereign Good and as the end of practical reason, practical reason's own function as pure function, namely Rectitude of Conduct. There is in Harris's "Praise" only a touch of the Kantian insistence on the merit of such righteous action. Harris's notion of Praise seems, so far at least, relatively undeveloped, though we shall see in Chapter V of the present Part how high a value he places on the agent's "acquiescence in the Consciousness of his own Rectitude" (cf. Part I, Chapter V, Section A.2, p. 141). Kant's notion of "the absolute worth of mere will" by contrast inflates itself swiftly and very dangerously; it can be diagnosed, quickly enough, as heterotopic.

Kant's insistence comes in the end to be on will's merit predominantly, and "good will" in its primitive sense is seen as a starting-point rather than as an end point. The merit of good will, the ineluctable goodness of good will, becomes for Kant the end of reason, and the centre of an axiology. One does not doubt that good will, in its primitive sense, has some further end: but the end that Kant would have it serve is altogether odd.

8. *The Axiology of Absolute Worth*

Kant's rationalistic teleology and its matching axiology seem, on the face of it, to have him denying the common sense of Shakespeare's:

> . . . for if our virtues
> Did not go forth of us, 'twere all alike
> As if we had them not . . .[1]

And this will not do. The curious situation in which Kant finds

[1] *Measure for Measure*, Act I, Scene i, line 33 (The Duke to Angelo).

himself, he has got into simply because the metaphysic has begun to run away with the morals of the *Groundwork*. The idea of the unconditioned has gone too far: it has run amok.

The axiology of the absolute value of good will is, clearly enough, what the difficult expressions "inner and unconditioned worth" and "absolutely good' in paragraph two of the *Groundwork* prefigure (p. 61: p. 11: A. pp. 9–10). The worth of "mere will" is 'unconditioned', at least in the sense that it is *not conditional* upon the success of the willed action. It is ineluctable, and it is ineluctable because it is *inner*, that is, immanent in the will of the agent. But whether or not these phrases in paragraph two prefigure Kant's assertion of the axiological supremacy of good will 2, the assertion itself is clear enough, when it comes in paragraph three.

We must consider Kant's explicit doctrine of absolute value at some length, and under two headings of his own devising.

(i) "*Something which has its full value in itself*"[1] Clearly there *is*, as we have seen, a sense, though a relatively trivial one, in which the ineluctable good of righteous willing is "absolute". Now the crucial question presents itself: "Can an axiological sense of 'absolute worth' be based on this sense of 'absolute'?" Kant answers "Yes" to this question, and draws a whole set of axiological consequences from his answer. We, on the contrary are forced to answer "No", and to reject the whole Kantian axiological deduction.

Kant has an axiology of absolute worth, though he introduces it in the first instance not with the phrase "absolute worth" itself, but instead by means of the invidious comparisons, which he draws in paragraph three, between *the will good in itself* and the other *goods* that the will might effect. These comparisons are various and complex, and they raise several kinds of issues.

The passage that we have so far omitted in our consideration of Kant's paragraph three, examined in Chapter III, Section B.2, pp. 65–69 above, now assumes a crucial importance. This passage itself consists of a particularly complicated set of

[1] Paragraph 3 of the *Groundwork*.

clauses, and even isolated from its dense and difficult context, it needs to be broken up into its simplest elements:

(*a*) "Considered in itself it [Good will, good through its willing alone] is to be esteemed beyond comparison as far higher than anything it could ever bring about—
(*b*) merely in order to favour some inclination—
(*c*) or if you like the sum total of inclinations".

(*G.*, p. 62: p. 11: A. p. 10.)

This raises, nicely, the issue between the two senses of "good will", good will 1 and good will 2. The passage asserts, in axiological terms, in terms of "esteem", that the function and purpose of good will 1 ("good will" taken in the primitive sense of 'practical reason') is primarily, if not solely, the generation of good will 2 ("good will" taken in the 'consequent' sense, the 'ineluctable-worth' sense).

"*Good will is to be esteemed far higher than anything it could bring about*"; this is the thesis (*a*). This thesis is modified by the two clauses (*b*) and (*c*). It is a thesis which might be contested, and one whose moral implications may turn out to be the reverse of edifying.

Let us deal with clause (*b*) first: "merely in order to favour some inclination". This suggests, perhaps, the old moral commonplace, that inclination must be subject to reason, and may relate to nothing more *outré* than the well-established notions that you must do what you ought before you do as you like, and that doing as you ought is altogether more important morally than getting what you want. Or it might simply be a reminder that the objects of inclination do not necessarily have any moral worth. All these material points could be conceded easily enough. However, the next clause goes further, and one might be prepared to concede what it claims if it is to be read in one way; but one will be forced to refuse the concession if it is read in another.

There are at least three possible ways of looking at clause (*a*) as it is modified by (*c*):

(i) If the expression "the sum total of inclinations" in (*c*) refers simply to the sum total of *one particular agent's* inclinations, then the favouring of them might be not only less valuable than good will, but even flat contrary to good will, or practical, 'universalizing' reason. If someone could "favour" all his own inclinations, but at the expense of other people (and the favouring of *all* one's inclinations would very possibly be at the expense of other people), then this end, though in a gross sense desirable for the agent, would not be morally valuable from any point of view at all. Kant may be concerned to remind us of this, and if so, what he says must be granted. The whole point of morality is that we cannot pursue the path of absolute egotism, and one is not going to contest this point here.

(ii) On the other hand, if an agent could favour the sum total of his own inclinations without trespassing on the rights of others, then he would have a perfect right to do so. It would be odd, too, to say that the good will exercised in bringing about this rare but happy effect was more valuable than the effect itself. Why should good will or prudence be 'esteemed beyond comparison, far higher than its results', even here?[1]

(iii) There is a third and quite different possibility however: "favouring the sum total of inclinations" might be taken in the sense of 'favouring the sum total of the inclinations of everyone involved', and read now as 'producing the greatest happiness of the greatest number'. Taken in this sense, the end of universal amelioration, an ideal which we do not very often realize in practice, is an essentially moral one. Indeed it defined the whole of morality, for Mill, and before him, perhaps, for Hutcheson.[2] Furthermore, it is an end which

[1] Kant's answer to this—because good will belongs to the noumenal world of freedom, while mere effects belong only to the phenomenal world—is one which we can note simply without discussing, in this essay.

[2] "That action is best, which procures the greatest happiness for the greatest numbers." Francis Hutcheson, *Inquiry into the Original of our Ideas of Beauty and Virtue* [1725] Treatise II *Concerning Moral Good and Evil*, Section 3, §8.

"The creed which accepts as the foundation of morals, Utility, or the Greatest Happiness Principle, holds that actions are right in proportion as they tend to promote happiness, wrong as they tend to produce the reverse of happiness . . . (J. S. Mill, *Utilitarianism*, Ch. II.)

". . . the end of human action, is necessarily also the standard of morality which may accordingly be defined, the rules and precepts for human conduct, by the observance of which an existence such as has been

Kant himself has at least acknowledged in the *Groundwork*, since it is no more or less than the 'adjustment of individual maxims to universal ends', and while this adjustment of personal ends into a public harmony may not be the whole of the law and the prophets, it remains an important part of them. Indeed so important a part is it that, if there *is* more, then it has to be shown that there is.

The other, and greater, part is, after all, essentially theological.

The question: "Which is of more value, the prudence or good sense or good will which brings about the universal adjustment of ends, or the state of affairs in which all ends are adjusted?" may be a meaningless one. But it is by no means evident that, if it is to be asked at all, then it is to be answered in Kant's way. We need not reply that: "Good will is to be esteemed beyond comparison as far higher than anything it could bring about . . ."

Is it, indeed?

Kant seems to take it as evident that good will, either good will 1 or good will 2 or both, is of greater value than any of the possible ends of will. His third paragraph closes with a comparison between good will and its ends which clearly favours good will; and there is no reference here to inclination, and no overtone of the possible conflict between passion and reason which a mention of inclination might introduce. When such conflicts do arise, then we must favour reason; but it does not follow from this that, when there is no conflict between what we would do and what we may do, the *willing to do* is somehow more estimable than the *getting done*.

Kant's view seems clearly eccentric when he says, in a passage already quoted in part above (pp. 65–6):

> [Good will's] usefulness [is] merely as it were the setting which enables us to handle it better in our ordinary dealings.

described [i.e. a happy one] might be, to the greatest extent possible, secured to all mankind . . ." (ibid., Ch. II.)

Mill explicitly uses the notion of "the end of human action", and locates the end, firmly, outside the will. And he locates it, of course, *in* "utility".

For Kant the "supreme good" is *virtue*: the *summum bonum* is only" the perfect good", the "supreme good" being the "condition" of the "perfect good", *C.Pr.R.*, A. pp. 206–7. See too A. p. 227.

This is not necessarily true at all. If good will's usefulness on a certain occasion comes to (for example) Jones's putting into effect steps to prevent Brown dying of cancer, then we do not say that the usefulness of Dr Jones's action—Brown saved—is a 'mere setting' for the incomparably more valuable and estimable thing, the good will of Dr Jones. "Good will" here can have either or both senses, 1 and/or 2, it makes no difference. We shall still be disposed to value the end at least as highly as the will which was the means. And "at least as highly" is a meiosis.

If Jones is a good surgeon and does his best but even so fails to save Brown, then that he tried is to his eternal credit, and here below it may be his consolation; but it is no more. It is not a precious diamantine thing compared to which Brown's recovery would be pinchbeck.[1]

Or, change the example and sharpen the eccentricity: a professional swimmer, Thompson, jumps into the river to save the Smith child. Thompson is inconvenienced by having to jump in in his lounge suit, but he is never in any real danger himself. Saving the child is easy enough for him, and no more than an inconvenient chore. Do we say here that the good will of Thompson is worth more than a child saved? We do not.

Why, is clear. These examples both involve persons, Ends-in-themselves, whose value is enough to render the actions both right and good, and even obligatory. The value of the end served, here an End[2]-in-himself, can easily outweigh the value of the agent's good will.

The kinds of value, good will and ends and Ends, might be said by some people to be simply incommensurable. It could be

[1] Consider also, "our ordinary dealings". What Kant says comes close to the notion—itself curious in the extreme—that the point of our "ordinary dealings" would be simply to produce settings for this 'jewel' of good will. Even if we take the 'great examination' view of life we must credit the Examiner with having set serious and interesting questions.

Whatever else one wants to say, this much is obvious: without our *ordinary dealings* there would be no occasion either for the functioning of good will or for the generation of good will 2. In whatever sense these kinds of good will are *unconditioned* they are essentially *conditional upon* there being things worth willing.

[2] The difference between ends and Ends will be specified further in Part III, pages 291 ff.

asked: "What sense does it make to balance the good of ends (one kind of value) or the value of persons (another kind again) against the 'value of mere will',"? We need not explore this possibility of incommensurability any further here. For our present purposes it is enough to notice that *if* the comparison is embarked upon at all, then it is by no means obvious that it falls out as Kant seems to think that it does. The contrary is true. Ends-in-themselves seem, self-evidently, always to be more valuable than the "absolute worth of mere will"; and ends, in the a-personal sense, may not always be less valuable than "mere will". The axiology of "the absolute value of mere will" is altogether odd.

(ii) "*This idea of the absolute value of mere will*". Kant makes his comparisons of value, which are far more open to question than he seems to imagine, in the context of the now familiar point about the ineluctability of the worth of willing. And he crystallizes this context itself in the first line of the next paragraph (*Groundwork*, paragraph 4), when he refers rather casually to "This idea of the absolute value of a mere will". The "absolute" in this phrase is dangerously ambivalent.

The notion of absoluteness has been defined by the ineluctability considerations. But it seems now in retrospect to have been used as a ground for those axiological comparisons which we have considered in (i) immediately above: comparisons that are seen in the light of ordinary common sense to be far from being evidently just.

Good will's worth which is absolute in the sense of being ineluctable is also apparently absolute for Kant in the axiological sense; but it is not clear how one gets this evaluative sense of "absolute" out of the metaphysical one. The expression "absolute value of mere will" looks to be no more than a dangerous equivocation.[1] Even reinforcing the virtually self-contained definition of "absolute worth" (which the ineluct-

[1] (i) Good will must be *valuable* before it can be *absolutely valuable*, i.e. valued-despite-its-ineffectiveness. That such a value is *absolute* makes it an absolute value (in the minimal sense in which it is "absolute"), but it does not make it a value.

(ii) That something is both absolute and a value does not make it the *absolute value*: see *Euthydemus*, 298–9, especially 298[e] ff.

ability considerations of paragraph three of the *Groundwork* give) with the assertion (at the top of paragraph one) that good will is the only thing "good without qualification", one can scarcely draw the axiological consequences which nevertheless seem so evident to Kant. The persuasiveness of a rationalist pattern seems to have prevailed over common sense, and Kant's notion of "absolute" in *absolute worth* turns out to be ambiguous. It is an Empsonian pun which we might welcome from Kant the professor of poetry, had he accepted that chair, but it is one which we must deplore in the professor of philosophy (see section B of the present chapter, below, pp. 116 ff.)

9. *The Function of Reason: the Ultimate Roots of the Axiology*

Kant does not dwell at all on the phrase "absolute value of mere will", though it crystallizes both the argument and the axiology of paragraph three. His particular use of it here in the first line of paragraph four of the *Groundwork* is simply as a rhetorical conjunction; it serves to tie the axiological comparisons into the full-dress discussion of 'the purposes of reason' which is about to commence. Even so, Kant's almost casual use of the phrase should not conceal from the reader the central role which this notion of absolute worth has in justifying—or in inspiring—those curious comparisons of value in the paragraph that has just closed. The question of the relative merits of good will and of its results has been settled in favour of good will; and this has all been done on the grounds of good will 2's unconditional coming-to-be. The pattern becomes even clearer later on in the argument when, talking about "that pre-eminent good which we call moral", Kant stresses, as something eminently worth notice and presumably of moral and axiological relevance, that this good "has not to be awaited merely from the result", being "already present in the person acting . . ." (*Groundwork*, p. 69: 20: A. p. 17; discussed below, Section A.12, p. 114 ff.). Now whatever one thinks about moral worth, and however highly one may value it, this fact that 'it has not to be awaited from the result' does not, as a rule, have much to do with the grounds of one's estimation of it. Nor, reading these particular passages of Kant, does one feel the slightest inclination to revise one's moral notions or to re-align them in the direction of the metaphysic of morals which the *Groundwork* is setting up.

10. *The Absolute Value of Mere Will, as the End of Reason*

Kant half acknowledges and seeks quickly to forestall the rebellion of common sense that his metaphysic of morals invites:

> Yet in this *Idea of the absolute value of a mere will, all useful results being left out of account in its assessment*[1] there is something so strange that, in spite of all the agreement it receives even from ordinary reason, there must arise the suspicion that perhaps its secret basis is merely some high-flown fantasticality, *and that we may have misunderstood the purpose of nature in attaching reason to our will as its governor.* We will therefore submit our Idea to an examination from this point of view. (*G.*, p. 62; p. 12: A. p. 10. Italics mine.)

Both Kant and Harris feel that they must meet suspicions of *fantasticality.* Harris is the more tender, and Kant the more resolute. Kant sweeps his axiological doctrine along together with his notion of 'absolute worth' in a series of teleological considerations which lead him to the inevitable conclusion that:

> In the natural constitution of an organic being—that is, of one contrived for the purpose of life—let us take it as a principle that in it no organ is to be found for any end unless it is also the most appropriate to that end and the best fitted for it. Suppose now that for a being possessed of reason and a will the real purpose of nature were his *preservation*, his *welfare*, or in a word his *happiness.* In that case nature would have hit on a very bad arrangement by

[1] See *C.Pr.R.* "We are here concerned only with the determination of the will and the determining principles of its maxims as a free will, *not at all with the result.*" A. p. 135 (italics mine). The question which Kant is interested in in this part of the *C.Pr.R.* is the one of 'the way pure reason can be practical, that is directly determine the will', i.e. by means of pure respect for—pure—universalizability. [See *C.J.* §29 on the "sublimity" of the—bare—'representation' of the moral law, M. pp. 127–8; B. p. 115.] Here in *G.* Kant stresses less the determination of the pure will, and more the immanent value of it.

> choosing reason in the creature to carry out this purpose. For all the actions he has to perform with this end in view, and the whole rule of his behaviour, would have been mapped out for him far more accurately by instinct; *and the end in question could have been maintained far more surely by instinct than it ever can be by reason.* If reason should have been imparted to this favoured creature as well, it would have had to serve him only for contemplating the happy disposition of his nature, for admiring it, for enjoying it, and for being grateful to its beneficent Cause—not for subjecting his power of appetition to such feeble and defective guidance or for meddling incompetently with the purposes of nature. In a word, nature would have prevented reason from striking out into a *practical use* and from presuming, with its feeble vision, to think out for itself a plan for happiness and for the means to its attainment. *Nature would herself have taken over the choice, not only of ends, but also of means, and would with wise precaution have entrusted both to instinct alone.* (*G.*, pp. 62–3: 12–13: A. pp. 10–11. Italics mine.)

Since happiness is not something that we can *with certainty* attain to, then it cannot be the end of reason. Further, if happiness were to have been the end of man, reason as we know it would not have been given to man, since it is a very poor means to happiness. From this it seems to follow that there must be some other end for reason, and the only proper end for it is the one end which it does attain infallibly: the production of good will:

> For since reason is not sufficiently serviceable for guiding the will safely as regards its objects and the satisfaction of all our needs (which it in part even multiplies)—a purpose for which an implanted natural instinct would have led us much more surely; and since none the less reason has been imparted to us as a practical power—that is, as one which is to have influence on the will; its true function must be to produce a *will* which is *good*, not as a *means* to some further end, but *in itself*; *and for this function reason was absolutely necessary in a world where nature, in distributing her aptitudes has everywhere else gone to work in a purposive manner.* (*G.*, p. 64: 14: A. p. 12. Italics mine.)

What can the end of reason be but a "good", which is "good in itself" because ineluctable? Teleology has found an infallible end for reason.

A good Aristotelian at heart though seduced by rationalism in the long run, Harris clings to the notion that happiness is the end of man the rational agent. When he comes up with Rectitude of Conduct as his Sovereign Good, Harris urges us to "fix our happiness" on it, even though this Good may not look like happiness as we usually understand it, and may indeed at times look more like Stoic renunciation. As a good rationalist Harris is very sensitive to the claims of the "Accommodate Self-derived and Indeprivable", and the identification of the Sovereign Good and Happiness with Rectitude of Conduct is forced on him. Kant, seeing that happiness is not in fact the infallible result of rational action, settles directly for what is: "the production of a will good in itself". And he lets happiness find its own place in the great scheme as best it can:

> Such a will need not on this account be the *sole* and complete good, but it must be the highest good and the condition of all the rest, even of all our demands for *happiness*. In that case we can easily reconcile with the wisdom of nature our observation that the cultivation of reason which is required for the first and **unconditioned**[1] purpose may in many ways, at least in this life, restrict the attainment of the second purpose—namely happiness—which is always **conditioned**[1] *and indeed it can even reduce happiness to less than zero*

[1] Notice the play on **"unconditioned"** and **"conditioned"** here. This particular pun is a complexity within a complexity:

(*a*) The end which Kant sees as *the* end of reason is unconditional: it is an unconditional purpose in the sense that its attainment is *not conditional upon* exterior circumstances. Fortune and chance are powerless to hinder it, since it remains, both in its beginnings and in its accomplishment immanent in the will of the agent. It is precisely because it is "*unconditioned*"/"*unconditional*" in this sense that Kant sees good will as the end of reason, i.e. sees good will 2 as this end.

Happiness, as a possible end of reason, is not so "*unconditioned*"/"*unconditional*" and so Kant rejects its claims to be *the/the prime, end* of reason. But further:

(*b*) happiness is in a clear, positive sense *conditional* on good will, that is

> *without nature proceeding contrary to its purpose.* (*G.*, p. 64: p. 14: A. p. 12.)

In so far as Kant may be read here as subjecting the claims of happiness to the prior and absolute claims of "the production of a will good in itself", we may accuse him of being a kind of rationalistic Pharisee. The production of good will is *not* what conditions human happiness, and it is not what can reduce it to zero. It is the claims of right action and the claims of the rights of others that can do this, but not any simple obligation on the agent to will well so as to produce ineluctably worthy will. There *is* no such simple obligation; good will 1 is not itself

on good will 1 or prudence; and in another sense again, (b1), it is conditional on good will 1.1, that is, upon prudence and a disposition towards moral action—happiness is dependent on the last, at least if it is to be 'deserved'.

But there is yet another sense in which happiness is *conditioned by*, *conditional upon* good will. This sense is led into by, but is stronger than, the sense of the 'conditioning' of happiness by good will 1.1:

(*c*) Crucially for the argument of the passage from Kant which we quote, happiness is '*conditioned*' by good will in the sense that our claims to happiness can be asserted only *after* the claims of duty have been met, or when there are no claims of duty to override them.

Anyone, Kantian or no, might admit that happiness was *conditioned* in the *b* sense, i.e. *conditioned by good will 1;* and it is only a moderate concession to the claims of the fitting, to concede that it is *conditioned in the b1 sense*, that is by good will 1.1.

Everyone must admit that happiness is *conditioned* by good will (i.e. by 1 and 1.1) in the *c* sense. To admit this *c* sense of conditioning is to admit no more than the inevitable, overriding claims of morality upon self-gratification.

But no one need conclude from *a* (i.e. that happiness is not inevitable in its coming-to-be) that it is conditioned in either the *b* and *b1* senses, *or* that it is conditioned in the morally crucial *c* sense. None of these senses of being *conditioned* seems to imply the other: the most that could be mounted would be an argument for some connection between *b*, *b1* and *c*: but *a* is empty of moral content. One does not get to *c* from *a*, nor does *c* imply *a*.

These points, *a*, *b*, *b1* and *c* might all be admitted, discretely, and without one's committing oneself to the large metaphysical doctrines and to the doubtful conceptual moves which are implicit in the persistent use of "*unconditional*", an expression which seems to answer more to an aesthetic than to a rational idea, and which is, at worst, a rhetorical device. See below, Part II, Chapter I, Section A, "Happiness as Conditioned", pp. 167 ff.

reason's end. Much less is good will 2 this end; and whatever conditions human happiness, it is not the prior claims of these things as pure ends.

Of course fortune too 'conditions' happiness, in that she may let it elude our grasp: but that is already well understood.

Good will, and good will simply in the sense of good will 1, recognizes the claims that others have on our action, and it shows us our duty. The point of good will 1 or prudence is that we may make a just estimate of values; it is not the point of values that they may determine prudence, and so produce the unconditioned good of good willing. There is, if we read Kant carefully, a suggestion of something literally preposterous in his priorities.

11. *Duty and the End of Reason*

It would not even be true to say that the end of good will 1 was simply that we should know our duty, as if duty were the end and *telos* of reason. It is quite false even to suggest that good will, now taken in the sense of good will 2, was the first, or the unconditioned, purpose of reason. To say that good will 1 was the end would be to forget, surely, that good will 1 obviously *is not* an end simply because it so obviously *has* ends.

The end of reason is not a unity. The notion of the '*end of reason*' may mislead us as it seems to have misled Kant; both happiness and duty may be pursued by practical reason, and both are ends. When one must give way to the other, the rationale of this renunciation of happiness is moral, and it is not a matter of rationalistic priorities, or of abstract teleologies.

When a duty is apparent to reason it is not for the sake, simply, of my seeing and so doing my duty that I can be said to have been given reason: here reason has an end which is beyond even duty. Reason has an end which is, if you like, duty's own end: that some act shall be done or undone, whose doing or not doing impinges upon the rights of some End-in-himself. Persons are indeed the Ends of duty. Duty is not in the last resort the end of anything, reason or anything else.

To turn Kant's teleologism back on himself we can ask: "What is the point of duty?" We can answer the question, too, in terms borrowed from himself: 'That Ends-in-themselves may be protected.' But we cannot answer the question as Kant himself answers it, with the reply that the point of duty is that moral agents may generate the unhinderable worth which accrues to dutiful action. Compared to the value of Ends-in-themselves, the mere accretion of worth in a moral agent is embarrassingly trivial. Is my "inner worth" or moral improvement, no matter how slight, worth more than the innocence which I must not seduce? Is my duty not to seduce the innocent determined by the worth-to-myself which I must forgo if I do the wrongful act? Is my duty not rather determined by the integrity of an End-in-itself, which I must, absolutely, not violate.

Kant's rationalistic argument was not, one supposes, intended to lead him into moral and axiological paradoxes, though it very clearly does. The essence of his central value, moral worth, lies in its ineluctability, and though ineluctable moral worth may be, morally speaking, a marginal value, it holds the centre of Kant's stage.

Kant's teleology and axiology of the ineluctable can be made plausible only when the ends of action, other than the end of good will itself, are morally trivial or can be made to seem so. The rationalist exaltation of good will 2 and the downgrading of other ends go hand in hand: we shall return to this question in Part Three.

12. "*Nature's Purposes*"

Nature's *telos* for any power, the rationalist argument premises, can never be something that might have been achieved as well or better by some other power; the end must always be whatever the faculty in question achieves *infallibly*. Pure instinct might have achieved happiness; reason can achieve only good will:

> . . . all these results (agreeable states and even the promotion of happiness in others)[1] *could have been brought about by other causes as well, and consequently their production did not require*

[1] The phrase "even the promotion of happiness in others" is, in this context, singularly monstrous. If we were not rational, then we would be incapable of charity and of rational love which are the two chief sources of such genuine happiness as there is in the world. See below Part II, Chapter III, Section C.4, pp. 274–75.

> *the will of a rational being*, in which, however, the highest and unconditioned good can alone be found. Therefore nothing but the idea of the law in itself, *which admittedly is present only in a rational being*—so far as it, and not an expected result, is the ground determining the will—*can constitute that pre-eminent good which we call moral, a good which is already present in the person acting on this idea and has not to be awaited merely from the result.*[1] (*G.*, p. 69: p. 20: A. p. 17. Italics in the last clause mine.)

This last quotation, dense and difficult, serves as a kind of summary of the whole argument so far. It states the teleological principle, and it defines *ambulando* the crucial notion of the unconditioned. The passage defines the *unconditioned* in the immensely symptomatic phrase in the last line, "and has not to be awaited merely from the result". This is the essence of one kind of *unconditionality*, that of the "absolute value of mere will" which is not conditional upon anything but the will. And Kant is never at pains to distinguish one kind of unconditionality from another. The value of mere will is *absolute* because unconditional/unconditioned; that is, it is absolute *because it does not have to wait upon the event* but is already incarnate in the mere act of willing itself. The metaphysical pattern is very elegant, but the conclusion is not one which common sense rushes to embrace. As we have already said above (p. 99), the metaphysical 'unconditionality' of good will 2 may seem to us totally without axiological—or moral—relevance.

For Kant, here, "that pre-eminent good which we call 'moral'" can be *constituted* ineluctably and with absolute ontological necessity within the will; it can be generated, with perfect assurance, beyond the reach of the malice of fortune and circumstance. Here we have the "inner and unconditioned worth" of paragraph two of the *Groundwork*. Or, by hindsight, we have here, now, whatever it was that these earlier phrases pointed towards, all fixed in the third paragraph's notion of unconditionality, which itself is tending to usurp the uniquely moral quality of moral goodness and of good will.

[1] The last phrase of this passage is discussed, again, below, Part I, Chapter V, Section A.2, p. 142, and Part II, Chapter III, Section C.4, p. 276.

Kant's use of "unconditioned" in the *Groundwork* answers to aesthetic rather than to rational, to poetic rather than to purely philosophical or to properly argumentative notions.

To use Coleridge's categories, and that not too inappropriately, one might say that the text of the *Groundwork* was less fanciful or fantastic, as Kant for a moment feared, than genuinely imaginative. The unconditioned is a poetical and gravid Idea: but, unfortunately, such aesthetic ideas are pregnant with ambiguity. The undoubted unity that they bring to their phenomena is one that analysis may all too easily dissipate: and here it is a unity which analysis must dissipate if the interests of morality are to be served.

B. THE UNCONDITIONED AS AN AESTHETIC IDEA

There is, in principle if not in detail, very little to be found in the poetic theory of Empson and his followers which had not already been foreshadowed by Kant in paragraph 49 of Book II of the *Critique of Judgment*. To say this is not in fact or in intention to detract from the genuine, creative originality of Empson. After all, in criticism the application of principles is everything, and the genuine critic is as much the man who shows us how to use the tool, as the man who first designed it.

If we forgive Kant his deplorable taste, or wink at his aesthetic patriotism, and permit him to illustrate a remarkably sound theory of poetry from a single and more than doubtful example, we can find the germ of the Empsonian method in his analysis of Fredrick's lucubration. Kant writes:

> When the great king expresses himself in one of his poems by saying:
>
> Oui finissons sans trouble et mourons sans regrets,
> En laissant l'univers comblé de nos bienfaits.
> Ainsi l'Astre du jour, au bout de sa carrière,
> Répand sur l'horizon une douce lumière,
> Et les derniers rayons qu'il darde dans les airs
> Sont les derniers soupirs qu'il donne à l'Univers;
>
> he kindles in this way his rational idea of a cosmopolitan sentiment even at the close of life, with the help of an attribute which the imagination (in remembering all the

> pleasures of a fair summer's day that is over and gone—a memory of which pleasure is suggested by a serene evening) annexes to that representation, and which stirs up a crowd of sensations and secondary representations for which no expression can be found.[1]

The germs of certain very influential contemporary theories of poetry are obviously here. Our minds grasp more than the poem *says*; the "rational idea" is the core, the flesh of the fruit lies all round the necessary armature: and what we grasp remains in a sense unsayable by us. "No expression can be found" as Kant puts it, though we know well enough what it is that we understand in the poem. What we understand can be explicated by criticism, though never caught in a paraphrase.

It is not to our present purpose to elucidate Kant's theory of poetry further, or to speculate on the critical works that he might have written had he accepted the Chair of Poetry at Königsberg. Clearly he would have filled it with immense distinction. Kant's notion of the aesthetic idea has been introduced, perhaps ungratefully to be used against its author in an analysis of some of his own more troublesome passages.

The following somewhat schematic analysis of the aesthetic notion of *the unconditioned* is offered in the belief that it enables us to make more sense than we otherwise might of the complexities and ambivalences of Kant's text. When we read the first few paragraphs of the *Groundwork* we feel, all the time, that we grasp something here, but we cannot say what it is.

1. *Recapitulation: The Idea of the Unconditioned*

Paul Klee remarked, acutely, on the difficulty that stands in the way of any clear explication of an aesthetic idea:

> It is difficult enough to survey the whole . . . but still more difficult to help another to such a comprehensive view.
>
> This is due to the consecutive nature of the only methods available to us . . . [it] results from deficiencies of a temporal nature in the spoken word.

[1] Immanuel Kant, *The Critique of Judgment*, trans. J. C. Meredith, Oxford (Clarendon Press), 1928/1961, p. 178 [trans. J. H. Bernard, New York, Hafner, 1966, p. 159.]

> For, with such a medium of expression, we lack the means of discussing in its constituent parts, an image which possesses simultaneously a number of dimensions.[1]

The analysis which follows will serve to recapitulate the chief points made in the present chapter and the one before it, and will provide a way into the other two Parts of the present essay. The analysis is set out schematically, and it attempts to show successively the simultaneities of Kant's Idea of the unconditioned.

The word "subject" is used in the following paragraphs in a sense which derives, somewhat remotely, from the musical one.

2. *The Idea of the Unconditioned: Analysis by "Subjects"*

We can trace the "unconditioned" Idea through its various transformations in the successive paragraphs of the first part of the *Groundwork*, seeing it as a kind of double or even triple *subject*, with a final working out which bears directly on the ontology of personal value as this is set out in the second chapter of the *Groundwork*.

The present analysis proceeds by paragraphs, that is according to the physical paragraphs of print as they appear in the relevant editions of the *Groundwork*, but it does not necessarily take into account Professor Paton's useful headings.

§1. *First Subject: Being unconditional because being-itself-a-condition: Good will 1*

(*a*) In paragraph 1 good will is said to be *unconditionally* good, "good without qualification". The sense of this is set, though only obliquely, by the consideration that good will itself is the *condition* of the goodness of anything else. Good will is the *unconditioned* good because it is the *condition* of the goodness of any other goods that we can think of, and it alone can "adjust" them to personal, and ultimately to

[1] Paul Klee, *On Modern Art*, trans. P. Findlay, London (Faber), 1958, p. 15. Klee is concerned, in this passage, with three-dimensional aesthetic images; but these present what is, in effect, only a special case. All explication of aesthetic ideas seems to face the same kind of difficulty: what comes as a whole must be dismantled, bit by bit, in a serial way. And, unlike motor car engines, or Bren guns, aesthetic ideas do not come with a handbook prescribing a rational order for demounting them.

"universal", ends. This is a way, if not an entirely satisfactory one, of setting up *a* notion of the unconditioned; what is itself a condition is therefore unconditioned. (But see above Section A.1 of the present chapter.)

(*b*) The moral-prudential sense of good will is given the faintest pietistic tinge by the phrase "a pure and good will" at the end of the paragraph.

(*c*) Or perhaps, it is simply modified by this notion of "a pure and good will", which serves to bring out the idea of the sound moral disposition which is itself an integral part of practical reason. (Good will 1 implies good will 1.1.)

§2. *First Subject.*

(*a*) Qualities which can be helpful to good will, helpful to practical reason or prudence that is, are nevertheless said to possess "*no inner and unconditioned worth*" themselves, and they are not to be regarded as "*absolutely good*". Their lack of *inner and absolute worth* is defined, so far, by their not being good unless they are qualified by the unqualified goodness of good will. Without practical reason even the qualities helpful to practical reason have themselves no unconditioned worth, "however *unconditionally* they have been commended by the ancients".

(*b*) To lack inner or absolute worth in this way is to be not-yet-qualified-by-practical-reason. The prudential moral notion of *good will* as practical reason itself is given, again perhaps, the slightest pietistic tinge by the phrase "*the inner worth of a person*": which phrase, as well, looks forward to the second subject. (What the *inner worth of the person* has to do with personal worth and the ontology of personal value we shall see in Part III.)

§3. *Second Subject: Being unconditional as not-being-conditional-upon-success: Good will 2.*

(*a*) The expression "*unconditional/unconditioned*" does not occur in the third paragraph at all. But this paragraph defines, nevertheless, a crucial *notion* of unconditionality, namely the notion of the value which is not-conditional-upon-the-success of the outward act willed. This notion of unconditionality is to dominate a great deal of the rest of the argument of the *Groundwork*.

This idea of unconditionality corresponds to those notions of "Accommodateness Self-derivedness and Indeprivability" which compel Harris to choose Rectitude of Conduct as his Sovereign Good. The notion of unconditional/ineluctable goodness is the notion which gets "good will" elected to the Kantian role of "the purpose of reason". The conjunction of the ineluctability of the goodness of *good will 2* with a teleological premise produces the Kantian conclusion that this good will, good will 2, is reason's end.

(*b*) This third paragraph contains (part of) the cash value of Kant's finding his axiological absolute in good will (i.e. in good will 2). The *unconditional* worth of *good will 2* gives it an axiological priority over the other goods which the will might effect, "its usefulness would be merely, as it were, the setting . . ."; and this unconditional worth is treated as axiologically absolute.

The transition from the metaphysical sense of absolute (which is defined by the ineluctability consideration) to the axiological sense is neither spelt out nor defended, and it seems to turn on an equivocation. Furthermore, in the light of the first sense of "good will" (good will 1 in paragraph 1) this transition looks extremely paradoxical. Why, if good will is the condition of the actual goodness of other goods, should "absolute worth" be identified with "mere", that is fruitless, "will"?

§4. (*a*) The unconditional value of mere will is now *referred to* specifically and for the first time as "absolute" in the first line of paragraph 4. The sense of "absolute" here has been defined, presumably, by the phrase: "good through its willing alone, good in itself . . . [even] if by its utmost effort it still accomplishes nothing", in paragraph 3 above. Certainly no other definition has been offered.

(*b*) And the phrase "all useful results being left out of account" refers back to the axiological implications which Kant has already derived in paragraph 3 from this notion of *absolute value*. The derivation is open to the severest criticism, and though the use of this expression "absolute" makes the drift of Kant's argument abundantly clear, it does nothing to make the argument itself convincing.

(*b*[i]) Indeed, the explicit use of the *expression* "absolute" to refer both to the ineluctability of good will's value and to its outranking all other good on the axiological scale, simply points up the equivocation on the *notion* of absolute worth which has occurred implicitly in paragraph 3.

(*c*) This fourth paragraph begins to develop the Kantian notion that the *unconditional* value of good will provides something that can pretend to fulfil:

> The purpose of nature in attaching reason to our will as its governor.

The production of this *unconditional/ineluctable* (Accommodate and Self-derived) worth of good will is later to be referred to as "reason's first and *unconditioned* purpose", and the Idea receives a superb literary or poetic, if not a satisfactory argumentative, development in this phrase "first and *unconditioned* purpose".

§5–6. These paragraphs develop the notion that the production of the unconditioned good of good will is the purpose of reason, by contrasting the infallible workings that instinct would have manifested *had* happiness been our end, with the fallible workings of reason when it is directed towards happiness as an end, in the world as it *is*. In the final sentence, having shown that happiness is not reason's end, Kant alludes to "a more worthy purpose" which is, indeed, "the supreme *condition*" of the [private] purposes of man. (See Third Subject: see also §7.)

§7. *Second, recalling First, and merging into Third Subject: the unconditioned as not-conditional-upon* and *the moral as conditioning the claims of happiness.*

(*a*) The "true function" of reason (which reason itself is not serviceable for guiding the will safely as regards its objects) "must be to produce a will which is good *not as a means to some further end but in itself*"; i.e. the *unconditioned* (= *unconditional*) good must be reason's *telos*. That is to say, good will 2 must be reason's *telos*.

The production of this good is reason's "first and *unconditioned* purpose", because a "first purpose" must, in Kant's hierarchical and rationalistic scheme, always be *unconditioned*, *eo ipso*. Happiness, for example, cannot be reason's first purpose, simply because it *is* conditioned—if only by chance, misfortune and miscalculation (and of course it is conditioned by duty. See Third Subject).

Reason, for Kant, not only must have a "first purpose" *a priori*, but it can be seen empirically or by inspection in fact to have one, namely the *unfailing* purpose of the production of good will, good will 2, which by virtue of its ineluctability must be acknowledged to be the required "*first purpose*".

And this ineluctable good must also be the highest good—here the axiology of paragraph three is reaffirmed—and "*the condition of all the rest*" (see the end of §6).

(*b*) This phrase "condition of the rest" recalls the *First Subject*: i.e. recalls the notion that good will 1, as practical reason, is the condition of the goodness of everything else; and the phrase also merges, as we shall see, into the *Third Subject*.

First and Second Subjects Worked Together.

(*c*) The production of the good of *good will* (and "good will" here has perhaps both the good will 1 and the good will 2 senses [cf. 7*a* and 7*b*]) is reason's first and unconditioned purpose; we have now the analogue in Kant of Harris's conclusion that the end of reason is Rectitude of Conduct.

The cultivation of reason, which is essential to the fulfilment of the first purpose, "may in many ways, at least in this life, restrict the attainment of the second purpose—namely happiness—which is always *conditioned*". Here the Third Subject emerges, and this is the *sole use of* "conditioned" to which a moralist need necessarily commit himself. It is a clearly *moral* use of a notion of conditionedness: the others are not.

Emergence of the Third Subject. This 7(*c*) sense of *being conditioned* is clearly enough the moral one, which we sum up in the important moral commonplaces: "You must do as you *ought* before you can do as you *like*", and "What you *ought* to do does not depend on what you *want* to do".

7(*a*, *b*, *c*). We have a kind of fusion now of the two senses of *good will*, the production of good will in either or both senses 1 and 2 is reason's "unconditioned purpose": good will 1 has an *unconditionality* defined in paragraph 1, good will 2 has an *unconditionality* defined in paragraphs 2 and 3; but by paragraph 7 these *unconditionalities* have merged, if only[1] in the sense that the one expression is used indifferently to cover both. This tends to bring together the two notions of *good will* (i.e. 1 and 2) into some kind of synthesis, and to play down the polarity that Kant has set up between good will as reason and prudence which looks towards ends ('universal adjustment'), and good will as the immanent and meritorious rectitude of a will which obtains regardless of the attainment or failure of any external end.

In 7(c) a "new" quite non-metaphysical sense of conditionality joins the other two, and expands the intentionality of the expressions *unconditioned/conditioned*. This new sense looks back, perhaps, to the faintly pietistic sense of inner worth as in "inner worth of a person" in paragraph 2, but it is capable of forcing its own definition, and of forcing its own acceptance upon us, quite regardless of these other notions. This "new" notion in 7(*c*), that duty is unconditional and that it conditions happiness, is one that need borrow no support from its more metaphysical neighbours. If we concede that there is any unconditionality in morals then it is this point that we shall be conceding, and not either of the more abstract, rationalistic ones.

The dominant element in the whole tripartite Kantian Idea of the Unconditioned, the dominant subject in the working out of the three together, is the unconditionality of *good will 2*, i.e. the unconditionality defined in paragraph 3 of the *Groundwork*; and this is the sense of *unconditionality* which we shall find recurring in later tracts of the *Groundwork*. The whole Idea remains essentially tripartite, however, even when all three subjects are running together, and overtones or undertones of the unconditionality of *good will as practical reason* (itself *the condition* of other goods) and overtones of the *unconditionality of*

[1] "If only": but this of course is the *only* way in which such disparate senses would merge: in an aesthetic Idea of the *unconditioned*, or in the ambiguity of the word "unconditioned".

duty emerge for a moment as they sweep on to the climax in the section on the value of the person in Chapter Two of the *Groundwork*.

It is precisely these notions, that prudence is necessary for the management of other goods, and that duty is not itself conditional and indeed conditions happiness (in the sense that duty does not depend on what we, as egotistical individuals, want, and can indeed override our desire), that carry the rather vapid metaphysical subject of good will 2 along with them.

The structure of the argument is, in so far as there is any argument, purely aesthetic, in that one ambiguous term holds it all together. The content of this gravid term derives, overwhelmingly, from the metaphysical "subject" defined in paragraph 3 of the *Groundwork*. (Later on, at the end of paragraph 16 this subject is expanded further, so that *the ineluctable* becomes *the moral*, or the essence of the moral, or seems almost so to do.)

The tripartite Idea of the Unconditioned, held momentarily in a synthesis at this point of the argument in paragraph 7, becomes itself in paragraph 8 the theme—or subject—of the subsequent paragraphs on *Duty* and the *categorical imperative*, "We have now *to elucidate* the concept of *a will estimable in itself and good apart from any further end*"—this is a concept that will be developed in the context of the discussions of Duty and of its formal principle, and it will affect, markedly, the ideas of duty and of the formal principle of morality which emerge.

They are discussed not, as one might expect, in their own right, simply: they are introduced as part of the "elucidation" of the notion of "absolute value of mere will" and of its cognate "a will estimable in itself, and good apart from any further end".

Kant's usage of the expression "*unconditioned*" answers, as we have said, to a kind of aesthetic Idea. His first and third "Subjects" (practical reason [good will], and the unconditionality of duty) are important and highly relevant to any theory of morals. The second Subject, good will 2, is lighter, more highly-coloured stuff, and it spins round in the solution after the weightier things have settled out: but simply because it is more highly coloured—more rationalistic—it reflects on all the rest, and gives the notions of practical reason and of duty and of the formal principle of morality a curiously rationalistic complexion. Though materially it is the least important of the three notions in Kant's triadic Idea of Unconditionality, as his theory is worked out, the Second Subject is the dominant one.

That good will as sense, prudence, or practical reason is the condition of the goodness of other goods is an evident truth. That duty is unconditional and so conditions happiness is another such. That the merit of good will as righteous striving after the right act is independent of the actual success or failure of that act is a truth too, but not a crucially important one: it is by no means as important as the other two, and it is neither their foundation, nor is it capable of adding anything to them.

It is however, the core of the *unconditioned* notion as Kant uses it.

It may be sensible to talk of the purpose of reason as being reason's own function when reason—i.e. good will 1—is seen as the adjudicator of all maxims, and as adjuster of all goods to universal ends. It makes much less sense to set up the ineluctable-unconditional praiseworthiness of rational action as the end of reason. It makes less sense, but there are strong rationalistic motives behind Kant's accentuation of the notion of ineluctability-as-"unconditionality".

It would have been better and more serviceable to morality to have stressed the two separate and categorically different points that (i) duty as duty is unconditional, i.e. makes demands with which we can not compromise, and that (ii) the goodness of everything else is conditional upon the presence of reason, that is, on good will 1. But Kant was, it seems, fatally tempted to throw the emphasis on the *unconditionality of the ineluctable*, and to combine the whole three ideas in a quasi-aesthetic, forceful, but finally unsatisfactory *Idea of Unconditionality* in which the ineluctability notion predominates.

No doubt *a* moral point is made when you say that: there is merit in trying whether you succeed or fail. But it is only a minor, peripheral point. It has nothing to do with the foundations of morality. Nor does it add anything of importance to the two more basic ideas: (i) that reason is the condition of the goodness of other things, and (ii) that duty is unconditional. When we finally unpack Kant's Idea, these two notions are seen to stand on their own merits and they neither need, nor can they gain from, association with the more rationalistically spectacular third notion, the "Second Subject", good will 2.

When we analyse out, one by one, the elements of Kant's brooding Idea we see how oddly they were combined, and with what little real profit to moral philosophy.

3. *Harris and Kant: a Difference in Emphasis*

Harris seems, if immeasurably the duller, even so the more prudent of the two men: his Sovereign Good is Rectitude of Conduct, "Accommodate, Indeprivable and Self-derived". And ineluctable too. But Harris's accent is always on "Conduct" as conduct, open essentially to outer consequences if these can be had. Kant throws the emphasis, for abstract rather than for concrete reasons, on the immanent, ineluctable, inner consequences of conduct, on "Praise" or praiseworthiness rather than on "Doing". The end which Kant seems to set up for reason, though perhaps metaphysically satisfying, appears in itself morally trivial. The suggestion that *good will* could be the *telos* of our rationality is, where good will 2 sets the tone and provides the concept-loading, quite monstrous. A dwarf, projected to make a colossus.

TABLE I: UNCONDITIONED/UNCONDITIONAL

The reader may find it convenient to have the crucial texts set out all in one place: this table gives both translations and the German text. Note that Paton uses "unconditioned" and Abbott "unconditional". (Italics mine, throughout.) Professor Paton's translation is cited first throughout this table.

Paragraph 3 is given in its entirety; the crucial latter half of paragraph 16 is given at length. Together these two paragraphs provide, we have argued, the specific intension of "unconditioned", as it is used in Chapter I of the *Groundwork*.

	English	*German*
§1	"a good will seems to constitute the indispensable *condition* of our very worthiness to be happy". *G.*, p. 61 "a good will appears to constitute the indispensable *condition* of our being worthy of happiness". *G.*, p. 10 A. p. 9	"und so der gute Wille die unerlassliche *Bedingung* selbst der Würdigkeit glücklich zu sein auszumachen schient" *G.*, p. 249
§2	"Some qualities are even helpful to this good will itself and can make its task very much easier. They have none the less *no inner unconditioned worth* but rather presuppose a good will which sets a limit to the esteem in which they are rightly held, and does not permit us *to regard them as absolutely good.*" *G.*, p. 61. "There are even qualities which are of service to this good will itself, and may facilitate its action, yet which have no *intrinsic unconditional value* but always presuppose a good will, and this qualifies the esteem that we justly have for them, and does not permit us *to regard them as absolutely good.*" *G.*, p. 10 A. p. 9	"Einige Eigenschaften sind sogar diesem guten Willen selbst beförderlich und können sein Werk sehr erleichtern, haben aber dem ungeachtet *keinen innern unbedingten Wert,* sondern stetzen immer noch einen guten Willen voraus, der die Hochschätzung, die man übrigens mit Recht für sie trägt, einschränkt und es nicht erlaubt, *sie für schlechthin gut zu halten.*" *G.*, pp. 249–50
	("However *unconditionally* they have been commended by the ancients") (". . . although they have been *unconditionally* praised by the ancients.") loc. cit.	("So *unbedingt* sie auch von den Alten geprisen worden.") loc. cit.

TABLE I—*contd.*

	English	German
§3	[*The good will and its results.*] "A *good will* is not *good* because of what it effects or accomplishes—because of its fitness for attaining some proposed end: it is *good through its willing alone*—that is, *good in itself.* Considered in itself it is to be esteemed beyond comparison as far higher than anything it could ever bring about merely in order to favour some inclination or, if you like, the sum total of inclinations. Even if, by some special disfavour of destiny or by the niggardly endowment of step-motherly nature, this will is entirely lacking in power to carry out its intentions; if by its utmost effort it still accomplishes nothing, and only *good will* is left (not, admittedly, as a mere wish, but as the straining of every means so far as they are in our control); even then it would still shine like a jewel for its own sake as *something which has its full value in itself.* Its usefulness, or fruitlessness can neither add to, nor subtract from, this *value.* Its usefulness would be merely, as it were, the setting which enables us to handle it better in our ordinary dealings or to attract the attention of those not yet sufficiently expert, but not to commend it to experts or to determine its *value.*" *G.*, p. 62. A *good will* is *good* not because of what it performs or effects, not by its aptness for the attainment of some proposed end, *but simply by virtue of the volition*, that is, it is *good in itself*, and considered by itself is to be esteemed much	"Der *gute Wille* ist nicht durch das, was er bewirkt oder ausrichtet, nicht durch seine Tauglichkeit zu Erreichung irgendeines vorgesetzten Zweckes, sondern *allein durch das Wollen,* d.i. *an sich, gut*, und, für sich selbst betrachtet, ohne Vergleich weit höher zu schätzen als alles, was durch ihn zugunsten irgendeiner Neigung, ja wenn man will, der Summe aller Neigungen, nur immer zustandegebracht werden könnte. Wenngleich durch eine besondere Ungunst des Schicksals oder durch kärgliche Ausstattung einer stiefmütterlichen Natur es diesem Willen gänzlich an Vermögenfehlte, seine Absicht durchzusetzen, wenn bei seiner grössten Bestrebung dennoch nichts von ihm ausgerichtet würde, und nur der *gute Wille*, (freilich nicht etwa ein blosser Wunsch, sondern als die Aufbietung aller Mittel, soweit sie in unserer Gewalt sind), übrig bliebe, so würde er wie ein Juwel doch für sich selbst glänzen, als etwas, das *seinen vollen Wert in sich selbst hat.* Die Nützlichkeit oder Fruchtlosigkeit kann diesem *Werte* weder etwas zusetzen, noch abnehmen. Sie würde gleichsam nur die Einfassung sein, um ihn im gemeinen Verkehr besser handhaben zu können oder die Aufmerksamkeit derer, die noch nicht genug Kenner sind, auf sich zu ziehen, nicht aber, um ihn Kennern zu empfehlen und seinen *Wert* zu bestimmen."

TABLE I—*contd.*

English	
higher than all that can be brought about by it in favour of any inclination, nay even of the sum total of all inclinations. Even if it should happen that, owing to special disfavour of fortune, or the niggardly provision of a step-motherly nature, this will should wholly lack power to accomplish its purpose, if with its greatest efforts it should yet achieve nothing, and there should remain only the *good will* (not, to be sure, a mere wish, but the summoning of all means in our power), then, like a jewel, it would still shine by its own light, as *a thing which has its whole value in itself.* Its usefulness or fruitlessness can neither add to nor take away anything from this *value.* It would be, as it were, only the setting to enable us to handle it the more conveniently in common commerce or to attract to it the attention of those who are not yet connoisseurs, but not to recommend it to true connoisseurs, or to determine its *value.* G., pp. 11–12 A. p. 12	

This Third paragraph (which connects up with the end of paragraph 16) is discussed above in the text: Part I Chapter III, Section B.2, pp. 65–69, Section C.3 and 6, pp. 82–83 and p. 86; Part I, Chapter IV, Section A.3 to 8, pp. 91–108: cf. especially 8(i), pp. 102–107.

	English	German
§4	"Yet in this idea of the *absolute value* of *mere* will . . ." *G.*, p. 62 ". . . this idea of the *absolute value* of the *mere* will . . ." *G.*, p. 62 A. p. 10	". . . in dieser Idee von dem *absoluten Werte* des *blossen* Willens . . ." *G.*, p. 250

TABLE I—*contd.*

	English	*German*
§7	"... but it must be the *highest* good and *condition of all the rest,* even of all our demands for happiness." *G.*, p. 64 "... must be the *supreme* good and *condition of every other*, even of the desire of happiness" *G.*, p. 14 A. p. 12	"... aber er muss doch das *höchste* Gut, und *zu allem übrigen,* selbst allem Verlangen nach Glückseligkeit, *die Bedingung sein* ..." *G.*, p. 252
	"... is required for the *first* and *unconditioned* purpose" *G.*, p. 64 "... is requisite for the *first* and *unconditional* purpose" *G.*, p. 14 A. p. 12	"... die zur *ersten* und *unbedingten* Absicht erforderlich ist" *G.*, p. 252
	"... of the second purpose, namely happiness—which is always *conditioned*" *G.*, p. 64 "... of the second which is always *conditional*, namely happiness" *G.*, p. 14 A. p. 12	"... der zweiten, die jederzeit *bedingt* ist, nämlich der Glückseligkeit ..." *G.*, p. 252
§14	"no *unconditioned* and moral worth" *G.*, p. 68 "no *unconditional* or moral worth" *G.*, p. 19 A. p. 16	"keinen *unbedingten* und moralischen Wert ..." *G.*, p. 256
§16	"Therefore nothing but the idea of the law in itself, which admittedly is present only in a rational being—so far as it, and not an expected result, is the ground determining the will—can *constitute that pre-eminent good* which we *call moral*, a *good* which	"Es kann daher nichts anders als die Vorstellung des Gesetzes an sich selbst, die freilich nur im vernünftigen Wesen stattfindet, sofern sie, nicht, aber die verhoffte Wirkung, der Bestimmungsgrund des Willens ist, *das so vorzügliche Gute,* welches wir *sittlich nennen,*

TABLE I—*contd.*

English	*German*
is *already present in the person acting* on this idea *and should not be awaited merely from the result*". G., p. 69	ausmachen, welches *in der Person selbst schon gegenwärtig ist,* die darnach handelt, *nicht aber allererst aus der Wirkung erwartet werden darf.* G., p. 257
"*The pre-eminent good which we call moral* can therefore *consist in nothing else than* the conception of a law in itself, which certainly is only possible in a rational being, in so far as this conception, and not the expected effect, determines the will. This is a *good* which is *already present in the person who acts* accordingly and *we have not to wait for it to appear first in the result.*" G., p. 20 A. p. 17	

For a partial resolution of the polarity between "the idea of the law" and the "absolute" good which does not have to be 'awaited from the result' of an action done for the sake of the law, see Part I, Chapter V, Section A.3; also Part II, Chapter III, Section C.4: see also Part III, Chapter II, Section A.4. "Mental Attitude or Moral Competence?", below, pp. 322ff.

The end of §16 is referred to above in the text:

Part I, Chapter III, p. 68.
Part I, Chapter IV, Sections A.9 and A.12, pp. 108 and 115. See below:
Part I, Chapter V, Section A, p. 134, A.2, p. 142, and A.3, pp. 143–144.
Part II, Chapter I, Section C, p. 190.
Part II, Chapter III, Section C.4, pp. 274–276.

CHAPTER V

THE NEW STRANGE DOCTRINE

> L'antiquité a beaucoup disputé sur le souverain bien. Autant aurait-il voulu demander ce que c'est que le souverain bleu, ou le souverain ragoût, le souverain marcher, le souverain lire, etc.
>
> Voltaire *Dictionnaire Philosophique*, "Bien, (Souverain Bien)"

The title of this Chapter is from Harris's *Dialogue*, and it comes from a passage which was to be echoed, curiously but perhaps inevitably, in the *Groundwork*:

> Your Doctrine, replied I, is so new and strange that though you have been copious in explaining, I can hardly yet comprehend you. (*D*., p. 106)

This remark, in which Harris plays the interlocutor to his own Socrates, matches Kant's curt acknowledgement of 'the suspicion of some high-flown fantasticality' in paragraph 4 of the *Groundwork*. Kant does not, unfortunately, equal Harris's copiousness and openness, and though he goes on to develop, he does little to explain and nothing to defend, his doctrine that the "absolute value of mere will" is the thing for whose production reason was given us by Nature.

What Kant keeps encapsulated in the aesthetic Idea of the Unconditioned, Harris spells out for us at considerable, even tedious, length. For all its tiresomeness, however, Harris's exposition has one great merit: at the end of the *Dialogue* we know precisely what it is that we would be agreeing to, if we were to fall in with 'the new strange Doctrine' of the Sovereign Good.

Harris, whether or not Kant had read him, is a most helpful pathfinder. He develops *in extenso* a rationalist, teleological, notion of a value or good whose ineluctability and infrangibility, let Fortune make to fall what blows she may, qualify it for the title of "Sovereign"; or to use one of Kant's expressions, which qualify it for the title of "absolute".

Kant and Harris agree on a central idea; the notion of an ineluctable, "Self-derived", "Accommodate, Complete", infrangible and irrefragable good. They disagree about this good importantly in one respect only. Harris wants his Good eudaemonic: Kant does not particularly care about eudaimonia as an element of his "absolute" good, not in the *Groundwork* at any rate.

Harris is concerned, if rather desperately, to show that his rationalist-Stoic Soverign Good can, despite all appearances to the contrary, be identified with Happiness. He is not, if he can help it, going to go back on his first axiom: "The sovereign good is what makes us happy." Kant, on the other hand, is not much concerned with happiness at all, and though it is allowed a short, parenthetical, appearance in paragraph 7, Kant is not especially anxious to make happiness central to his sovereign or absolute good. He concedes that good will need not be the only good, but his concessions to ordinary eudaemonism are less than generous:

> [A will which is good in itself] *need not on this account be the sole and complete good*, but it must be the *highest good* and *condition* of all the rest, even of all our demands for *happiness*. (*G.*, paragraph 7, p. 64: p. 14: A. p. 12. Italics mine.)

Happiness is admitted as an end, but its *conditionality* is insisted on. And that Kant is substituting, here, a bogus for a genuine conditionality makes the matter worse still from the eudamonists' point of view. Happiness is being sacrificed, if only in a theoretical sort of way, less to duty than to rationalist teleology. The absolute good of good will, and not the absolute value of persons or Ends, is being set up as that which conditions our strategies for happiness.

Happiness makes its appearance from time to time in the *Groundwork*, but it always vanishes again quickly, buried under talk about unconditionality and 'the motive of duty'. "A will which is good in itself" need not, even for Kant, be the sole good: but it is always for him the central good, the sun around which everything revolves.

A. THE BURDEN OF THE DOCTRINE

Harris, looking towards Happiness as well as towards accommodateness and absoluteness, puts his doctrine very plainly:

> It amounts all, said he, but to this—Place your *Happiness* where your *Praise* is. I asked, Where he supposed that? Not, replied he, in the Pleasures which you feel, more than your Disgrace lies in the Pain—not in the *casual* Prosperity of Fortune, more than your Disgrace in the *casual* Adversity—but in *just complete Action throughout every Part of Life, whatever be the Face of things, whether favourable or the contrary.* (*D.*, pp. 106–7. Italics partly mine.)

Happiness is not to be placed in what is "casual" but in what is "complete": in what is immanent and absolute, and not in what, to borrow Kant's phrase without his precise context, "has to be awaited merely from the result". Happiness must lie in what is itself *absolute* and beyond time and chance: and Harris dwells on this at length, saying very clearly indeed what Kant comes at rather more obliquely.

Harris is, as we have already said, infinitely more concerned than Kant to show us that Rectitude of Conduct is a hedonic as well as an absolute good. Having fixed happiness in the absoluteness of the worth of Conduct, *faute de mieux et pas en piété*, Harris tries to reconcile us to our situation, offering us happiness on ordinary terms whenever he can, and stressing the resemblances, faint though they may be, between his 'absolute' happiness and ordinary happiness when he cannot. This quixotic eudaemonism, however, is always less interesting than Harris's consistent rationalism, to which indeed the quixotry inevitably gives way in the end.

Harris does his best for happiness, and he is always at pains to show how his absolute good, Rectitude of Conduct, can co-exist amicably with other goods, goods that are more satisfactory in a worldly sense if not as certain in their coming-to-be, or as irrefragable.

Harris, though he believes as much in duty as most men, is not concerned, as is Kant, to talk largely about Rectitude of Conduct as "the condition of all the rest", so giving duty some high but ill-defined sovereignty in the realm of value. Harris's will, of course, has all strategies for happiness overriden by "Moral Office", but he puts his point about Office and its claims clearly enough for us to see where the limits of moral censorship lie. It is Kant who allows the necessary notions of duty-as-censor and duty-as-commanding-the-rational-will to spread without limit, and beyond their reasonable confines, under cover of the splendidly 'philosophical' but disastrously equivocal language of "condition"/"unconditioned"/"unconditioned purpose"/"condition of all the rest".

Nor is Harris inclined to make the kinds of pejorative axiological comparisons that Kant is so free with. For Harris the Sovereign Good is not allowed to become "the highest good" displacing all the others. Happiness, the ordinary man's 'highest good', must be shown somehow to merge into the Sovereign Good of "Conduct", if the thing is at all possible.

That, and how, the absolute good of good will is not the sole good for Harris comes out in passages like this one:

> But why then, said I, such *Accuracy* about *Externals?* So much Pains to be informed, what are *Pursuable*, what *Avoidable?* It behoves the Pilot, replied he, to know the Seas and the Winds the Nature of Tempests, Calms and Tides. They are the *Subjects*, about which his Art is conversant. Without a just Experience of them, he can never *prove* himself an *Artist*. Yet we look not for his *Reputation* either in *fair* Gales, or in *adverse*; but in the *Skilfulness of his Conduct*, be these Events as they happen. In like manner fares it with this the *Moral* Artist. He, for a *Subject* has *the whole of Human Life*—Health, and Sickness; Pleasure and Pain; with every other possible Incident, which can befal him during his Existence. If his *Knowledge* of all these be accurate and exact, so too must his *Conduct*, in which we place his *Happiness*. But if this *Knowledge* be defective, must not his *Conduct* be defective also? I replied, so it should seem. And if his Conduct, then his *Happiness?* It is true.
>
> You see then, continued he, even tho' *Externals were as nothing;* tho' it was true, in their own Nature, they were neither *Good* nor *Evil*; yet an *accurate knowledge of them* is, from our Hypothesis, absolutely *necessary*. Indeed, said I, you have proved it. (*D.*, p. 107.)

The moral artist needs other goods than good will itself as materials to work on, and for Harris these goods and their management are absolutely empirical. Since happiness, if it can be had, always remains a proper end for "the Moral Art" as Harris conceives it, the will of the moral artist has, to determine it, the ordinary concerns of life. These ordinary concerns must always be gone about according to the dictates of "Moral Office", but it is ordinary exterior goods, and not the necessity to produce bare inner good will, which provide the agent with his reasons for acting. The moral agent's will is moved by these exterior goods according to principles of experience, "accurate and exact" compilations from life, and not by anything *a priori*. For Harris, the moral agent's acts *are* determined by "the result expected from [the action]", (cf. *G.*, p. 69: 20: A. p. 17); and they may very well "borrow [their] motive[s] from this expected result" (*G.*, p. 69: 20: A. p. 17). For all that the Sovereign Good itself is immanent, the will as will remains, for Harris, very much engaged in the world: and indeed Kant's disengagement of the will from the world and from the empirical is no more than an illusion, though it is one that Kant cherished.

Harris is concerned, when he can be, more with good will 1, that is with prudence, than with good will simply as "Accommodate, and Indeprivable". However absolute Rectitude of Conduct may become as an immanent act of the will, it begins in and with the empirical and in no sense *a priori* concerns of ordinary life. Kant's bare formal principle of action (cf. *Groundwork*, pp. 68 ff.: 20 ff.: A. p. 17 ff.), has no precise analogy in Harris, and Harris has no use for such a principle. The pursuit of happiness as governed by the cardinal virtues will serve for Harris to guide the will in "Conduct", and to produce its inner "Rectitude".

The will of Harris's agent is not determined *a priori* and, materially speaking, *in vacuo* by a formal moral law, but it is moved by the ordinary claims of appetite and of reason, nicely and prudently balanced against "Office" to produce Conduct. When Kant asks:

> What kind of law can [it] be the thought of which, *even without regard to the results expected* from it has to determine the will if this is to be called good absolutely and without qualification?" (*G.*, p. 69: p. 21: A. pp. 17–18.)

he is putting a question which Harris would hardly have understood. Harris's metaphysics do not fly so high. They rise no further than the teleology of the Pre-conceptions and the aptness of Righteous Conduct to meet them. For Harris, the getting of happiness, in either the ordinary or the "new" sense, is a matter more of the Prudence of the Ancients, than it is of obedience to a formal, end-indifferent Law of Duty. For Harris, neither the agent's will nor the Law of his action prescind from the results; and why should they?

1. *The "Noble Prerogative of Moral Artists"*

However, for all that Harris's Moral Artist may be determined not *a priori* but empirically enough and by skilfulness of Conduct rather than by a luminous, transparent Law, the exercise of his Moral Art itself, considered as a purely immanent function of the will, is as absolute as Kant's "absolute worth of mere will". And for the same reason. The quotation from the *Dialogue* continues:

> . . . Inferior Artists may be at a stand, because they *want* materials. From their *Stubbornness* and *Intractability*, they may often be disappointed. But as long as *Life* is passing, and Nature continues to operate, the *Moral Artist of Life* has at all times, all he desires. He can never want a *Subject* fit to exercise him in his proper Calling; and that, with this happy Motive to the Constancy of his Endeavours, that, the crosser, the harsher, the more untoward the *Events*, the greater his *Praise*, the more illustrious his *Reputation*. (*D.*, pp.107–8.)

Inferior Artists are the practitioners of those inferior arts whose canon is success. The Moral Art may, of course, aim at success and at happiness; and though these things are not to be commanded, they still remain the aims of rational action.

Action itself, however, and the Moral Arts, are always to be commanded in a way in which ends are not; the Moral Artist as Moral Artist "has at all times all he desires". The Moral Art is immanent.

The ever-present availability, the absoluteness of the moral art itself, quite apart from the absoluteness of the worth which its exercise generates, makes it an obvious rationalist candidate for the title of our "proper Calling".

When Aristotle said that "nothing human is so constant as the excellent exercise of our own faculties", he thought in terms rather of the possible success of actions, than in terms of eudaimonia as a pure moral function; and Aristotle's theoria is selected as the proper end of man rather for its intellectual essence and its hedonic tone than for its relative accommodateness. Harris knows this, and knows that his reader does too, and he tries to meet the obvious objection that an Aristotelian eudaemonist—or the natural man—will raise to his identification of happiness with pure righteousness or the bare exercise of the Moral Art. Harris knows that, as Moral Artist in his sense, a man may 'have all he desires', yet feel as *un homme moyen sensuel* that he would like a little more. The *Dialogue* takes up again:

> All this, said I, is true, and cannot be denied. But one Circumstance there appears, where your Similes seem to fail. The *Praise* indeed of the Pilot we allow to be in his *Conduct*; but it is in the *Success* of that Conduct, where we look for his Happiness. If a Storm arises, and the Ship be lost, we call him not *happy*, how well soever he may have conducted. It is then only we contratulate him when he has reached the desired Haven. Your Distinction, said he, is just. And it is here lies the *noble Prerogative of Moral Artists*, above all others—But yet I know not how to explain myself, I fear my Doctrine will appear so strange. You may proceed, said I, safely, since you advance it but as an Hypothesis." (*D.*, p. 108.)

This "Prerogative" looks as though it is going to turn out to be as paradoxical as the "new doctrine" is strange. And remarkably uncomfortable it looks to be going to be, too.

"Prerogative" seems all too amiable a title for it, if the prerogative should prove to be what we suspect it to be, namely, a licence to call ourselves 'happy in the attempt' even if we fail to gain the end attempted.

It seems as though the eudaemonists' objections to a doctrine of fruitless happiness will not really be met. Even so, at least for Harris, Rectitude of Conduct is not simply to be called the "highest good" (*G.*, p. 64: [Abbott, "the supreme good" p. 14: A. p. 12]), as if this were axiomatic and self-evident. Harris knows that what we would have if we could is success, Kant's setting rather than his jewel; and he knows that if we are wrong about this then we want to be shown why we are wrong.

Harris treats our ordinary predilections less cavalierly than Kant does; if we ought not to 'look for Happiness in Success', but rather in the mere Rectitude of our Conduct, then we need to be instructed in this obligation. It is not self-evident.

2. "*The Very Conduct is the End*"

Harris instructs us with rationalistic argument. Though he insists that ordinary goods are the necessary materials of the Moral Artist, and stresses, when he can find it, the confluence of ordinary happiness and of righteousness, even so the innermost core of his doctrine is a piece of rationalism.

The quotation from the *Dialogue* goes on again, recommending our "Prerogative" in rationalist terms which tend to overbear rather than to meet the obvious objections of the ordinary, commonplace eudaemonist, who would like to be both good *and* successful. Harris finds himself, for all his willingness to concede what he can to our prejudices in favour of success, in much the same position as Kant, insisting, though with more overt rationalism and less covert pietism, on the claims of the metaphysical goodness of something which is, as he writes, "perpetually complete in every Instant". This good with its peculiar absoluteness, absoluteness defined now in terms of its completeness, overbears all our objections that it is not really what we would like to mean by "happiness".

Invoking this complete good, Harris can give the Moral Art an absolute end, and set up a Sovereign Good in which it will find its unfailing *telos*. But he cannot so easily show that this absolute end is identical with Happiness—happiness which is so noticeably neither absolute, nor so inevitably attainable, and whose very fragility set the whole of the problem in the first place. The *Dialogue* mounts this argument:

> Thus, then, continued he—*The End* in other Arts is ever *distant* and *removed*. It consists not in the *mere Conduct*, much less in a *single Energy*; but is *the just Result of many Energies*, each of which are essential to it. Hence, by Obstacles unavoidable, it may often be *retarded*: nay more, may be so embarrassed as *never possibly to be attained*. But in the *Moral Art* of Life, the very CONDUCT is the END; the very *Conduct*, I say, itself, throughout every its *minutest* Energy; because

> each of these, however *minute*, partake as truly of *Rectitude*, as the *largest Combination of them*, when considered collectively. Hence of all Arts is this the only one *perpetually complete in every Instant*, because it needs not, like other Arts, *Time* to arrive at that Perfection, at which in *every Instant* it is arrived already. Hence by *Duration* it is not rendered either *more* or *less* perfect; *Completion*, like Truth, admitting of no Degrees, and being in no sense capable of either *Intension* or *Remission*. And hence too by necessary Connection (which is a greater Paradox than all) even that *Happiness or Sovereign Good*, the End of this Moral Art, is itself too, in *every Instant*, *Consummate and Complete*; is neither *heightened* or *diminished* by the Quantity of its *Duration*, but is the same to its Enjoyers, for a *Moment* or a *Century*. (*D*., p. 109.)[1]

"*The very Conduct is the END*." This, now, is what the rationalist can offer us: happiness, "in every instant Consummate and Complete" and "admitting of no Degrees" and of no "Intension or Remission". This happiness is a mundane, secular analogue of the Beatific Vision itself, and its supreme excellence is in its *consummateness*. That its hedonic tone may be rather low is by now neither here nor there.

Time, the great enemy, cannot touch the Sovereign Good, "by Duration it is not rendered more or less perfect", and it rises above all the shocks and chances of everyday life.

This consummate complete "happiness" is an analogue of the Beatific Vision in so far as its consummateness and completeness are the nearest we can get, here below, to the positive eternity of heaven. While Harris's "END" may not be Boëthian, *interminabilis vitae tota simul et perfecta possessio*,[2] it is the best that the world can offer. And if, as happiness, it seems very thin in tone, this is the best the world can afford, on these particular terms. A livelier happiness, if we may put it this way, is always in danger of lacking the precise consummateness of "Conduct".

[1] Harris's idea of an "Energy", which engaged Herder's attention in the *Kritische Wälder*, is developed in the two aesthetic *Dialogues*; here in the *Third Dialogue* it recurs, but is neither effectively used nor further developed. One can see how Harris might have made a great deal more of it, in the heart of the *Third Dialogue*.

See above, Part I, Chapter I, Section 3, and footnote 1, p. 25.

[2] Boëthius, *De Consolatione Philosophiae* 5, 6.

What is crucial here is not, really, the attempted identification of happiness with the Sovereign Good—we see this as foredoomed to failure anyhow—but the way in which this Sovereign Good or "END" is described. It is, like eternity, "perpetually complete in every instant", "Consummate and complete", and "neither heightened nor diminished . . . the same for a moment or a century". Harris has all the stops pulled out as far as they will go.

Nor are our parallels with Boëthius' eternity and with the Beatific Vision idle commentary. The latter comparison at least is Harris's own idea; and though he makes it somewhat offhandedly in a parenthesis, the context has us in no doubt about the seriousness of the analogy. The rationalist Sovereign Good is to be, beneath the moon, as much "Complete" and above Fortune's flux as is the vision of the blessed in heaven. Harris says of his "System", that is of the view of the Sovereign Good which he proposes, that:

> If its aims are successful it is thankful to Providence. It accepts all the Joys derived from their Success, and feels them as fully, as those who know *no other* happiness. The only Difference is that having *a more excellent Good* in view, it fixes not, like the Many, its *Happiness* on *Success* alone, well knowing that in such case, if Endeavours *fail*, there can be nothing left behind but Murmurings and Misery. On the contrary, when this happens, it is then it retires into itself, and reclining on what is *Fair*, what is *Laudable*, and *Honest* (*the truly beatific Vision, not of mad Enthusiasts, but of the Calm, the Temperate, the Wise and the Good*) it becomes *superior to all Events; it acquiesces in the Consciousness of its own Rectitude;* and like that Mansion founded not on the Sands, but on the Rock, it defies all the Terrors of Tempest and Inundation. (*D.*, p. 121. Italics of parenthesis mine.)

The will of a rational agent[1] who is convinced by Harris's system may seek exterior goods: but if baffled, "it retires, into

[1] Harris's "it" is troublesome here. One often has to search about in his paragraph to find the antecedents of his pronouns: it is annoying to have to do this in so crucial a passage. Our own phrase "The will of a rational agent . . ." is an interpretation: the thing to which Harris's "it" seems in his text to refer, is his system or his 'new doctrine' of the "END".

itself"; and so retired, it 'reclines on what is Fair, Laudable and Honest' enjoying "the truly beatific Vision" and becoming "superior to all Events". Here is the rationalists' absolute as absolute as one could hope to find it. If Kant had expressed his notion of "the absolute worth of mere will" as copiously as this, it might have been apparent to himself and to his readers that the cash value of it was indeed a "beatific Vision". A beatific Vision which dispenses, at a stroke, with one of the conventional capital letters, and with beatitude.

Harris's Sovereign Good is Sovereign Good because "perpetually complete in every instant"; it is a good, as Kant would put it, "good not as a means to some further end but in itself" (*G.*, paragraph 7, p. 64: p. 14: A. p. 12). And it is pre-eminently a good which "has not to be awaited merely from the result" (*G.*, paragraph 16, p. 69: p. 20: A. p. 17). It is the good of a will which, when circumstances are frowning, "retires *into itself*". Here Harris's language and Harris's notion both strike echoes in Kant. For example, they seem to be taken up in phrases like Kant's "*inner* and unconditioned worth" (*G.*, paragraph 2, p. 61: pp. 10–11: A. pp. 9–10), and in other phrases and notions in the *Groundwork*.

Harris chooses "Conduct" as the "more excellent good" precisely because it does not rely on success, and here he and Kant are in perfect accord. Rationalist immanentism can go no further than to make "Sovereign" or "absolute" the good which the will finds in itself when it 'retires into itself'. Conduct and the will's "acquiescence in the consciousness of its own Rectitude" become the inner, immanent "END" of reason. This "END" is, to borrow a phrase from Kant, the good of "a will good in itself", and triple armed against fate and fortune.

Heralds cannot be taken as prophets, their view is always backward-looking. Yet it is curiously apt that Harris, whose Sovereign Good is impregnable as "Accommodate, Self-derived and Indeprivable", should bear on his shield three hedgehogs *or*. And there is a fourth on his crest.[1] This last, somewhat larger, hedgehog symbolizes, perhaps, *Durability*, as this is realized by the Sovereign Good, according to the 'new, strange

[1] Harris's arms: *argent, a chevron ermine noir, between three hedgehogs or*, are reproduced beneath the portrait-frontispiece to Volume I, of the *Works*.

Doctrine'. Here in this shy but well-protected animal we have a metaphor for a Sovereign Good that, "if Endeavours fail", can 'retire into itself'.

These emblems are all happy coincidence; but they would have made an elegant conceit for canting arms.

3. *Moral Good and the Perpetually Complete, Absolute Good*

As in Kant there is in Harris too, a tendency for a constellation of superior moral notions to form around the rationalistically excellent good which 'has not to be awaited in the Event'. Harris may not identify this good, as Kant seems to identify it, by osmosis, with moral goodness, *tout simple* (*G.*, paragraph 16, p. 69: p. 20: A. p. 17), but he gathers around it, nevertheless, whatever is "Fair, Laudable and Honest".

This is a natural enough process, since fairness, honesty and the rest are conditions of Rectitude of Conduct as rectitude. Even so, we must beware of letting the 'availability' of Conduct, or its 'absoluteness' usurp the moral point of Rectitude itself.

There is, in rationalism of Kant's and Harris's sort, a tendency for the 'absolute', the 'accommodate' and the ineluctable to displace the properly moral itself. The centre of gravity, the sun, in a rationalist system becomes, not the moral at all, but the '"absolute" good' as "absolute".

Rationalism seems in the end to overlay with pure metaphysics the very moral point of righteousness itself. We ought indeed to pursue righteousness, but for righteousness sake, or, to be precise, for the sake of the values that it serves. We should not seek righteousness, simply because it alone of all earthly things is unfailing. It may indeed be unfailing, from a certain point of view, but our obligations are towards it in itself as righteousness, and not towards it as the only indeprivable good to be found beneath the heavens.

Kant is in grave danger of letting the very moral itself be replaced by the "absolute": and we have already seen a marked symptom of this in the last clauses of the sixteenth paragraph of Chapter I of the *Groundwork* where he talks of:

> . . . that pre-eminent good which we call *moral*, a good which *is already present in the person acting*, . . . and should *not be*

awaited merely from the result. (*G.*, p. 69: p. 20: A. p. 17. Italics mine.)[1]

The expression "*moral*" is in grave danger (here, and by implication elsewhere) of becoming defined in terms of the other two expressions in italics. Moral worth may be ineluctable, but it is not *moral* in virtue of this ineluctability: nor has the pre-eminence of moral goodness over other goods anything to do with its 'not having to be awaited from the result'. The moral is moral, and pre-eminent, for reasons which have nothing to do with this rationalistic kind of absoluteness.

There is a passage in one of the Psalms which may help to bring out this last point; the final phrase of the verse gives us a kind of model of the rationalists' "absolute". The *Vulgate* reads:

> Jucundus homo qui miseretur, et commodat,
> disponet sermones suos in judico,
> Quia in aeternum non commovebitur.
>
> (Psalm 111: 5–6.)

The Prayer Book version contains the same instructive phrase:

> A good man is merciful and lendeth: and will guide
> his words with discretion.
> For he shall never be moved . . .
>
> (Psalm 112: 5–6.)

We must show mercy. We must "lend". These are, presumably, for the author of the Psalms, absolute moral principles. And if we do show mercy, then we "shall not be moved for ever". But the point of our showing mercy, and the point of its being our duty, is not that we may not be moved for ever.

Kant has, so to speak, given up external ends only to fall victim to an internal and immanent one, precisely because it is internal and immanent, and *in aternum non commovebitur*. The end is "beatific" in Harris's lax and empty sense; and it is not morality's specific end.

The point of mercy and of lending lies in themselves; that is to say in the good that may be done to persons, to Ends-in-

[1] See above, Part I, Chapter III, Section B.2, p. oo; Part I, Chapter IV, Section A.9 and A.12, pp. 108–115. See below, Part II, Chapter III, Section C.4, pp. 274–6, and Part III, Chapter II, Sections A.3–4, pp. 319 ff.

themselves, by acts which are guided by principles of long-suffering and of benevolence. The point of mercy is not that the merciful man shall be not moved. The point of morality is not that agents shall become worthy, even 'unconditionally' so: and the point of moral worth itself is not its ineluctability.

We have two "absolutes" in this context; on the one hand the moral absolutes "Be merciful!" and "Lend!", which relate in turn to persons as absolute in the realm of value; and on the other hand we have the "absolute" of '*being not moved*'. Now by an accident of language, this second "absolute" will stand well enough as a kind of model for the ineluctable infrangible Accommodate absolute and Complete Sovereign Good, and we can see that it is, though "absolute" in a sense, and absolute in a rationalist sense, neither the ground of, nor as important as, the moral absolutes. Who would have thought that it was? Kant? No, perhaps not if one takes him as entertaining the notion explicitly. But in so far as he is caught in the grip of his own metaphysic of morals, just this startling reversal of values is implicit at every turn. In Part III of this essay we shall see how far Kant is prepared to take his rationalist axiology, and his metaphysic of moral absolutes.

To borrow Kant's own terminology of hypothetical and categorical imperatives: the Moral Law does not say, "*If* ye would not be moved for ever, *then* 'act only on that principle . . . '". It says simply, "Act only on that principle . . . ". The Moral Law is absolute: but not because its end is an absolute-of-ineluctability. One can never be certain that Kant in the *Groundwork* at least is doing justice to this fact.

Though Kant provides the language of categorical and hypothetical imperatives in which we may put the point that we are going to make, the point may be made against him, and there is at least a case *prima facie* to be answered by him.

Kant, as we shall see in a later Chapter[1] talks, in the *Groundwork*, first about duty and action for the sake of the law, and only then about the simple form of the law itself. And his first enunciation of the categorical imperative is cast not in terms of an obvious question such as, "If I want to do the right thing, how do I know what the right thing is?", but in terms of talk

[1] See: Part II, Chapter III, Sections B and C, pp. 234 ff and pp. 248 ff respectively.

about good will. If we look at the text we find that good will is in this context, as highly charged with good will 2 and with the *soi-disant* absoluteness of ineluctability, as it is with good will 1. Kant says:

> ... I need no far-reaching ingenuity to find out what I have to do *in order to possess good will*. Inexperienced in the course of world affairs and incapable of being prepared for all the chances that happen in it, I ask myself only '*can you also will that your maxim should become a universal law?*' When you cannot it is to be rejected ... (*G.*, paragraph 18, p. 71: p. 23: A. p. 19. Italics mine.)

What is meant by "*good will*" here? If I want to possess good will 1, that is practical reason, or the will which adjusts my maxims to universal ends, then the question "Can I will my maxim universally?" is the way in which to possess it. The way to bring into action the potential good will or reason with which nature has already endowed me, is to ask the question which the categorical imperative sets before me. The categorical imperative is indeed, if anything is, the Form of good will 1.

But if, bearing in mind the ineluctability talk in paragraph 3 of the *Groundwork*, and the exposition of the doctrine of the end of reason in paragraphs 4–7, we take the question adumbrated in Kant's eighteenth paragraph to mean, "What must I do if I would possess [*the merit of*] good will?", then we cannot avoid the suspicion that Kant thinks the point of the categorical imperative itself to be, not so much the good that might be done by following it, not so much the Ends-in-themselves protected by it, as the ineluctable good will which, under its guidance, an agent may generate within the immanence of his own psyche. Such a doctrine would be altogether odd. And it would make the categorical imperative itself hypothetical, in so far at least as my asking, "Can I will *m* universally?" would be contingent upon my wishing to attain the end of 'possessing good will'.

It makes some sense at least to ask, "Why should I concern myself with having good will 2?", while it makes none at all to ask, "Why should I concern myself with good will 1?" Simply being reasonable in either the reflective/discursive or the practical way carries its own evident and uncontestable *ratio*, in a way in which even being full of the "absolute" merit of righteousness does not. Thus the categorical imperative seen as having its *end* in *good will 2* would be a *condition* of something that might be allowed to be called into question:[1] how categorical would it then be?

Whether or not one can use, successfully, against Kant a knockdown argument of the sort just sketched, one wants to insist, at the very least, that Kant's language here, on pp. 71: 23: A. p. 19 of the *Groundwork*, is indiscreet. In these passages "good will" answers both to the notion of regulative practical reason, and to the special rationalistic idea of an absolute worth. When any of us ask ourselves, "What must I do to possess good will?", if any of us ever do, surely what we mean, in the context of talk about the categorical imperative is, "How can I find a right principle of action?" We do not mean: "How can I be 'absolutely good', ineluctably worthy?"

The categorical imperative does not say, "If you want to be worthy, then, act only . . .". It says: "Act only. . . ." So it should.

Indiscreet though Kant may be here in the eighteenth paragraph of the *Groundwork*, there is a kind of consistency about the pattern. If indeed the end of reason is good will, i.e. good will 2, then the end of anything which conduces to this must itself be good will 2; the categorical imperative and its being followed are both conducive in just this way.

If Kant wants to maintain that the *telos* of good will 1 and of the categorical imperative itself is good will 2, then he is saying not simply that man is made for the sabbath, but that he is made ultimately for the Lord's Day Observance Society. A monstrous conclusion: but monstrous only when it is brought out. The trouble with so much of the doctrine of the *Groundwork* is that Kant never brings it out at all. It lies in the text, like forgotten objects in a time capsule.

All that the critic can say here is this: Kant has already

[1] In a theological context, of course, the question "Why do you want to generate good will?" gets the answer, "Because such righteousness 'avails to eternal life'." In such a perspective acts for the sake of good will become, even for Kant, acts conditional upon an end, if an eternal End. On this, see below: Part II, Chapter II, "Virtue and Rewards".

committed himself falsely to the doctrine of the end of reason, and that is in itself bizarre enough. If he seems, on the face of it, to be compounding yet another oddity in his notion of the "end" of the categorical imperative, the seeming at least may be looked into. Perhaps if Kant had thought that his text bore the interpretation which we put on it, then he might have explicitly ruled this interpretation out: but the text as it stands is not entirely clear, and it is even troubling.

4. *A Variety of Absolutes*

The intension itself of the categorical imperative ought, perhaps, to define the sense of "good will" in paragraph 18 (*G.*, p. 71: 23: A. 19–20) for us. The expression "good will" here, we feel, can properly mean only good will 1: and perhaps it does. But the context of the *Groundwork* exposition of the categorical imperative is at best ambiguous: at worst it is plain confusing.

The interpretation of the categorical imperative in terms simply of good will 1 is certainly borne out by the phrase ". . . inexperienced in the course of world affairs . . .", which suggests that the categorical imperative will fill in for that prudence to which we cannot lay much claim. And what we are being offered seems, if certain phrases are stressed and others suppressed, to be simply a moral touchstone, and a useful one.

This "formal" principle of action, this touchstone of maxims, is a great deal more helpful than Harris's talk about skill and experience in conduct. Likewise, as a rule of socially, responsible prudence, or if you like of moral prudence *tout simple*, the first formulation of the categorical imperative is as elegant and as useful as one could want.

It is cast in the form not only of a category or form of all acts of moral prudence, but as well in the form of a categorical, that is, absolute and no-buts-and-ifs-about-it moral command. It is simply the meta-moral command, under which all particular commands can be made to fall, and is therefore doubly and elegantly categorical. "Categorical" here is a fruitful paranomasia.

Given the ambiguity of Kant's use of "good will" and the heavy involvement of one sense of it with notions of ineluctability, the difficulty is to disentangle the strands of intension.

Is Kant concerned chiefly with the *absoluteness of the moral Law as morally absolute*, and with the *absolute value of Ends-in-themselves* (the thing which itself determines which maxims shall fall under or fail to fall under the category of universalizable), or is he concerned rather with the *absoluteness* of the "absolute worth of mere will"?

The question can be asked, but not answered. Kant himself never quite faced it in the *Groundwork*, as far as one can see, and so he never made up his mind. He left us with a text that forces us to try to make up our minds. There is, surely, in the whole matrix of ideas with which the first chapter of the *Groundwork* provides us, a polarity between two absolutes. There is a polarity between (i) the absoluteness of moral principles,[1] their being able to command categorically, against inclination, and contrary to interest, and (ii) the rather empty absoluteness of acts of will which are, to use Harris's expression "perpetually complete in every instant", or which are, to use Kant's terms, acts of a will "which is good in itself" and "always good". The polarity can be traced in the text: and it can be applauded as poetical, or deplored as confusing. The one thing we do not seem to be able to do with this polarity is to resolve it. All that can be done is to confront Kant's readers with it, and let them do what they can to disengage the morals from the metaphysics of the *Groundwork*.

Are the agents in Harris's and Kant's systems concerned to be merciful because morally one must? Or are they concerned to be merciful because this is the only way in which they may be 'unmoved for ever' in a rationalist sense? The question can be opened, but perhaps not ever quite closed. Very little escapes the chances of the world, or attains to an absoluteness even as modest as that of the Moral Art which "is arrived at every instant in its perfection". And a kind of intellectual thrift might impel a philosopher to make sure that even this slenderest of absolutes should not go to waste. Well and good; if it can be turned to account, then it can be. This particular absolute, however, offers no support to, and certainly no

[1] The absoluteness of moral principles itself derives, in the last resort, from a third absolute, i.e. from the absolute worth or value of Ends. Such, at any rate is our thesis: how far was it Kant's? For a discussion of this, see Part III.

alternative to, the absolutes of morality and the absoluteness of the worth of persons.

Kant seems to be in danger, if only because his ideas and his language are not quite worked out in the *Groundwork*, of confusing and conflating the two, a-categorical kinds of absolute, the moral and the merely metaphysical.

Harris, who is much less concerned with duty and with the claims of moral action as absolute claims, grapples manfully with the thankless task of identifying the rationalistic absolute, by hook or by crook, with happiness. And we may leave Kant's difficult and pregnant text for a while, and return to Harris and watch him struggle to make a happiness as 'unmoved for ever' as is Rectitude of Conduct.

5. *The Sovereign Good as Happiness*

When we left Harris he had just reiterated that "*Happiness* or *Sovereign Good*, the End of [the] Moral Art, is itself too, *in every instant Consummate and Complete*". But Harris the author is probably aware that this suggestion that Happiness is in every instant consummate simply begs the very question which lies at the root of his whole *Dialogue*. He allows Harris the faithful interlocutor and good listener to raise a silent objection:

> Upon this I smiled. He asked me the Reason. It is only to observe, said I, the Course of our Inquiries—a new Hypothesis has been advanced—Appearing somewhat strange, it is desired to be explained—You comply with the Request, and in pursuit of the Explanation, make it ten times more *obscure* and *unintelligible*, than before. It is but too often the Fate, said he, of us Commentators. But you know in such cases what is usually done. When the Comment will not explain the Text, we try whether the Text will not explain itself. This Method, it is possible, may assist us here. The Hypothesis, which we would have illustrated, was no more than this—That the *Sovereign Good lay in Rectitude of Conduct*; and that *this Good corresponded to all our Pre-conceptions*. Let us examine then, whether, upon trial, this Correspondence will appear to hold; and, for all that we have advanced since, suffer it to pass, and not perplex us. Agreed, said I, willingly, for now I hope to comprehend you. (*D.*, p. 109.)

As long as the Sovereign Good is called "Rectitude of Conduct", then the Rationalist-teleological argument will work; that is, its conclusion may not seem totally unacceptable. However, when the Sovereign Good, Rectitude of Conduct and Happiness are all to be identified with one another, then experience stands in the way. Happiness is *not* "consummate in every instant", and all the rest. And here is the problem, where it was all the time: here is the problem which occasioned the *Dialogue on Happiness* in the first place.

Harris must do what he can to make his reader swallow, along with the rationalist Sovereign Good, this identity between it and Happiness. The best he can do now is to find ways of persuading us to allow this paradoxical identification: he tries to reconcile us to it, as well as he can.

B. THE DOCTRINE RECOMMENDED

The 'new strange Doctrine' is recommended by Harris in terms of an image that eighteenth-century Stoics borrowed often enough from the antique sources. The poet Mackenzie puts what is indeed the essence of Harris's matter in two couplets:

> The friend of Pyrrhus bade him feast and live,
> Possessed of all the finished war could give.
> Vain were his banquets, had not Pyrrhus fought;
> The chace, and not the quarry, Pyrrhus sought.[1]

Harris expresses himself more largely.

Part Two of Harris's *Dialogue* begins with a recapitulation: the Pre-conceptions of the Sovereign Good are rehearsed again, and Rectitude of Conduct is shown to match up to all of them. Then the text continues (§3 of the *Dialogue*):

> You see then, said he, how well our Hypothesis, being once admitted tallies with our *Original Pre-conceptions* of the *Sovereign Good.*
>
> I replied, it indeed appeared so, and could not be denied. But who think you, ever dreamt of a Happiness like this? A Happiness dependent, not on the *Success*, but on the Aim? Even common and ordinary Life, replied he, can furnish us

[1] Henry Mackenzie, *The Pursuits of Happiness* (1770).

> with Examples. Ask of the Sportsman where lies his Enjoyment? Ask whether it be in the *Possession* of a slaughtered Hare, or Fox? He would reject with Contempt, the very Supposition—He would tell you, as well as he was able, that the Joy was in the *Pursuit*—in the Difficulties which are obviated; in the Faults, which are retrieved; in the *Conduct* and Direction of the Chace thro' all its Parts—that the *Completion* of their Endeavours was so far from giving them Joy, that instantly at that Period all their Joy was at an End. For Sportsmen, replied I, this may be no bad Reasoning. It is not the Sentiment, said he, of Sportsmen alone. The man of Gallantry not unoften has been found to think after the same manner.
>
> Meus est amor huic similis; nam
> Transvolat in medio posita, & fugientia captat.[1]
>
> To these we may add the tribe of Builders and Projectors. Or has not your own Experience informed you of Numbers, who, in the *Building* and *Laying-out* have expressed the highest *Delight*; but shown the utmost Indifference to the *Result* of their Labours, to the Mansion or Gardens, when once finished and complete? (*D*., p. 111.)

This set of notions: Pursuit, Projection and Conduct, is nicely exploited, despite the whiff of aristocratic world-weariness in the examples. Even so, these notions do less than we would like to reconcile us to 'putting our Happiness not in Success but in the Aim'. Where we aim we would like to hit too, occasionally. Projectors, particularly those of modest means, sometimes delight in the success of their schemes, more than in the projection of them. Some of Harris's own tenants might have found a more healthy relish than he in "a slaughtered Hare": the image of "the chace" convinces only where there is no pinch of necessity, and so it convinces only where there is least need of conviction.

Harris tries another tack again: he puts forward quite a different kind of example, and one which brings out rather

[1] Horace, *Satire* I, II, verse 107. "My love is like unto this, for it passes over what is served to all, and chases flying game." Translation by H. Rushton Fairclough, London (Loeb/Heinemann), 1926, p. 26.

more strongly the *moral* nature of the Moral Art. He attempts to recommend the paradox of rationalistic happiness, not by showing that the moral art and happiness are the same in eudaemonic tone, and not now by stressing 'Accommodateness', but by getting us to swallow at a draught the identity of morals and happiness—after we have poured out meet libations to moral greatness:

> If you are for Numbers, replies he, what think you of the numerous Race of Patriots, in all Ages and Nations, who have joyfully met Death, rather than desert their Country when in Danger? They must have thought surely on *another* Happiness than *Success*, when they could gladly go, where they saw Death often inevitable. Or what think you of the many Martyrs for Systems wrong as well as right, who have dared defy the worst, rather than swerve from their Belief? You have brought indeed, said I, more examples than could have been imagined. (*D.*, p. 114.)

The trouble with this example is that it is altogether too heroic in its morality, and it tells against rather than for the thesis that is being recommended, namely, that Harris's Moral Art and the art of eudaimonia or successful living are the same. It is one thing to remind us that the Patriots and Martyrs find their end in pure Rectitude of Conduct, even when this brings not only no hope of success but the certainty of pain and persecution. It is another thing again to suggest that *l'homme moyen sensuel* is prepared to acknowledge that his view of the Sovereign Good and of happiness is at bottom the same as the Martyr's or the hero's.

Harris's example of 'the Assassin of the first Prince of Orange' who, "though brought by his Conduct to the most exquisite Tortures, yet *conscious of what he had done*, could bear them all unmoved" (*D.*, p. 112), and his example of the dying Epicurus, point the difference between Epicurus and the Assassin of the Prince on the one hand and the rest of us on the other. If not quite impossible to most of us, the Stoicism of Epicurus is still less than congenial:

> ATTEND too to Epicurus dying, the Founder of a Philosophy, little savouring of Enthusiasm—'*This I write you* . . .

> *while the last Day of Life is passing and that a HAPPY one. The Pains indeed of my Body are not capable of being heightened. Yet to these we oppose that Joy of the Soul which arises from the memory of our Past Speculations*'—Hear him, consonant to this, in another Place asserting that a *Rational Adversity was better than an Irrational Prosperity.* (*D.*, pp. 112–13.)

We have come quite a way from the 'numerous sportsmen and gallants', well contented by the excitements of the chase.

Nevertheless there is something in righteousness that even the least heroic of us must acknowledge as making for our own comfort:

> Besides, continued he, what is that *Comfort of* a GOOD CONSCIENCE celebrated to such a height in the religion which we profess, but the Joy arising from a Conscience of right *Energies*; a Conscience of having done nothing, but what is consonant to our Duty? (*D.*, p. 114.)

The justice of the observation may be conceded. And had Harris left the matter here we might have been convinced, or at least silenced; but the argument is pushed a little further, and a little too far:

> I replied, It indeed appeared so.
>
> Even the vulgar, continued he, recognize a *Good* of this very Character, when they say of an Undertaking, tho' it *succeeds not*, that they are *contented*; that they have *done their best*, and can accuse themselves of nothing. For what is this, but placing their *Content*, their *Good*, their *Happiness*, not in the Success of Endeavours, but in the *Rectitude*? If it be not the Rectitude which contents them, you must tell me what it is else. It appears, replied I, to be that alone. (*D.*, pp. 114–15.)

The objection to this can be put just by changing "they are contented" to "they are consoled". Consolation rather than contentment is what the ordinary man finds in Rectitude without profit. Likewise, the ordinary man can easily say 'what it is else' that would content him: it would be profit along with Rectitude. This, Harris has already allowed as a possibility, though he knows as well as anyone else that the happy conjunction of righteousness and prosperity occurs less often than we would like. There is all the difference in the world between the egoist or the cynic who is concerned only for profit, and the good eudaemonist who expects his profit along with his righteousness, and as a consequence of it rather than as a reward. For the eudaemonist the very point of all conduct is its end, and happiness is the only end which common sense and philosophical reason can both see as evidently final. That what is so evidently final, to ordinary and to philosophical reason, should not be by any means final in the economy of the world is the essence of the whole paradox with which Harris wrestles in the *Dialogue Concerning Happiness*.

The trouble with Harris's argument is that as his moral tone rises, so the plausibility of his identification of Happiness and the Sovereign Good in Rectitude of Conduct *tout simple* plunges. We can admire the moral enthusiasm which leads him to quote Socrates:

> "Oh Crito, if it be pleasing to the Gods this way, then be it this way."

> "Anytus and Melitus, I grant, can kill me; but to hurt or injure me is beyond their Power." (*D.*, p. 113.)

But we can see ourselves less able than Socrates to make this noble, necessary, saving, distinction between killing and injuring!

Harris knows as well as anyone how bad a fist he has made of recommending his 'new strange Doctrine', and as his Friend he asks for a concession which as himself he grants:

> I hope then, continued he, that though you accede not to this Notion of Happiness which I advance; you will at least allow it not to be such a Paradox as at first you seemed to imagine. That indeed, replied I, cannot be denied you. (*D.*, p. 115.)

"Not *such* a Paradox." With this particular paradox we can hardly hope for a resolution, and we ought to be grateful for any mitigation of it that we can get.

1. *Two Goods, Rectitude of Conduct and Success*

There are, for Kant, and Harris, and for anyone else, apparently two rather different goods, neither sole and neither complete. And nothing that can be said will reconcile us to less than their fullest combination. We all esteem Rectitude of Conduct, righteousness, and we would all like endaimonia, happiness, as well.

There is indeed, as Kant says, "a peculiar kind of contentment proper to reason" which reason itself finds 'in fulfilling its highest practical function, the establishment of a good will', but this is *a* kind of contentment, and peculiar to reason: it is not all that there is to contentment. It may even be *part* of a eudaimonia such as Aristotle's, but it cannot be the whole of it. There is enough of Aristotle in most of us to make us object that the consciousness of rectitude is not all that we mean by *happiness*, and neither rationalistic arguments, nor rationalist and persuasively moral ones elegantly combined, will quite convince us that we should mean no more.

What we should value in rectitude, however, is rectitude itself, and not the ineluctability of its worth. There is a kind of moral idolatry about the rationalist system which would elevate good will's moral worth to the role of reason's end, not because it was moral, or because it was worthy, or because it serves the worth of Ends, but simply because it alone of all human things escapes the universal condition of mutability.

We may worship goodness: but there is no virtue in worshipping teleology. It is clear enough that Kant's good will 2
is not the highest good, and that Harris's "more excellent good" is simply *not* the Beatific Vision. Harris's comparison is frivolous, both to the eudaemonist who would have happiness—and eternal happiness at that if he is a Christian or a Moslem—and to the moralist, who can see some point in Conduct more germane than its rationalistically conceived quasi-'eternity'.

The eudaemonist will not be satisfied if rational, moral, prudent action produces anything less than happiness. The moralist sees obligation as binding, however it affects happiness: but like the eudaemonist the moralist laments the failure of rational, moral action to produce happiness. Duty certainly 'conditions' happiness, but this conditioning has very little to do with the failure of that eudaimonia, which it is Fortune's to give or to withhold.

Nor, when Fortune is kind, and moral action is crowned with happiness, does duty suffer one whit.

In our "sublunary state" we are subject both to Duty and to Fortune: and these are separate and discrete subjections. Rationalist arguments which tend to assimilate the two, one to the other, and aesthetic notions like 'the conditioned', which tend to conflate these subjections, merely add intellectual confusion to a situation that has, at best, to be borne with patience.

We must pass now to Coleridge's and to Green's criticisms of Kant's treatment of ends: these form a kind of tailpiece to the present Part of the essay, and a prolegomena to Part II.

APPENDIX TO PART ONE

S. T. COLERIDGE: T. H. GREEN: A POSTSCRIPT FROM HUME

[See above: Part I, Chapters III–IV, pp. 79 and 91]

S. T. COLERIDGE

As J. H. Muirhead shows in the chapter on Coleridge's moral philosophy in his *Coleridge as Philosopher*,[1] S. T. C. was very sympathetic to a morality that could unite, under one single principle, the rightness of acts and the goodness or moral worthiness of agents. Whether such a principle is or is not chimerical is not our present concern. It is to our purpose however that Coleridge, who thought that such a union of rightness and goodness was desirable, should not have accepted what he found offered to him by Kant. Kant's Stoic-rationalism he rejects as firmly as he rejects Paley's empiricist semi-utilitarianism.

Professor Muirhead recounts in some detail Coleridge's criticism of Paley, and of Kant, summing up with the remark:

> . . . Coleridge's criticism, both of the current empiricism and of Kantian rationalism strikes deeper than the rejection of the treatment of pleasure. Beyond this there was the acceptance by the former [Paley] of the "consequences" as the ultimate criterion of the goodness of an action, *the total rejection of them by the latter* [Kant] . . .[2]

Coleridge seems to have read Kant as we read him, seeing in his doctrine a notion of the will-as-prescinding-from-ends which threatens to reduce moral philosophy to an absolutely sterile formalism.

There is a passage from Coleridge's marginal annotations to his copy of Kant's *Vermischte Schriften* (which Muirhead quotes in part), which relates the notion of prescinding-from-ends to the notion of the formal moral law, though the immediate

[1] J. H. Muirhead, *Coleridge as Philosopher*, London (Allen & Unwin), 1930, pp. 137 ff.

[2] Muirhead, pp. 150–51.

occasion of Coleridge's annotation is a passage from Kant which is not concerned with this formal moral law.

It is not anything from the *Groundwork*, but a sentence from *Dreams of a Spirit-Seer* which touches off Coleridge's reflection. Kant wrote:

> Does man's heart not contain immediate moral precepts, and is it absolutely necessary to fix our machinery to the other world for the sake of moving man here according to his destiny?[1]

Coleridge answers the question on the flyleaf of his copy of the *Vermischte Schriften.*[2] His style is headlong, and some of the sentences are obscure, but the general sense is plain:

> Let the Heart answer in silence to these questions—a cultivated Heart, to which Vice in its ordinary shape is hateful on its own account. Will it not say—True! What I do, I would fain do well—it is not any Hope of future Reward that impels me, nor any Fear of future Punishment which keeps me in the Road—but the thought that all I can do, is but a dream, and that not myself only but that all men and all things are but Dreams, that nothing is permanent which makes the mortality of man a stupefying thought to me. I cannot conceive a supreme moral Intelligence, unless I believe in my own immortality—for I must believe in a whole system of apparent means to an end, which end has no existence—my Conscience, my progressive faculties, etc. But give up this, and Virtue wants all Reason—Away with Stoic Hypocrisy! I know that in order to [gap in MS.] the idea of Virtue we must suppose the pure good-will, or reverence for the Law as excellent in itself—but this very excellence supposes—consequences tho' not selfish ones—Let my maxim be capable of becoming the Law of all intelligent Being—well! but this supposes an *end* possessible

[1] Immanuel Kant, *Dreams of a Spirit-Seer, Illustrated by Dreams of Metaphysics,* trans. E. F. Goerwitz, ed. F. Sewall, London (Swan, Sonnenschein), 1900, p. 120.

[2] Asterisk with a note, "See the blank leaf at the end of the Volume" against this passage on p. 344 of the *Vermischte Schriften,* volume II, in the collection of the British Museum.

> by intelligent Beings—For if the Law be barren of all consequences, what is it but words? To obey the Law for its own sake is really a mere sophism in any other sense—: you might as well put abracadabra in its place—I can readily conceive that I have it in my nature to die a martyr, knowing that annihilation followed Death, if it were possible to believe that all other human Beings were immortal, and to be benefited by it—but any benefit that could affect only a set of transitory animals [word obscure in MS.] I could not deem myself wasting of any exertion in my behalf, how can I deem others of the same lot?—Boldly should I say—O nature! I would rather not have been—let that which is to come so soon, come now—for what is all the intermediate space, but sense of utter worthlessness. Far far below animals—for they enjoy a generic immortality, having no individuality, but man is truly and solely an immortal series of conscious mortalities, and inherent Disappointments.

Coleridge *is* right, surely, when he insists that ends and Ends are the concern of the law. "If the Law be barren of all consequences, what is it but words?"[1]

Coleridge's views of the notion of 'reverence for the law' and of the formal nature of the reverenceable law are very like those which we shall put forward in Part II, Chapter III below. What is crucial about Coleridge's testimony here is that he was extremely sympathetic to Kant's enterprise. But, clearly, viewing the texts that he had before him, Coleridge found 'prescinding' notions in Kant, and he saw the objections to these notions. A law that is without ends is abracadabra: it cannot even be reverenced 'for its own sake' since, without end or content, it has nothing in it to be reverenceable. The "very excellence" of the law "supposes consequences, tho' not selfish ones": the fact that some consequences may be selfish does not entail that all are.

"Away with Stoic Hypocrisy": the concern of action must always be with ends and with Ends, and not with a bare and empty law. Nor, indeed, is the concept of "a possible *pure* will" (*G.*, p. 58: 7 A.p.6), on which this law is supposedly

[1] See Muirhead, op. cit., p. 154.

based, at all viable. A 'will' that is so "pure" that it ceases to concern itself with ends, is no longer will.

Besides making the obviously true point about the moral law Coleridge seems to be saying, in this annotation, that action is important only if it is concerned with ends or Ends that are more than "only a set of transitory animals". Now this might be contested.

Even if we are, none of us, immortal surely we must treat one another as Ends, for "the intermediate space" of time between birth and annihilation. This recognition of personal worth is central to morality, and it stands apart from any assertion of the eternal nature of the person who has worth.

We might or might not concede Coleridge his notion that a life that did not open into eternity would be "worthless": but such worthlessness, even conceded, would not count against the worth of the person, the worth against which I must not act. A person, even if not eternal, remains a person.

It is a commonplace of Christian thought that in some sense the worth of man lies in his eternal destiny, and there may well be such an eternally-conditioned worth: but moral value, the worthiness-to-be-treated-as-an-End, though historically it may have been made manifest in a Christian context, is distinguishable from the notion of a transcendental worth made actual in an eternal end. This distinction is one which humanists, Christian and non-Christian, ought clearly to make.

Christian humanism preaches the fellowship of the immortal sons of God: non-Christian humanism must preach the fellowship of "conscious mortalities". Personal worth is the worth which a person has, quite apart from his putative eternity. If personhood is not, indeed, the image and mirror of ultimate Personhood, and if it is not, like God, eternal, then I must still reverence it: *Ich kann nicht anders.*

These issues will be taken up again, and at greater length below: Part II, Chapters II and III, and in Part III.

T. H. GREEN

As it stands in the *Lectures on the Principles of Political Obligation*, the following passage of T. H. Green's is not offered, specifically, as a criticism of Kant, or of any particular passage in the *Groundwork*. Nevertheless, as the editor's note tells us, the *Lectures* follow upon a course on Kant's moral theory and 'the two courses are directly connected'. T. H. Green writes:

> In previous lectures I have explained what I understand moral goodness to be, and how it is possible that there should be such a thing; in other words, what are the conditions on the part of reason and will which are implied in our being able to conceive moral goodness as an object to be aimed at, and to give some partial reality to the conception. Our results on this question may be briefly stated as follows.
>
> The highest moral goodness we found was an attribute of character, in so far as it issued in acts done for the sake of their goodness, not for the sake of any pleasure or any satisfaction of desire which they bring to the agent. But it is impossible that an action should be done for the sake of its goodness, unless it has been previously contemplated as good for some other reason than that which consists in its being done for the sake of its goodness. It must have been done, or conceived as possible to be done, and have been accounted good, irrespectively of the being done from this which we ultimately come to regard as the highest motive. *In other words, a prior morality, founded upon interests which are other than the pure interest in being good, and governed by rules of conduct relative to a standard of goodness other than that which makes it depend on this interest*, is the condition of there coming to be a character governed by interest in an ideal of goodness. Otherwise *this ideal would be an empty one*; it would be impossible to say what the good actions were, that were to be done for the sake of their goodness; and the interest in this ideal would be impossible, since it would be an interest without an object.[1]

The point which Green makes here, that something has first to be good before its goodness can become our own good

[1] T. H. Green, *Lectures on the Principles of Political Obligation*, reprinted from Green's *Philosophical Works*, Vol. II; introduction by Lord Lindsay of Birker, London (Longmans), 1941/1950, pp. 29–30. (Italics mine.)

motive for doing it, may be taken as an implicit if not explicit commentary on Kant's *Groundwork*, paragraphs 15–17 (pp. 68–70: 19–21: A. pp. 16–18).

Kant's ideal of 'a law the thought of which even without the results expected from it' has 'to determine the will if this is to be called good absolutely and without qualification' is, to borrow Green's phrase, "an empty ideal". The Law has to show us a good other than the Law before we can make ourselves righteous to the extent of letting that good, alone, determine us. The formal Law as 'determining' is an illusion: certainly we know 'in advance of the maxim' that we must obey the Law; but what we must *do* to obey it depends on the maxim put to the test by the Law. And what we must *do* is concerned with results, with ends and with Ends.

If we have not got an idea of a good to be done, then we cannot do it for its own goodness' sake: we must know the difference between right and wrong before we can perform right actions for disinterested motives.

DAVID HUME

Hume makes a similar point in the postscript of the letter to Francis Hutcheson which was quoted above in Part I, Chapter I. He writes:

> You are a great Admirer of *Cicero*, as well as I am. Please to review the 4th Book, *de finibus bonorum & malorum*; where you find him prove against the *Stoics*, that if there be no other Goods but Virtue, tis impossible there can be any Virtue; because the Mind woud then want all Motives to begin its Actions upon: And tis on the Goodness or Badness of the Motives that the Virtue of the Action depends. This proves, that to every virtuous Action there must be a Motive or impelling Passion distinct from the Virtue, & that Virtue can never be the sole Motive to any Action. You do not assent to this; tho' I think there is no Proposition more certain or important. I must own my Proofs were not distinct enough, & must be altered. You see with what Reluctance I part with you; tho' I believe it is time I should ask your Pardon for so much trouble.

The goodness of will depends on the goodness of what is to be willed. This point is inescapable, though Hume's talk of "a Motive or impelling Passion" might with profit give place to less sentimental talk about reason. But it is clear, Hume's own morality of the feelings aside, that "Virtue can never be the sole motive to any action".

What is good in the sense of will-able or ought-to-be-willed, is what is, in a sense, useful. The earlier part of the same postscript reads:

> Actions are not virtuous nor vicious; but only so far as they are proofs of certain Qualitys or durable Principles in the Mind. This is a Point I shou'd have establish'd more expressly than I have done. Now I desire you to consider, if there be any Quality, that is virtuous, without having a Tendency either to the public Good or to the Good of the Person, who possesses it.[1]

First we have good will to order other goods: then we have virtue, but even virtue, admired apparently for its own sake, is valued in so far as it is a disposition towards ordered, rational action between persons. The values served by right action are prior to Virtue: Virtue itself has a value that lies in its utility. Whatever tends to "the public good or the Good of the Person" is "good": and even Virtue is "good" by the same token.

Hume's statement of the position is not without its own difficulties, but the point about the priority of ends over virtuous dispositions is clear enough.

[1] *The Letters of David Hume*, ed. J. Y. T. Greig, Oxford (Clarendon Press), 1932, Vol. I, Letter 13, p. 35. Greig draws our attention to Hume, *Treatise*, Bk. III, Pt. II, Sect. I, especially p. 479 of the Oxford edition.

PART TWO

CHAPTER I

THE ENDS OF REASON, OF LIFE AND OF DUTY

> Ce M. Esprit commence par dire que la prudence n'est pas une vertu, et sa raison est qu'elle est souvent trompée. C'est comme si on disait que César n'était pas un grand capitaine parce qu'il fut battu à Dyrrachium.
>
> Voltaire, *Dictionnaire Philosophique:* "Fausseté des vertus humaines"

Kant's elevation of the ineluctable goodness of good will—good will 2—to the role of reason's end has consequences which go beyond the doctrine of the end of reason itself. The immanence which is characteristic of that *end*, conceived as Kant conceives it, is carried over, rather oddly, into the whole structure of the moral philosophy of the *Groundwork*.

The postulation of an immanent act of the will's own as reason's end, tends to remove ends in the ordinary sense both from their accustomed function as movers and determinants of the will, and from their status as things relevant to the maxims of morality. Both the will, which Kant would have determined solely by the moral law, and that 'formal' law itself, are made to prescind, as far as is possible, from ends. The will, a formal law, and an inner, absolutely-valuable act are set up as a kind of *trimurti*, a three-faced idol, of absolute immanence.

There are two further and altogether curious consequences to Kant's overrating of immanence. The first is this: not only are the ends of the will allowed to drop out of sight, but Ends, persons who by their presence in any situation limit the possible pursuit by an agent of his private ends, drop out too. This may sound odd, since Kant is as famous for his formulation of the moral law in terms of the End-in-himself, as he is for any of the other things in the *Groundwork*. However, as we shall see in Part III, the ontology of personal value, with which Kant seeks to underpin his formula of the End, is itself open to the gravest objections. This ontology is more conditioned by the immanentist notion of absolute worth than is either appropriate or prudent, and the Endship of Ends is made to rest on a foundation which is at once irrelevant and insecure.

The issue of the End and its value must be left to one side for the present however: it will be taken up again in Part II, Chapter III, Section C.4, and in Part III.

The second and highly unexpected consequence of Kant's elevation of the immanent good of good will to the role of reason's end is that his account of duty and of duty's conditioning of happiness becomes ambiguous.

It may seem odd to impute ambiguity to Kant's doctrine of duty, since his *Groundwork* is supposed to make plain one thing, the ground and the nature of duty. But it is just because Kant gets other things out of focus that his doctrine of duty, too, becomes blurred.

There are three large themes which run through moral philosophy: (*a*) the theme of ends, states of affairs which the will would make or un-make; (*b*) the theme of personal value, End-being, which limits any agent in his pursuit—or his avoidance—of ends or states of affairs; (*c*) the theme of duty, where a duty, too, is something which limits or hinders action. Morality is no more than the organization of the *Achtung!* of innumerable monads of value into a system, a 'legislation for a Kingdom of Ends'.

The grounds of duty itself lie, one can only suppose, in the value of persons. Duties must arise from and only[1] from, the bearing of states of affairs as envisaged by an agent's will, upon persons: upon persons whose interests must be respected, and who can therefore give value, or disvalue, to mere 'factual' situations over and above the value that these have as 'mere objects of desire'.[2]

[1] Speaking, that is, humanistically. Duties towards God may be more than, or other than, personal. The relation between Creator and creature *may* be different from a moral one: e.g. see Kierkegaard, *Fear and Trembling*. This question goes far beyond our present scope. Cf. below, p. 309n.

[2] There are two 'transitions from fact to value', if there is any at all: one has to get from "This is D" (where D = any description) to "This

Duty's conditioning of happiness may be seen, if one takes the view just adumbrated, as a limitation put upon the *prima facie* and natural end of practical reason, namely: the production of the happiness of each agent who is endowed with practical reason.

Happiness, any agent's happiness, is conditioned by two things: (*a*) by chance and fortune, hence the Stoic problem; (*b*) by the demands of duty. And practical reason itself may be seen as having two ends: (i) the conditioned one of producing happiness (where happiness itself is doubly conditioned); (ii) the conditioning one, of perceiving where duty lies. Practical reason looks both ways, towards eudaimonia, and towards duty: and to talk in an abstract way of "the end of reason" without doing justice to reason's twin functions, is to commit a fatal blunder.

Reason's end is double: to produce happiness, and to perceive duty. The 'conditionality' of happiness is double; happiness waits both upon fortune and upon duty. When the first has done her worst, and the second has settled all her claims, then "Let happiness be unconfined!", as it is at the end of all good comedies.

A. HAPPINESS AS "CONDITIONED"

Happiness is "conditioned" in two separate, indeed in two disparate ways,[1] and it is important to insist on the categorical difference between the two kinds of conditionality. Kant's use of the expressions "conditioned" and "unconditioned" does not provide for this necessary distinction.

is D and wanted, want-able", etc.: and from D to "This is D and involves a moral value", is morally-able-to be wanted, etc. 'Desire' allows us to make the first transition: the second transition turns on the bearing of what comes under D upon the Endship of some End.

The whole notion, however, of "mere facts" is one which is open to question. The notions of mere fact and of pure description are useful to philosophers who wish to ask: "How do we get from fact to value?" They are of less use in practical life, where we already know how we "get to" one from the other. This may be instructive.

[1] The present section develops, further, points made in Part I, Chapter IV, Section A.10 q.v., see also footnote 1, pp. 111–12.

In the first place, happiness is conditional upon fortune. Any strategies for achieving happiness must succeed as best they can in a world which does not seem to be arranged so as to ensure that attempts at happiness shall succeed. This we shall call, henceforth, conditionality-*f*[ortune].

In the second place, happiness is conditional upon, or conditioned by, duty. Duty conditions happiness in the sense that any strategy for happiness, conceived by any individual, must wait not only upon its own success, but even more importantly, must submit itself to the overriding scrutiny of duty, before it can or may be embarked upon. This we shall call henceforth, conditionality-*d*[uty].

These two kinds of "conditionality" which govern happiness have in fact little or nothing to do with each other. That "The best laid schemes o' mice an' men gang aft agley" has really nothing to do with the fact that, before even I set about acting on my plan, I must ask, "Is the maxim of this act compatible with universal willing?"

It is an accident of rationalism that Kant set up duty, or at any rate good will, as the end of reason; it is an accident within an accident of the system that has him set up as this "end" the precise, pietistic, concept of duty which he has. Kant sees, like Harris, that happiness, conditional-*f* fails as a candidate for the role of end of reason, simply because it can fail as the end of a strategy. But, the argument runs: if something unfailing must be the true end of reason and happiness-conditioned-*f* cannot be this end, then something less fragile must be. The obvious candidate now for reason's end is *good will* ambiguously posed between (i) the perception of duty, (ii) the effort to do one's duty, (iii) the ineluctable worth of such an effort. All this is, as has been noted already, confused still further by Kant's pietistic[1] definition of duty in terms of pure motivation, a notion which, like the notion of "absolute worth", involves a sense of prescinding-from-ends.

It happens that good will, in one sense, can be found to be unfailing; and it happens that good will in this sense, and in

[1] 'Pietistic' is too strong, perhaps, and too pejorative a word. Kant's talk about pure motivation is of course not entirely moral, or moralistic, but derives from the official metaphysic. This metaphysic might justify the moral talk—but it itself is hardly recommended by it.

cognate ones, has to do with duty: so *good will-duty* becomes for Kant the end of reason, as this end is rationalistically conceived. What conditions happiness-conditioned-*d* is duty; so duty, or some function of it becomes the rationalistic end. The moral and the ineluctable become related not simply through their real connection (ineluctable worth is in fact moral worth),[1] but through a factitious relation as well, one which has no more content to it than a pun on "conditionality".

There are two separate issues to be considered under the general rubric of the present section, and their consideration will form divisions A.1–2 and A.3 of the section. They are (1) the issue of Kant's conflation of conditionality-*f* and conditionality-*d*, and (2) the issue of the value and status of an argument of Kant's about duty's determinateness of concept, which is an argument deriving in part at least from a consideration of conditionality-*f*. The burden of the argument runs thus: since happiness often fails, so no recipes for happiness can serve adequately to guide our life; consequently, a notion of duty must guide our actions instead.

We must consider also the precise notion of duty which Kant puts forward, but that matter can wait until our next chapter.

Briefly, we want to argue that as far as issue 1 is concerned, Kant is in the wrong. The conditionalities-*f* and -*d* of happiness must both be admitted; but one does not imply the other. A notion of "conditionality" which involved them together would be no better than paronomastic. As for issue 2, Kant is of course in a sense right—though one's agreement must be qualified by one's reservations about the precise notion of duty which Kant puts up.

The second issue, 2, is considered below in Section A.3. "Duty, but not happiness can guide action", pp. 175 ff. However, before we can consider duty as a guide to life we must consider, first, some notions which Kant puts forward about duty's conditioning of happiness.

[1] That moral worth is both *moral* and *ineluctable* seems to be a perfectly contingent matter. The ineluctable does not imply the moral, and how far 'moral worth' implies 'ineluctable worth' is not at once evident. The ineluctability of moral worth may turn as much on the concept of *worth* or credit ('to-be-allowed for cashing whether cashed or not') as on the *moral* half of the notion *moral worth.*

1. *Duty Conditions Happiness: that is, the claims of Duty take priority over the claims of happiness, or over claims to happiness*
It is paradoxical, perhaps, that we should be accusing Kant of mishandling this theme. He is notorious for the severity of his views on the unconditionality of duty, or notorious anyhow for the apparent severity of his views. And the notion of duty at least might be thought to be something that Kant got right, if uncomfortably right.

Nevertheless we find Kant's doctrine of duty and his account of its 'conditioning' of happiness both unacceptable and wrong. The doctrine has, in fact, a deep conceptual confusion in it, and part, though not all, of this conceptual confusion can be traced to the aesthetic idea of the unconditioned.

Certainly duty conditions happiness in the sense that we must do our duty before we seek, or even if it prevents our seeking, our happiness: but this moral fact does not justify, and justice is not done to it by, Kant's multifarious usages of "*unconditioned*"/"*conditioned*".

In paragraph 6 of the *Groundwork* Kant has this to say about the *un*conditionality of duty and the conditioned-ness of happiness. He adumbrates, and seems to favour, the "Idea" that:

> . . . our existence has a different and far nobler *end* [than happiness] for which, and not for happiness, reason is properly intended, and which must therefore, be regarded as the *supreme condition*[1] to which the private ends of man must, for the most part, be postponed. (*G.*, pp. 63–4: *13–14*: *A. p. 12*, translation cited, Abbott's. Italics mine.)

Kant is doing two things here. He is (i) repeating in effect (taking the whole context into account) his highly contentious and doubtful doctrine of the single end of reason. He is repeating his doctrine that reason's end is to produce good will because good will is itself ineluctably and absolutely good. And (ii) Kant is perhaps making a valid moral point; the point namely that happiness must often be postponed or sacrificed in deference to the claims of duty. However, though

[1] Cf. again *C.Pr.R.*, A. pp. 206 ff, 'Virtue' is the 'good will' of *G.* developed further, and more plausibly moralized.

these points are run together in the complex and dense early paragraphs of the *Groundwork*, (ii) has nothing to do with, and certainly owes nothing of its validity to, (i). Happiness is not subject to conditionality-*d* because it is subject to conditionality-*f*, nor has the *un*conditionality of duty which implies the conditionality-*d* of happiness, anything at all to do with conditionality-*f*.

One could imagine a world of unfailing rational strategies for happiness, and one could still postulate a moral censorship of these strategies. If, after I had subjected a well-conceived maxim to the moral censor and found it good, the strategy also always worked eudaemonistically, then this would be a fact about the world quite without prejudice to my obligation actually to subject my maxims to moral censorship.

I do not have to universalize my maxims because happiness may fail, or because reason's end is not happiness, or because instinct rather than reason would have been a better guide if happiness were the human end: I have to universalize because of the point of universalizability.

Now it is a criticism of Kant to point out that (ii) owes nothing to (i) here, that is that conditionality-*d* in no way depends on conditionality-*f*, only if he says, or suggests that there is a material connection between the two conditionalities.

Suggestion is easier to bring home to him here than explicit statement; though one, often enough repeated, tends to merge into the other. And there is certainly suggestion. Furthermore, this suggestion is carried, precisely, by the reiterated linguistic device of the use of "unconditioned/conditioned", and by the subtle, aesthetic, interplay of this with its chief defining notion, the notion of the ineluctable.

Kant has this to say about *good will*, that is, about his rationalistically conceived, unfailing good will 2, the will which is itself free from any suspicion of conditionality-*f*:

> Such a will need not on this account be the sole and complete good, but it must be the **highest good** and the **condition** of all the rest, even of all our *demands for happiness*. In that case we can easily reconcile with the wisdom of nature our observation that the cultivation of reason which is required for the **first and unconditioned purpose** may in many

ways, at least in this life, restrict the attainment of the *second purpose*—namely, happiness—which is always *conditioned*; and indeed that it can even reduce happiness to less than zero without nature proceeding contrary to its **purpose**; for reason, which recognizes as its highest practical function the establishment of a *good will*, in attaining this **end** is capable only of its own peculiar kind of contentment—contentment in fulfilling a **purpose** which in turn is determined by reason alone, even if this fulfilment should often involve interference with the *purposes* of inclination.

We have now to elucidate the concept of a **will estimable in itself and good apart from any further end.** This concept, which is already present in a naturally sound understanding and requires not so much to be taught as merely to be clarified, always holds the highest place in estimating the total worth of our actions and constitutes the **condition** of all the rest. (*G.*, p. 64: pp. 14–15: A. p. 12. Italics and bold mine.)

What we are faced with here is not in any sense a philosophical argument, or a philosophical exposition. Rather, language is being used in this passage as it is used in literature; the reiterated expressions "purpose", "unconditioned", "conditioned", are like "words which talk back and forth to each other in [a] poem":[1] the pattern is highly suggestive, but it is in no sense conclusive. Whatever is or can be meant by "the notion of a will which . . . is good without a view to anything further", a will which is in an obvious sense an *unconditioned* good, one must insist that this will has less than nothing to do with the properly moral notions of (1) the unconditionality of duty and (2) the duty-conditioned-ness of happiness. The other ends of the will are, one agrees, conditioned by duty. But this is *not* because duty is the ground of unconditioned, that is, ineluctable, good will: and though the ends of will are 'conditioned' by duty, this is *not* because happiness, unlike good will 2, is subject to conditionality-*f*. The ends of will are conditional-*d*, but this conditionality has nothing to do with,

[1] This phrase is borrowed from Lawrence Thompson, *Fire and Ice: a study of the poetry of Robert Frost*, New York (Henry Holt), 1942, p. 21.

much less does it derive from, the unconditionality of reason's **"end"**.

The ineluctability of the goodness of will ('good without a view to anything further') is what had this "absolute" and so "unconditioned" goodness and its production elected to the highest possible status in Kant's system. The unhinderable coming-to-be[1] of the goodness of good will secured for good will the coveted role of the *end of reason*. However, the sense in which this good will by being the highest, 'the first' and 'the unconditioned' *end*, so makes all other ends *conditioned/conditional upon* it, must remain for ever unclear. One has of course to acknowledge that happiness is, always, alas, subject to conditionality-*f*. But the fact that good will 2 is not subject to conditionality-*f*, does not serve either to make good will 2 that "end of reason" which happiness-conditioned-*f* cannot ever be, nor does it serve to make the conditionality-*d* of happiness a consequence of itself.

Happiness is conditional-*d* not because there is something in this world, namely good will 2, which escapes being conditional-*f*. Happiness is conditional-*d* for a profounder and more important reason: for every agent there are other persons in the world.[2] For any agent it is necessary that he remind himself that his ends must be articulated to, and subjected to, universal ones; and this is because "Universal ends" is a way of putting "The ends of Ends".

The good will to which I may have to sacrifice my happiness is not good will 2, not the ineluctably-worthy-thing, at all. Good will 1 as prudence and moral awareness may show me my duty; and a duty may require me, if not always and of its essence at least sometimes and contingently, to sacrifice (or at least to postpone) my own happiness in deference to its unconditional claims. So in a sense good will "conditions" happiness: but it is not good will 2 that does this. It is practical reason, as consciousness of the claims of persons upon my

[1] How such an unhinderable-coming-to-be merges aesthetically with "self-existence" considered as a predicate of rational Ends (cf. *Groundwork*, Ch. II) we shall discuss below, in Part III, cf. pp. 293, 327 ff.

[2] There is also, of course, the Agent-considered-as-Person who limits his own actions morally just as if he were the Other to whom his inclinations must, on occasion, defer.

actions and my omissions, that "conditions" my happiness. Good will 1 conditions all conduct: good will 2, though itself "unconditioned" conditions nothing in particular; and it conditions nothing at all, perhaps.

The conditioning-good-will conditions not because it itself is *un*conditioned or 'good without a view to anything further', but precisely because it *is* good with a view to certain things. Practical reason is good with regard to the rights and demands of others, that is to the claims of Ends-in-themselves: practical reason makes me act on maxims only that are *allgemein-zweckmässig*. Ends-in-themselves make unconditional demands on my conduct, and good will 1 enables me to see, and disposes me to meet, these demands: good will 2 may be unconditional in a quite different sense, but this sense has nothing at all to do with the absoluteness of duty, or with duty's unconditionality.

Kant's vision of the ineluctable end of reason is an illusion: the unconditionality of duty is not. And it is only compounding illusion with itself to try to derive the unconditionality of duty from the absolute, inner, and unconditioned worth of reason's alleged end.

The unconditional ground of the unconditionality of duty is either the unconditional value of Ends-in-themselves, or it is nothing.

Happiness is conditional upon duty when duty has its "unconditional" and "categorical" prior claims on our action. This is a simple moral fact and not a fancy metaphysical one.

It is important to realize that this moral fact is not reinforced by talk about action-from-duty being the *condition* of the production of "good will" which is itself, because *unfailing*, reason's first and *unconditioned* end. On the contrary, such talk can do the unconditionality of duty no good at all. A truth turned into a mystery may seem to be done away with when the mystery is exploded: but we can easily jettison Kant's "unconditioned" talk, without duty becoming a whit the less unconditional. So much the worse, then, for the talk: it must be cut short. But duty remains.

2. *The End of Duty*

That duty conditions happiness and inclination is an evident truth. If we want to bring out its evidence further, then we must talk about the kind of thing which a duty turns out to be, namely, the adjustment of our private maxims of action to universal ends. Likewise we must, to justify duty, show that the point of duty, the end of it, is that we shall behave fittingly towards Ends in themselves, whether these Ends are ourselves or others.

The end of practical reason is reasonable conduct: it is not the merit of reasonable conduct. The end of practical reason is works and not the saving value or the credit of works. This is so, whether this saving value is seen in the perspective of Christian theology, or through the eyes of a rationalist concerned above all with whatever absolute the world may withhold from the scythes of chance and fortune and failure.

3. *Duty, but not Happiness, Can Guide Action*

A severe moralist might, perhaps, object to the classical eudaemonistic systems of morality: but a moralist's objection would not rest on the fact that happiness is conditional-*f*. The severe moralist does not object to eudaemonism, if he does, because even the best calculated eudaemonistic strategies may fail. He bases his objection on the suspicion that eudaemonistic systems overlook that happiness is conditioned-*d*. One sometimes feels that the trouble with Aristotle and with his followers is that they are writing about happiness, simply, and not about morality at all.

One must be terribly careful, at this point, to do justice to the part that both conditionalities-*f* and -*d* play in the argument. And one must be careful not to confuse the conditionalities or their roles.

The severe moralists' objection to simple eudaemonism is that it is eudaemonism simply, and that it does little or no justice to the 'real' issue of morality, namely to the fact that happiness is conditional-*d*. The objection takes two forms: (*a*) the moralist suggests either that no real attention has been paid to conditionality-*d*, for example by Aristotelians, or (*b*) the moralist is scandalized a little to find that if and when such attention *has* been paid, then somehow the conditionality-*d* of happiness is absorbed into the content of happiness. There is the feeling that the unconditional claims of duty are to some extent got round by the invention of such virtues as magnanimity, which certainly involve other-regarding attitudes, but which are practised by individual agents for the status they give, and for the eudaimonia implicit in that status.

There may be something in the uneasy feelings that we, or moralists, sometimes have about eudaemonism. We shall see.

The Stoic objected against eudaemonism that happiness was conditional-*f*. He objected that the strategies of eudaimonia did not by any means guarantee success, and so he "fixed his happiness" in something else. This something else was usually ineluctable or accommodate in the first place, and moral in the second. Occasionally the order was reversed—*properly* reversed one would like to add. But the Stoic was often as not the father of the rationalist, and talk of virtue often tends to be talk of that which "the soul discovers for itself, within itself" rather than talk of some positively moral thing.

Virtue seems quite often to be valued because it escapes conditionality-*f* and not valued simply because it is always exquisitely sensitive to conditionality-*d*.

There is an argument in Kant which combines the points about conditionality-*f* and conditionality-*d* in an odd but quite valid way. He argues in effect from the conditionality-*f* of happiness to the notion of duty as the chief, even sole, guide to action, without stressing—at this particular point—that duty is and must, on any account of the matter, be a guide along with happiness, since happiness is conditioned-*d* by duty.

Kant extrapolates, in effect, from the conditionality-*f* of happiness to show that happiness cannot *be* a sound guide: then he produces duty as the alternative guide. The argument is, notice, not a moral one, nor even, quite, a Stoic-rationalistic one. It is essentially epistemological or gnoseological:

> To assure one's own happiness is a duty (at least indirectly); for discontent with one's state, in a press of cares and amidst unsatisfied wants, might easily become a great temptation to the transgression of *duty*. But here also, apart from regard to duty, all men have already of themselves the strongest and deepest inclination towards happiness, because *precisely in*

> *this Idea of Happiness all inclinations are combined into a sum total.* The *prescription* for happiness is, however, often so constituted as greatly to interfere with some inclinations, **and yet man cannot form under the name of 'happiness' any determinate and assured conception of the satisfaction of all inclinations as a sum.** Hence it is not to be wondered at that a single inclination which is **determinate** as to what it promises and as to the time of its satisfaction may outweigh a wavering Idea; and that a man, for example, a sufferer from gout, may choose to enjoy what he fancies and put up with what he can—on the ground that on balance he has here at least not killed the enjoyment of the present moment because of some possibly groundless expectations of the good fortune supposed to attach to soundness of health. But in this case also, *when the universal inclination towards happiness has failed to determine his will*, when good health, at least for him, has not entered into his calculations as so necessary, *what remains over*, here as in other cases, *is a law*—the law of furthering his happiness, not from inclinations, but from duty; . . .[1] (*G.*, p. 67: pp. 17–18: A. p. 15. Italics and bold mine.)

Duty becomes a guide where happiness cannot be one, for the plain reason that there is no determinate[2] concept of happiness. But it happens that there is a determinate, or a determinating, concept of duty which we have in the categorical imperative. Here, in the case of the gouty man we have a specific rule which derives, how it is not absolutely clear, from the categorical imperative: what-is-to-be-done is determined not by any problematic strategy of eudaimonia, but by duty.

Duty becomes the guide here for a contingent reason. That there can be no determinate concept of happiness is contingent

[1] The final clause ". . . and in this for the first time his conduct has real moral worth", has been omitted, since it is germane rather to the issues raised in our next chapter than to the present argument. But it is useful to note, yet again, the *density* of Kant's writing, and to see how issues pile upon issues as clauses pile upon clauses. The texture is beautifully woven: it is the pattern that one may object to. See below, Chapter III, Sections B.2 and C. ff.

[2] The issue of there being no "determinate concept" of happiness is raised by Kant again in Chapter II, p. 85: 41, A. p. 35.

upon a number of factors, and Kant refers us to some of them: many of these factors might fit under the rubric of happiness-being-conditional-*f*. That is to say: one of the reasons that we can have no determinate concept of happiness is that happiness may fail, strategies may cancel one another out, things may for ever be going wrong. Thus we may come to prefer small advantages that we may have now, to greater benefits that lie in the uncertain future.

The argument in Kant's paragraph is plausible, and probably valid enough as a practical persuasion; but it is an argument in the epistemological or gnoseological realm, rather than one in the moral realm. What is apparent here is not the content of duty, not the importance of duty, not the importance of persons whom duty serves, but simply the fact that duties can be found out in some sense *absolutely*, whereas strategies for happiness cannot. That Kant's gouty man does not exhibit an absolutely clear case of a duty, deriving lucidly from the categorical imperative, does not tell, very heavily anyhow, against Kant's general point here. It would not be difficult to find other rather clearer examples.

4. *Eudaemonic Theories and the Conditionalities of Happiness*

In our reading of eudaemonists of various complexions we may have, by and large, two objections always in mind: (i) that these men talk as though happiness were both (*a*) less fragile (less conditional-*f*) than it is, and (*b*) more capable than it is of providing a determinate concept for action; and (ii) we may add a further objection that as eudaemonists, they really miss the moral point, the point that happiness is conditional-*d*.

It is perfectly true, as Kant says, that:

> . . . reason is not sufficiently serviceable for guiding the will safely as regards its objects and the satisfaction of all our needs (which it in part even multiplies). (*G.*, 64: 14: A. p. 12.)

Even so, he draws too many consequences from this, too quickly, and with too little sensitivity to the differences—often categorical differences—between them. That reason is "not sufficiently servicable . . . " in this way has something to do with happiness's conditionality-*f*. But one cannot conclude from the mere fact that happiness is conditional-*f* to the idea that some other thing duty-as-good-will, must be practical reason's unconditional end and purpose. All that one can conclude from the failure of happiness is that practical reason may have no infallible end, where infallibility is conceived in terms of a naive teleology.

All the philosophical capital that can be made out of the conditionality-*f* of happiness is made when one sees that this conditionality-*f* accounts at least partly for the gnoseological or epistemological point that one cannot have a determinate concept of happiness. This point, then, conjoined with the demonstration that there is a determinate, or determining, concept of duty, gives duty the edge. But it is not, given the context and the considerations, any kind of moral edge: it remains, essentially, an epistemological advantage which duty enjoys over happiness.

We shall take this point up again in the next chapter but one.

Neither duty ('Because we can have a determinate concept of it') nor good will (i.e. good will 2, 'Because it is ineluctable') is or can be argued to be the "end" of life or of reason. Duty is, because of its epistemological clarity, a better, surer guide than happiness. But it is a *moral* guide for quite other reasons again—and these have nothing to do with good will 2 and its ineluctable worth, any more than they have to do with the epistemological issue.

That is to say, the moral importance and the moral absoluteness of duty owes nothing to the epistemological absoluteness of its concept *vis à vis* happiness; nor does it owe anything to the other, quite different, absoluteness of the "absolute worth of mere will". We have, simply three kinds of absolute. One has to say this obvious thing because, in Kant's vocabulary and in the presuppositions on which it is based, there seems to be confusion about and conflation of these three discrete absolutes.

If indeed "Duty" *is* "the necessity to act out of reverence for the law",[1] it is the necessity to act out of reverence for a law which specifies morally important things: the abstentions

[1] Cf. *Groundwork*, p. 68: 19; A. pp. 16–17; discussed below in Chapter III, Section C.3, pp. 268 ff.

enjoined by the Decalogue for example. Duty is not either: (i) a necessity to act on a 'determinate concept' simply because it is determinate or (ii) the necessity to produce the ineluctable goodness of good will 2 because this ineluctable goodness is "absolute". Duty is the necessity to act on good will 1, that is to be reasonable just because one can be reasonable: it is the necessity to act properly towards Ends.

There are ultimate irrelevancies and categorical confusions set all about Kant's doctrine of duty as we find it in the early passages of the *Groundwork*; conditionality-*f* becomes confused with conditionality-*d*; or, another side of the same coin, the ineluctable becomes the end of reason, because it is ineluctable. Duty becomes the guide to life not simply because it—and morality—are the conditions of a kingdom of Ends, but because we can have a determinate concept of duty, while we cannot have such a concept of happiness.

It is characteristic of Stoicism that it displaces happiness in the ordinary sense by a "happiness" determined in terms of the inner integrity of the agent, since this inner integrity is all that we can command with any security in this life. It is characteristic of rationalism that it displaces the properly moral in favour of an accident of the moral, namely that it can always be commanded. When a man is, as is Kant, both something of a Stoic and very much of a rationalist, then the displacements occur in a complex, interrelated kind of way.

Harris the Stoic eudaemonist replaces ordinary happiness with the "Happiness" of Rectitude of Conduct, because this alone is "Accommodate" or ineluctable. Kant does the same, in a deontological mode, making morality and not happiness the end of action; *but he does this not for morality's own sake*. Kant selects good will 2-Duty as the end of reason, not because of the importance of duty, but because of its accidental freedom from conditionality-*f*, and because of its accidental epistemological clarity. That is, the *good will* element of *good will2-duty* is elected to the role of reason's end because good will can always come to be. *Duty* is elected because, as well as being a condition of this ineluctable goodness (and as well as conditioning happiness) it, unlike happiness, is something of which we can have a determinate practical concept.

5. *Eudaimonia, and the Claims of Duty over Happiness*

We can say that Kant and Harris come only relatively closer than did Aristotle to a "true" notion of morality. Where Aristotle underplays the conditionality-*d* of happiness, Kant misconstrues it. Happiness is conditional-*d* not for gnoseological or rationalist-immanentist reasons, but precisely because the Conditions of happiness's being conditional-*d* exist. Happiness is conditional-*d*, because personal existences have an absolute axiological importance. His own exclusive happiness is not the sole end of any one agent's practical reason, just because there are other persons besides himself, or because he, himself, as person, has claims on his own action, which limit certain strategies for gratification.[1]

Happiness, that is the happiness of agent NN, cannot be the *sole* end of his practical reason if there are Persons (other Persons, himself-as-Person) to be considered. The Person is the Condition of all action.

Perhaps the most important thing to bear in mind when reading the *Groundwork* is that happiness is conditional-*d* not because something else, namely good will, is *un*conditional, or because this happiness itself is conditional-*f*, but because Persons exist and are Conditions which must be taken into account by all agents before they can act upon their own, individual, eudaemonistic strategies.

To misinterpret the point of happiness's absolute conditionality-*d* because of a rationalist obsession with another absolute—"the absolute worth of mere will"—is to err almost as seriously as Aristotle may be thought to have erred in not taking up the point of happiness's conditionality-*d*, at all.

The end of practical reason is reasonable conduct: and the end of reasonable conduct is the End in the Kingdom of Ends. Nothing else has an absolute value: or if it has, the "absolute" is vacuous and morally null.

The only other absolute[2] is happiness, and this one is tempted

[1] A clear contemporary and topical example: I must not experiment with drugs or take drugs for mere pleasure, because of the risk of addiction. To become, wilfully or carelessly, a drug addict is to commit a moral crime against my own person.

[2] Happiness or eudaimonia is, as Aristotle points out, not only the practical end that action has in view, it is also the only one about which further

to call, with calculated paradox, a *conditional-absolute*. Happiness is conditional-*f* and conditional-*d*, but it is absolute even so, in that it is the only end or point to action which does not require a justification. It is the only self-validating end, as Aristotle discovers and demonstrates in the *Nichomachean Ethics*.

Fortune, and the conditionality-*f* of happiness may be allowed perhaps to drop out of sight for a moment, and we may ask: "What of *happiness conditional-d* but still absolute, faced by the *unconditional* claims of a duty *conditioning-happiness-d?*" How do these absolutes fare when confronted? Curiously, they fare well enough. For what, if not happiness in some ultimate sense, are we acting for the sake of, when we defer to another's claim on us, as it is put by duty? When I act morally towards another, answering the call of duty, and defer my happiness to his claim, what can be the point of, the end of his claims, if not his happiness?

Some people might want to answer this rhetorical question not with "happiness" as it expects but with something like "moral goodness": but that just will not do: or, if it will do, the endaemonist is not routed by the reply.

The reason why "moral goodness" will not do as an answer to our question, "To what of NM's do I defer when I postpone my happiness in obedience to his moral claim?" we shall discuss in our next section; i.e. Section B immediately below.

B. MORAL GOODNESS AN ILLUSION?

There is no way at all of assuring our happiness here below: happiness is conditional-*f* and neither consistent morality, nor for that matter consistent immorality, will ensure happiness for us. This fact of the conditionality of happiness may even appear to be edifying, at least to those who think that to be moral is simply a different kind of thing from embarking on a eudaemonic strategy: if virtue were always rewarded, then we might be virtuous for the reward, and not for virtue's own sake.

It must be admitted that to be moral is a different thing from

questions need not be asked. Happiness is the only thing of which we do not ask, "What is the point of it?", "What is it for?", "What is the good of it?" It is the *good*, the *aim* of all action. Aristotle takes very seriously indeed his own first sentence in the *Nichomachean Ethics*.

pursuing a pure eudaemonic strategy, but unless we specify this difference with some care, we may end up both by denigrating happiness as a human end, and by miscalculating the business itself of being moral.

An agent acts morally when, plotting a eudaemonic strategy for himself, he subjects all its maxims to the principle of universalizability before he acts; and the moral man acts, then, only on maxims which are universalizable. That is to say, in general terms, the moral man adjusts his ends to universal ends, his ends to the ends of Ends.

The world might have been arranged as certain rather Leibnizian Sunday-school books used to suggest that it is, in such a way that even here below a man will be rewarded for his morality with a commensurate portion of happiness. In such a world—not the world which we inhabit of course—even renunciations and postponements of one's own happiness carry an assurance of eudaemonic recompense.

Such an arrangement would realize the eudaemonists' ideal, and leave morality in a very happy state indeed. Or would a severe moralist feel, perhaps, a little uneasy in such an ideal world?

The ideal world of the eudaemonists is too good of course, to be true: some people might think it even too good to be good. "Surely", someone might ask, "isn't it just the point of morality, that it need not pay?" To this one would have to answer, "No, it isn't: you have managed to get it slightly but disastrously wrong."

The hard fact about morality is that we would have to be moral even if morality were not profitable: we must be moral even if morality is not profitable.

We have to be moral even though it sometimes is not profitable to be so. But the real point of morality does not lie in *its not being always profitable and its always being obligatory:* the point lies simply in *its always being obligatory.* The 'point' in the sense of 'end' of morality is that Ends in-themselves must be treated as Ends; and the profit, or loss, to the agent who meets this obligation has nothing to do with the case. It has nothing to do with it, notice, either way.

It is not true to say either that "the point of morality is that in the end it leads to the moral agent's happiness", or that "it can/should command us against our happiness", or again that "it can be/should be unprofitable to the agent." Whether a moral act makes me happier or sadder is, as far as morality is concerned, quite indifferent: and one means *indifferent*.

The point of morality is to get *one* to adjust to *universal* ends; and this, for the sake of those whom one accommodates. One must adjust to others for others' sakes. The point of morals is not to make me as agent happier, or as some seem to think, to make me as agent sadder. The point of it is to get End-as-agent to treat any other End as an End, with what Kant so aptly calls "practical love" (*Groundwork*, p. 67: p. 18: A. pp. 15–16.)

1. *The Roots of an Illusion*

All that has been said is obvious enough. Nevertheless, it needs to be stressed, since perhaps Kant and certainly some Kantians tend to get it all subtly wrong. There is a kind of priggish "moral goodness" talk which one sometimes encounters that, though it is no doubt intended to stress the indifference of morality to any one agent's eudaimonia, ends up by supposing that if acting morally did happen to further Agent NM's eudaimonia on *x* occasion, then the moral act of NM would be less moral, or somehow spoiled. We shall look at Kant's grocer and at his would-be suicide in our next chapter but one, and try to decide how far, if at all, Kant himself fell into the trap of making moral action essentially anti-eudaemonistic.

One sometimes comes across talk about Christian eudaemonism being disedifying: "Oh, Christians are moral for the sake of rewards and punishments." The burden of the accusation being that the Christians do not understand morality. And they may not either: but then, neither, by and large, do the people who make this sort of remark.

It is essential that we see precisely what the Christian "hope and expectation" comes to. According to the orthodox account of the after-life the happiness of the saved will be, unlike earthly happiness, happiness totally un-conditional: and it will *a fortiori* be happiness un-conditional-*f*. It *will be* unconditional. There is, now, here below, however, a condition of ultimate and unconditional happiness, namely that all happiness and all eudaemonistic strategies here below, be seen and be treated as conditional-*d*. 'Practical love' for others must govern self-love.

The Christian account is seen quite simply—or seen too simply—as a projection on to a higher plane of the optimistic story of virtue rewarded, which is not true when it is told of this world below.

As virtue is not inevitably profitable here below, the projection is necessary if any general theory of eudaimonia is finally to hold; perhaps all eudaemonic theories are over-optimistic then? This is another question, and one into which we cannot go here.

Notice that the Christian picture of the after-life is essentially a eudaemonic one; "just deserts", a notion which we find in both theology and in literature, is a notion which is highly theory-impregnated with eudaemonic presuppositions: and eudaemonism produces just this demand for this kind of justice.

The story is not—essentially—one about morality at all. People who criticize it as somehow a-moral, or as somehow showing moral insensitivity, understand neither it, nor, one suspects, morality. A story about the end and point of life need not be a story about morality, even though morality is the form of life.

It is not enough to say, "Morality is not eudaemonic, *so* all eudaemonic talk spoils the purity of morals": one has to say why and how talk about morality is not eudaemonic talk.

Any moral act of obligation, for instance, of not seducing this innocent NM, is an act (or an abstention) of necessary obligation. It is an act with absolute claims, whether or not the seduction would make me happier now, or sadder later, or much sadder later on still.

The point of my obligation not to seduce this innocent NM is not my happiness, one way or the other: it is that the innocent NM be not seduced.[1]

If morality is in my interest here below, or hereafter, this is, eudaemonically speaking, a bonus, and eudaemonistically it is

[1] My obligation is to NM the person, not to NM's innocence. How far innocence is a moral predicate, and how far a psychological one, and how far it is related to the range of hedonic strategies from which the innocent is forced to choose, these are complex and important questions, beyond our present scope.

edifying. That morality is in my interest, here or hereafter, is morally indifferent. The indifference of morality cuts both ways; it is true to say both that *even if any moral act* (or all)[1] *was not in my interest, I would still have to do it,* and that *if a moral act is in my interest, then it is still as much a moral act as if it were not.*

A moral act's being or not being in my interest—as agent—is neither here nor there as regards its being moral. If the Christian story about ultimate eudaimonia being conditional upon my treating earthly eudaimonia as conditional-*d* is false, then I am still obliged to be moral. If the story is true, then what I am obliged to be as being moral is no less moral for the eudaimonia that will accrue to my moral acts in an eternal eventuality.

There are two discrete, but tonally similar facts: (i) that happiness fails and is conditional-*f*; and (ii) that virtue is not in fact always rewarded here below. These two facts tend to become, in some philosophies, assimilated to the point of morality. This is surely a mistake: the point of morality is something quite different from either of these things.

There are two realms, intersecting but at least notionally separate, eudaemonics and morality. Simplifying, we may say that nobody does anything except for the sake of eudaimonia: but what is done for the sake of eudaimonia must be done under the censorship of morality.

Could one say, then, that: "No one does anything except for the sake of eudaimonia, *or* for the sake of morality"?[2] One could, but it would still be slightly misleading.

"For the sake of eudaimonia" is a phrase which has an ordinary enough translation, "I did it to be a bit happier: I did it because I wanted to get . . ., &c." But, "for the sake of

[1] How far can we admit this parenthetic "or all"? If I am an End in a Kingdom of Ends then it is logically odd to suppose that no moral act by *anyone* ever benefited me: how far can I envisage the possible case of all moral acts by me as being to my disadvantage? Moral acts by other people would be bound, sooner or later, to conspire to my benefit. I still might not benefit from my moral acts. This ought, perhaps, to be gone into further. See P. Foot, "Moral Beliefs", *P.A.S.*, Vol. 59 (1958–59) and in Foot, ed., *Theories of Ethics*, O.U.P., 1967.

[2] Or charity, or love. But these are at least moral; and they are in effect more than moral, often 'beyond' morality, in many cases.

morality/moral goodness" is less clear, and perhaps we ought not to use or coin the phrase. I refrain from seducing the innocent NM not "for the sake of morality": NM has her own "sake", "for the sake of which" I do not seduce her. I can act, in an ordinary sense, for her sake or for mine: but only in a strained sense of "sake" can I act (or refrain from acting), either for morality's or for goodness' sake.

Morality is not itself an end, as Kant himself says perceptively enough; it is the condition or form of a Kingdom of Ends. But that he saw this in at least one place in the *Groundwork* did not prevent Kant, as it has not prevented some who might be described as being in his tradition, from forgetting it.

There are two strands in what we have been discussing: (i) the strand of the indifference of morality to eudaimonia, *one way or the other*; and (ii) the strand of 'for-the-sake-of-ness' which tries in effect to give to morality or to moral goodness the kind of *sake* or *end* (or perhaps even End-ship) that belongs to persons. We might bring the threads together here by some device such as this; by saying, or sloganizing: "Eudaimonia is concerned with what I do for my sake, morals are about what I do for other peoples' sakes. Nobody who is not mad fails to act for his own sake; nobody who is not a moral imbecile fails to act with regard to, and on occasion just *for*, the sakes of others." And we may add: "If acting for others' sakes happens to make me happier, then this is fortunate: if it does not, then it is unfortunate. But to act with regard to/for the sake of others is an obligation, willy nilly."

2. *An Illusion Dispelled*

For all that we have said, we must conclude that moral goodness is not an illusion: but we must be careful not to make it into one.

The difference between moral value and other kinds of value, between moral good and other goods, cannot be denied, though it is more often flatly asserted than convincingly and carefully specified. A consequence which is often drawn from this difference between moral and non-moral value, namely that moral good, unlike other goods, is something that can, and must on occasions, be pursued for its own sake, may not indeed be a consequence of this simple distinction of kinds at all, but of something else again, related to, but not identical with it.

The central notion of action is acting for an end.[1] But when we consider ends "for the sake of which" we act, and when we reflect on this use of "sake", we see clearly enough that the agent as enjoyer or obtainer of the end, is himself that for the sake of what, or whom, the end is sought. Agents have "sakes", and so do Ends. But ends do not: not even when they are absolute *ends*, such as "the worth of mere will", "good in itself, and always good".

The central notion of morality is that of action done or refrained from for the sake of persons—for the sake of the person of oneself, or of another.

We might, perhaps, distinguish moral from non-moral goods on these grounds: moral goods are essentially those from the pursuit of which "*Achtung, und die Würde der Menschheit*",[2] "Reverence, and the dignity of Man", do not deflect us, either in principle, or on occasion.

"*Achtung*" can warn us off, but it can also beckon us on; and the connection between moral and personalistic or altruistic action is plain enough. The 'dignity of man' can command not only abstention, but positive action, and charity or at least altruism and positive concern for others can be of obligation.

All moral action, conceived in these terms—and it is not clear *prima facie* that we need conceive it in any others—is for the sake of *persons*, and not for the "sake" of moral goodness as such.

Moral, like non-moral goodness, has as it were *no sake* for which we can act: "sake" talk extrapolates from, and is essentially parasitic upon, the persons who are involved in, and who determine, an end-seeking or end-abstaining situation as moral. The moral is concerned with the person. Even when I do pursue "moral goodness for its own sake" I do this for the sake of my own Person: my moral improvement is *mine*, and no impersonal talk of "goodness for its own sake" will serve to evaporate this intrusive personal pronoun.

We must, in the light of what we have just said, modify

[1] Even, in his less metaphysical moments, for Kant: cf. *Groundwork*, p. 95: 54: A. pp. 45–6.

[2] Cf. *Groundwork*, p. 107: p. 70: A. p. 59. Cassirer, Vol. 4, p. 299.

something which we said a little earlier, at the end of Section A5 of the present chapter. What I sacrifice my happiness to when I sacrifice or defer my happiness to another's moral claim may, and for the most part will in effect be, the happiness of that other. But it is not the happiness of another simply *as happiness* which binds my will with duties: it is the happiness of another *as another's*.

It is respect for another person which is the ground of my practical obligation to respect that other person's happiness. In so far as we are all informal, undoctrinaire Aristotelians and tend to see eudaimonia as the end of each person's actions, then we will see respect for the person as coming to respect for the person's happiness. But in so far as we may have some notion of the person as having some other end besides, or apart from happiness, so will respect for the person entail respect for that other end.

Philosophically speaking, one is in a curious situation here. What is one to say that "respect for the person" means unless one gives "person" some content and some context: and how is one to do this without talking about his life's aims, that is his happiness?

Talk about "the good of the person" will help here, of course, but simply because *good* is a wider notion than is *happiness*, and this device of wider talk is very useful. Even so, we must insist that if anyone gives "good" a content, either (i) other than eudaimonia, (ii) incompatible with eudaimonia, then he must be called upon to defend his content. *Prima facie*, the good and the *telos* of the person is eudaimonia. What else could it be? It is the only end that an End can entertain for himself as self-evidently worth being an end; and it is the only end that makes being at all worth the candle.

C. THE IDEAL AS PERFECTION: THE AGENT AS STOIC

At this point of our essay the parallels between Harris and Kant become less striking and much less important than they have been heretofore. Nevertheless, though he is much less *apropos* now, Harris still occasionally says things which help throw into relief aspects of the *Groundwork*. Having begun with him as a man who said some Kantian things in advance of

Kant, we may keep him as a representative man, from whom a background, a parallel, or a contrast can be taken.

What Harris has to say of Perfection as an Ideal, may throw some light on the issue of the person and the eudaimonia of the person, as objects of moral concern. The rationalistic emptiness of Harris's "Perfection" should warn us against setting up something other than personal eudaimonia, or persons simply, as the moral end.

If the Greeks made Olympus all too human, the Stoic rationalist has to make his men a little too god-like. Harris develops, in the eighth section of his *Dialogue*, a notion of human perfection which owes much more to Stoic rationalism than it does to Aristotelian eudaemonism:

> By means then, said he, of our Hypothesis, behold one of the fairest, and most amiable of Objects, behold THE TRUE AND PERFECT MAN: that Ornament of Humanity; that Godlike Being, who, *without regard either to Pleasure or Pain uninfluenced equally by either Prosperity or Adversity, superior to the World and its best and worst Events, can fairly rest his All upon the Rectitude of his own Conduct; can constantly, and uniformly, and manfully maintain it; thinking that, and that alone, wholly sufficient to make him happy*. (*D.*, pp. 122–3.)

It is not quite clear here whether Rectitude of Conduct is to be pursued because it is Rectitude: or whether it is the end of action because it alone is always "Accommodate", &c. This kind of fatal ambiguity hangs equally over Kant, and especially over the celebrated passage at which we have already looked (*Groundwork*, p. 69: p. 20: A. p. 17), in which he seems in effect to conflate the essence of the moral with its "not having to be awaited from the result [of the action]". This is a confusion of a significant, highly rationalistic sort, which we must discuss again in the next chapter but one: Chapter III, Section C.4.

Harris's "happiness", in the passage which we have just quoted, is of course a "placed" happiness. It is not eudaimonia; it is the one ineluctable thing, the one accommodate, labelled "happiness" in a desperate, paradoxical, attempt to produce a Stoic eudaimonia. Furthermore, when Harris goes on to talk of the "true and perfect man", moral considerations and the paradoxical Stoic eudaimonia are inextricably mixed. The confusion is useful, by way of example.

Harris does not expect his moral Ideal of the "The True and Perfect Man" to have ontological reality in the sense of its being realized in any human individual. But he insists nevertheless—or the cynical might say *therefore*—on its higher reality:

> I might add, said he, if there were Occasion, other Arguments which would surprise you. I might inform you of the natural Pre-eminence and high Rank of *Specific Ideas*—that every *Individual* was but their *Type*, or Shadow;—that the *Mind* or *Intellect* was the *Region of Possibles*;—that whatever is *Possible*, to the *Mind*, actually *Is*; nor any thing a *Non-entity* except what implies a *Contradiction*;—that the genuine Sphere and genuine Cylinder, tho' *Forms* perhaps *too perfect*, *ever to exist conjoined to Matter* were yet as *true and real* Beings, as the *grossest objects* of Sense; were the *Source* of infinite *Truths*, which *wholly* depend on them, and which, as Truth, have a Being most *unalterable* and *eternal*. But these are Reasonings which rather belong to *another* Philosophy; and if you are satisfied without them, they are at best but superfluous. (*D.*, pp. 125–6.)

We are beyond Harris's rationalism now, and launched into a metaphysic more Platonic than Aristotelian. Perhaps wisely, Harris does not press it:

> He waited not for my Answer but proceeded as follows. It is thus, said he, have I endeavoured, as far as in my power, to give you an Idea of the *perfect Character*: a Character, which I am neither so absurd, as to impute to myself; nor so rigorous and unfair, as to require of others. We have proposed it only, as an EXEMPLAR OF IMITATION, which tho' *None* we think can *equal*, yet *All* at least may *follow*—an Exemplar of Imitation, which in proportion as we approach so we advance proportionately in *Merit* and in *Worth*—an exemplar, which, were we more *selfish*, we should be Fools to reject; if it be true, that *to be Happy*, is *the ultimate Wish of us all*, and that *Happiness* and *Moral Worth* so reciprocally correspond, that there can be no Degree of *the one*, without an equal Degree of

> *the other*. If there be Truth, said I, in your Reasonings, it cannot certainly be otherwise. (*D*., p. 126.)

We are left, here below, with the correspondence of Happiness and Moral Worth as an ideal. But the source of the whole problem is that happiness and moral worth do not seem at all to correspond here below. This is the root of the paradox of happiness, that this ideal pre-ordination is less realized than it might be. Even on the most accommodating definition of "moral worth", even when we equate it to the apparently selfish and egocentric prudence of Aristotle's splendid citizen-philosopher, the correspondence between moral worth and happiness is at best incomplete. The most prudent man can never be sure that he will enjoy the fruits of his prudence, and so, if Harris is right, he should set his enjoyment in prudence itself. The "sake" of morality, perhaps, replaces the "sake", "for the sake of which" eudaimonia is sought. But the displacement does nothing useful, either for morals or for happiness.

1. *Eudaimonia as a Stoic Problem*

There is no solution to the eudaemonistic problem in Stoic-rationalism. We have not solved either the problem of happiness or the problem of making happiness and moral goodness or worth commensurate, when we have tracked down the one thing that is always accommodate and ineluctable here below, namely, a man's credit accruing to him for righteous effort. Credit is a deserving, but not always a getting of deserts, and eudaimonia turns upon gettings rather than on deservings.

Nor have we, having isolated a man's ineluctable credit, his good will 2, done anything for morality, either. The juggernaut-like worth of righteousness is, if anything at all, an accident of morality, not its substance. When we talk of a man oppressed by fate and his fellows, as nevertheless worthy and deserving, we are talking in terms of the eudaimonia that we think his good acts *would* merit, a eudaimonia which, precisely, he lacks. Moral goodness, credit, praise, are indeed uncashed or uncashable tokens for eudaimonia which our good acts have earned us. They are not anything that we would particularly want in themselves: or, as soon as they themselves become objects of desire, then a meta-eudaimonia reasserts the eudaemonist's account of ends.

D. THE LIFE OF CONSISTENCY

There is nothing in Harris's *Dialogue*, as we have noted already, to match exactly Kant's doctrine of a formal moral law, (a law whose "formal" nature we shall explore in Chapter III below). However, there is in the *Dialogue* something quite minimal which may stand in for Kant's formal categorical imperative. This is the notion of 'Consistency in Life'. It is to some degree "categorical" as is Kant's idea, in its power to give moral form to human conduct, and it is as unconditionally binding as Kant's too, no doubt. Harris, however, is too urbane to feel that the absoluteness of obligation needs to be insisted upon too far: we are all well enough acquainted with that fact.

Harris's notion of consistency is not categorical, of course, in the high, critical, sense at all. That is, there is no model of an *a priori* formal determination of moral phenomena. However, Harris's notion of "Consistency" has something of the indefinite application which is the characteristic of Kant's more elegant categorical form:

§4 of the Dialogue:

> We have supposed the *Sovereign Good* to lie in *Rectitude of Conduct*. We have. And think you there can be Rectitude of Conduct, if we do not *live consistently?* In what Sense, said I, would you be understood? To *live consistently*, said he, is the same with me, as *To live agreeably to some one single and consonant Scheme or Purpose*. Undoubtedly, said I, without this, there can be no Rectitude of Conduct. *All Rectitude* of Conduct then, you say, implies such *Consistence*. It does. And does all *Consistence*, think you, imply such *Rectitude?* I asked him, Why not? It is possible, indeed it may, said he, for aught we have discovered yet, to the contrary. But what if it should be found that there may be numberless Schemes, each in particular *consistent with itself*, but yet all of them *different*, and some perhaps *contrary?* There may, you know, be a *consistent* Life of Knavery, as well as a *consistent* Life of Honesty; there may be a *uniform* practice of Luxury, as well

> as of Temperance, and Abstemiousness. Will the Consistence, *common to all of these Lives*, render the *Conduct* in each *right?* It appears, said I, an Absurdity, that there should be the same Rectitude in two Contraries. If so, said he, we must look for something more than mere Consistence when we search for that Rectitude which we at present talk of. A *consistent* Life indeed is requisite, but that alone is not enough. We must determine its *peculiar Species*, if we would be accurate and exact. It indeed appears, said I, necessary. (*D*., pp. 115–16.)

The 'something more than *mere Consistence*' which forms the firm ground of obligation and rectitude turns out to be, not surprisingly, Nature:

> Nor is any thing, continued he, more easy to be discussed. For what can that *peculiar Consistence* of Life be else, than a Life, whose several Parts are not only consonant to *each other*, but to the *Nature* also of the Being, by whom that Life has been adopted? Does not this *last* Degree of Consistence appear as requisite as the *former?* I answered, it could not be otherwise.
>
> You see then, said he, the true Idea of right Conduct. It is not merely, *To live consistently;* but it is *To live consistently with Nature*. Allow it. (*D*., p. 116.)

The true Idea of Righteous Conduct is "*to live consistently with Nature*". However indulgently one reads this part of Harris's treatise, and however much it may remind one of Kant's formulation of the categorical imperative in terms of laws of nature, Harris's treatment of the question is bound to appear more than a little perfunctory.

Harris's concern is not to rework for himself a plot of moral philosophy already well enough cultivated by his classical predecessors, but simply to get something out of the usual commonplaces which he thinks he can use in his mitigation of the paradox of Happiness and Rectitude of Conduct. Harris takes for granted what he expects his readers to concede, namely that the classical philosophers from whom he borrows his idea of nature have established obligation on this foundation as firmly as it can, or need be, established. Harris's interests are not primarily in obligation as such, but in effecting, by means of his talk about Nature, whatever reconciliation he can between his doctrine of Righteous Conduct as Sovereign Good, and a rational eudaemonism.

"To live consistently with Nature is to live agreeably to a just Experience of those things which happen around us" and consequently "the Essence of Righteous Conduct" lies "in SELECTION and REJECTION": "such Selection should be *consonant with our proper Nature.*" The whole affair is circular, but not without a certain appearance of point.

Harris's aim is simply to re-assert the nature of the situation within which the "Moral Art" is practised, the world of empirical facts through which we make our way as reason best dictates. By insisting that Rectitude of Conduct depends, like all practical eudaemonism, upon selection and rejection in accordance with Nature, Harris hopes to soften or perhaps simply to gloss over, the uncomfortable difference in hedonic tone that there is between Rectitude of Conduct in itself and such Conduct crowned with "outward" success:

> See then, said he, the Result of our Inquiry—The SOVEREIGN GOOD, as constituted by *Rectitude of Conduct*, has, on our strictest Scrutiny, appeared to be this—TO LIVE PERPETUALLY SELECTING, AS FAR AS POSSIBLE, WHAT IS CONGRUOUS TO NATURE, AND REJECTING WHAT IS CONTRARY, MAKING OUR END THAT SELECTING AND THAT REJECTING ONLY. It is true, said I, so it appears.
>
> Before we hasten then farther, said he, let us stop to recollect and see whether our present Conclusions accord with our former. We have now supposed the *Sovereign Good* to be *Rectitude of Conduct*, and *this Conduct* we have made consist in a certain *Selecting* and *Rejecting*. We have. And do you not imagine that the *Selecting* and *Rejecting*, which we propose, as they are purely governed by the Standard of *Nature*, are capable in every instance of being *rationally justified*? I replied, I thought they were. But if they admit a *rational Justification*, then are they *Moral Offices* or *Duties*; for thus you remember . . . a *Moral Office* was defined. It

> was. But if so, *To live in the Practice of them*, will be *To live in the Discharge of Moral Offices*. It will. But *To live in the Discharge of these*, is the same as *Living according to Virtue*, and *Living according to Nature*. It is. So therefore is *Living in that Selection, and in that Rejection, which we propose*. It is. (*D*., pp. 117–18.)

What Harris is forced to say, for all that his ethics move in a material context and not in the pure realm of formal principles, is very like what Kant is to say. Harris's " . . . making our End that Selecting and that Rejecting only" makes good will (in the primitive if not in the consequent sense) both the content of happiness and the end of reason. In Harris's system whatever ends we would have and may possibly attain, we are entitled to, as long as the initial pursuit of them is consonant with Moral Office: ends remain to determine the will, and good will 1 becoming itself the "point" of practical reason does not displace ordinary ends in the way in which good will 2 would.

We must set our hearts on pure action itself, simply in case we fail in our ends. However, should we succeed in our ends, then we may rejoice as much as we please in what we have contrived to get. Righteousness and eudaimonia may not always run together, but if we do contrive, selecting and rejecting rationally, to be both righteous, and happy in the eudaemonists' sense, then we are entitled to our happiness.

To will at all we must venture on some end, selecting this thing or rejecting that, and hoping by the one to gain, by the other to be free, of something. But we must set our hearts, Harris thinks, on the venture itself, and not on the end if we are to have the happiness that Fortune cannot take from us. Harris does not have Kant's notion of a formal determination of the will, prescinding from the expected results of action; but like Kant and for half of Kant's reason, he is forced to fix the *end* not in the ends of action but in action itself.

What determines the will for Harris is not "the idea of the law in itself . . . present only in a rational being" (*Groundwork*, p. 69: p. 21: A. pp. 17–18), but precisely "the expected result" of an action; what is to be gained from it or prevented by it, when this result is itself compatible with Moral Office.

The Sovereign Good itself lies not in what might be gained or might be prevented by action. It lies simply in the actions of Selection and Rejection, when these are governed by Nature and the Discharge of Moral Office. For Harris ends are proper to the will, eminently so, and determine the whole action of willing; but in so far as they are not inevitably to be attained, they cannot be the Sovereign Good. The eudaemonics of Rectitude of Conduct must replace ordinary rational eudaemonism, but only because this is a harsher, more uncertain world than it might have been, and because the rationalism of Harris will have eggs much fresher than the hens can lay them.

That part of action itself which can be wholly commanded by the agent, his own rational willing, and the practical steps which circumstances allow him to attempt to bring about whatever it is that he rationally wills, is Kant's "good will". And it is Harris's Conduct and his Sovereign Good. Both are commanded by the agent, absolutely, because they remain immanent in him, and do not suffer the chances to which the "external" is inevitably subject.

What kind of view of life does this metaphysic of the inevitably possible leave us with? Harris himself makes some attempt to characterize it:

> I cannot deny, said I, but that as you now have explained it, your Hypothesis seems far more plausible, than when first it was proposed. You will believe it, said he, more so still, by considering it with more attention—In the first place, tho' perhaps it esteem nothing *really* GOOD but VIRTUE, nothing *really* EVIL but VICE, yet it in no manner takes away the *Difference*, and *Distinction of other Things*. So far otherwise, it is for establishing their Distinction to the greatest Accuracy. For were this neglected, what would become of *Selection* and *Rejection*, those important Energies, which are its very Soul and Essence? Were there no DIFFERENCE, there could be no CHOICE. It is true, said I, there could not. (*D*., p. 119.)

Though it looks paradoxical, if "nothing is *really* Good but Virtue", everything nevertheless remains the same. Choice and rejection proceed according to the old rules of prudence, and the conduct of life is unaltered. The only thing that is changed is the locus of our happiness, which moves from success to pure immanent action. But we need deny ourselves nothing that we would have if we could. Virtue is the only good of the "Indeprivable" and "Accommodate" kind, but there are other goods besides, and though neither "Indeprivable" nor "Accommodate" they remain goods:

> AGAIN, said he. It is no meagre, mortifying System of *Self-denial*—It suppresses no Social and Natural Affections, nor takes away any Social and Natural Relations—It prescribes no Abstainings, no Forbearances *out of Nature*; no gloomy, sad, and lonely Rules of Life, *without* which it is evident Men may be as honest as *with*, and be infinitely more useful and worthy Members of *Society*.—It refuses no Pleasure, not inconsistent with *Temperance*—It rejects no Gain, not inconsistent with *Justice*—Universally, as far as *Virtue* neither *forbids* nor *dissuades*, it endeavours to render Life, even in the *most vulgar* Acceptation, as chearful, joyous, and easy as possible. Nay, could it mend the Condition of Existence in any the *most trivial* Circumstances, even by adding to the amplest Possessions the poorest meanest Utensil, it would in no degree contemn an Addition even so mean. Far otherwise—It would consider, that to neglect the least Acquisition, when fairly in its power, would be to fall short of that *perfect* and *accurate Conduct*, which it ever has in view, and on which alone all depends. (*D.*, pp. 119–20.)

If Kant's jeremiads against "dear self" in the second chapter of the *Groundwork* (p. 75: pp. 27–8: A. pp. 23–4), do stem at least in part from the metaphysics of the necessarily-possible, it is obvious from Harris that they need not. If you can be happy in the most eudaemonic, even in the most sybaritic way, while observing Moral Office, then this is your good fortune. The only reason you have for looking for another kind of happiness again is not that *this* one is unfitting, but simply that it may fail.

What Harris advocates—on metaphysical grounds—is an ethic, eudaemonistic in aim and determination, but Stoic in tone and content. Harris advocates this from hard necessity, not from misanthropic inclination.

Nor does Harris think, as Kant does, that the notion of duty needs to be set in sharp opposition to all notions of possible interest, even when these interests are clearly private ones.

Harris's attempt to persuade us that we do already, in some sense, fix our happiness in action and not in success began, as we remember, with the sportsman's example with parallels from hunting and gallantry. The notion behind these examples recurs again at the end of his discussion, transformed from frivolity to high seriousness. He says of his system:

> It teaches us to consider *Life*, as one great important *Drama*, where we have each our *Part* allotted us to act. It tells us that our *Happiness*, as *Actors* in this *Drama*, consists not in the *Length* of our Part, nor in the *State* and *Dignity*, but in the *just*, the *decent*, and the *natural Performance*. (*D*., p. 120.)

We can command this, our 'just, decent and natural Performance'; and if we achieve nothing else besides, we can rest happy in it, or at the very least, not unhappy.

1. *The Paradox of Happiness*

Harris knows the human situation well enough, and although he begins his *Dialogue* with the Aristotelian axiom of eudaimonia, "The good is that which makes us happy"; yet the facts of life and the rationalist rebellion against them grip him at once, and make him turn the aspirations of eudaemonism inwards towards the immanent action of willing itself:

> ALL MEN PURSUE GOOD, and would be *happy*, if they knew how; not happy for Minutes, and miserable for Hours, but *happy*, if possible, *thro' every Part of their Existence*. Either therefore *there is a* GOOD *of this steady durable Kind*, or *there is none*. If *none*, then *all Good* must be *transient and uncertain*; and if so, an *Object of lowest Value*, which can little deserve either our Attention, or Inquiry. But if there be *a better Good*, such a Good as we are seeking; like every other thing, *it must be derived from some Cause*; and that Cause must be either *external*, *internal*, *or mixt*, inasmuch as except these three, there is no other possible. Now a *steady*, *durable Good*, cannot be derived from an *external* Cause, by reason all derived from *Externals* must *fluctuate*, as they *fluctuate*. By the same Rule,

> not from a *Mixture of the Two*; because the Part *which is external*, will *proportionately destroy its Essence*. What then remains but the *Cause internal*, the very Cause which we have supposed, when we place the *Sovereign Good* in *Mind*; in *Rectitude of Conduct*; in just *Selecting* and *Rejecting*? There seems indeed no other Cause, said I, to which we can possibly assign it. (*D*., pp. 121–2.)

Here, the rationalist in Harris will have either more than we can reasonably expect here below, "a Good of [a] steady durable Kind", or if not this, then he will have much less; if all sublunary good must be transient and uncertain, then it is "an Object of lowest Value". The compromise between these impossible extremes cannot but seem eminently reasonable now: "*the Cause internal*", beyond sublunary chance, must determine the only good, immanent in "Mind" and "Rectitude", "in just Selecting and Rejecting", which can be "steady" and "durable", above transience and uncertainty.

Even rationalism involves a compromise, and Harris and Kant make the only choice possible to them. Despite its low eudaemonic tone, they place the sovereign good in Rectitude of Conduct, in a just Selecting and Rejecting and in good will.

The Sovereign Good "retires into itself": Kant extols the 'absolute worth of mere will' because it has this absoluteness of total retirement.

Rectitude and good will are steady and durable; and they are "beatific" in the toneless sense of enjoying their own kind of negative "eternity". What is to the point, further, they are always within the competence of our will. So if we would be happy, "not for minutes . . . but through every Part of our Existence", then we had better compound these eternities and fix our happiness here, in Conduct, "eternal" and always to hand, no matter how low the eudaemonic tone of Righteous Conduct seems to be:

> FORGIVE me then, continued he, should I appear to boast—We have proved or at least there is an Appearance we have proved, that *either there is no* GOOD *except this of our own; or that, if there be any other, it is not worthy our Regard.* It must be confessed, said I, you have said as much as the Subject seems to admit. (*D*., p. 122.)

Moral athletes and hard-pressed rationalists choose the same *summum bonum* in the end. Though they have different motives, they both settle for Righteous Conduct or 'good will', leaving the middling sensual man with a sense as much of grievance as of shame.

CHAPTER II
VIRTUE AND REWARDS

> . . . If we were born for virtue or honesty, and this be the only desirable good, as Zeno would have it, or at least so much more so than everything else, as to outweigh all that can be put in the scale against it, which was Aristotle's opinion; it must certainly follow, that honesty is the only, or however the greatest good: now whatever is good must certainly be profitable; whence it follows, that whatever is honest must certainly be profitable.
>
> Cicero, *The Offices*, VIII, Thomas Cockman's translation, 1699

The notion of virtue to which a Stoic is driven is perforce a notion determined by happiness' being conditional-*f*: if happiness may fail, then something else, again, must be found that will not fail: virtue is always available, and it is immanently ineluctable.

Sometimes, however, one finds people who talk as though it were the point of virtue as virtue that it need have nothing to do with happiness. Where Stoic-rationalism elects virtue to the highest role simply because it alone is unfailing while happiness is always conditional-*f*, there is a kind of Stoic-anti-eudaemonism that sees in the disengagement of virtue from happiness, virtue's real point and value. The contest is all, the bays are nothing. There is, that is to say, a class of persons who seem to value virtue for its own sake, when this comes to taking it to be the mark of virtue that it leads, or may, or need lead, to nothing but itself. "Virtue is its own reward" can be said not only with a wry cadence, but also in tones of high moral enthusiasm.[1] But, though the higher tone may seem altogether

[1] See *M.E.E.* ". . . although virtue may now and then be called meritorious . . . and be worthy of reward, yet in itself, as it is its own end, so also it must be regarded as its reward". A. p. 317. And see the earlier: ". . . when compared with *human ends* all of which have their obstacles to be overcome, it is true that the worth of virtue itself, which is its own end, far outweighs the end of all utility and all the empirical ends and advantages which it may have as consequences". A. p. 308. These texts must, of course, be set against e.g. *C.Pr.R.*, V, cf. A. pp. 227 and 243, etc.

more appropriate, we must remember that moral enthusiasm, when it is misplaced, can injure morality.

Perhaps, though it is to some extent parenthetical, we might usefully look into this question of virtue and rewards. The question is already in the air; and although we cannot go exhaustively into all aspects of it in this essay, frankness as well as some attempt at completeness, compels us to put our own position on the issue of virtue and its putative rewards.

Whether Kant was or was not, in his *Groundwork* phase, an anti-eudaemonist, we cannot, perhaps, decide: but, since we are criticizing him, it is only fair that we should give some sketch, even if a very brief one, of our own views on this issue of virtue and its rewards.

Though it is an undeniable fact that virtue is often as not, not crowned with eudaimonia, this has always seemed to most people a fact about eudaimonia. It is certainly not the point of virtue; even so, so evident a truth has not always, it would appear, seemed evident to everyone.

A. "THE UNENDING DEVELOPMENT OF THE POSSIBILITIES OF THE SOUL"

That eudaimonia is a proper end of life, and that morality is concerned with each agent's moral censorship of his own strategies for eudaimonia, not because renunciation is a good thing, or because virtue itself is the ultimate value, but because Ends must be respected, are commonplaces which must be insisted upon, if we are to escape the illusory notions of virtue which, while failing to solve the eudaemonic problem, also and just as seriously fail to come at the point of morality.

It may be instructive to look at some extreme views on this matter; the limits must be plotted, if one is to fix the mean.

In the Drew Lecture for 1929 entitled "The Destiny of the Soul", the Reverend Professor W. R. Matthews contrived to produce a notion of virtue or of moral activity as its own end, which combines all the elements of Stoic rationalism, along with a renunciation, very curious in a Christian context, of Christian finalism. Matthews wrote:

> We may ask whether we can represent the future life as a sphere of rewards and punishments. Undoubtedly popular religion has seized upon this aspect of the Christian doctrine to the exclusion of most of the rest, and the preaching of heaven and hell has often been little better than a frank appeal to the simplest kind of self-interest. In contrast to this style of eschatology the disinterested pursuit of virtue as preached by Spinoza has seemed an infinitely higher doctrine. But the idea of reward is not necessarily immoral and unspiritual, nor need the God who rewards the righteous be regarded as a celestial school-master who hands out prizes at the end of the school year. The real ground for an objection to the idea of reward is that the prize is thought of as something of a different character from the achievement which earns it. If we are told to serve God for the sake of sensual happiness, the doctrine is plainly immoral, for it implies that sensual happiness is more valuable than virtue. Doubtless many who have represented the service of God as a good investment have really meant something like this. But not necessarily. The reward need not be in a different category from the activity which it crowns. The good man really loves goodness for its own sake, and his reward is the "wages of going on and not to die", the opportunity of proceeding further in the unending development of the possibilities of the soul.[1]

The idea "unending development of the possibilities of the soul" which this passage exhibits, looks suspiciously like an eternity of moral activity and of moral effort, a heaven of

[1] W. R. Matthews, "The Destiny of the Soul", *The Hibbert Journal*, Vol. XXVIII, No. 2 (1929). Notice how phrases like "goodness for its own sake" tend, in such a context, to limit the intension of goodness to virtue and to virtue-as-striving. What Matthews writes here might have been suggested by certain things, e.g. in section IV of Kant's *Dialectic of Pure Practical Reason*, ". . . the perfect accordance of the will with the moral law . . . is required as practically necessary [and] it can only be found in a *progress in infinitum* . . ." A. p. 281, etc. See too, footnote A. p. 220. Even so, in the end, Kant seems to allow the *summum bonum* or kingdom of God to be eudaemonic, A. p. 224, p. 227, etc.

precisely those felicities of Harris's "Choice" and "Conduct" which we find too thin on earth. There is something ominous in the sentence:

> ... The reward need not be in a different category from the activity which it crowns.

If, as the liturgy of the Church assures us, this is indeed "a vale of tears" it would be disquieting to think that heaven (if there is one), may be no less tearful and no less strenuous than earth.

The reason why the traditional orthodox theologian has made "the prize something of a different character from the achievement which earns it" is obvious enough; and Professor Matthews seems to have overlooked the evident here. Prizes are generally different from efforts, and athletes get medals at the Olympics, and not merely permission to compete again next time. Heaven is different from earth in that there we will all get the prizes we deserve, and more than we deserve, whereas here below we have so often to console ourselves simply with deserving what we may very well not get. Virtue must be its own reward "in this sublunary state" not because there is nothing that would fittingly reward virtue, but simply because what might do this does not in fact do it. The virtuous man would not feel affronted were he offered prosperity or eudaimonia: it just happens to be the case that the offer is much rarer than it might be.

There is a sense, of course, in which traditional theologians have made the prize and the achievement the same. In so far as virtue is thought of as partaking of the love of God, then it is in a sense the same as the reward of virtue, which is God Himself, enjoyed in the Beatific Vision: but this kind of identity does not seem to be what Professor Matthews had in mind.

Again: one would like to know what Professor Matthews meant by his reference, in the last line of the passage quoted, to "the possibilities of the soul". If he meant *all* the possibilities of the soul, and all the possibilities of an embodied one, then these will, indeed, orthodox theologians assure us, be satisfied by the infinite possibilities of heaven. Matthews seems, on the face of it, however, to be offering us an eternity of Harris's "Conduct", and not of his "welfare", keeping the strenuous "possibilities" while denying us the delightful ones.

If sensual happiness is, somehow, to be part of heaven (and St Thomas for one seems to think that it is), then the mere abstract reflection that this might make sensual happiness "more valuable than virtue" looks too abstract to carry much weight. Heaven will not be all sensual—the theologians stress the intellectual nature of its delights—but if it is partially so, then part of the aim of virtue too is sensual pleasure.

And why should it not be?

That virtue is an absolute in the rationalistic sense, and that it is all that we may be sure of here below, does not make it more important then sensual pleasure. And when sensual pleasure, here below, 'must be sacrificed to virtue', this is only a *façon de parler*; and one which may deceive us. The pleasures which I have now to forgo for virtue's sake must be forgone for reasons that can be given at length; and in the list of reasons that I give, the phrase "for virtue's sake" will cease to figure. The sakes of some persons will, soon enough, be introduced into the account. Virtue itself is not the end, even of heroic righteousness: look long enough and you will find an End. You will find Ends loved, and God as the End-of-Ends, if you look at the saints of religion. If you look to humanists, you will find man, taken as an Ideal and as an End, as the point of righteousness, or particular human beings taken as contingent yet absolute Ends.

Professor Matthews presents us with an interesting example of a confusion into which a surprising number of people fall: he makes virtue, and virtue defined as moral striving rather than as *areté* or right functioning, the central and all-important notion. Virtue becomes absolute axiologically and every other way, when in fact it is absolute only in the rather empty rationalistic way. Professor Matthews shows us clearly how virtue can be over-valued or misvalued, that is how it can be made an axiological absolute when it is not one. Matthews does not show us, as Kant does, how the confusion arises; but he is instructive in that he takes the absolutist axiology of value to lengths that are, given a context of Christian belief, quite quixotic.

To offer no rewards to virtue within a story part of whose point seems to be to reassure us that virtue will be rewarded, is either heroic, or bizarre. Quixote was both: heroic, and bizarre.

B. THE PROBLEM OF EUDAIMONIA AS A MORAL PROBLEM

For all that one must insist that eudaemonics is one thing, and morality another, it must be admitted that the problem of eudaimonia is itself, perhaps in a second-order sense, a moral problem.

It is, precisely because (i) we, ordinary virtuous people, not only want happiness itself (and not some mere "placed" happiness which rests in our own ineluctable credit), and (ii) because we also think that we deserve happiness, that our not getting it generates a sense not merely of frustration but of injustice. If the good man always prospered and the bad always came to an unpleasant end, then our sense of eudaemonic justice would be satisfied. Or, to put it more boldly, our sense of justice, simply, would be satisfied.

The point of morality would not, then, become the prosperity of the righteous: the point would remain as it is. Nevertheless, we would be relieved of a great portion of what we now bear with: the problem of evil in its moral aspect. We would no longer be disedified by the spectacle of the suffering of the good man and the prosperity of the wicked one, a spectacle which raises at once our eudaemonic and our moral bile.

To say that the sufferings of the righteous and the prosperity of the wicked pose a moral problem is not by any means to say that morality is concerned *au fond* with reward and punishment: these, prosperity and punishment, are what moral or immoral acts merit, and they are the sanctions of morality, if indeed it has any. But they need not be the point, or the sole point, of morality.

The point of morality, of sanctioned as well as of sanctionless morality, is the respect by Agents of the End-ship of Ends. What else could it be?

The great moral problem that the failure of the moral ideal—virtue rewarded and vice punished—presents is, let us say, a moral problem of a special kind and order. Questions about 'the fairness of things' may come after questions about conduct, and be rather different from them: but they are still, in a sense, moral questions. In heaven both moral questions will lapse: there will be no need to insist on respect for persons, since, among "holy wills" this will be a matter of course: and the problem set by a universe which seems "unfair to people" will lapse in the face of absolute eudaimonia.

C. ESCHATOLOGY, EUDAIMONIA AND MORALITY

Christian eschatology seeks to perform a double task: (i) to complete the eudaemonic account that remains for ever incomplete here below as long as happiness is conditional-*f*, and (ii) to do this in such a way that the moral impropriety of the imbalance between righteousness and prosperity will be redressed.

Classical eudaemonism, and the particular second-order moral problem that the failure of the eudaimonia of the just man presents, are susceptible of a solution, if only of a transcendental and other-worldly one. Kant himself recognizes this, if not in the *Groundwork*, at any rate in the *Critique of Practical Reason*.

St Augustine, a severe moralist in many ways, is most concerned to complete the eudaemonic pattern in this, perhaps his most quoted sentence:

> Thou has made us for Thyself O Lord, and our hearts are restless till they find rest in Thee.[1]

This can be read as a prayer, or set up as an argument. As an argument it gets a great deal of its force from our sensitivity to the paradox of happiness: that the good do good and may get no good from it themselves.

St Augustine appeals at once to the natural man, and to the man with doubts about Stoicism; he is at once commonsensical and eudaemonist. Indeed Stoic rationalism of Epictetus'

[1] Augustine, *Confessions*, Bk. I, Ch. I.

and, one may suppose, of Harris's sort is rejected, unequivocally enough by Augustine:

> The rational creature . . . has been so made that *it cannot itself be the good by which it is made happy.*[1]

Is this eudaemonic realism? Or is it a critique of the Stoic, and implicitly of the rationalist notions of man as his own "Cause internal" of his own good?

That his remark about the 'otherness' of human good is intended as a critique of Stoicism, comes out in another passage of St Augustine's:

> It is not the virtue of thy soul that maketh thee happy, but He who hath given the virtue . . .[2]

Clearly Augustine understands happiness in the ordinary man's sense. He knows that we think of it as something over and above, and different from, our virtue. Of course the realistic reflection that we are not our own happiness can be shaped up into a eudaemonistic apologia, and it can become part of a proof for the existence of God. This is indeed how the passage from the *Confessions* is often used: and, in the same way one might quote this:

> The striving after God is, therefore, the desire of beatitude, the attainment of God beatitude itself.[3]

Whether this apologetic will do, is not our present concern. The interest to us of these fragments from a severe Father lies in the frankness with which St Augustine recognizes as legitimate the claims of eudaimonia. The attainment of God would, indeed, be the attainment of Virtue itself; but the attainment would be, by the same token, a Beatitude, the expansion and flowing of *areté* and not the re-enactment of acts of "virtue" in the narrow, moralists' sense, the sense that is full of necessary renunciation, and of the contingent failure of happiness. Renunciation is necessary for morality: the failure of happiness is an accident. This failure is due to the flaw in the universe,

[1] Augustine, *Serm.* 150, 7, 8. [2] *Ibid.*, 150, 8, 9.

[3] *Ibid.*, *De moribus eccl.* 1.11.18. All these quotations are cited and commented upon in F. Copleston's *History of Philosophy*, London (Burns Oates), 1950, Vol. II, Ch. VII, q.v.

Augustine thought, left by an aboriginal calamity. The Fall is not from all points of view a "happy fault".

Two alternatives present themselves: we may place happiness in mundane righteousness, despite the notorious fact that even if virtue is its own reward, we would still prefer profit as well. Or, we may postulate or argue for the resolution of the whole eudaemonic paradox of deserving and deserts in some future state, where happiness will be as complete and unfailing as we could wish, and, as well, commensurate in some way with our righteousness. We may take, that is, the tragic or the Christian view of life. But we may not, in a sense, take the Stoic view: virtue is at once too much an end, and too little an end to be the crown of action: it has the end-likeness of eudaimonia, but it lacks the self-justification, the self evidence of eudaimonia as an end.

We can ask of virtue: what is the point of it? When this question is asked of happiness it is altogether odd.

Stoicism must, it seems, be purged of its rationalism, or it is no more than the eudaemonics of the consolation prize.

If St Augustine is quite deceived, and there is no God, then, in a sense, action has no final end. But it has ends still, though these may fail, and it has Ends. These Ends, like the poor, are always with us, and they give to humanism a better rationale than virtue and the worth of virtue give to Stoicism.

As we remarked in the Appendix to Part I, Coleridge seems to have conflated the notions of personal worth and personal, immortal, destiny. When he writes:

> I cannot conceive of a supreme moral Intelligence, unless I believe in my own immortality.[1]

he seems to be involving the notion of morality with the notions of eternity and immortality in a way which may strike us as very odd, even if it is traditional enough.

The Burial Service in the Prayer Book states the human condition exactly:

> Man that is born of woman hath but a short time to live,

[1] S. T. Coleridge, flyleaf annotation to Kant's *Vermichte Schriften*, quoted above, Appendix to Part I, pp. 159–60.

and is full of misery. He cometh up, and is cut down, like a flower; he fleeth as it were a shadow, and never continueth in one stay.

But, though this is our situation, we are not worthless to ourselves, or to others: and morality is based on the realization that others cannot be worthless to us. The "sure and certain hope of the Resurrection to eternal life" may console us, and it may give to life a point that it otherwise lacks, utterly: but such a hope might be an illusion without morality being an illusion.

Whether we are immortal or not we must behave to one another with decency, for as long as our *stay* may be.

1. *The Idea of a Future Life*

To those who believe in an after-life, and notably to Christians, the postulation of transcendent eudaemonics has seemed not only convenient but necessary. However, to those who do not have this kind of belief, the whole thing takes on the look of an argument or a persuasion, which indeed it sometimes is. For Kant in the *Critique of Pure Reason* of course, there was a curiously ambivalent way out which was provided by the regulative employment of the Ideas. In Kant's middle way, justice and a concern for the metamoral problem of ultimate justice, rather than a concern for eduaimonia as such, sets the tone: the solution is, even so, Augustinian in essence. The resolution of life's imbalances and injustices will come, not here but hereafter.

As Dryden's Deists have it:

Our reason prompts us to a future state
The last appeal from fortune and from fate:
Where God's all-righteous ways will be declar'd,
The bad meet punishment, the good reward.[1]

Kant is concerned less with eudaimonia than with a kind of moral book-keeping, and less with this, even, than with a kind of teleologism, parallel to if different from St Augustine's. The upshot, however, is the same in the end. Though in Kant's critical system we cannot know, we can and must think accord-

[1] John Dryden, *Religio Laici*, lines 58–61.

ing to an Idea of justice and of happiness and unhappiness commensurate with desert.

Kant's view in his critical period is stated in these terms:

> If we judged according to *analogy with the nature* of living beings in this world, in dealing with which reason must necessarily accept the principle that no organ, no faculty, no impulse, indeed nothing whatsoever is either superfluous or disproportioned to its use, and that therefore nothing is purposeless, but everything exactly conformed to its destiny in life—if we judged by such an analogy we should have to regard man, who alone can contain in himself the final end of all this order, as the only creature that is excepted from it. Man's natural endowments—not merely his talents and the impulses to enjoy them, but above all else the moral law within him—go so far beyond all the utility and advantage which he may derive from them in this present life, that *he learns* thereby *to prize the mere consciousness of a righteous will as being*, apart from all advantageous consequences, apart even from the shadowy reward of posthumous fame, *supreme over all other values*; *and so feels an inner call to fit himself*, by his conduct in this world, and by the sacrifice of many of its advantages, *for citizenship in a better world* upon which he lays hold in idea. This powerful and incontrovertible proof is reinforced by our ever-increasing knowledge of purposiveness in all that we see around us, and by contemplation of the immensity of creation, and therefore also by the consciousness of a certain illimitableness in the possible extension of our knowledge, and of a striving commensurate therewith. All this still remains to us, but we must renounce the hope of comprehending, from the merely theoretical knowledge of ourselves, the necessary continuance of our existence.[1]

And very equivocal terms these are. At one moment Kant has the "mere consciousness of a righteous will" as supreme over

[1] *C.P.R.* B. 425–6 K–S edition, pp. 379–80 (Italics mine). Though Kant's remarks in the *C.Pr.R.* seem less equivocal—cf. e.g. A. p. 227—the whole matter is as it were bracketed by the reservation that God and immortality belong to the realm of the reflective and the regulative, and not to the constitutive principles of reason. There is always an 'as if' in Kant which would have been foreign, for example, to St Augustine.

all other values; at the next "citizenship of a better world" is what justifies, that is, gives teleological point to 'the sacrifice of many advantages' in this one. If the phrase "a better world" is a euphemism for the older and bolder "heaven", then Kant's finalism ends up with the same end as does St Augustine's. If, on the other hand, "a better world" refers simply to a Kingdom of Ends taken as an Ideal, then indeed Kant has expressed, here, the essence of the moral: its end is not virtue or 'the mere consciousness of a righteous will' but Ends, and a possible Kingdom of Ends.

Whether a Kingdom of ends is possible in this world, or only in another (conceived either as the Christians conceive it or, as for example McTaggart conceived it), it remains an Ideal, and one in accordance with which we may regulate our conduct. Even so, one feels more drawn to concern for Ends-as-Ends, than to concern for an Ideal, albeit one so exalted.

It is important to notice that, even for Kant, the righteous will which is valuable, as he says in the *Groundwork*, "apart from all advantageous consequences", comes in the end to have a further, teleological, eudaemonistic role or value, in that it fits us for this higher citizenship, whatever that may be. Righteousness is seen in the *Critique* passage less as a rationalist absolute worth than as "availing to salvation", and the notion of good will, mere good will, as "reason's *end*" collapses: it is crucial to our understanding of the *Groundwork* that there is indeed no such collapse in that book.

We need not conclude that the passage from the *Critique of Pure Reason* shows a falling away from a purer teaching. The collapse threatens nothing but the rationalist doctrine of absolute value. Morality, properly conceived, remains unthreatened by the admixture of the transcendental and the eschatological; interest in 'citizenship of a higher world' does not threaten or weaken morality. Conceived in transcendent or non-transcendent terms, morality is a matter of Ends, not of the mere, disinterested, forgoing of ends.

It is interesting to see Kant, in one place at least, abandoning the rationalist absolutism of ineluctable moral value, and embracing what may even be the traditional eudaemonics of

Christianity. The passage from the *Critique of Pure Reason* contrasts sharply with some of the doctrines implicit in the *Groundwork*, where, as we shall see, Kant comes dangerously close to identifying virtue with absolute disinterestedness, adding this curious moralized notion of prescension-from-ends to the teaching, already odd enough, about absolute "good will" as reason's "unconditioned" end.

2. *An Ambiguous Finalism: an Ambiguous Axiology*

When Kant suggests in the *Groundwork* that we may already have an Idea that:

> . . . our existence has a different and far nobler *end* for which, and not for happiness, reason is properly intended . . . (Abbott, p. 13: Paton, p. 64; cited above, Part II, Chapter I, p. 170.)

his doctrine, in so far as it specifies that *end*, is caught uneasily between pure humanism and that strand of Christian or transcendent humanism which adds to the value of works the extra dimension of a value "availing for salvation". Kant rests, in the *Groundwork*, on the ineluctability of credit, and not on its ultimate cashability; and this makes the *Groundwork* much more rationalistic a work than are the ethical fragments of the *Critique of Pure Reason* or indeed than the *Critique of Practical Reason*. Kant keeps as his chief value, in the *Groundwork*, an end which is immanent—good will 2—though the whole point even of this immanent-worth notion seen as regards its content, is that good will is something-availing. Praiseworthiness implies, at least ideally, praise. Credit is always credit for something, and credit is ideally redeemable.[1] The ghostly analogue of the Christian notion of the value of virtue as "availing" is implicit even in so thin a notion as praise, and it hovers faintly but clearly present over the final half of "praise*worthiness*".

There is never any question about our valuing good will 1.

[1] The concept of credit seems logically to involve that credit is redeemable There may be uncashed cheques, but there cannot be necessarily uncashable ones: cheques may "bounce" of course, but 'that there cannot be uncashable cheques' is no doubt the principle behind the law that bankrupts cannot write cheques.

If I ask, "Why should I be reasonable?" what can anyone answer? *I* must fall silent. However, if I ask, "Why should I pursue good will 2, this rationalistic 'absolute'?" there is no knockdown answer, and it is not obvious at all that I can be shamed into silence. Unlike good will 1, good will 2, though "absolute" needs a point, a justification, if you like an end. And it is only in so far as we may still be haunted by the ghost of the end that righteousness has in theology, that we allow ourselves to be silenced when we ask, "What, apart from its serving Ends, is the *point* of the so-called '*end*' which Kant finds for reason?" The old-fashioned Christian could tell you the point of righteousness: even if it should prove fruitless here, and of no benefit to us, or to those whom we would serve, it will be rewarded hereafter.

The point of fruitless rectitude lies not in any insipid "beatific vision" of Harris's sort but in the Beatific Vision of the Christian theologian. One cannot ask of this, "What is its point?" since unconditional/unconditioned eudaimonia is its own point: and so one cannot ask of the righteousness which secures it, "What is the point of the righteousness?" Or, if one does ask one can be told: and the Beatific Vision provides a sense for righteousness which no "Cause internal" can.

In his *Epistle to the Romans*, St Paul uses the language of "finality" as neatly as any pure philosopher; but he is not writing as any kind of rationalist:

> Now being made free from sin, and become servants to God, you have your fruit unto sanctification and *the end of life everlasting*. (6. 19–23.)

There is no doubt here about the true end of life, it is for St Paul "life everlasting", and the system of final causes is unequivocal. Works, in this system of final causality, come to be seen as things which avail us towards the *true end*. Seen as availing towards a transcendent end, works and their merit take on a life of their own; and their availing value is in danger of splitting itself off from the works themselves, and from their rationale. This has happened in the history of Christian thought, sometimes to the point of scandal. But even the most interested doctrines of works remain parasitic on works themselves. The Ten Commandments had to be worth keeping before even Omnipotence itself could make it, eternally, worth our while to keep them. Kant in the *Groundwork* stumbles, as many Christians before him had, and sets up the supervenient value of works rather than works themselves as the end of reason. But, and here is the paradox, he does not refer, at least in the *Groundwork*, to the whole scheme of finality in terms of which this value-of-works notion takes its meaning. If merit earns us eternal bliss, then merit is a very interesting concept: but if all that we can say about merit is that it is ineluctable, then we would have to be extraordinarily enthusiastic rationalists before we found that particularly interesting. Kant values the merit of works more than works: but, though merit is essentially cashable, he makes no allusion in the *Groundwork* to the cashing of it. He is like a man just interested enough to expect to be paid for some service: but disinterested enough to take the banknotes of the Confederacy or the bonds of Imperial Russia.

There are two good reasons for valuing works: (1) one can value them because they avail to our true end which is eternal life, or (2) one can value works because of the ends which they serve, namely the preservation of, and the amelioration of the condition of, Ends-in-themselves.[1]

These two points of view represent perhaps a complementarity, perhaps a disjunction requiring choice. But they represent two viable world views. We do good works for the sake of the good they will do us in the kingdom of heaven, or for the sake of the good which good works do. Or we do them for both reasons.

If the *unco guid* are scandalized by the first of these alternatives (or by the conjunction of the first with the second), then they will have to wait till our next chapter for whatever balm we have to pour on their irritation. Those readers who are Christians will perhaps acknowledge that they regard works both ways. Those who are atheistic humanists will have no way but the second in which to regard works.

[1] Notice how Kant's expression "End-in-itself" keeps the language of finality, while not conforming to any of the classic themes of final causation. See Part III of the present essay.

Kant however, takes a third view of it all, or finds a new reason for valuing works, when he sets up good will, righteous effort, as reason's end.

Certain exegetes might choose to see Kant, simply, as seeking to disembroil himself from the interestedness of Christian doctrines of availing works, in favour of a purer, more disinterested humanist morality. Such an interpretation however lies uneasily to the text of the *Groundwork*. The absolute value of works-as-availing remains in Kant, but it is attenuated and pale, with the sure availing of works to salvation replaced by the ineluctability of the credit due to them. This is neither plain Christian finalism, nor humanist finalism either. One's eye is neither on one's own eternal good, nor on anyone else's good here below. One's eye is simply on the ineluctable worth of one's own will, where all that can really be said for this worth is that it is ineluctable. This being so, the ultimate axiology of the *Groundwork* must remain essentially unsatisfactory.

Christian interestedness or humanist disinterestedness come to the same in practice, in so far as the immediate point of each is moral, personalistic conduct. That moral conduct may be the condition of unconditional eudaimonia in one case, and the condition of nothing but itself in the other, is neither here nor there. What both Christians and humanists have to do remains the same—treat persons as Ends for the person's sake, and with/without hope of a future reward.

What Kant seems to want us to do, in the *Groundwork*, is neither to act clearly as Christians, nor straightforwardly as humanists. Our obligations are towards good will as an *end* rather than towards Ends. In Kant, what we can hope for is not praise or credit cashed, but praiseworthiness and credit as a mere potentiality made actual only within ourselves: and we are the only audience that can applaud our own moral performances.

This view seems eccentric: and even if it issues in the same kind of conduct as Christian or agnostic humanism, the eccentricity is somewhat disquieting. Two obvious *points* of action seem to have been suppressed in favour of a third, which is neither eudaimonia nor Endship, but only the rather sterile "good will" of the agent himself.

The *Groundwork* is essentially equivocal in its axiology. Or, if not equivocal, then trivial.

D. "MAN'S FINAL HAPPINESS DOES NOT CONSIST IN MORAL ACTIVITY"

Against the passage from Professor Matthews's Drew Lecture with which we began this present chapter, we can set another authority, from the opposite camp, St Thomas Aquinas. St Thomas writes:

> Man's final happiness does not consist in *moral* activity, for it is ultimate and not subservient to a higher end, whereas *moral* activity is directed to something above itself. We may draw a comparison; a soldierly effort is subordinate to victory and peace; it is foolish to fight for the sake of fighting.[1]

The form of this is splendid, and it will do to refute opinions like Matthews's. The question remains: is Aquinas right about the matter of it? Is there indeed this something above moral activity which can give it its teleological, eudaemonic, point? We can solve this question only, in the last resort, by faith: or by eschatological positivism, that is by waiting and seeing.

The only scandal implicit in St Thomas's remarks may be occasioned by his flatly eudaemonic use of "moral": moral acts are 'acts for the sake of a higher [eudaemonic] end', and so—the modern critic is likely to object—they are not really *moral* acts at all, but acts of transcendental, eschatological self-interest.

Perhaps they are acts of self-interest: but this is so only when the large eudaemonic view is being taken. Seen as acts here and now and seen in terms of their own particular *raisons d'être*, these eschatologically interested acts are as moral as may be. They are acts authorized by the principle of universalizability: they are other-regarding acts: they are acts whose agents adjust their ends to Universal ends, and who respect the Endship of Ends. And this respect of Ends is the point of morality. Morality is not necessarily in principle, or always in fact, a matter of being disinterested—though such disinterestedness is generally the condition of being heroically or un-

[1] St Thomas Aquinas, *Summa Contra Gentiles*, III, 34.

commonly good. Morality is a matter of doing what is right. What is right is, in the last resort, what is 'a possible legislation for a Kingdom of Ends'.

And, for all that it is impossible consistently to conceive of a worldly and non-Utopian morality which does not require disinterestedness, eschatological interest is not ordinary interest, and may go along with *ordinary* disinterest, perfectly well.

If any moral act is in my interest, here or hereafter, then I cannot be totally disinterested in all possible senses when I perform it: but is the disinterestedness of the agent taken in the highest of high senses the essence of the being moral of his act?[1] It is not.

However, just in so far as Kant seems, in the *Groundwork*, almost to make disinterestedness of the essence of morality, frankness compels us, before we analyse his view, to make plain our own position. We want to maintain a point of view which may be put shortly and not too misleadingly, in terms such as these: the right is prior to the good; the first question in morality is to settle what must be done/left undone; questions of motive, and the issue of interested or disinterested compliance with the claims of morality are essentially secondary.

The Christian sees the end of life as eudaimonia: here below such eudaimonia as can be had by moral and prudent acts, and hereafter the transcendent eudaimonia assured by a promise. He sees morality as, here below, adjusting individual agents' eudaemonistic strategies to universal ones: and as providing each agent with a rule for determining lines of conduct which will eventually secure his own interest, as well as securing the immediate interests of others.

The atheist humanist believes the first part of the story, that morality accommodates individual to general ends; but

[1] If disinterestedness is absolutely essential in Kant's system, this is ultimately for metaphysical and not for moral reasons: Kant's real contention is not a moral one, but one about 'a causality which is determined wholly by itself', A. p. 138, cf. also pp. 155–6. That is a noumenal causality, or one as near noumenal as may be. "When I subsume under a *pure practical law* an action possible to me in the world of sense, I am not concerned with the possibility of the *action* as an event in the world of sense . . ." Kant writes—A. p. 160.—But this world of sense, is for all that, the world, or part of the world, we live in and in which action has its meaning.

he cannot believe the second part. This means that the atheist humanist cannot complete Aristotle's eudaemonic account of the world—any more than Aristotle could. It does not mean, though, that the humanist necessarily differs from the Christian on the nature of morality, or on the content of most moral obligations. If there are differences of view, then these arise from dogmatic rather than from general considerations.

The atheist must of course be eschatologically disinterested perforce, just as the Christian must be so interested perforce: but it would be odd to say, even if one believed that the eudaemonic circle could not be completed, that the essence of moral action lies in the total and 'eternal' disinterestedness of the agent.

What is so special about being disinterested?

1. "*Moral Good*" *and* "*Eternal Interests*"

There is nothing ultimately scandalous in St Thomas's articulation of the idea of moral activity into a scheme of final happiness—or if anyone is scandalized, then he is sensitive to a fault. However, what St Thomas puts with a cold-blooded realism can be put less well: and put less well it can look less acceptable, much less so.

The French neo-Thomist Jacques Maritain has a short passage in his *Introduction to Philosophy* which is, at first reading, so strikingly indiscreet that it might throw the over-sensitive, by sheer reaction, into the camp of Professor Matthews. Maritain writes:

> By . . . constantly raising the question of man's last end, and directing men towards the sovereign good, [Socrates] went beyond utilitarianism of every description, and, with the full force of a sane common sense, vindicated the supremacy of *moral good* and our own great *eternal interests*.[1]

[1] Jacques Maritain, *An Introduction to Philosophy*, trans. E. I. Watkin, London (Sheed & Ward), 1946, p. 51. M. Maritain's account of Socrates' contribution to moral philosophy is thoroughly, and quite inappropriately, impregnated with Christian terms and Christian presuppositions. Kant would not have approved, at all, of M. Maritain's phrase "our eternal interests", see e.g. *C.Pr.R.* A. p. 227 where he says, "Morality should never be treated as . . . an instruction how to become happy".

This is piquant in the extreme: "moral good" is equated with "eternal interests" in an extraordinarily offhand way, "utilitarianism" is excluded as something that eternal interests leave behind them, yet the doctrine itself of M. Maritain looks like the baldest eschatological utilitarianism.

This passage of Maritain's seems confused, perhaps on the face of it contradictory, and altogether highly scandalous: but it may be instructive. It throws into relief the way in which Christian expectation can render morality an interest to the agent. If my eternal eudaimonia, incommensurably greater than any happiness I could experience here below, depends on my acting morally *now*, then present sacrifice is given a sense as profitable hereafter. But: the point, now, of other-regarding actions seems to be not the Others for whom I have a regard, but my own, ultimate and eternal interest.

This looks scandalous, and it makes "morality" very much a matter of self-*interest*: right action is only, now, a function of eschatological egoism, that is of *an* egoism.

How scandalous, though, is this, in the last analysis? The chief stumbling-block may be linguistic and philosophical, and not material at all.

The definitions of "morality", especially the informal, implicit ones, with which we operate nowadays, have notions built into them not only of respect and regard for others, but something more again, something more like *concern*, where this has a sense even of selfless concern. To be told that our moral actions are, in the long run, the eternal run, self-regarding, shocks us; excluding egoism in the ordinary sense from morality, for tender or tough-minded reasons or both, we are shocked if any kind of egoism comes in again by the back door.

Even so, our shock may be mitigated, when we reflect that we may be including under "morality" part at least of what M. Maritain might want to reserve for inclusion under "charity": we may be concerned with the exclusion of egoism, under one concept, where he would be concerned to stress positive love, under another concept.

If part of the intension of "charity" has somehow been included in our notions of "morality", the affair takes on an air of paradox. Christianity, above all religions and above all ethical systems, has insisted always on charity. Yet M. Maritain, a noted Christian apologist, seems to be suggesting an ultimately egocentric notion of morality. The paradox is there, but it may be dissolved if we reflect that morality and charity may be more strictly delimited concepts for M. Maritain than they are for speakers of the philosophically normative dialects of Anglo-American.

The paradox is resolved when we see that what is in issue *is*, really, definitions.

In one sense "Love thy neighbour as thyself" can be read as the form of morality: read this way it is satisfied by respect, forbearance and rational altruism shown to others. And such morality may, for all we can presently tell, be rewarded by God hereafter.

In another sense "Love thy neighbour as thyself" is the formal law of charity: and charity is a virtue that goes, mysteriously, beyond rational altruism; and in a sense, beyond care for, if not hope of, a reward:

> Charity is not altruism. In the end altruism expects a return: we are ourselves other people's other people. We wish to be done by as we do. Political reformers always want their share of their own reforms. It's the saints who renounce everything for themselves who work effective reform, because they work through charity.[1]

Here, it is argued that charity is not altruism: but it is also argued that it is, for that reason, more effective in a utilitarian way even than altruism. Altruists are reproached for their self-interest. The whole set of notions can be read two ways, depending on where you view them from, and the characters in Mr Scott-Moncrieff's novel take a religious, not a simply philosophical view; and they elevate charity above morality, more confidently than Professor Matthews might have elevated morality or virtue itself above interest.

Morality, the form of a Kingdom of Ends, is certainly concerned with reciprocal advantage: this much is obvious. There is no reason why it should not be concerned with

[1] George Scott-Moncrieff, *Death's Bright Shadow*, London (Allan Wingate) 1948, pp. 124–5. Of course disinterestedness, altruism and suppression-of-egoism expect, in a Kingdom of Ends, some "return". Such a kingdom is, even at its most ideal, a polity like any other.

eschatological interest as well, if only since this would establish a perfect, ideal, reciprocity or balance of 'goods forgone and good gotten' which the world, as we see it, cannot exhibit.

Charity, though it may be rewarded, is like its psychological analogue love, not concerned with reward, or even with self: it finds its *ratio* in the Other as Other. This sounds altogether mysterious, but we, each of us, have some inkling of what charity is. It is higher than, and different from morality: and for everyday purposes, morality must do when charity wears thin.

Charity goes beyond respect: morality may stop at respect. But we will confuse issues, terribly, if we allow "charity" and "morality" to seep into each other's spheres of intension.

The present essay cannot even begin the fine discriminations, logical and phenomenological, that are necessary if we are properly to delimit charity from morality. And in the last resort the task may be impossible: we may be for ever approaching a boundary, but never finding or fixing it.

In a sense, though, we may even be happy to keep the issues a little "confused".

If a man is not a Christian, and has, in his own view, no "eternal interests", then he must practise morality—'charity', 'altruism'—with total eschatological disinterestedness. Morality must remain, even when the agent's other-worldly interest in it has evaporated; and the moral atheist can lay claim to a kind of disinterestedness which is bleaker, if not higher, than the disinterestedness of the Christian saints.

The definition that we, now, in secular societies of the twentieth century, want to give of morality, is one which disengages it from the interests, eternal or otherwise, of the agent, and which directs our attitude towards the others with whom he has to deal. The other becomes the point, the end, of moral action, either for his own sake, and, after all he has a 'sake', or because, eschatology being bankrupt, there is no other point for moral action.

The adjustment of our private maxims to universal ends is the crux of morality: and the crux of the crux, is that universal ends are the ends of Ends. What is really at issue is respect for

Persons, for Ends-in-themselves. This is something that the Enlightenment, and the subsequent drifts towards agnosticism and towards atheism, have brought out; and to this degree these trends have had a positive—a positive moral—value. They have not simply secularized charity, as the Christian might object. They may, by a curious paradox, have put charity, or love of some order, into *mere* morality.

The present chapter is, as we have said, no more than a parenthesis; and the matters that it has raised cannot really be dealt with in a parenthesis; they deserve a full development in another place, in another essay.

Clearly, a whole phenomenology of conduct could base itself on the exegesis of St Paul's sentence to Timothy:

> Dearly beloved: Godliness is profitable to all things, having promise of the life that now is, and of that which is to come. A faithful saying, and worthy of acceptation. (I *Timothy*, 4. 8–16.)

And the exegesis would need to be a double one: Christian and secular humanisms will no doubt find this saying "faithful" in two rather different, but perhaps not totally disparate ways.

2. *The Two Ends of Reason*

Reason has two ends, not one as Kant suggests in the *Groundwork*. One of reason's ends is that its possessor may secure his happiness, here if he can and hereafter if there is a hereafter, making the best of both worlds, if this is possible.

It is also an end of reason that the reasonable agent, as well as securing his own happiness, do nothing to jeopardize, and in certain cases do something positively to assure, the happiness of others. And the conflict between the two aims, securing our own happiness, and respecting the happiness of others, while it will demand disinterestedness on many occasions, does not make disinterestedness either the point or the essence of reasonable conduct. One can always ask: what is the point of disinterestedness? And one can easily see the point, too.

But while duty and disinterestedness both have a point, *happiness* is its own point: the happiness of others, or our own happiness.

3. *Kant: the Pure Notion of Personal Value*

The essential idea of morality must be disembroiled from notions of eternal reward and eternal punishment, especially when we are dealing with people who do not believe in such things. And—a quite different point—the idea of personal worth or value must be seen to stand apart from the putative eternity and eternal worth of the person.

Kant is, one senses, working towards these disembroilments: he is attempting, if unsuccessfully, to free morality from any involvement with interest—and presumably from any involvement with eternal interest. He is, too, attempting to give some account of the value of the person which will not involve it, with the putative eternity of the person. Kant's instincts were, from the modern point of view, excellent: but his arguments were not always very convincing. His account of the value of the person is not only no better than the Christians': it is, as it stands, demonstrably worse.

CHAPTER III

INTEREST OR DISINTERESTEDNESS AT THE ROOT OF MORAL CONDUCT?

> . . . Utilitarian moralists have gone beyond almost all others in affirming that the motive has nothing to do with the morality of the action, though much with the worth of the agent.
>
> J. S. Mill *Utilitarianism*, Chapter II

> The Stoics, indeed, with the paradoxical misuse of language which was part of their system, and by which they strove to raise themselves above all concern about anything but virtue, were fond of saying that he who has that has everything; that he, and only he, is rich, is beautiful, is a king. But no claim of this description is made for the virtuous man by the utilitarian doctrine. Utilitarians are quite aware that there are other desirable possessions and qualities besides virtue, and are perfectly willing to allow to all of them their full worth. They are also aware that a right action does not necessarily indicate a virtuous character, and that actions which are blamable, often proceed from qualities entitled to praise. When this is apparent in any particular case, it modifies their estimation, not certainly of the act, but of the agent. I grant that they are, notwithstanding, of opinion, that in the long run the best proof of a good character is good actions; and resolutely refuse to consider any mental disposition as good, of which the predominant tendency is to produce bad conduct. This makes them unpopular with many people; but it is an unpopularity which they must share with every one who regards the distinction between right and wrong in a serious light; and the reproach is not one which a conscientious utilitarian need be anxious to repel.
>
> J. S. Mill (ibid.)

Harris has something to say on two important topics, self-denial and interest. What he says Kant might well have rejected, but equally, what Harris says provides a background against which we can see, perhaps a little more clearly than we otherwise might, what precisely Kant himself *is* saying about interest and disinterestedness, and about the bearing which both have on duty.

A. "HONOUR AND JUSTICE ARE MY INTEREST": HARRIS

Harris's Friend's Friend Theophilus addresses a long deistic apostrophe to his Maker, and in the core of it he foreshadows his argument for something that Harris (in his guise of the Friend) is later to say straight out, namely, that the only possible guide for conduct is our own Welfare or Interest, where this is set off, of course, against "Moral Office":

> In as much as Futurity is hidden from our Sight, we can have no other *Rule of Choice*, by which to govern our Conduct, than *what seems consonant to the Welfare of our own particular Natures*. If it appear not contrary to Duty and moral Office, (and how should we judge, but from what appears?) Thou canst not but forgive us, if we prefer Health to Sickness; the Safety of Life and Limb to Maiming or to Death. But did we know that these Incidents, or any other were appointed us; were fated in that Order of incontroulable Events, by which Thou preservest and adornest the Whole, it then becomes our Duty, to meet them with Magnanimity; to co-operate with Chearfulness in what ever Thou ordainest; that so we may know no other Will, than thine alone, and that the Harmony of our *particular* Minds with thy *Universal*, may be steady and uninterrupted thro' the Period of our Existence. (*D.*, pp. 132–3.)

If Providence disposes against our interest, then indeed we must accept this as the superior wisdom of the Deity: but human wisdom has no other guide than interest. What else could guide our action?

Kant thinks that he can, indeed, supply us with a surer guide to action than interest, and he puts forward what is in effect a three-pronged answer to the question: 'What, if not interest, can guide our action?' He says: (i) that our actions should be governed by principles of self-denial and by disinterestedness; (ii) that our actions should be guided finally and fundamentally by the formal Moral Law; and (iii) that this Law itself is 'disinterested' in the sense of not concerning itself with ends.

The aim of the *Groundwork* is, as Kant says, "to examine the idea and the principles of a possible *pure* will", (*G.*, Pref; p. 38: 7: A. p. 6). This "pure" is as ambiguous as is his "unconditioned". It puns, dangerously, on "the idea" as *a priori*, and the "principles" as disinterested; it conflates issues best kept separate.

Kant's notion of the pure, formal and unconditioned Moral Law is inextricably bound up with categorically-displaced notions about self-denial and disinterestedness; and Harris's colder, more prosaic morality, in which concern for our own "Welfare" is merely set off against "Office", presents a useful contrast. It is profitable, perhaps, to consider Harris's doctrine, briefly, before we look more closely at Kant's.

The Christian resignation of Harris-Theophilus is urbane without enthusiasm, deferring to the Deity's greater wisdom, and to the "Universal Mind", in terms of rational, but not necessarily here of rationalistic, Stoicism:

> Be these our Morning, these our Evening Meditations—with these may our Minds be unchangeably tinged—that Loving Thee with a Love most disinterested and sincere; enamoured of thy Polity, and thy DIVINE ADMINISTRATION; welcoming every Event with Chearfulness and Magnanimity, as being *best* upon the Whole, because ordained of Thee; proposing nothing of ourselves, but *with a Reserve* that Thou permittest; acquiescing in every Obstruction, as ultimately referable to thy Providence—in a word, that working this Conduct, by due exercise, into perfect *Habit*; we may never murmur, never repine; never miss what we would obtain, or fall into that which we would avoid; but being happy with that transcendent *Happiness*, of which no one can deprive us; and blest with that Divine *Liberty*, which no Tyrant can annoy; we may dare address Thee with pious Confidence, as the *Philosophic Bard* of old,
>
> *Conduct me, Thou, of Beings Cause Divine,*
> *Where-e'er I'm destin'd in thy great Design.*
> *Active I follow on: for should my Will*
> *Resist, I'm impious; but must follow still.*
>
> (*D.*, p. 134.)

Harris's Friend was "sensibly touched" by this apostrophe when he first heard it: we are more likely to be struck by the frigidity of its piety. But it is precisely this coldness, and the coldbloodedness of rational virtue which consorts with interests and which takes our "Welfare" as its guide, which contrasts so instructively with Kant's enthusiasm—an enthusiasm which rises above a mere apostrophe, and wraps itself in the baffling form of a metaphysic of morals. Harris's love of God may be "most disinterested", but his everyday actions are not: nor does he see why they should be, unless indeed "Office" should demand it.

1. *Self-Denial*

The key to the moral life for Harris is Habit, and he is orthodoxly Aristotelian about this:

> . . . tho' the Difficulty of *acquiring* Habits be great and painful yet nothing so easy, so pleasant, as the *Energies*, when once wrought by Exercise to a due Standard of Perfection. (*D.*, p. 135.)

The acquisition of habits can be painful, and the root and ground of any morality, even the coolest, seems to be some degree of self-denial.:

> . . . Does not *the Difficulty of attaining habit* too well support a certain Assertion that *defend Virtue as we will it is but a Scheme of Self-Denial?* (*D.*, p. 136.)

The phrase "defend Virtue as we will" is quite splendid: and one feels it would have shocked Kant profoundly. Harris and his Friend would be as deeply shocked to find that all virtue was at bottom "Monkish".

The hard truth about self-denial and its connection with virtue is cast into an elegant paradox, calculated to put as good a face on the matter as can be put:

> By *Self-denial*, said he, you mean, I suppose, something like what follows—*Appetite* bids me eat; *Reason* bids me forbear—If I *obey* Reason, I *deny* Appetite; and Appetite being *a part of myself*, to *deny* it, is a *Self-denial*. What is true thus in *Luxury*, is true also in other Subjects; is evident in Matters

> of Lucre, of Power, of Resentment, or whatever else we pursue by the Dictate of any Passion.
>
> You appear, said I, to have stated the Objection justly. To return then to our Instance, said he, of Luxury. *Appetite* bids me eat; *Reason* bids me forbear—If I *obey Reason*, I *deny Appetite*—and if I *obey Appetite*, do I not *deny Reason?* Can I *act either way, without rejecting one of them?* And is not *Reason a Part of myself*, as notoriously as *Appetite?*
>
> Or to take another Example—I have a Deposite in my Hands *Avarice* bids me retain—*Conscience* bids me restore. Is there not a *reciprocal Denial*, let me obey *which I will?* And is not *Conscience a Part of me*, as truly as *Avarice?*
>
> Poor Self indeed must be denied, take which Party we will. But why should *Virtue* be arraigned of thwarting it, more than *Vice* her contrary?—Make the most of the Argument, it can come but to this—If *Self-denial* be an objection to *Virtue*, so is it to *Vice*—If *Self-denial* be no Objection to *Vice*, no more can it be to *Virtue*. A wonderful and important Conclusion indeed! (*D.*, pp. 136–7.)

The self-denial of Vice: this is a nice touch, and not without strict justice either. Bad habits are as enslaving as good ones, and what we deny ourselves for the sake of our vices can sometimes be more than they are worth.

This is all rational morality at its coldest; but it is by no means rational morality at its worst:

> He continued by saying, that the *Soul of Man* appeared not as a *single Faculty*, but as *compounded* of many—that as these Faculties were not always in perfect Peace one with another, so there were few Actions which we could perform, where they would be *all* found to *concur*. What then are we to do? Suspend till they agree?—That were indeed impossible.—Nothing therefore can remain, but to weigh well their several Pretensions; to hear all, that each has to offer in its behalf; and finally to pursue the Dictates of the *Wisest* and the *Best*. This done, as for the *Self denial*, which we force upon the rest; with regard to our own *Character*, it is a Matter of Honour and Praise—with regard to the *Faculties denied*, it is

> a Matter of as small Weight, as to contemn the Noise and Clamours of a mad and senseless Mob, in deference to the sober Voice of the worthier, better Citizens. And what Man could be justified, should he reject these, and prefer a Rabble? (*D.*, pp. 137–8.)

Self-denial may be "a Matter of Honour and Praise", but its *raison d'être* is our Welfare. Self-denial, like virtue itself, serves eudaimonia: a eudaimonia which is available to the man who can "weigh well" the "several Pretensions" of his own competing faculties. Virtue can be defended.

2. *Interest*

Harris foresees that his cold, rational morality may seem scandalous, but he is confident that, even when he has stated it as boldly and provocatively as he may, he can remove the scandal. He is confident that on reflection we shall find what he has to say only reasonable:

> I dare say, continued he, you have seen many a wise Head shake, in pronouncing that sad Truth, *how we are governed all by* INTEREST.—And what do they think should govern us else? Our Loss, our damage, our *Disinterest?*—Ridiculous indeed! We should be Ideots in such case, more than rational Animals. The only Question is, *where Interest truly lies?* For if this once be well adjusted, no Maxim can be more harmless. (*D.*, p. 138.)

If "Interest" cannot be our guide, must "Disinterest" be? Curiously enough Kant *was* to say, or to seem to say forty years later, that it *is* our "Disinterest" that should govern us (though not our loss), even when duty and happiness do happily coincide. Recall the case of the grocer in the *Groundwork*, who seems almost excluded from the possibility of morally-worthy action, simply because, in the grocery business, honesty pays.

Which doctrine is the more reasonable? Kant's looks on the face of it absurdly severe, Harris's irresponsibly optimistic. Will either really do?

Kant makes his best point, not by shaming us into accepting the governance of "our Disinterest", but by reminding us that, as Harris says, "The only Question is, *where* Interest truly lies."

There is a great deal to be said for our interest, if we can be sure where it really lies.

But is interest consonant with morality: could it be the moral man's guide? On this question, Harris covers himself with a typically eighteenth-century definition of "interest", one which enables him to have it both ways. Interest is quickly enlarged to include all the necessary virtues:

> I find myself existing upon a little Spot, surrounded every way by an immense unknown Expansion.—Where am I? What sort of a Place do I inhabit? Is it exactly accommodated, in every Instance, to my Convenience? Is there no Excess of Cold, none of Heat, to offend me? Am I never annoyed by Animals, either of my own kind, or a different? Is every thing subservient to me, as tho' I had ordered all myself?—No—nothing like it—the farthest from it possible—The World appears not then originally made for the *private Convenience of me alone?* It does not.—But is it not possible so to accommodate it, by my own particular Industry?—If to accommodate Man and Beast, Heaven and Earth; if this be beyond me, it is not possible—What Consequence then follows? Or can there be any other than this—*If I seek an Interest of my own, detached from that of others; I seek an Interest which is chimerical, and can never have Existence?* (*D.*, pp. 138–9.)

And a few sentences later Harris writes:

> Is a SOCIAL INTEREST joined with others such an Absurdity, as not to be admitted? The Bee, the Beaver, and the Tribes of herding Animals are enough to convince me, that the thing is, *somewhere at least*, possible. How then am I assured, that it is not equally true of *Man?* —Admit it; and what follows? —If so, then HONOUR and JUSTICE are my INTEREST—then the WHOLE TRAIN OF MORAL VIRTUES are my INTEREST; *without some Portion of which not even Thieves can maintain Society.* (*D.*, p. 139.)

The device is Aristotle's, of course. The Aristotelian life of praxis in particular presupposed social relations and depended upon socially glorious virtues; and it assimilated to eudaimonia both the self-denial and the other-regarding sentiments and principles which a doctrine of naked, quite selfish, interest would exclude.

Harris, like Aristotle, solves the problem "Why should I not pursue my naked interest?" simply by denying that there can be any such thing as a totally separate egoistic interest: "... if I seek an interest of my own, detached from that of others; I seek an Interest which is chimerical ...". as a large, general move this will, perhaps, do: but its application to matters of detail is notoriously taxing. The history of moral philosophy has shown that interest and happiness, socially defined, will make excellent abstract, philosophical ends both for individual and for collective action: the difficulty is, however, to apply the notions, and to reconcile the existentially disparate interests of person and society, person and person.

Just as there is no definite concept of happiness, so there is no determinate concept of interest or of general eudaimonia, from which we can safely deduce, or conclude, our duties in every particular case. This uncertainty of interest faces the man who is concerned, immorally, to procure his own happiness simply, and faces equally the moral man who would serve the common good if he could. Kant writes about all this in his gnoseological submission that duty can be the only sure guide to conduct (*Groundwork*, p. 67: 17–18: A. p. 15), in an argument which we have already considered in Part II Chapter I Section A.3 above, pp. 175 ff.

Though we may agree with Harris that our "Welfare", defined in his urbane terms, should indeed be the guide to our actions, we may agree with Kant that it is often easier to discover our duties than our interests. Harris's doctrine is the more congenial: Kant's, on this point, the more realistic. But Harris might accept this realism, too, with every sign of complaisance and resignation.

Faced with the notorious difficulties which lie in the way of discovering true social interest, we might fall in completely with Kant's notion of life guided by duty, if only he did not introduce the notion of a pure determination of the will by duty. Even Harris, who has us ruled by "Interest", "and rightly", has us overruled by "Moral Office": and it is easier to know our

Office than to know what, indeed, will make us happy. But to demand a pure determination of the will by duty seems, on the face of it, to be altogether too severe. The will has ends besides the ends of duty, and surely it is entitled to them.

Kant tries to persuade us that only pure determination by duty will do, and he has the will prescinding quite from its ordinary and accustomed ends. The will is to be determined simply by the Law: but, to add subtlety to subtlety and severity to severity, Kant has his Law, itself, prescinding from ends. This is not only severe, it is odd.

Kant's "possible *pure* will" becomes altogether too "pure"; it almost ceases to be *will* at all.

Formal principles, duty as disinterestedness, and the goodness of good will independent of success: all the notions of ends-not-mattering rush in to fill for Kant the vacuum set up by the practical realization, that, though we would be eudaemonists if we could, even the concept of eudaimonia is as indefinite as the substance of it is elusive.

Bearing in mind the trite, commonplace, things that Harris has said about Interest and Office we can appreciate more fully perhaps the extreme way in which Kant removes interest and ends from the determination of the will.

The rather languid Aristotelianism of Harris is an excellent background against which to examine Kant's moral severities and his metaphysical flight into the absolute of unconditioned values and unconditioned laws. These we shall consider in our next Sections B and C, immediately following.

B. THE CATEGORICAL IMPERATIVE: KANT

In a crucially important passage of the *Groundwork* Kant writes as follows:

> ... the ground of obligation must be looked for, not in the nature of man, nor in the circumstances of the world in which he is placed, but solely *a priori* in the concepts of pure reason. (*G.*, Preface, p. 57: p. 4: A. p. 4).

What can be meant by an *a priori*, other-than-natural, a-circumstantial determination of the will? That something can and must be meant by an *a priori* or pure determination of the will is part of Kant's doctrine of freedom as a noumenal possibility. This doctrine is one which we are not examining in the present essay. What we shall argue is that, even if the categorical imperative is useful, as indeed it is, as a test of maxims, this fact may be given a very minimal interpretation.

That the categorical imperative works as a touchstone is accounted for when one sees it as a device for focusing the agent's attention on the consequences of his action, when these are seen as 'universalized'.

The categorical imperative determines neither laws nor wills *a priori* or in a pure fashion. It simply puts us in the posture of a kind of negative utilitarianism. Kant writes in the *Critique of Practical Reason:*

> If the maxim of the action is not such as to stand the test of the form of a universal law of nature, then it is morally impossible.[1]

One can agree to this, but it is not at all clear that such an agreement brings any metaphysical, or indeed any other more-than-utilitarian consequences with it.

Kant refers in the *Metaphysic of Morals* to the elective will as being determined properly only by "The form, consisting in the fitness of the maxim of the elective will to be a universal law."[2] But this "form", this "fitness", depends itself on the content and the end of the maxim. And if content is what actual universalizability depends on, how is the "form" or "fitness" of a maxim any purer under Kant's rules than it would be, for example, under J. S. Mill's?

As Kant says in the *Critique of Practical Reason*, "On the notion of an interest is based that of a maxim."[3] And one might argue, as we do: on the notion of maxims is based the possibility of a law of maxims, a categorical imperative. Even the Law, if not rooted itself in interest, is bottomed on what is so rooted.

Kant's great contribution to the eighteenth-century moral debate was that he found a determinate concept of, or rather a categorical form for determining concepts of, action. It may

[1] *C.Pr.R.*, A. p. 161.

[2] *M.M.*, A. p. 269.

[3] *C.Pr.R.*, A. p. 172, and *G*, Ch. III, p. 128*n*: pp. 96–7*n*: A. p. 80*n*.

not have been absolutely original,[1] but it is effective. Whether or not it was what Kant thought he had found, or whether it worked for the reasons he thought, these are different matters again.

The first clearly intelligible statement of the categorical imperative in the *Groundwork* comes in Chapter II: the adumbrations of it in Chapter I, in paragraphs 17 (pp. 69–70: pp. 19–20: A. pp. 17–18), 17a,[2] and 18 (p. 71: p. 21: A. pp. 18–20) are extremely confusing to the reader, if they are not themselves positively confused. They raise every issue at once, self-denial, disinterestedness, and unconditionality; and they are bedevilled by Kant's unfailingly ambiguous use of the expression "good will".

The first chapter account of the categorical imperative has the mind desperately engaged in sinuosities of thought, like Laocoön with his snakes, and one escapes to the second chapter, and to the second half of that, with a sense of relief. Here at last is a clear statement of the principle of action:

> *Act only on that maxim through which you can at the same time will that it should become a universal law.* (*G.*, p. 88: p. 46: A. p. 38.)

If I see myself as obliged unconditionally to act in accordance with this general principle, then I have a clear guide to particular actions. Any maxim that I can so will, this I *may* act on: any maxim that I cannot so will I *must not* act on.

A vast amount has been written, and no doubt will go on being written, about the principle of universalizability. This principle seems to answer to an ideal of the human mind that there should be some simple and entirely logical test for rightness and wrongness: it is a simple test, and valuable, but whether or not it is "logical" in the required sense is open to dispute.

If one is not prepared to contribute to the continuing debate about the principle of universalizability, one may at least declare one's position and remind one's reader, that, at the

[1] See Matthew, 7: 12 and Luke 6: 31.

[2] The German text and Paton's translation have a paragraph-break which Abbott ignores: Abbott's §17 should be broken into 17 and what we shall call 17a, at the phrase, "Let the question be . . .", Abbott, p. 21, last line, A. p. 18, 13 lines down.

practical level, a naive interpretation of universalizability may even have something to recommend it. After all, in "the Passage from Ordinary Rational Knowledge of Morality to Philosophical" we are not by any means obliged to forget what we already know perfectly well.

Everyone knows, not to put too fine a point on it, how and why the categorical imperative works. It is efficacious because it draws our attention to the elements in moral decision to which Burke referred in our quotation in Part I, Chapter III, Section C.2, pp. 81 ff. That is, it draws our attention to equity and to utility. And it does this because of the pregnant, and this time useful, ambiguity of one of its terms.

"Act only on that principle that at the same time you can will to be a *universal* law" makes a double use of "universal", getting out of it, at once, notions both of equity and of utility.

Faced by a prospect of action I, obedient to the categorical imperative, find the maxim of my envisaged policy, and I embark on the reflections which are occasioned by a confrontation between any maxim and the categorical imperative itself: "Can I will *m* universally?" Let us see what happens, in fact, when I ask: "Can I will *m* universally?"

The content of this question splits on two senses of "universal" willing: (1) Going back to what I learnt in the nursery I ask first, "Can I will *m* universally, that is allow others, and not only myself, to do what it authorizes or embodies?"

The essence of morality, and the essential thing that one learns about morality as a child, is that exceptions are not to be made in one's own favour. It is not all right for me to do *x*, "Because *I* am *me!*", where it would be wrong for others to do *x*. *Being me* does not somehow dissolve the wrongness of acts, wrong when considered as 'done by anyone you like to name'. *I* can be named, and the act is as wrong for me as for anyone. This kind of universality: "If it's wrong for NM then it's wrong for me, for my name can go in the space NM" is what we learn about as small children as we learn about conduct itself.[1]

[1] From this consideration we exclude, of course, any reference to acts justified by status. Children may be puzzled by status-rights, but adults by and large are not. And, all status-rights are parasitic on more basic morality and subject to it: and subject to a utilitarian critique as well as to a critique of equity.

But what *is* a wrong act? (2) Again, unless our upbringing has been at the hands of the excessively deontological, we have a second resource to universality. "Is *x* a bad act?" is the kind of question that can be settled often enough, and is settled for the most part, by envisaging the consequences of the act. Allowing, for the sake of argument, "That *x* be done", we authorize, in our imagination, anyone to do *x* as the mood moves him: and then we regard the consequences to be expected from any, or all, such acts when they are done. If harm will come, then the act is bad: if not, it is at least not bad.

Of course it all depends on what we mean by "harm", and endless practical and philosophical questions may present themselves, unbidden or invited; but we at least know where to start from.

Philosophical doubts notwithstanding, if and when any adult agent goes through the Kantian categorical imperative drill, he gets an answer quickly enough: having already some rather firm notions of what he means by "harm", he is in a position to decide on the universalizability or otherwise of his maxim.

This last point can be illustrated best perhaps from cases where an appeal is made to the principle of universalizability in order to block an act or a maxim, and the appeal fails. In C. P. Snow's first novel the central character, Finbow, an urbane detective of the 1930s' sort says, apropos of an unsuccessful appeal by another character to the principle of universalizability:

> That reminds me of the remark that sergeant-majors used to make to youths who'd got dirty buttons 'what would happen if every soldier in the British Army came on parade with his buttons as dirty as yours?' There is only one answer, but so far as I know it was never made: it is, of course: 'There would be a number of dirty buttons in the British Army'.[1]

Since nobody but a sergeant-major, or some functionary of that sort, has anything morally against dirty buttons, one can universalize one private's conduct with nothing but morally indifferent consequences. The functionaries' argument, if there is one, will have to relate buttons to some matter of recognized

[1] C. P. Snow, *Death Under Sail*, London (Heinemann), 1932/1961, p. 96.

importance before the appeal to the principle of universalizability can work. There is nothing in buttons as buttons for which we need care—a button.

What we are trying to find out when we ask, "Can I universalize *m*?" is whether *m* involves anything against which moral objections are known to exist, or against which moral objections can henceforth be seen to exist as the result of the reflections forced on us by this particular use of the categorical imperative. The categorical imperative serves, indeed, to focus moral reflection.

It is not *a* moral objection to *m* that *m* cannot be universalized, but it is a mark of there being such objections. "Universalize!" invites us to consider whether in any case there is anything morally odd about the maxim of a proposed act, anything morally undesirable about the consequences of action in accordance with it.

The morally odd always comes, in the end, to have something to do with a tendency on the part of certain acts to cause harm to people, to Ends. We know, already, before we apply the principle of universalizability, what will count as "harm" in the required sense: if we did not, then the principle would not help us at all.

G. E. Moore's famous argument in Chapter V of the *Principia Ethica* is to the point here. He takes seriously, or at least pretends to take seriously, the possibility that universal extinction might be desirable; but he fails, even so, to universalize murder, since murder would not effectively attain this end, but would, however, produce other, clearly undesirable consequences:

> Where the best is not attainable (assuming extermination to be the best) one alternative may still be better than another. And, apart from the immediate evils which murder generally produces, the fact that, if it were a common practice, the feeling of insecurity, thus caused, would absorb much time, which might be spent to better purpose, is perhaps conclusive against it. So long as men desire to live as strongly as they do, and so long as it is certain that they will continue to do so, anything which hinders them from devoting their energy to the attainment of positive goods, seems plainly bad as a means. And the general practice of murder, falling so far

> short of universality as it certainly must in all known conditions of society, seems certainly to be a hindrance of this kind.[1]

One may find Moore's philosophical seriousness here ironic or comic: but the burden of his argument remains the same. We do judge by consequences, and the test of the universalizability—the *very* universalizability—or otherwise of a maxim lies in the consideration of the consequences apt and liable to follow from its universal or at the least its general adoption.

There may be a sense of good will, good will 2, which can in a way prescind from ends: but neither good will 1, the adjuster to universal ends, nor the Law, which is no more than the principle of such a rational good will, can be unmindful of the ends of action and the putative consequences.

Neither prudence nor the moral law can be made sense of unless we consider, in concrete terms, the adjustment of our particular maxims to universal ends. This adjustment can be considered only if it is made quite concrete: the disadvantages, vividly held before the mind, which would flow from the universalization of certain maxims are precisely what fault faulty maxims. And the expression "disadvantages" becomes a meiosis, when they are such as they would be, were murder a custom. That is, the expression becomes a moral meiosis. Men not only "desire to live", but as Ends, they have a right to do so: morality is the strategy for the management and articulation of such rights.[2]

If this is utilitarianism then it is minimally so, and we can allow Mill his celebrated point against Kant, even if we doubt whether this, and Mill's own arguments, can prove the full utilitarian doctrine as it is put forward in the classic texts.

Mill wrote of his predecessors, and of Kant in particular:

> It is not my present purpose to criticise these thinkers; but I cannot help referring, for illustration, to a systematic

[1] G. E. Moore, *Principia Ethica*, Cambridge (University Press), 1903/1951, pp. 156–7. [This utilitarian passage might, one feels, have been more in place in his little *Ethics*, in the Home University Library.]

[2] As Kant correctly points out, *C.Pr.R.*, A. pp. 257–8. The Moral Law enables me, among other things, to sort the *Rights* of Others out from their mere *wants*. See below, p. (251), 292 ff. 303 n, 309, 311 ff.

> treatise by one of the most illustrious of them, the *Metaphysics of Ethics*, by Kant. This remarkable man, whose system of thought will long remain one of the landmarks in the history of philosophical speculation, does, in the treatise in question, lay down a universal first principle as the origin and ground of moral obligation; it is this: "So act, that the rule on which thou actest would admit of being adopted as a law by all rational beings." But when he begins to deduce from this precept any of the actual duties of morality, he fails, almost grotesquely, to show that there would be any contradiction, any logical (not to say physical) impossibility, in the adoption by all rational beings of the most outrageously immoral rules of conduct. All he shows is that the *consequences* of their universal adoption would be such as no one would choose to incur.[1]

Utility may[2] not be the whole content or sole ground of the rightness of acts: but Kant takes advantage of our natural utilitarianism more effectively even than Mill. The categorical imperative *says* nothing about utility, but it *draws our attention to it* most efficiently by requiring us to test maxims against their own possible harmfulness. Showing something to be harmful makes, perhaps, a stronger *prima facie* case for its being wrong, than showing it to be useful does for its being right. This kind of negative utilitarianism is effective, while making smaller claims, and needing infinitely less elaboration and defence, than does Mill's rather more ambitious scheme of positive utilitarian morality.

1. *How 'Formal'?*

The categorical imperative itself can be formal, prescinding from and not concerning itself with (any particular) ends, for a quite unmysterious reason. It is a test of maxims, and it need mention no ends since the maxims themselves will. The test is

[1] J. S. Mill, *Utilitarianism*, London (Longmans), 1901, Chapter I, pp. 5–6.

[2] We may, and sometimes do, lay claim to deontic intuitions which forbid us to do *x* even when we cannot specify the damage which would result from *x*. However, in so far as utilitarianism provides a critique of other systems, we do tend, when we can, to back up our deontic intuition with utilitarian instances. Injunctions against doing things that we 'see no harm in' are obeyed, if at all, with murmurings.

in some sense *a priori*, but what it tests is full of quite empirical content. There is no other kind of content, after all: not, that is, in the world of human concern and human action.

The formal nature of the categorical imperative lies in this, and simply in this: that it applies a touchstone to all and to any specific maxims of action. One can see how formal/categorical can pun to some degree on "Categorical" in the sense of categorical as this expression is used in the *Critique of Pure Reason:* but there is no great mystery in the matter, and none to be made out of it. The categorical imperative is not concerned with the content of any particular maxims as particular, but with the universalizability of any or every maxim that may occasion action.

Kant misleads his reader, and himself perhaps, about the way in which the categorical imperative prescinds from ends, when he writes in Chapter II of the *Groundwork:*

> Finally, there is an imperative which, *without being based on, and conditioned by, any further purpose to be attained by a certain line of conduct*, enjoins this conduct immediately. This imperative is *categorical. It is concerned, not with the matter of the action and its presumed results, but with its form and with the principle from which it follows;* and what is essentially good in the action consists in the mental disposition,[1] let the consequences be what they may. This imperative may be called the imperative of *morality*. (*G.*, pp. 83–4: p. 39: A. p. 33. Italics mine.)

The categorical imperative is not concerned with the 'purpose to be attained by a certain line of conduct' simply because not it, but the maxim of the conduct (which the imperative tests), alludes to this purpose. Nevertheless, the aim and point of the categorical imperative is to get us to look at our particular purposes in the light of "universal ends". As Kant puts the matter, in this passage which we have just quoted, everything tends to become more mysterious than it need be. The idea of being "conditioned", and the ambiguous and bedevilling notions of prescinding from ends come into play; and the quite

[1] The altogether curious remark about "mental disposition" is taken up below in B.2 immediately following the present section, and it is considered again in section C.1 (ii), pp. 255 ff.

unviable distinction between the form and principle of an action and its presumed results is put up, yet again.

This distinction comes to nothing, if any attempt is made to make anything of it. It remains what it is, and as unavailable to metaphysical ethics as it ever was. The categorical imperative does not concern itself with the presumed results of *any* action, because, and simply because, it concerns itself with the presumed results of *all:* it is concerned not with any particular set of results, precisely because it is concerned with just any results you like to specify. The categorical imperative can avoid the particularity of the Decalogue, simply because it claims to show us in a perfectly general way what there is against each of the various sins listed as not-to-be-done. Or, rather, it claims less to show us what is wrong about any acts, than to put us into such a posture that we can see for ourselves. Even the categorical imperative cannot show us anything that we could not already see: though on any particular occasion when we use it sincerely, it may 'make us see', for the first time.

Provide the maxim that, acted on, would lead to ϕ results: the categorical imperative will then pass or fail the maxim, on its universalizability—that is on its presumed results, "If everyone were allowed to do it".

Kant is, in substance if not in intention, a kind of utilitarian, since it is reflections about the effect of actions on the general happiness that his categorical imperative occasions in those who make use of it.

It is extremely interesting to recall, here, that J. M. Keynes in his essay "My Early Beliefs" couples Bentham with Kant, casually and as a matter of course: he refers to ". . . the universal ethics of Kant and Bentham which aimed at the general good".[1] Mill's point about utility and the categorical imperative had been taken, it would seem, by 1903. What Keynes

[1] John Maynard Keynes, "My Early Beliefs" in, *Two Memoirs*, London (Hart-Davis), 1949, pp. 98–9.

Curiously, the distinction between "being good" and "doing good" which Keynes and his circle drew—cf. op. cit., p. 84—is one which might have appealed to Kant. Indeed, it is one that they might easily have found foreshadowed in Kant. The concern of Keynes and his friends was not with ends at all, but with some quasi-aesthetic, or psychological analogue of good will 2. Like Kant, they pursued intrinsic, immanent values: but, less tough-minded than he, they thought of this disengagement

goes on to say shows that he and his friends may have over-interpreted this point, but that is another matter.

Kant, if a substantial, was not a declared utilitarian, and he clearly thinks that a great deal more might be made of the formal nature of the categorical imperative than can be. In this regard his best example is the one of promise-keeping. There is a sense in which the maxim of false-promising does contradict itself. Following the principle of breaking promises, people would soon destroy good faith, and cut the ground from under the whole business of promise-making. This is, if you like, a contradiction: but it is also a consideration of consequences. It happens that in this sort of case the contradiction is particularly sharp and that one is inclined to stress this quasi-logical element, and not simply to dwell upon the deplorable consequences as deplorable.

It is nice to be able to face someone who is about to embark on a piece of wickedness with the reflection that, sooner or later, his action will turn out to be self-defeating. And indeed, a bilker cannot bilk too often: the institution of promise-keeping may, in a stable society, be safe enough, but *his* particular credit will not be. His credit gone, he at least will not be able to exploit any further the institution of promise-making which he has abused.

This particular reflection operates on the level of mere interest, but it can, possibly, force an agent to consider what Kant would have him consider, that though a particular "will to lie" is possible, a universal "will to lie" is not (*Groundwork*, p. 71: p. 23: A. p. 19). The universal practice of false-promising would have just the result that the occasional and particular episodes of faith-breaking may not have, the subversion of the very institutions of promise and of trust. These gone, lies would be no longer possible. Mendacity itself would be bankrupt.

The elements of contradiction and self-defeatingness in this kind of case can be—and have been—analysed at length. The only observation that one wants to make here is that Kant seems to throw light on the peculiar status of the jurisprudential and

from "the life of action, and from the pattern of life as a whole" as a "religion" (Cf. op. cit., p. 92). For Kant it was, even at its worst, no more than a "metaphysic".

political principle *pacta sunt servanda;* this principle assimilates all kinds of behaviour to *a contract to abstain from*, which contract itself becomes the locus of obligation.

The peculiar tenacity with which the idea of social contract holds on, despite the well-known objections to it, is perhaps accounted for largely by its simplicity. There is no need to argue the specific morality, expediency, or allowableness of particular kinds of actions, murder, judicial murder, perjury and the rest: all are excluded under the contract.[1] The contract binds you, and it alone stands between you and just those actions which you might otherwise do, and which you would almost certainly suffer. One cannot consistently both make use of, and do things that would undermine, an agreement or an institution: not, that is, without contradiction—and wickedness.

For all that Kant hoped to make morals absolutely *a priori*, it is "the nature of man" and "the circumstances of the world in which he is placed" that finally determine rightness and wrongness. What is right can be universalized, what is wrong cannot: but this is as far as one can speak *a priori*. What can be universalized and what cannot, depends on the contingencies of the economy of the human situation: how man is made, and to some degree, how and where he finds himself.[2]

In the *Metaphysical Elements of Ethics* Kant gives us a formula

[1] The Bill of Rights appended to the Constitution of the United States of America lists the inconveniences from which the citizens agree mutually to protect one another under their new institutions. It was the author of the Declaration of Independence who insisted that the Bill of Rights should be drawn up: Jefferson had a lucidity and a consistency that make him one of the most perfect representative figures of the Enlightenment. If there is to be a written Constitution—a contract—then self-evident rights should be made evident under it. They are the *ratio* of the contract: it is a pact designed to protect them.

[2] Here one may recall St Thomas Aquinas's curiously empty remark that "The first precept [of the Natural Law] is to do good and abstain from evil". *Summa II, I Q. 94, a.2.* This principle of the Law conceded, one has then to discover what is good and what is evil. That is, we have to discover the nature and end of man, and map the human situation as best we can. Aquinas, of course, knew this. Kant thought that his test of universalizability made the determination of the will a-circumstantial, and freed man from human nature. Or, at any rate in the *Groundwork*, he professed to believe this. The "possible pure will" is as 'pure' as is universalizability: but what universalizability takes as its concern, what it spotlights, is 'impure', 'practical' and contingent. How could it be otherwise?

which, if we read it in a resolutely unmetaphysical way, would yield a simple utilitarianism. He writes:

> The supreme principle of Ethics . . . is: Act on a maxim, the *ends* of which are such as it might be a universal law for anyone to have.[1]

And against any metaphysic of ethics, the official one of the whole Kantian corpus, or the rather more domestic one of the *Groundwork*, one might simply put an Occamist kind of objection: "If this 'Act on a maxim the ends of which . . .' *can* indeed be regarded as 'The supreme principle of Ethics', it can be so recognized in utilitarian terms: and this being the case, one need go no further".

It is difficult to see how the simple recognition of the viability of the 'supreme principle' forces one into metaphysics.

By mentioning ends in the formula of the categorical imperative given in the *Metapyhsical Elements of Ethics*, Kant has broken his usual rule of tact which keeps the notion of ends out of formulations of the Imperative: but this momentary lapse underlines that it is no more than a rule of tact.

Maxims always refer to ends, so the imperative need not.

And, to use a simple simile: Whether or not any particle will pass through a sieve, depends not simply on the size of the holes in the sieve, but also on the size of the particle. Whether or not a maxim of the will will "pass", depends not only upon the form of universalizability, but on the ends of *that* maxim.

2. *What is 'Essentially Good' in an Action?*

To return again to the passage, from pp. 83–4: p. 39: A. p. 33 of the *Groundwork*, which we have been discussing: when Kant says that, "what is essentially good in the action consists in the mental disposition, let the consequences be what they may", we see conflations and confusions loom again. The phrase "let the consequences be what they may" looks towards the ineluctability notion; and the assertion that the 'essential goodness' of an action lies in the agent's mental disposition, exhibits a confusion of questions about the rightness of actions and the goodness of agents which bedevils the whole structure of the *Groundwork*. What *is* "essentially good", one must insist, is what

[1] *M.E.E.*, A. p. 306.

is right, or the good that may be done by an act: and if this essential good were not *given*, then the "absolute" merit of righteous willing could not even be generated.

At the risk of tedium, one must reiterate these three things: (*a*) If the categorical imperative concerns itself with no ends, this is only because it can concern itself with *all*, and '*no* end' means simply 'no *one* particular end'; (*b*) What is "essentially good in an action" need not be identified with the agent's disposition or his righteous effort, for all that the merit of this effort is ineluctable. (And, it must be noted, this unhinderable-coming-to-be supplies Kant's only ostensible reason in the *Groundwork* for thinking a good disposition to be "essentially good"); (*c*) An agent's mental disposition is not strictly relevant to the rightness of his act (as even Kant himself recognizes, if only momentarily elsewhere), and tests for the rightness of acts have nothing to do with, and need not mention, agents' motives or dispositions.

To identify, as Kant does, "the imperative of morality" with something that is "concerned not with the matter of the action and its presumed results", and to embroil the "imperative of morality" with the question of the agent's "mental disposition" is simply to confuse two levels of morality. It is in fact to take the second level for the first, to take the less fundamental for the more so. What "the imperative of morality" is concerned with, essentially, is the act-to-be-done, and this is the first good in any situation. Confront an agent with this-requiring-to-be-done and he can either do it, and be good; or he can not do it, and be bad; or he can do it in bad faith, and be in another sense bad; or he can not do it in good faith, and be in this sense good. But agents' dispositions are not morally primitive, and they are not the first or the "essential" goods in moral situations. They themselves are only good or bad *vis à vis* goods-to-be-done or evils-to-be-avoided. This point has been made already in Part I, Chapter IV, Section A.8(i), where we discussed the relative values of the lifeguard's good will on one hand, and the end of a child saved on the other, and suggested that a child saved is of more worth than the good will generated in the act of saving him.

Taking, then, a pragmatic and perhaps simple-minded view of the workings of the categorical imperative, and seeing it as concerned rather with what is to be done than with the agent's disposition as he does it, we can return to the first chapter accounts of it, and try to see precisely what it is that Kant is advocating in these difficult pages.

Throughout the following paragraphs we might well bear in mind Coleridge's observation quoted in the Appendix to Part I of the present essay:

> Let my maxim be capable of becoming the Law of all intelligent Being—well! but this supposes an *end* possessible by intelligent Beings—For if the law be barren of consequences, what is it but words?

What, indeed, could it be but words?

C. "BUT WHAT KIND OF LAW CAN THIS BE?" OR, THE RIGHT AND THE GOOD CONFLATED?

T. H. Green pointed up a possible confusion in moral philosophy when he wrote:

> . . . it is important to bear in mind the two senses—the fuller and the more restricted—in which the question, What ought to be done? may be asked. It may either mean—and this is the narrower sense in which the question may be asked—what ought an action to be as determined in its nature by its effects? Or it may be asked with the fuller meaning, what ought the action to be with reference to the state of mind and character which it represents?[1]

It is a confusion between what we may call 'primitive right', "What ought I do?", and right-and-right-dispositions, "What ought I to do, and what should be my dispositions/motives?" which we must beware of in Kant.

Kant's first enunciation of the categorical imperative is what we have labelled the "adumbration" of it in Chapter I of the *Groundwork*, in paragraph 17 (pp. 69–70: p. 21: A. pp. 17–18): the enunciation is in itself clear and unequivocal:

[1] T. H. Green, *Prolegomena to Ethics*, Oxford (Clarendon Press), 1890, Book IV, Ch. I, p. 315.

> I ought never to act except in such a way *that I can also will that my maxim should become a universal law.*

The meaning of this is clear enough: but it is clear only if we read the formulation of the law out of its context.

That is, the formulation of the categorical imperative is unequivocal only if we remove it from its immediate surroundings, and look, simply, to its double in Chapter II. In its specific context in Chapter I, the first enunciation of the categorical imperative is mixed in inextricably with the most doubtful teaching about motives, moral dispositions, and the rest. This teaching is itself open to all kinds of objections, and in the context it is simply irrelevant.

Even if it were in itself acceptable, the talk of motive is not to the point of a discussion of the categorical imperative.

The context in which the first formulation of the categorical imperative occurs, and which seems to determine the sense which Kant gives to the principle of universalizability, is set by what Kant calls his "three propositions". These propositions, the first of which Kant does not state specifically, have been a scandal to certain of his readers. And succeeding generations of students of the *Groundwork* have quoted, in exasperation or with passion, Schiller's ironical:

> I love to serve my friends, but unfortunately I do this from inclination. And so I often feel guilty that I am not virtuous.

Whether Schiller's gibe is just or not, it seems, as one reads what Kant wrote, to be apt. It seems indeed to have been invited.

Professor Paton in his Notes to his translation of the *Groundwork* denies that Kant is in fact saying what Schiller and others have taken him to be saying. But the puzzle remains: why if he did not want to maintain the things that Schiller and common sense rebel at, did Kant use the extraordinarily misleading terminology that we find in the *Groundwork*? The following considerations may begin at least to answer this question.

1. *The First Proposition*

Kant does not, as we have said, state his "first proposition" explicitly, as he does the second and third; but we may presume that its substance is what is involved in paragraphs 7, 8, 9 and 10 (pp. 64–7: 14–16: A. pp. 12–14).

Kant begins his tripartite argument leading up to the first enunciation of the categorical imperative (*Groundwork*, p. 70: 21: A. p. 18) by talking of motive (*Groundwork*, p. 65: p. 15: A. p. 13), and the whole intended substance of his assertions may be no more than this: that motive is irrelevant both to the *claims* of duty and to the *grounds* of duty. Kant may be saying no more than that duty can command us unconditionally and quite independently of any inclination of ours towards the act of duty: and indeed that duty may command us in the very teeth of our strongest disinclination. If this is what Kant is saying then it is clearly true. And it is a truth to which Harris and his mentor Aristotle might be said to have done less than justice, with their bland homogenization of private and public interests into a single social synthesis. Kant however manages to mistake and to mis-state the point which he sees more clearly than the eudaemonists. The capacity that duty has to overrule inclination may be underrated by eudaemonists, but it is fatally overdeveloped by Kant.

For one reason or another Kant contrives to suggest that the essence of duty lies in its conflict with inclination; but, despite his suggestion, the truth is not quite this. Duty is essentially *indifferent* to inclination but need not be opposed to it. If *x* is my duty, it is as much my duty if it is also in accord with my inclination and interest, as it would be were it quite out of accord with interest and inclination. The essential bite, so to speak of duty, is that it can command us unconditionally against all inclination: nevertheless, that is not to say that any act *must* make such a claim as a condition of its being a duty.

Duty is surely above private inclination, as indifferent to its opposition as to its concurrence.

The essence of duty lies not in opposition to interest, not in concurrence with it, and not even in its indifference to interest: the essence of duty lies in the relation, *sui generis*, of command which duty sets up between an agent and the right, that-which-must-be-/done/refrained-from. The essence of duty lies in the proper nature of these things that are duties—ultimately acts of a kind which bear on states of affairs in a world in which these states of affairs bear upon persons, and where persons are Ends.

The concept of a duty is the concept of something which you must do, whether you like it or not, *because of what it is that you must do or refrain from*, where this is judged in terms that, in the end, devolve on respect for persons.

The idea that duty is in no way grounded on inclination is one that it is difficult to assent to, if it is stated quite abstractly. Of course the grounds of my duty are not my inclinations—I am not obliged to do things because I want to. Nor is my wanting to do something the ground of my obligation to do it, should I in fact be obliged to. Again, I am not obliged to do what you want: your wanting, simply, is not the ground of any obligation I may have actually to do what you want. But in a broader and more general, one might say, more Aristotelian sense of "inclination", inclination is at the ground of all duty. That is, the inclinations and disinclinations natural to the human rational animal as such do indeed determine the contents of duty. This must be said, if only to remind ourselves that universal ends, for all that they may be universal remain, still and essentially ends. Both agents and the law of action must come, at last, to a consideration of ends.

Now it is worth saying this last thing, since it is just possible that Kant wants to deny it—or would deny it if he thought he could. We shall discuss this a little later on.

Whatever Kant wanted to assert in these paragraphs 7–10 of the *Groundwork*, he appears at least to be asserting just the sort of things that friendly commentators seem to feel that they must be at pains, on his behalf, to disclaim.

Kant begins his exposition of his notion of duty in paragraph 9 (*Groundwork*, p. 65: p. 15: A. p. 13), with the example of the grocer [Abbott, the 'prudent tradesman']; this example illustrates for Kant a distinction that he sets up between acts (*a*) *done from duty* (*b*) *done from some purpose of self-interest.* If an act "accords with" duty but might, as well, serve the agent's interest, then it is difficult to decide whether it should be classed under (*a*) or under (*b*). And this seems, somehow, to matter rather a lot to Kant. He writes:

> For example, it certainly *accords with duty* that a grocer should not overcharge his inexperienced customer; and

> where there is much competition a sensible shopkeeper refrains from so doing and keeps to a fixed and general price for everybody so that a child can buy from him just as well as anyone else. Thus people are served *honestly*; but this is not nearly enough to justify us in believing that the shopkeeper has acted in this way *from duty* or *from principles of fair dealing*; his *interests* required him to do so. We cannot assume him to have in addition an immediate inclination towards his customers, leading him, as it were out of love, to give no man preference over another in the matter of price. Thus the action was done neither *from duty nor from immediate inclination, but solely from purposes of self-interest.* (*G.*, p. 65: pp. 16–17: A. p. 13. Italics mine.)

As Paton remarks, "a grocer might have a conscience", but we can't be sure. On the other hand, we cannot be as certain as Kant seems to be, that the honest grocer acts "solely from purposes of self interest".

The trouble, the theoretical trouble, about cases where duty and interest run together is that the situation does not bring out either (*a*) that duty depends in no way on the agent's mere interest, or (*b*) that duty can command an agent contrary to his mere interest.

And this important idea is perhaps what Kant is trying, not altogether successfully, to bring out in his second and more serious example of those who take care to preserve their lives:

> . . . to preserve one's life is a duty, and besides this every one has also an immediate *inclination* to do so. But on account of this the often anxious precautions taken by the greater part of mankind for this purpose *have no inner worth*, and the maxim of their action is *without moral content*. They do protect their lives *in conformity with duty*, but not *from the motive of duty*. When on the contrary, disappointments and hopeless misery have quite taken away the taste for life; when a wretched man, strong in soul and more angered at his fate than faint-hearted or cast down, longs for death and still preserves his life without loving it—not from inclination or fear but from duty, *then indeed his maxim has a moral content.* (*G.*, pp. 65–6: p. 16: A. pp. 13–14. Italics mine.)[1]

[1] See *C.Pr.R.* ". . . the purity of the moral principle . . . can only be strikingly shown by removing from the springs of action anything that men

This perhaps means no more than (i) men are so inclined to preserve their lives that, when they do so, we need not credit them with having acted simply from duty (they have done what they wanted to anyhow, and this happened to be their duty), and (ii) it being one's duty to preserve one's life is quite independent of one's being also inclined to do so. But Kant's text appears to say more than these two things. Much more.

Kant defines two important notions here in this passage: they are the notions of *inner worth* and of *moral content*. However, the very passage which serves to define these crucial notions for Kant also seems, on the face of it, to conflate them. Moral content is one thing: inner worth is another. Neither of these notions, despite what Kant seems to suggest, is or can be the other: neither depends, essentially on the other. Or, if this puts it too loosely, one can say, in sharp disagreement with Kant, that though a maxim with moral content may be needed to determine a will if this will is to have inner worth, even so,the inner worth of a will is not what determines the moral content of a maxim. This point must be expanded, at some length.

C.1(i) *Inner Worth.* The precautions that most men take to save their skins "have no inner worth" Kant writes. That is to say, presumably, these precautions are not purely dutiful. This passage about those who preserve their lives defines a notion of "inner worth" which makes 'inwardly worthy' actions conditional upon their being disinterested.[1]

Now this is perhaps too severe a definition of "inner worth", since it brings this "worth" closer to the counsels of perfection

may regard as part of happiness. Morality then must have the more power over the human heart the more purely it is exhibited." A. p. 254. 'Purity' here is a complex notion: and noumenality is part of that complex, along with a moral sense of 'purity', and with a sense relating to the exigencies of 'showing strikingly' that the principles of action are not based on mere and sheer self-interest.

[1] Kant's very tough view, as expressed in the example of those who preserve their lives, is a possible, but not altogether a traditional one. Even the severest moralists of the Middle Ages, for example, seem to have taught that any act of a rational creature, not sinful, and done while in a state of friendship with God, is to some degree meritorious: it has, that is, an "inner worth", and, as well, avails to salvation. Heroic sanctity is one thing: the saving merit of good works another and less arduous matter.

and to works of supererogation than may be strictly necessary or prudent. The grounds for Schiller's gibe are obvious.[1] The man who loves his friends and helps them is surely virtuous and "worthy". Likewise, the mountaineer who has no inclination at all towards suicide is acting morally as well as merely prudently when he looks to his equipment, checks his oxygen bottles, and makes sure that he has all his special foods in their accustomed pockets.

We would certainly blame the healthy, young, and altogether cheerful climber for not taking these recognized precautions. Why can we not praise the moderately sad man for taking them? Must he 'long for death' before his care over nylon ropes and nailed boots can be considered morally relevant? Are such precautions the ground of "worth" only when one would much rather not take them?

If the condition of "inner worth" is to be total disinterestedness or a positive clash between duty and inclination, then we shall have to find some other label than "inner worth" for the worth of ordinary moral conduct. It is difficult to see why an act becomes morally estimable only when it becomes difficult or onerous. Existence may be a burden: but this does not mean that life is a simple obstacle race.

Even the more amiable case which Kant sketches (*Groundwork*, p. 67: 18: A. p. 15), of the man who furthers his own happiness "not from inclination but from duty" is a little too extreme. The phrase, "The law of furthering [one's] happiness not from inclination but from duty" seems to put too severely the point that it makes. It is only when the agent has specifically followed this law that his conduct "has a real moral worth" in Kant's eyes. But for most of us, the pursuit of our own happiness is rational and pointful, and perfectly moral as long as it does not infringe on duty. To make a duty to further one's own happiness the first reason for such action, or to make a bow to such a duty the necessary condition of the being-morally-worthy of one's action, all this is utterly ultramontane.

[1] See also the phrase "then for the first time his action has its *genuine moral worth*" (*G.*, p. 66: 17: A. p. 15). Perhaps there were for Kant two kinds of moral worth the more and the less "genuine": the distinction would seem to match, fairly closely, the distinction between the necessary precepts and the precepts of perfection.

One sees the point, in a sense, of what Kant is saying; but he overstates his point terribly.

Happiness can give an act its moral *ratio*, and the act does not have, in this sense, to wait upon duty. Duty must censor any tactic of happiness, but this is another matter. Kant seems to have mixed matters up, and not to the ultimate good of morality. That happiness must wait upon duty does not entail that only dutiful acts can be rational, and so, moral acts. And: any act that can be moral can surely have some "inner" or moral worth.

Kant's idea of *inner worth* seems, as set up in the passages at which we have glanced, to be unnecessarily and even imprudently severe. But this is not all.

The same passages set up, as well, a notion of *moral content* which appears to arise, obscurely, out of the concept of inner worth, or to conflate with it. And this notion looks to be shot through with a disastrous category mistake.

Kant writes of any less-than-disinterested action done 'in accordance with duty' that "the maxim of this action is without moral content". What can this mean?

C.1(ii) *Moral Content.* The term "moral content" is Kant's own and he may define it as he pleases, but one might expect it to refer to that *in* a maxim which enables it to pass through the sieve of the universalizability test. For example:

> "Let me visit the sick" has "moral content", and passes;
> "Let me renege on my promises" has 'immoral content' and fails.

But Kant seems here in paragraphs 10 and 11 of the *Groundwork* to be defining "moral content" in terms not of what would be found *in the maxim* of the act, but rather in terms of what would be found in the *agent's dispositions seen as his motive for the act.* That is to say, questions about the rightness of acts seem, and the impression is strengthened as we read on in the passage (paragraphs 10–11), to have become confused with quite different questions about the purity of the motives of agents, and with quite irrelevant questions about the goodness of agents' wills and their "inner worth".

Furthermore, as we have seen, Kant's notions about the degree of purity that a motive must have if it is to generate "inner worth" are altogether too severe. The notion of moral content is conflated, therefore, with notions about motive which: (*a*) have nothing, categorically, to do with moral content: and which (*b*) are eccentric and over-severe in themselves.

The category mistake is, perhaps, of more serious concern than is the excessive severity of Kant's notions about pure motivation and "inner worth". Kant's chief defect in the passage which we are examining is that he brings *goodness of motivation,* quite irrelevantly, into the question of a test for the *rightness of maxims* or the *rightness of acts.*

This is very important. If the categorical imperative is to tell me simply what is my strict duty, if it is to show me what is the specific cash value of the universal adjustment of my principles on any particular occasion, then my motive need not be mentioned at all.

My duty can get done, whatever my motive; and it is my duty quite apart from all talk of motives.

The categorical imperative should—and indeed does—simply show me what would have to be done or refrained from, if my duty were to be done by me on occasion. It should show me my plain duty. The duty shown me, I may or may not, then, make what the categorical imperative shows me also, now, the motive for doing what it shows me. This depends. It depends probably (*a*) on the circumstances and (*b*) on my character. But the first job, so to speak, of the categorical imperative is not to improve my character or to give me access to possible acts of a disinterested sort: it is to show me my duty, and to adjust my occasional end to universal ones.

If my duty is to do what I am already inclined to do, then I cannot make duty my sole motive. I cannot be disinterested when my interests run along with my duty, and the grocer who realizes the truth of his trade association's motto, "Fair Dealing is Good Business", cannot perform disinterested acts of fair dealing during business hours. This does not mean that he is or must be honest only from the deontologically irrelevant motive of interest, or on that deontologically irrelevant ground.

It means, simply, that, to the relevant grounds of obligation, his interests have added themselves as a-categorical and further inducements to the act of duty. But obligation and its grounds remain the same, whether or not private interest provides an inducement to duty. Duty cannot be affected by private interest either way. That is, private interest can make a duty neither more of one nor less of one: and interest-as-motive is, surely, irrelevant to the being-a-duty of whatever is one.

The grocer example was an ill-chosen one, if it was intended to make clear the independence of duty of the interests of the agent. Kant might well, in view of the extreme optimism of some eighteenth-century notions of the automatic confluence of private and of general interest, have wished to stress that duty can command a man against his interests. The last example which will make this kind of point however is the grocer's shop example; it illustrates, if any one does, the cheerful view that honesty is the best policy.

It is interesting, again, to look at Keynes's view of Kant. Not only did Keynes find Kant a kind of utilitarian, but Keynes glosses his own phrase about "the universal ethics of Bentham and Kant which aimed at the general good" with this remark:

> . . . and it was because self-interest was *rational* that the egoistic and altruistic systems were supposed to work out in practice to the same conclusions.[1]

Now whatever point Kant is labouring to make in his grocer example, and in his example of those who would save their lives, he is not trying to show that self-interest is either altruistic *or* the ground of duty. It is precisely the opposite of this optimistic view that Kant is putting here. Shaftesbury is by no means Kant's model when he puts, firmly if not very clearly, the point that duty can cut across, or run counter to the interests of the man who has the duty. If Keynes was right in finding Kant a utilitarian, he was wrong in supposing that Kant was either a willing one, or a sanguine one.

Kant tried not to be a utilitarian, but the categorical imperative itself forces anyone, Kant included, into a utilitarian posture. Kant tried not to be, and succeeded in not being, a

[1] Keynes, p. 99.

moral optimist of the kind that Shaftesbury was, even if he could not avoid altogether the utilitarianism of Hutcheson. It is not, after all, very difficult to show that there need be no pre-established harmony, here below at least, between a man's duties and his own interests. It is evident enough that duty and private interests, especially as Coleridge puts it "selfish ones", need not by any means run together. It is, on the other hand, extremely difficult to find a sense in which an act could be right, or even pointful, if no interest of any sort were served by it.

We must disagree with Kant when he says—or seems to say—that the condition of true moral action lies in the kind of purity of will which is incompatible with our having any interest in the act of duty: we must agree with him when he stresses that the classic case of a duty is, all too often, a case in which our private interests are not consulted, and indeed are outfaced by a categorical, unconditional claim.

One can, of course, always construct marginal cases, of a more subtle kind than Kant's grocer example, where interest not only runs with, but even provides the ground of a duty. It might be argued that a romantic attachment and shared interest could set up for a couple, if not a duty to marry, then something rather like one. Such cases, however, are hardly the pure paradigms of duty; a duty as often as not leaves out of account the agent's own interest and concerns itself with the interests of others.

Kant conflates with the categorical imperative his notion of purity of motive; he runs together his rather ultramontane idea of disinterestedness, and the purely deontic notion of the moral content of maxims. His potential-suicide example states that, in the passage from which we have already quoted:

> When . . . disappointments and hopeless misery have quite taken away the taste for life; when a wretched man, strong in soul and more angered at his fate than faint-hearted or cast down, longs for death and still preserves his life without loving it—not from inclination or fear but from duty; then indeed his maxim has *a moral content*. (*G.*, pp. 65–6: pp. 16–17: A. p. 14.)

This passage seems to define a notion of "moral content" which is at once rigoristic and confused: Kant is over-severe. And he seems, as well, to be making a category mistake. When a man "preserves his life without loving it, not from inclination or fear but from duty", "*alsdenn hat seine Maxime moralischen Gehalt*".

The definition of *moral content/moralischen Gehalt* which this passage sets up may be criticized on two grounds:

(*a*) The definition is rigoristic if it suggests that right acts have for, or generate within, their agents "moral worth" *only* when they are performed in a state of pure disinterestedness.

(*b*) And the whole passage is the reverse of useful if it suggests, as indeed it does suggest, that the question of motives has anything at all to do with the moral content of maxims. The matter looks even odder when we consider Abbott's translation. He renders the last phrase of paragraph 11 of the *Groundwork*:

> . . . then his maxim has *a moral worth.* (*G.*, p. 16: A. p. 14.)

Can *maxims* have moral worth? Is not moral worth essentially a predicate of agents? Abbott has simply mistranslated *moralischen Gehalt* here writing "worth" instead of "content": but how simple, indeed, is his mistake?

It is symptomatic of the general drift of Kant's own passage: it is Kant, not Abbott, who makes the *Gehalt/content* of a maxim depend, in some obscure fashion, on the will and on the feelings of the man who entertains the maxim. It is the *man* who must preserve his life "not from inclination or fear/*nicht aus Neigung oder Furcht*" but "from duty/*aus Pflicht*" before his *maxim* can have "moral content". For Kant *sittlichen Wert* seems to determine *sittliche Gehalt/moralischen Gehalt*:[1] to our ordinary way of thinking, the determination is the other way about.

Surely the "moral content" of a maxim is, and must be, a quite different kind of thing from the moral content of an agent's will. To conflate the 'contents' of maxims with motives as 'contents' of wills is simply to muddle one's categories; and this seems to be just what Kant does here. One cannot compare the content of wills with the 'content' of propositions or maxims,

[1] *Moralischen Gehalt*, para. 10: *sittliche Gehalt*, para 11: cf. *C.* p. 254.

any more than one can compare the contents of a diplomatic dispatch with the contents of the ambassador's trousers pocket.

If *Wert* and *Gehalt* stand in a relationship, then it is *Gehalt*, taken as something of moral consequence, which moves a will, and produces *Wert*. But what can *Wert* do for, or to determine, *Gehalt*?

Kant reinforces his curious, rigoristic and categorically confused definitions of "moral content" in his next example: reiterating again the ultramontane notion of *moral worth*, and making it quite clear that a right action done from inclination not only need have, but indeed can have, no moral worth. The suggestion conveyed by the passage is almost that inclination spoils moral worth.

And so inclination must spoil moral worth, of course, if moral worth is to be defined in terms of disinterest:

> To help others where one can is a duty, and besides this there are many spirits of so sympathetic a temper that, without any further motive of vanity or self-interest, they find an inner pleasure in spreading happiness around them and can take delight in the contentment of others as their own work. Yet I maintain that in such a case an action of this kind, however *right* and however amiable it may be, has *still no genuinely moral worth.* [Abbott: *no true moral worth.*] It stands on the same footing as other inclinations—for example, the inclination for honour, which if fortunate enough to hit on something beneficial and right and consequently honourable, deserves praise and encouragement, but not esteem; for its maxim lacks *moral content* [Abbott: lacks the *moral import*], namely, the performance of such actions, not from inclination, but from *duty.*[1] (*G.*, p. 66: p. 16: A. p. 14.)

There is something odd about admitting that an act may be *right* or *plfichtmässig* while denying it *moral worth*, *sittlichen Wert*. What is *right* surely has, in some sense, "moral worth": and it is only if "moral worth" is defined in terms of something over and above rightness, for instance, defined in terms of rightness

[1] The German of this runs: ". . . denn der Maxime fehlt der sittliche Gehalt, nämlich solche Handlungen nicht aus Neigung, sondern aus **Pflicht** zu tun". *C.* p. 254, line 13 of last para.

plus disinterestedness, that the right can be less than 'morally worthy'.[1]

Even granted that "moral worth" might require both rightness of action and a certain quality of attitude, it would still be odd to talk of the "moral content", the "*sittliche Gehalt*" of the *maxim* of a right act, as though *it* depended on the motive of the agent. But for Kant, before the maxim can have "moral content" it seems that the agent must act "not from inclination but from duty".

Rigorism about "genuinely moral worth" and confusion about the worth of wills and the moral content of maxims are both patently present in this example. The use of the expression "moral content" here provokes the obvious and necessary objection: that the being a duty of an action and the moral worthiness of a putative agent of that duty are two different things, and ought to be kept quite separate from one another. The moral content or import of a maxim should, one feels, refer simply to its ability to pass the test of the categorical imperative.

The moral worth of the characters of agents does, indeed, call for assessment of motives, but this is simply another issue again.

We may repeat here what we have already said more than once, that what is "essentially good" in an action is not, as Kant would have it (*Groundwork*, pp. 83–4: 39: A. p. 33), "the mental disposition [of the Agent]"; it is the thing-to-be-done

[1] It must be admitted that a right act done with a thoroughly bad motive or even with a very egoistic one, would be spoiled: that is, the goodness that a right act should generate in the agent's will would be lost or spoiled. But the act would still be good/right. The philanthropist who endows hospitals simply or chiefly to advertise himself, or his business, or in hope of a knighthood, is perhaps lacking in true "moral worth": but the act describable as "endowing hospitals" is right in itself. What is wrong is the inner action of the man, rather than the act which he does. He lacks purity of heart, but his town gets hospitals, and that is something gained. One might even, as a humanist, prefer that one man's heart should be impure, but that the sick should be cared for, to a state of affairs where the vain man conquered his vanity, but the sick had a less efficient hospital. Theologically, this presents a classical problem: but we are not concerned with theology here. The notion that a concurrence of inclination might spoil a good act by robbing it of its purity has a nice parallel in Kant's remark about a *pure judgment of taste* as one uninfluenced by charm or emotion, in *C.J.* §13 M. p. 65: B. p. 59.

which he does. On the primitive rightness of the act is based all or any righteousness which may be displayed in the doing of it. This right alone is what the categorical imperative is concerned with, and the imperative commands our act, not our motives or our dispositions. The imperative is content to show us what to do: it does not preach purity of motive in the doing. The homiletic tone is all Kant's, not reason's. It belongs not to Morality, but to Metaphysics.

C.1 (iii) *A Third Sense of Good Will.* What has happened in Kant's unsatisfactory "first proposition" is, perhaps, that he has introduced, or been seduced by, a third possible sense of good will and one more removed from the primitive sense of practical reason even than is good will 2, though in a way much closer to it.

There is a sense of "good will" which we all apply to acts of disinterestedness; and there is *a* sense in which we must all, sometimes at least, be disinterested and show "good will". "Peace on earth to men of good will" may not mean peace on earth to saints only, but the saintly sense, the disinterested sense, is implicit occasionally in every sense of good will. That is, the high sense of "good will" is implicit in good will 1 itself. This is so, since sometimes I will have to act disinterestedly *if I am to do my duty at all*. And on these occasions, I am being required to show the same disinterest that a very virtuous man might go out of his way to show, often, and for its own sake.[1]

What one wants to object is, simply, that though:

good will 1 (i.e. practical reason)	entails having	good will 3 (i.e. acting against my own interest)

is a valid scheme, it must be qualified "not always". My duty does not always require that I act disinterestedly: "Blessed is the cheerful giver" indeed, since he has inclination and duty running together. The entailment in the schema ought to have

[1] Disinterestedness has, of course, no "sake". The highly disinterested man would be a Schweitzer or a Father Damien, doing heroic things, against inclination and self-interest, for the sakes of others, i.e. for Ends-in-themselves.

some kind of statistical operator on it: for such-and-such a number of cases of duty, duty will imply disinterestedness: while for so-and-so a number of cases the agents of the acts dictated by good will 1 will all be like cheerful givers.

Though duty and inclination do not always accord, a duty is no less my duty if it runs with my inclination: I am obliged to cherish my wife even though I love her in the sentimental and romantic sense. Nor is a duty any more my duty if I dislike it, though it may occasion more moral effort. An uncongenial duty may be more of a test of character, more of an occasion for heroic virtue and the rest, but these are, if certainly important, nevertheless still peripheral matters. The right is more important than the righteous.

Kant would be in an impregnable position if he were to stress that a characteristic thing about duty is that it (i) can, and (ii) often does, require a sacrifice of interest. And he would be correct if he said that (i) was an essential characteristic of duty. But he is wrong if and in so far as he allows himself to say, or to seem to say, that (ii) the actual conflicts of duty and inclination, are essential to the nature of duty itself.

The issues which Kant conflates, and the practical as opposed to the theoretical drives which there are towards such a conflation, all come out in a passage from Countess Tolstoy's diary:

> 'I nursed [Leo Tolstoy] day and night', she wrote, 'it was such a happy natural thing—the only thing I can do really well—to make a personal sacrifice for the man I love. *The harder it was on me the happier I felt*. But now that he is up again he no longer needs me. I am cast aside as of no further use except that I am still expected to do the impossible.'[1]

"The harder it was on me the happier I felt"; this is human enough avowal, but we must not be misled. No doubt it was the unfortunate Sofya Andreyevna's duty to nurse her impossible husband, but its being hard or easy to do her duty made it no less or more her duty. She rejoiced in the hardness simply, as is clear enough from the biography, because it enabled her to prove something.

Now it is not the first or most important point of a duty that

[1] Quoted in Cynthia Asquith's *Married to Tolstoy*, London (Hutchinson), 1960, p. 129.

it enables us to prove something: and what we ought for the most part to be doing is our duty, and not proving things. Nor, unless there were duties in the first place, could they be dramatized in this way.

The ground of Sofya's duty to nurse Leo Tolstoy was not that this enabled her to show a love that he seemed to be rejecting, or that it allowed her to be disinterested, or that it was an occasion for putting down inclination. All these are irrelevant. The ground of her duty was his need, and the special relationship in which they stood to one another.

Countess Tolstoy's maxim need not, and should not, have contained anything about unrequited love, the chance to rise above inclination, or anything of the sort. It should have been: can I will 'universally' that a wife nurse her sick husband?[1]

Motive does not enter into the maxim of an act: nor does mention, even, of motive.

Kant seems to have been inclined to extend good will 2 to good will 3, and to suggest that the end of reason is duty—which indeed in a sense it is—and this as always and necessarily disinterested duty—which indeed it is not in any clear sense at all.

If duty and rational action are the same, then the end of reason lies in men being rational in their action; the end of reason is in a sense duty, but only in a sense. Rational action, which is indeed "the" end of practical reason if it is to have *one* end, includes in its intention both duty and private happiness.

Duty does not have always the sense that it has sometimes, the sense that is of a command contrary to the agent's own interest. Kant is right to insist that this may be what any duty involves on any occasion. But a complete falsification of Kant's own position can arise from an imprudent enlargement of the notion of good will 1 to include other notions of good will, especially if what are included are ideas of goodwill-as-disinterestedness. All too often in the *Groundwork*, the extension

[1] That the situation between Leo Tolstoy and his wife went beyond questions of duty is without prejudice to the ultimate fact that there are certain basic duties, and that the categorical imperative can show us what would at least be *against* duty. Of course the marriage relationship is not one of duty exclusively; a lot of duty talk will simply be irrelevant in this kind of context. On "super-meritorious" actions see *C.Pr.R.*, A. pp. 178–9 and p. 253.

of good will 1, or practical reason, is precisely in the direction of good will 3; but—and this is the rub—the occasional necessary disinterestedness of the moral agent becomes absolute and universal. Good will 3 is over-developed, and as a consequence the true point of it tends to become lost.

When "good will", read simply as good will 1 or practical reason, includes always the notion of disinterestedness, it includes too much. Sometimes our very duty is to do what will make us happy, and we can be virtuous eudaemonists. Sometimes our duty is to do what will not make us happy, and we must be virtuous and let eudaimonia go. But if duty always required us to be disinterested, then happiness would hardly get even that low second place that Kant gives it. It is one thing to say that duty can cut across inclination: it is quite another to define it in such a way that it must.

The extension of senses of good will from 1 through 2 to 3 is perhaps the most plausible account that one can give for Kant's notoriously apparent, and materially quite needless, moral severity. Since Kant himself was not aware, as far as one can see, of the systematic or aesthetic ambiguities of the expression "good will", he could always defend himself against imputations of severity in terms of his first paragraph. In the first paragraph of the *Groundwork* 'good will' issues in no more than the simple obligation of rational, moral, action, an obligation that it would be eccentric, and patently absurd to deny.

2. *The Second Proposition*

The upshot of Kant's first proposition which, if he had enunciated explicitly he might himself have modified profoundly, is to embroil the notion of the moral law itself with notions of disinterestedness. It tends, fatally, to mix up the content of maxims with the contents of agents' wills. This comes out still more clearly in the "second proposition", where moral worth seems to be something that lies in maxims, and where some of the old ineluctability and formal law notions raise their heads again. Kant writes:

> Our second proposition is this: An action done from duty has its *moral worth* [Abbott: *derives its moral worth*] not *in the*

> *purpose* to be attained by it, but *in the maxim* [*from the maxim*] in accordance with which it is decided upon; it depends therefore, *not* on the *realization* of the object of the action, but solely on the *principle of volition* in accordance with which, irrespective of all objects of the faculty of desire, the action has been performed. (*G.*, pp. 67–8: pp. 18–19: A. p. 16. Italics mine.)

Two notions seem to preside over this passage: (i) the notion that maxims,[1] and not ends, must determine the virtuous man's actions (a notion which, for all that it is stressed and reiterated, must remain empty), and (ii) the notion that success or "realization" is irrelevant to the generation of good will 2 in the agent. Clearly the spirit of unconditionality hangs over all.

What Kant goes on to say becomes more and more confused and more and more puzzling, and at the heart of the puzzle lies, as usual, the expression "unconditioned" in the phrase "unconditioned and moral worth". Kant goes on to write:

> That the *purposes* we may have in our actions, and also their *effects* considered as *ends* and *motives*[2] of the will, can give to actions no *unconditioned and moral worth* [Abbott: *unconditional or moral worth*] is clear from what has gone before. Where then can this worth be found if we are not to find it in the will's relation to the *effect* hoped for from the action? It can be found nowhere but *in the principle of the will*, irrespective of the *ends which can be brought about by such an action*; for between its *a priori* principle, which is formal, and its *a posteriori* motive, which is material, the will stands, so to speak, at a parting of the ways; and since it must be

[1] Maxims taken, too, as Kant insists in the *C.Pr.R.*, purely under the aspect of their universalizability. This is 'pure' determination, and as-near-noumenal-as-we-can-have, should we want noumenal-determination at all. For the official metaphysic as it bears on morals, see for example, A. pp. 168–74, *178–9*, 185, 189 ff., *204*. See too *G.* pp. 69–70: 21–2: A. pp. 17–18, discussed below, pp. 277 ff.

[2] It is significant, of course, that Kant runs "ends or motives" together like this, as though they were the same kind of thing. They are not. If the 'official' metaphysic of the phenomenal and the noumenal has as its consequence this kind of humping together of different *sorts* of things, then so much the worse for the metaphysic.

> determined by some *principle*, it will have to be determined by the *formal principle* of volition when an action is done *from duty*, where, as we have seen, *every material principle is taken away from it.* (*G.*, p. 68: pp. 18–19: A. p. 16. Italics mine.)

The notions of three sorts of prescinding from ends are now kept in play at once: (*a*) the virtuous will is determined by the *formal principle* and not by ends; (*b*) the principle which determines good will 1 is itself not concerned with ends but is formal; (*c*) no ends need be *attained* by the action of the good will 1 for this will to be, or to produce, good will 2. And to *a* we may add its own expansion: (*d*) that it is not either ends or motives, "effects considered as ends or motives of the will", which determine the virtuous man, but simply the, itself prescinding, formal principle.

This last notion is perhaps the most surprising of all. Kant writes: "[moral worth] can be found nowhere but in [adherence to] the principle of the will, *irrespective of the ends which can be brought about by such an action* . . ." Here one protests that neither (i) the will, nor (ii) the principle of the will, can be thought of "irrespective of the ends" which its action *may be presumed* to bring about. And this is the case whether or not the actions bring their ends about on a specific occasion. The expected ends or results of an action—whether they eventuate or fail to eventuate does not matter—are absolutely crucial to our judgment of an act as a right or wrong act.

If we did not know what results to expect from the following of maxim *m*, then we could not decide whether or not the categorical imperative test would let it pass.

The principles of the Decalogue itself are determined by the ends which actions forbidden in it would have. Certain effects would be brought about by murder, theft and covetousness which could not be rationally justified, so murder and the rest are forbidden. The forbiddings of the Decalogue are achieved by specific mention: but that the categorical imperative avoids this kind of specific mention makes it no less, itself, concerned with ends.

The will is the faculty of end-seeking in man, and its proper principles are those maxims whose form is the categorical imperative, which "adjusts" particular maxims to universal ends. There is nothing else to be said.

Kant however, with his notion of the opposition of right acts and willed-contradiction, seems to be dividing principles from "the ends which can be brought about by action", just as, with his extension of the notion of good will from 1 to 2 and then to 3 he divorces the will acting in duty from its possible ends. But none of these divorces is possible, except in the sense in which 3 is sometimes possible and sometimes the upshot of having a duty. When a duty makes me abandon my own ends, I am not being forced to give up ends as ends: I sacrifice my ends to another's ends. Still, ends remain; my private ones give way to some that are more universal. "Pure will" cannot, as *will*, be quite empty.

The notion of end-seeking is implicit in the very notion of will, even of "pure will", and the notion of rational action as end-seeking action is paradigmatic. Moral action/rational action sometimes involves us in seeking ends other than those of inclination, certainly. Altruism, duty and the needs of society make claims on us. But we can abstain from seeking our own ends and secure those of others only because there *are* ends to be sought, for ourselves and for others. Duty, when it involves abstinence, calls us from the quest of ends which we may fancy, and sends us off after others to which we may not be inclined. Even so, ends remain.

That Kant did less than justice to this fact was, it would seem, the opinion of T. H. Green. It is apparent, too, from the text of the *Groundwork* and from Kant's first enunciation of the Categorical Imperative. This we shall consider in the next section but one.

We must examine now, as a kind of parenthesis and recapitulation, Kant's short "third proposition".

3. *The Third Proposition*

Kant's third proposition is offered as an inference from the two preceding ones:

> *Duty is the necessity to act out of reverence for the law.* [Abbott: *Duty is the necessity of acting from respect for the Law.*] (G., p. 68: p. 19: A. p. 16.)

The proposition looks two ways: obviously enough, towards the ideal of pure motive, and less apparently towards the notion of the law itself as formal and undetermined by empirical considerations. Read simply as a definition of duty, the proposition seems quite unintelligible; read more largely it begins to have some meaning.

It is difficult to decide what, precisely, Kant wants to say about motive when he says that "Duty is the necessity to act *out of reverence for the law*". There are at least three *prima facie* possibilities:

(i) That we must act out of reverence for the law and do our duty for duty's sake, when there is either: (i*a*) no inclination present towards the act in question; or (i*b*) when there is a disinclination, no matter how strong.

(ii) That we must act with some degree of rational conviction of duty when we do a duty, even if it happens to be a congenial one.

(iii) That we must, to do our duty at all, act *only* from motives of respect for the law and must exclude from our motivation any inclination towards the act which is our duty.

The first proposition, (i), is clearly true, and it makes the essential point about duty, that it commands us; and just as it is not based on any mere inclination, duty can override any mere disinclination. But what of the other two propositions?

The last, (iii), is clearly too extreme a view to command assent. Even so, it seems to be implicit in Kant's would-be suicide example. And it represents the kind of view which Kant has often been criticized for holding: a view which may follow from the official metaphysic of noumenal freedom, but which does not chime in with ordinary moral intuition. When indeed Kant is forced to write in the *Metaphysical Elements of Ethics*, ". . . reason commands how men should act, although no instance of such action could be found . . ."[1] he dramatizes for us the oddness of a metaphysic which can generate so ultramontane a view of the morally possible.

It could be maintained in ordinary moral discourse that all

[1] A. p. 271. See too, "For it is not enough to do what is right, but we should practise it solely on the ground of its being right," *C.J.*, §53, M. p. 192: B. p. 171.

duties implied some further meta-duty of the 'disinterested' or 'distanced' doing of one's duty. But the arguments for this view, taken in a high severe form, would seem to centre on a discussion of the counsels of perfection rather than on any exposition of the necessary precepts. The severe form of the view is one for which there are precious few arguments in ordinary ethics.[1] For most of us it is enough that we have our duty to do: we do not particularly value this having-a-duty as an occasion for still further supererogatory acts of the will. Nor is it evident to ordinary moral consciousness that we must consider ourselves as morally slack if we do not seek to make of every work a work of supererogation.

The furthest that ordinary common moral sense could go, perhaps, would be to concede *ii*; that is to admit that some reverence for the law must enter into an action before it is unequivocally an action of NM's doing his duty. Even this might be a trifle further than some people would want to go. Need I, when I embark on an act of congenial duty, advert to and make a motive of the dutifulness of my act before I can consider myself a worthy or fully rational agent? It seems odd to say "yes": but there is something not quite satisfactory about saying "no", too.

Kant's example in the *Groundwork* (p. 67: 17–18: A. p. 15) of the man who furthers his own happiness "not from inclination but from duty" is, as we have already said, too harshly put. If we allowed ourselves to be over-persuaded by Kant, we might just admit that "for the first time his conduct has *real moral worth*" when it is done "from duty". If "real moral worth" means 'a specific kind of moral worth' we shall concede Kant his point: if on the other hand all that it means is 'now for the first time his act is really moral' then there is no reason at all to concede Kant anything. To pursue my own happiness, censoring my strategies by the categorical imperative, is rational: and, on our ordinary definition of "moral", moral. And if moral, it can surely be morally worthy.

What we are really concerned with when we use the categorical imperative test is moral action: and what concerns us about

[1] Likewise, ascetic theology, and other systems of special ethics which concern themselves with the works of perfection, are said to warn us against spiritual pride and against taking on too much.

moral action, at this point of our argument, is the question: "How far must an action to be rational/moral be done in advertence to its being rational or being-a-duty?" Talk about "moral worth" can only confuse this rather delicate issue, and though we must insist that if any act is moral, then it can have moral worth, we ought perhaps to agree to keep talk about moral worth out of contexts where what is really central is the moral, the right, itself.

It is possible that Kant's third proposition, "Duty is the necessity to act out of reverence for the law", is not introduced to make a point about motivation at all. That is to say, it is possible that it makes such a point more by the accidents of its verbal expression and of its context than by intention. It may not express Kant's considered doctrine of motivation. The central point of the third proposition may be simply: that the law and what is reasonable, and not inclination or interest, is the core of morality. Now this is itself a very reasonable doctrine. But that "*duty*" is, in any plain sense of the words, "the necessity to act out of reverence for the law", one denies. Duty is the necessity to do the necessary thing, which is by and large to perform acts which aid, or to refrain from acts which harm, one's fellows: we have *a* duty to do *one or more* such acts on *a* specific occasion. We must treat persons as Ends, whether these persons are others, or ourselves seen as the patients of our own acts. Occasions for meeting this obligation to treat people as Ends present themselves to us, from day to day.

It is clear to ordinary moral consciousness that, despite Kant's definition, the "necessity to act out of reverence for the law" is not what constitutes "duty". Considered formally my duty is to "Act only on that principle, &c."; and taken materially my duty is to do whatever thing constitutes 'acting only on that principle' in a specific case at a specific time. There is nothing in the notion of duty taken in itself which says that we must act out of pure reverence for the law; and whatever one can say about there being a further possible duty or meta-duty to act out of pure or even minimal reverence, it does not constitute the real essence of duty itself. The point of *a* duty is the End, the other person, served, rather than my-rationality-exercised: and the last thing that can be the point of a duty, in the primitive sense of "duty", is the moral improvement of me as a dutiful agent. The inwardly righteous may have "absolute worth": but this absolute worth is not the real point of anything, and certainly not of duty.

Kant gives *a* reason why duty must be the necessity to act out of pure reverence for the law. It is that there is nothing else out of reverence for which one could act. He says that there is, in effect, nothing else other than duty worthy to be a ground for action for a rational will. He is simply wrong about this, as we shall see in Part III of the present essay.

What Kant means by saying that only reverence for the law is worthy to determine a rational will is obscure, or mistaken, or both. But what Kant says in support of this odd doctrine is of great interest in itself. He writes:

> For an *object*[1] as the *effect* of my proposed action I can have an *inclination*, but *never reverence*, precisely because it is merely the *effect*, and not the *activity*, of a will. (*G.*, p. 68: p. 19: A. p. 16.)

The point seems to be this: that only two things have absolute value for Kant: (i) the *activities of wills*, (ii) *persons*. The activities of will have "absolute value" for the reasons given in paragraph 3 of the *Groundwork*, and at the end of paragraph 16. Persons too have absolute value, and this is asserted, if not further explicated, in Chapter II when we are introduced to the formula of the End-in-Itself.

The only things that can be reverenced, and so form the basis for rational action, are activities-of-will (*Groundwork*, pp. 67–8: p. 19: A. p. 16), and persons. Hence derives Kant's disinclination to think of the law itself as dealing with mere ends, ends which may be neither will-activities, nor persons.

Kant does not talk in the *Groundwork* of the will as dealing,

[1] Notice that Kant uses the word *object* here, and "effect"; later on in the same paragraph he is to use "results". The equivalence is not without its own interest. One cannot, indeed, reverence objects as such: but results as affecting persons can elicit 'reverence' in the sense, at least, of making unconditional claims upon us. See Part III, Chapter I, Section B.1 at p. 301 and Section B.2 at pp. 304 ff., for some elucidation of the Kantian conceptual schemes: not-needing-to-be-produced, *implies* value; being-able-to-be [or needing-to-be]-produced, *implies* disvalue.

explicitly, with ends even when these are Ends, or when ends involve Ends. In this omission lies the key to the weakness of his ontology of personal value.

We shall see in Part III that there is ultimately a conflict even for Kant between his two 'absolutes', *will-activity* and *the person;* and rationalism seems to triumph over humanism in the long run, will-activity trumping personhood.

Will and its activities seem to take a higher place in Kant's axiological scale than do persons and rational nature as such. Ordinary ends come nowhere at all on the scale.

Despite the too elevated and altogether too confused role given to good will in Kant's axiology, there is some sense in his refusal to let the will be determined, in the high sense, by objects.

Objects[1] of the will do not command us, as long as they are simply objects. What we could or would do we are not obliged to do, unless either as implementing a moral law, or—to put it another way—as part of a policy of "treating human nature as an End and not simply as a means". We are not indeed, nor should we be, commanded by mere things.

Kant quite obscures his own doctrine on this point however when he says a few sentences further on:

> ... the moral worth of an action does not depend on the result expected from it ...

This has nothing at all to do with the unworthiness of mere things to command the will. That the moral worth of an action,

[1] Even the claims of aesthetic objects, claims to admiration, intelligent reading, etc., are, though strong, not "compelling". There is no moral defect in not listening seriously to Bach, or in scribbling upon reproductions of the "Mona Lisa". We must not, of course, destroy unique copies of Bach scores or deface the "Mona Lisa" in the Louvre, but this may be, in the last resort, because other people as possible valuers of these things make a claim on our action. It is difficult to see how an aesthetic object itself and 'for its own sake' could make such a claim. On the other hand, though there are utter daubs that we know to be valued by others, *we* do not value them: still, we do not, by and large, destroy them physically (critical destruction is another thing again). No objects, as objects, have absolute claim on us: and if there *are* aesthetic claims, simply, we are disinclined to admit that these can be absolute, in the sense in which moral ones can.

that is, credit for trying, does not depend on the actual attainment of that end *tells us nothing at all about the worthiness or otherwise of objects to determine the will.* And this fact about the immanence of credit, "inner worth", cannot for a moment count against the point that, in general, it is ends which determine the will. As determining a rational will, these ends are indeed mediated through the categorical imperative; this imperative may raise their solicitations to the status of a command, or it may put the ends down with a flat "Thou shalt not!". Even so, without ends as envisaged in maxims, there are no maxims for that categorical imperative itself to act as the touchstone of: and the imperative "Act only on that maxim . . .", deprived of all maxims, can determine nothing at all. It cannot move any will to any thing whatever. It is altogether too "pure".

Moral laws, as opposed to the Moral Law, are determined by results as they bear upon persons: and the Moral Law tells us, precisely, to look to results, and in this light. Results then are, at a remove, the ends of the Moral Law itself.

The rule for lifeguards, "Jump in and try to save swimmers in distress" is derived from the results which can be achieved by experienced swimmers diving into the surf with ropes and lines and pulling out other, less amphibious people who are thereby saved from drowning. Such results determine the rule, and give it whatever moral force it may have. We have the rule to get the ends: and the rule has moral force because the results that can be had are of this kind: people are saved. If standing on the shore spinning a prayer-wheel had the same results, then we would have prayer-wheels at the seaside instead of, or as well as, lifeguards; one would be obliged to spin a wheel, when now one is obliged to jump into the surf, run for the lifeguard, or take whatever other action lies in one's power to take. What determines the will of a lifeguard is reverence not for the Law, but for life, the life of persons. And this reverence for persons determines, or should determine, all laws.

4. *Results: Production and the Will*

One of the motives which Kant has in playing down the importance of *results* as such, comes out in his next sentence again:

> For all these results (agreeable states and even the promotion of happiness in others) could have been brought about by

other causes as well, and consequently their production did not require the will of a rational being . . . (*G.*, p. 69: p. 20: A. p. 17.)

The trouble with this sentence is that what it says is not true; or rather, it is true, if at all, only for a possible universe. It is not true for this one. The happiness of one's wife and one's children and one's friends might, in some other possible world, have been provided for by nature. In this actual and present world their happiness is partly at least a matter of love and nurture and of kindness. What one does has a causal, and so morally relevant, bearing on the well-being and happiness of others. The happiness even of one's most casual contacts may be touched by one's action. The reason why I must not snap at the girl in the neswpaper shop when my detective magazine has not come in is that I can hurt her feelings. Even if, by smiling at her, I cannot assure her happiness in any very positive way, I can still upset her by being boorish, so minimal politeness becomes a moral obligation.

Kant's rationalism goes far too far. Granted that in some remotely possible way such results as he lists—"even the promotion of happiness in others"—*might* have been brought about by other causes as well, nevertheless the fact remains that both these results, and even more obviously moral ones like the saving of men's lives, are brought about, in this universe, by human action.

A phenomenological account of happiness would, of course, show that Kant's very "possibility" is in fact null, as far as the production of happiness is concerned. Happiness in human beings is to a very large degree a function of interpersonal relationships, and so it does essentially require just this very thing that Kant now goes on to deny that it does require, "the will of a rational being", to produce it. One cannot be happy in love without loving and being loved by another person: and love manifests itself, not in a mere will but in action, and not immanently but in the world.

The "*first*" purpose of reason as this is rationalistically determined (that is, good will 2) is ousting for Kant the "*second*" purpose, which is happiness; and good will ousts the second purpose, even when this second is quite as much a function of reason itself as is the first. Kant tends to reject the dualism of the actual universe, in which the will has external ends, in favour of the tidier functional monism of an ideal universe where the ends of will are immanent in will itself. In the world as it is, both reason's infallible and ineluctable ends, good will 1 and 2, and its fallible ends, of which "the production of happiness in others" is one, are equally and essentially functions of reason and of rational action. That the external ends of reason sometimes fail is an argument against the rationalistic dogma that reason could not have proper ends that failed; it is no argument at all against reason's having the ends that it does have.

Reason could not have ends that *might* fail. But it has! And they sometimes *do* fail; and that is the end of it.

The rationalist dogma, and the impressive ineluctability of one of reason's practical generations, weigh more heavily for Kant than they need; and the notion of ineluctability presides over the final sentence of the paragraph at which we are looking. Having maintained what is almost certainly not the case, that even human happiness might have been produced by causes other than the rational action of reasonable beings, Kant goes on to say:

> For all these results (agreeable states and even the promotion of happiness in others) could have been brought about by other causes as well, and consequently their production did not require *the will* of a rational being, *in which, however, the highest and unconditioned good can alone be found*. Therefore nothing but the idea of the law in itself, which admittedly is present only in a rational being—so far as it, and not an expected result, is the ground determining the will—can constitute that pre-eminent good which we call moral, a good which is already present in the person acting on this idea and *has not to be awaited merely from the results*. (*G.*, p. 69: p. 20: A. p. 17. Italics mine.)

This is all very curious. The activity of will which here seems central is not autonomy, the giving to oneself or the seeing for oneself one's duty by means of good will 1 and by the testing of one's maxims; the central value is not as it should be, the person.

The accent is, oddly, but as we might by now expect, all on the good will 2. The accent is on that ineluctable worth of a righteous will which "has not to be awaited merely from [its] result": this is "the highest and unconditioned good", if only because of the fatal pun on "unconditioned". The pun is fatal: and the unconditioned goodness of good will 2 is axiologically vapid.[1]

This good 'that need not be awaited' is, and determines for Kant the notion of, 'the highest and *unconditioned good*', a good which can be found only in a human will. This good, and its real but trivial ineluctability, tend (*a*) to oust all other *acts* of the will, that is to displace good will 1 as will's function; (*b*) to oust all *ends* of will; (*c*) even (as we shall see in Part III) to oust the value of persons itself as an absolute value.

The will dwells alone with the Law; the Law dwells alone with the will. A pure, if still dualistic, immanence has been achieved; the immanence of the good which need not be awaited satisfies the demand that there shall be, here below, some "absolute", "accommodate" and "indeprivable" good. The pattern is elegant, but it is not for a moment convincing.

5. *Conclusion*

Having considered the general pattern of the "three propositions", dominated as they are by the twin notions of prescension from ends and the absoluteness of the worth of mere will (itself a classic prescension notion), we can come now, finally, to the question which stands at the head of our present Section, C. We can come, at last, to the question, "*What kind of a law can this be?*", which '*has to determine the will without regard to the results*'.

Kant writes:

> *But what kind of law can this be* the thought of which, *even without regard to the results expected from it*, has to determine the will if this is to be called *good absolutely* and *without qualification?* Since I have robbed the will of every inducement that might arise for it as a consequence of obeying any particular law, nothing is left but the conformity of actions to universal law as such, and this alone must serve the will as

[1] Cf. above Part I, Chapter V, Section A.3, pp. 143 ff.

its principle. That is to say, I ought never to act except in such a way that I can also will that my maxim should become a universal law. Here bare conformity to universal law as such (without having as its base any law prescribing particular actions) is what serves the will as its principle, and must so serve it if duty is not to be everywhere an empty delusion and a chimerical concept. The ordinary reason of mankind also agrees with this completely in its practical judgements and always has the aforesaid principle before its eyes. (*G.*, pp. 69–70: 21–2: A. pp. 17–18.)

One might answer, as even the rationalist Harris almost certainly would have, that there is no kind of law, "the thought of which even without regard to the results *expected* from it" can determine the will. No practical law can be as "pure" as that.[1]

Kant's example of false-promising itself turns on the results of false promising. These happen to be spectacular, the destruction of the agent's credit (which may provide both a reason and a 'mere motive' for his refraining), and, ultimately the practically-possible and in-theory-inevitable destruction of the institution of promise-keeping itself. These two spectacular results can be brought, somehow, under the notion of self-contradiction, but they turn, even so, on the effects of "particular actions".

By now one suspects that it is not simply the positive claim of the notion of self-contradiction which has defined Kant's view of the formal categorical imperative, but that it is as much the very doubtful claims of the notion of "absolute" worth as

[1] In *C. Teleolog. J.* Kant has the moral law formal, as ever, and the will acting 'irrespective . . . of any end whatever', §30 = 91, M. p. 145*n*: B. p. 323*n*. In the *Introduction* to *C.J.* Kant insists that "practical precepts" are "morally practical" as ". . . laws independent of all antecedent reference to aims or ends". M. p. 11: B. pp. 9–10. The official doctrine of "suprasensible" freedom demands that there be these precepts: but the categorical imperative by acting as a test of maxims, far from showing that there must be such precepts, calls their very possibility into question. What it judges is ends—with regard to their universalizability indeed—but ends, nevertheless. And ends whose universalizability or otherwise depends as much on *their* nature as on that of universalizability. (This we tried to show above, p. 241 ff.) One might say of "suprasensible" purity of will what Kant said of mundane innocence ". . . a splendid thing, it is very sad that it cannot well maintain itself". (*G.*, Ch. I, penultimate para.)

absolute and *prescinding-from-ends* which weigh with Kant in this matter of the formal Law.

The question "What kind of a law . . . ?" sweeps along in its rush the highly doubtful presupposition that the thought of a law *can be* without regard to the results of it. One does not quite know whether Kant is saying the objectionable thing he seems to be saying, or simply making yet again the point that might be better put, about a law "the thought of which without regard to the results" as objects of my possible self-interest serves to command my conduct. It is one thing for the Law not to concern itself with the results that *I* would like to enjoy on some occasion: it would be quite another for it not to concern itself at all with results. There cannot be a law of action which does not concern itself with results, for action is always and necessarily concerned with them.

Again, as we read this complex passage from the *Groundwork*, the point of the law and the aim of the categorical imperative seems, for Kant, not to be the determination of a rational will, the actualization of good will 1, but the production of good will 2. The tension of the good, "to be called good absolutely and without qualification", determines the whole structure of the set of ideas.

One is in a literary rather than a philosophical realm with all this. Kant does not put up a series of propositions and arguments; rather he puts down a number of highly suggestive and completely ambiguous sentences, that he who runs may read. And the pace is so hot, that we run faster than we can read.

Rationalistic arguments which are explicit in Harris, and explicit too in Kant, have also an inexplicit form in Kant. The Idea of the unconditioned carries, in a suggestive, poetic, ambiguous way, certain notions that might be set out, quite explicitly, in argumentative form.

The trouble is that when the hidden contents of the Idea of the unconditioned are unpacked, the doctrine which is brought to light seems so curious that one wonders that Kant should even entertain it, much less advocate it.

It might be argued that even Kant himself was a victim of his own obscurity in the *Groundwork*: or, to put it another way, it might be argued that the force of his imagination led him to set down, in a compressed and aesthetic form ideas which must, on cool reflection, be divided, distinguished, and even divorced from one another.

6. *Summary and Final Analysis*

If anyone still remains to be convinced that Kant did use the aesthetic notion or set of notions of unconditionality, or needs to be shown that his use of it was more enthusiastic than sober, then the only argument that there is left to bring lies in the last paragraph of the section on the categorical imperative which we have been considering. The quotation and analysis of this passage will do as a final rehearsal and final recapitulation of the argument of the present chapter. Kant writes:

> Thus I need no far-reaching ingenuity to find out what I have to do in order to possess *a good will*. Inexperienced in the course of world affairs and incapable of being prepared for all the chances that happen in it, I ask myself only '*Can you also will that your maxim should become a universal law?*' Where you cannot, it is to be rejected, and that *not because of a prospective loss to you or even to others*, **but** *because it cannot fit as a principle into a possible enactment of universal law*. For such an enactment reason compels my immediate reverence, into whose grounds (which the philosopher may investigate) I have as yet no *insight*, although I do at least understand this much; *reverence* is the assessment of a *worth* which far outweighs all the worth of what is commended by inclination, and the necessity for me to act out of *pure* reverence for the practical law is what constitutes duty, to which every other motive must give way *because it is the condition of a will good in itself, whose value is above all else*. (*G.*, p. 71 : p. 23 : A. pp. 19–20. Italics mine.)

Here, the slide in the senses of 'good will' follows the classic pattern set up in the first three paragraphs of the *Groundwork*. A good will begins in lines one and two as good will 1 : if, "inexperienced in the course of world affairs", I want to have an informed practical reason, then I must frame the question of the categorical imperative and ask, "Can I will the maxim of such-and-such a proposed action universally?" This is all very reasonable, and very profitable. So far we must follow Kant.

But at once the clouds of doctrine begin to gather: "where you cannot [will it universally your maxim] is to be rejected, and that *not because of a prospective loss . . .*". But, surely, it is just because certain actions *do* result in certain sorts of damage and loss to others (and even to myself) that I must refrain from them. And it is—and here is the rub—because of this possible damage that such envisaged actions will not fit into any universal enactment of law. Kant's disjunction is false: one cannot set *loss* against *non-universalizability* in this way; they are not opposed but co-ordinate notions and the "but" which we have set in bold is misleading. It is just "prospective loss", specified in certain ways,[1] which is the bar to the universalizability of certain maxims. The acts caused by following these maxims would give rise to consequences not compatible with "universal ends". Mill is closer to being right than Kant here: I cannot will, "Let me drive as fast as I please and as drunk as I please", simply because of the possible loss to my wife and to bystanders, and to myself, which this would involve. I cannot universalize: "Let anyone (myself or another) drive as fast and as furiously as he pleases", because this could not fit into any possible traffic code of any Kingdom of Ends. The prospects to which this maxim gives rise are all of loss: the maxim, therefore, cannot be universalized. It is loss envisaged which precisely bars my principle of drunken driving as "a possible enactment of universal law".

That Kant was lured into setting up his misleading disjunction between *prospective ends* and *universalizability* under the influence, at least the partial influence, of the true reflection that duty can command an individual contrary to his own interest and to his "prospective loss", makes the disjunction no less misleading. When I forgo my own ends in deference to universal ones, these themselves are still none the less ends, prospective gains to someone.

It is possible that, insufficiently instructed in Kantian moral

[1] If "prospective loss" could be taken to refer simply to loss of things that would be had only on *mere inclination*, then of course we could concede Kant his phrase. But it is not at all clear that Kant is saying anything as simple as this here, or as clear. A loss to my self-interest, merely, does not count against an action, morally: but there are some losses, even to self, that make the acts which end in them morally unacceptable.

theory, I may have no "complete insight" into the reverence which reason has for the principle of possible enactment: but I know already—as a matter of that ordinary practical reason which Kant is attempting to make more explicit—what possible universal enactment has to do (*a*) with the possible and probable results of my actions and (*b*) with their bearing on the treatment of persons as Ends.

What indeed has a worth which far outweighs the worth of the mere objects of inclination is the *person*, and his claims are what bind my action through the categorical imperative. But it is not this worth which seems, for Kant, to determine the will which obeys the categorical imperative. The last line of our section from the *Groundwork* ends with a reference to "a will good in itself", whose condition "pure reverence for the practical law" is. The classic slide from good will 1 at the beginning of the section to good will 2 at the end of it, has been achieved. An empty Law now commands a possibly fruitless, but still absolutely worthy, will. Immanence is all.

The necessity to obey the categorical imperative is the necessity to respect the claims of persons upon action. This is indeed for ordinary moral consciousness "what constitutes duty", and every other motive must give way to this. If the question of other motives arises, then we must obey the command of duty, not because duty is "the condition of a will good in itself", and not because the value of 'a will good in itself' is 'above all else', but simply because persons are persons and exercise an absolute claim on the practical reason of rational agents.

The ineluctable worth of a righteous will is not at the centre of morality: it is a mere and peripheral detail. It may be "absolute" but its absoluteness is utterly incommensurable with the serious and properly absolute absoluteness of the claims of a person on the acts of other persons.

"Everyone will acknowledge this" it may be objected: Will they? Would Kant? In Chapter II, where he is talking about the value of persons as persons, he says a number of things which must make the attentive reader uneasy. Kant seems indeed, to be grounding the value of persons on the absolute value of good will, making the morally crucial absolute depend upon the axiologically vapid "absoluteness" of "the worth of mere will".

This will not do.

7. *Interest or Disinterest? Our own Question Answered*

The answer to the question which we have set at the head of the present chapter is that it is neither mere pure personal egoistic interest, nor pure altruistic disinterest, nor yet a pure formal disinterested Law, which is the root of moral conduct.

The root of moral conduct lies, as Kant sees in his first paragraph, essentially in the adjustment of private to universal ends: it lies, as he says later on in the *Groundwork* in forming enactments for a Kingdom of Ends. Without interest there would be no private ends, and no universal ones to adjust them to.[1] And without the real possibility of disinterested action, there could be no such adjustment.

If we could never be disinterested, then public and private ends could be reconciled only by chance or by a pre-established harmony. Such a harmony does not obtain. Nor do we depend simply on chance for our actual reconciliations, such as they are. Disinterestedness is both possible and actual, and it is presently useful to us: ordinary "kingdoms" reflect, however imperfectly, a Kingdom of Ends, ordinary politeness this polity.

We see the point of the question in the title of our chapter only when we reject its implicit "*either/or*", and realize how complicated and how qualified must be the answer which we give to it. Interest lies at the root of all moral action: but action

[1] See *G.* Ch. III, p. 128*n*: pp. 96–7*n*: A. p. 80*n* and A. p. 69*n* also A. p. 37*n*. But it is significant that Kant should in the *C.Pr.R.* write an encomium to freedom, meaning at least in part freedom from inclinations, which ends with the remark that such a state of independence would be enjoyable with "an enjoyment . . analagous to the self-sufficiency which we can ascribe only to the Supreme Being", A. p. 215. Here indeed is the Stoic as Christian, the Christian as Stoic, enjoying for a moment a glimpse of a Vision as odd, and as oddly beatific, as Harris's. See too the remarks on the 'sublimity' of *apatheia* in *C.J.* §29, M. pp. 124–5: B. p. 113, and Kant's sentence in the *C.Pr.R.* ". . . [inclinations] are always *burdensome* to a rational being", A. pp. 213–14. Kant's notions of interest and of inclination are less than satisfactory. See below, p. 305 & 305 n.

could not be moral were we quite incapable of present disinterestedness.

When Kant writes, in Chapter II of the *Groundwork*, that:

> . . . because the Idea of making universal law is *based on no interest* and consequently can alone of all possible imperatives be *unconditioned* . . . (*G.*, p. 99: 60: A. p. 50)

we may agree with him in so far as "*no interest*" means 'no merely private, merely personal, as-yet-ununiversalized interest'. But the "*unconditioned*" imperative of universal law itself must be conditioned by interests. We would not know what to legislate, even for a kingdom as ideal as a Kingdom of Ends, if we did not know the interests which Ends have, the interests, which in the interests of all, any enactment must universalize. The aim of a Kingdom of Ends is, indeed, not too unlike that "Social Interest" by which Harris would have us governed: and enactments designed to serve this Interest are as conditioned as is anything else "sublunary".

Interests are discovered: laws are enacted. Even so, the autonomy of the rational will legislating for a Kingdom of Ends is not unconditioned: it must 'find out' enactments, much as the famous men of the Bible "found out musical tunes". Morals, for all that the rational will may be autonomous, is more like discovery than it is like improvisation. The rules of composition condition music: the economy of human nature and of the human situation condition even the autonomous enactment of laws for a Kingdom of Ends.

A Critique of Pure Reason may be possible, but a critique of "pure" will fails for want of a subject. The will is always concerned with ends, simply as will. And the Moral Law is "pure", 'categorical' and empty only in a Pickwickian sense—as Mill saw.

Furthermore: in so far as the notion of 'purity' of will may invite, by aesthetic or free association, the ventilation of notions of purity-as-disinterestedness it simply invites us, if not to jest, at least to pun on altogether serious matters.

CONCLUDING NOTE TO PART TWO

There is one passage of the paragraph from the *Groundwork* (pp. 68–9: 19–20: A. pp. 16–17) which we have been discussing at length, which is not treated in our last chapter in Part II. The passage reads:

> Only something which is conjoined with my will *solely as a ground* and *never as an effect*—something which does not serve my inclination, but outweighs it or at least leaves it entirely out of account in my choice—and therefore only bare law for its own sake, can be an object of reverence and therewith a command. *Now an action done from duty has to set aside altogether the influence of inclination, and along with inclination every object of the will;* so there is nothing left able to determine the will except objectively the *law* and subjectively *pure reverence* for this practical law, and therefore the maxim of obeying this law even to the detriment of all my inclinations. (*G.*, pp. 68–9: pp. 19–20: A. pp. 16–17. Italics mine. See also, e.g.: *G.*, p. 94n: p. 60n: A. p. 44n.)

What Kant says might do if he were simply defining what he means by "an action done from duty". However, what is suspicious here is that "grounds" alone and not effects of the will may command the will; the only "ground" that is available to command the will is a Law which, like the will itself, *does not concern itself with effects*. Immanence broods.

We must remind ourselves that all actions of a dutiful sort need not fall into the class of "action done from duty", and though inclination is neither the *ground* of duty nor of any moral command, it is still, if not the ultimate *reason*, a perfectly proper *motive* for acts of duty and may properly accompany any properly dutiful motive. We must concern ourselves with ends, and we may, on occasion, concern ourselves with our own ends, even the ends-of-inclination. Duty is not pure disinterestedness, nor is the Moral Law itself totally end-prescinding, totally 'disinterested'.

If the Law were 'to the detriment of' "all" of *everybody's* "inclinations", then it would not be a Law for a kingdom, of Ends, or for anything else. The Law may command any man at any time against his interests: but it would be logically odd to conceive of a law, as a law, which always commanded everybody against their interests, and secured, with each act of obedience to it, nothing for anybody. Such a conception would be logically odd because 'the end of every law is the common good': a law that compelled renunciations while securing no goods, would not be a law. Just as duty is concept-bound to some notion of disinterestedness, so law is concept-bound to some notion of a 'public', 'universal' or 'general' interest. That it is universal does not make it any less an interest.

But of course, as Kant may be insisting, that something may be a universal interest does not guarantee that it will be my present and immediate interest as well. If only we could be sure that this *was* all that he was saying.

PART THREE

CHAPTER I

KANT'S ONTOLOGY OF PERSONAL VALUE: A FALSE ABSOLUTE

. . . . and having gain'd
A more judicious knowledge of what makes
The dignity of individual Man,
Of Man, no composition of the thought,
Abstraction, shadow, image, but the man
Of whom we read, the man whom we behold
With our own eyes; I could not but inquire,
Not with less interest than heretofore,
But greater, though in spirit more subdued,
Why is this glorious Creature to be found
One only in ten thousand? What one is,
Why may not many be? What bars are thrown
By Nature in the way of such a hope?
William Wordsworth, *The Prelude*, Book XII

The value of the person, of the End-in-himself, is absolute. Persons are limits to action, and their claims on action are absolute in the negative sense of setting up the *Achtung!*, and often in a positive sense of compelling action. I must not push an uncongenial colleague off the edge of the wharf, however much I may be tempted to. If he falls in by chance it may even be my duty—for want of a better swimmer than I—to dive in and try to save him. Respect for the worth of being-human commands both abstention and positive action.

The "value of mere will' is also in a sense "absolute", and though there is no connection between these two absolutes, Kant seems determined to find one. Furthermore he seems determined in the *Groundwork* to ground the value of Ends-in-themselves on the "absolute" value of the will's own ineluctable *end*, its own worth or value, generated within itself, by righteous willing.[1]

[1] Contrast *C.Pr.R.* A. pp. 152–3 and 163 and 181. Again contrast A. pp. 225 and 259. The dangerous side of Kant's doctrine of "worth" in the *C.Pr.R.* is summed up in his remark that "*Respect* is a *tribute* which we cannot refuse to merit". A. pp. 169–70.

This metaphysic of morals carries a step further Kant's pejorative axiology, in which the ends of the will are seen as of less value than the will's own absolute goodness. The playing down of the ends of will, and the final grounding of personal value on the "absolute worth of mere will" are intimately related to one another.

As we have already seen, the suggestion that the ends of will are of less value than the righteousness of will itself, looks highly implausible when one defines "end" in terms of states of affairs which involve the good, or happiness of other persons. But Kant, instead of valuing ends for the bearing that they may have upon Ends, seems in the last resort, to value Ends because of the possibility they themselves have of generating ineluctable, end-less, absolute, worth.

To our ordinary way of thinking the ends of will become objects of reverence and effect an absolute determination of the will, in so far as they bear on Ends: and we already know this as a matter of the "ordinary rational knowledge of morality". There is a double paradox in Kant's doctrine of will: (i) he plays down the importance of external ends as determinants of the will; (ii) he grounds the value of Ends on the value of will's immanent *end*, the "absolute" value of mere possibly-end-deprived, but ineluctably-worthy, will.

The notion of the person as End-in-himself which Kant sets up in the *Groundwork* Chapter II must, if it is to be of any use to morality, be disengaged from the rationalistic metaphysic which surrounds it. The absolute value of Ends must be disengaged from "the absolute worth of mere will".

A. THE LANGUAGE OF "ENDS": ENDS AND ENDS

In his lucid and incisive commentary on Kant's *Groundwork*, Sir David Ross has this to say about the formulation of the categorical imperative in terms of humanity as an End-in-itself; the quotation is lengthy, but all of it is important:

> Kant distinguishes between independently subsisting and non-independently subsisting ends. This is forced upon him by the fact that he has already described man, i.e. all men, as ends. This, in the ordinary sense of the word, men are not.

> For an end is an object of desire, and an object of desire is something that does not yet exist. He therefore has to justify this description of man as an end by describing him as an end of this very exceptional kind, an end which already exists. The notion of self-subsistent ends is nothing but an embarrassment to Kant. When he remembers that men are (according to his use of words) self-subsistent ends, he interprets 'treating them as ends' merely as not interfering with them. But that just means recognizing their rights, and belongs to the conception of duty rather as obedience to law than as the seeking of an end. At other times, . . . he interprets "treating men as ends" as the positive "advancement of humanity"—a stimulating ideal, but one that would be unmeaning if humanity were a self-subsisting end. The plain fact is that in strictness man is not an end at all, and the description of him as an objective and at the same time as a self-subsistent end can be understood only if we take this as a way of expressing the fact that there is something which can be realized in any man and is worthy of being an object of desire to every man. From the beginning of the *Grundlegung* we know that in Kant's view good-will is just such a thing. In Kant's attitude towards his second formula two strains may be distinguished. He has expressly told us that when he has offered his first formula of duty he has only shown that *if* duty is an objective fact, it must take the form assigned to it in the first formula. He has still to show that there is such a thing as duty, and it is in the attempt to do this that he puts forward the second formula. *His thought is this: If there is something that has absolute value, there must be a duty to conserve this and to promote it to the best of one's ability. Now there is such a thing, viz good-will, and it exists either actually or potentially in every man; therefore in all our actions we must treat neither ourselves nor others as mere possible enjoyers of pleasure, but as beings in whom good will may be and should be conserved and promoted.*[1]

One might agree with Sir David Ross that "the notion of self-subsistent ends" is not as clear as it could be. One might very

[1] Sir David Ross, *Kant's Ethical Theory: a commentary on the Grundlegung zur Metaphysik der Sitten*, Oxford (Clarendon Press), 1954, pp. 51–2. (Italics mine.)

well agree with Ross's judgment that "in strictness man is not an end at all"; and one might substitute for the notion of end more explicit notions. Yet although the notion of self-subsisting or self-existing ends may be, in the short run, confusing, in the long run it may have some positive value.

If one puts the accent on "*self*-existing", a kind of proto-Existentialist sense emerges, and this sense, which may be of considerable importance, will be explored, if only briefly, in the last chapter of this essay.

If one puts the accent on "self-*existing*", then, it seems, confusion follows. Let us begin with the short view of Kant's idea of self-subsistence, and give our attention to the power which it has to confound the issue of personal value.

The value of the person, conceived of negatively, may be thought of in terms of '*the limitation of all end-seeking*': the person is the value which, being higher than all subjective ends, limits our seeking of them.

Taken positively, the value of the person makes him worthy not merely of our forbearance, but of our active help and encouragement. Both 'recognizing rights' and 'advancing humanity' are commanded by the injunction to treat men as Ends in themselves. This is clear; but what is not clear is the precise significance of the notion of **end** as it is conceived by Kant.

And here the double paradox shows itself. Kant has played down the ordinary ends of will, in Chapter I of the *Groundwork*, in favour of the one unfailing and immanent *end*, the ineluctable worth of a worthy-will; now it is this *end* which is to serve as the ground of the value of Ends.

We may mark the three important notions of end which are in play here by typographical devices, formalizing usages which have been followed, if only approximately, so far in this essay: "end" in the ordinary sense of "something which might be the object of and achieved by the will" can be marked by end, printed without typographical modification; for persons, Ends-in-themselves, we may put, as we already have, End; and for the immanent end of the will, its own ineluctable worth, the *end* which is both the supplanter of ends and the ground of the value of End, we may put *end*. For the family of notions of end we shall write **end**, where this signifies by-and-large an aesthetic idea of end-ship which holds other senses in an uneasy tension. With these conventions set, we may pursue our argument.

1. *The Idea of an End: Ends and* **end**

Ross, following Kant as closely as he can, settles on good will as the end potentially in man, which transmits its absolute value to man. This certainly keeps Kant's large philosophical, quasi-aesthetic, notion of **end** relatively tidy, but it has an unfortunate moral and axiological consequence.

As Ross points out, the notion of **end** is altogether odd in the context; and the oddness goes, we suggest, beyond grammar and into metaphysics.

The notion of end usually means "something which can be realised".[1] But we ought not to conclude from this fact about the grammar of "end", that we can speak of man as an End-in-himself only if we can find something which, in the words of Ross's commentary, "can be realized *in* man, and something which is worthy of being an object of desire *to* every man". The use of "end" in the idea of an End-in-himself, is already linguistically or conceptually odd; we can hardly be forced to compound one eccentricity for another, allowing the first to persuade us that the second must be conceded too. That is: having allowed Kant his odd use of "end", we need not feel forced to follow him in his search for **ends**-in-man which can justify man's Endship.

There is nothing *to-be-realized* in a man which, in the ordinary way, we consider to be the ground of our obligation to treat a man as an End: each man exists-as-an-End, and this is the fact, the proto-moral piece of axiological ontology which we mark by the moral concept of *person*. If the notion of independently-subsisting ends marks any important fact, then this indeed is it: that men are simply "given" as Ends.

If I treat some particular man on a particular occasion as a *limit* to my proposed action, then I am not strictly realizing anything *in* him, though, in a real and psychological sense, I may allow him to realize something in himself.[2] Even when I am

[1] Kant himself makes something of this, see below, Section B.2.

[2] The end which all men would realize in themselves is of course, happiness: cf. *Groundwork*, p. 83: pp. 38–9: A. pp. 32–3.

advancing humanity and helping someone to attain an end, this end may be "in" him or "external" to him. It is hardly plausible to say that whenever I treat men as Ends, either 'negatively' by regarding them as limiting my action, or 'positively' by helping them, so I am realizing something *in* them. It is even less plausible to say that I am realizing good will in them.

The conceptual drag of "end" is something realizable, and this, and the eminent realizability of good will (in one sense of "good will") conspire to mislead Kant and some Kantians. Man as an End-in-himself becomes conflated with the notion of a possible "end" to be realized in all men, namely the always-realizable *end* of good will. Such a conceptual and moral scheme will not do.

Persons or Ends are such not because of *ends*. Persons may have ends, and these ends must be respected, if at all, because they are the ends of persons: 'simple' ends or states of affairs may set up absolute limitations or absolute demands on the will, but if and when this is so, it is because of a particular relation between the end and an End. If I have to produce the state of affairs or end, "Jones saved from drowning", this obligation obtains not because of the demand of an end as an end or as an *end*, but because of the presence-in-that-state-of-affairs, of an End. If I have to put myself out on occasion for the sake of my children's happiness, take them to the Zoo, suffer their little friends, make sure that they are not wretched at school, then this is because their happiness is the end of Ends, and because I can take steps to secure this end for them which they cannot (and because it is *my* specific responsibility to take these steps). My children as Ends make certain ends morally important for me.

While Ends may transmit their value to ends, the value of Ends derives in no way from that of *ends*. Persons or Ends, given as absolute, may make certain specified ends, in certain specified situations, absolute too, in the same moral sense: but *ends*, though metaphysically absolute, do not communicate their absoluteness to Ends. If *ends* communicate anything at all, what they communicate is by no means the quite other moral absoluteness of Ends as Ends. This absolute moral value of Ends is, and must be, given as the first moral *datum*. I must attempt to save Jones from drowning because he is an End, not because I hold him capable of realizing the *end* of ineluctable worthiness of will. If Jones is a notorious burglar, and singularly devoid of such present *end*-seeking, he still demands, morally, to be saved from drowning.

2. *Self-subsistent Ends*

There seems to be some connection, if an obscure one, between the notions of self-existence and of a limit to possible actions by others, when these are taken as predicates of "man". The idea of man as an End-in-himself connects up if inchoately both with the usual notion of an end as something sought, and with the notion of a limit, as when we think of our obligation to do as we would be done by. A man 'would be done by' in accordance with certain notions of himself as an integral and self-regarding person, and it is the fact that a man has ends for himself which makes him *un*usable by others simply as an instrument: part of treating a man as an End-in-himself lies in letting him pursue at least some of his self-chosen ends for himself.

Furthermore, the obligation to respect the fact that men or Ends have ends for themselves, other than the ends or purposes that we may have for them, seems to rest on nothing more than this fact itself, self-subsistent and self-validating. Men have their own ends, and these ends are the ends of Ends. Since men are 'just *there*', and since it happens to be the case that they are self-regarding and set their own ends, so we must respect them as Ends, and we must respect such of their ends as may be required under this rubric of End-respect.

The existence of rational nature, the existence of beings having this autonomous, self- and other-regarding nature, is the central fact which constitutes value and the possibility of value. Rational nature, or personhood, is the fact from which value derives.[1]

[1] The 'rule' of Empiricist moral philosophy that 'You cannot get value out of fact' and the rider, 'so you cannot get it out of *this* fact either' is a rule of which Kant seems to have been ignorant, and is one of which the existentialists are simply not convinced. Hume himself ignored the rule too: value for him seems to be founded on the simple, psychological and practical fact of our *valuing*, and some values fit into what he is pleased to call "morals". The existentialists have a similar strategy to Hume's in all this, though their view is much more complex than his: it is more complex

None of this is quite as clear, perhaps, as we would like it to be, but one feels that an existentialist phenomenology of value ought to be possible, and ought to make the notions of self and of value a little less obscure. There may be some strain of quite positive existentialism in Kant, but if there is, it is likely that the formidable difficulties which stand in the way of its development conspired with his early rationalism, to turn him from the existential analysis of value into the *cul-de-sac* of rationalistic ontologism. And there is one line of thought in Kant that clearly does end up in this *cul-de-sac*: his ontology of personal value is, in one version of it at least, as trivial as his formula of the End-in-itself is existential and forward-looking. The rationalism of the metaphysic of absolute value almost cancels out the existentialist possibilities of the formula of the End-in-itself. Almost, but not quite. The *Groundwork* is a work which modern moralists should 'prize as emeralds': but like all very big emeralds, it is flawed. Let us look at the flaw.

The notion of *self-subsistence* or of "self-existence" is present in Kant but it does very little work (see *Groundwork*, p. 105, line 13).[1] Nevertheless it is essential to note that this idea of self-subsistence forms a kind of aesthetic affinity with the ineluctability, the virtual- or as-good-as-self-subsistence of the *end*. And the given-ness, the "*independence*", the axiological "self-subsistence" of Ends becomes itself identified with, or worse, grounded on, the ineluctable-to-be-hadness of *ends*. That is, the "end"-ship of Ends becomes identified with the goodness of the only good acts which cannot fail, acts of good will seen as immanent, and as 'absolutely' valuable.

For the present it is sufficient to notice that the self-subsistence of man gives place, on Ross's reading of Kant, to the notion of good will as "an object of desire to every man". Talk about the self-subsistence of man as a value is of less importance

too than Kant's, and fortunately without his rationalism. If Hume can ignore *Treatise*, Book III, Part I, Section I, so can the existentialists. See George A. Schrader, *Existential Philosophers*, New York (McGraw-Hill), 1967, pp. 41 ff. See below, Chapter II.

[1] Abbott, p. 67, line 17, uses the perhaps weaker phrase "independently-existing end" to render Kant's "*selbständiger-Zweck*": see *Cassirer*, p. 296: A. p. 56, ll. 12–13.

to Kant than is the notion of man possibly possessed of good will. It is clear that Ross is right when he sums up Kant's "thought" as this:

> *If there is something that has absolute value, there must be a duty to conserve this . . . now there is such a thing, viz. good will, and it exists actually or potentially in every man.*

Ross is also right in thinking that for Kant, man himself derives his value from his possible possession of good will, a will whose value is "absolute": Ends are Ends, because of the possibility of *ends*. Kant says as much.

In a passage that is highly ambiguous, if not downright contradictory when read as a whole, Kant makes one statement which seems clearly enough to put the value of man in his good will:

> Now this end [i.e. the end against which we should never act] can be nothing other than the *subject* of all possible ends himself, *because this subject is also the subject of a will that may be* **absolutely** *good*, for such a will cannot without contradiction be subordinated to any other objects. (*G.*, p. 105: p. 67: A. p. 56. Italics and bold mine.)[1]

This quotation seems to confirm Ross's opinion that Kant indeed maintains that the value of 'self-subsistent' man lies in his possible possession of **absolutely** valuable good will. Granting that Ross's view of Kant is borne out, we must ask: *is Kant's doctrine itself true?*

Ross apparently thinks that it is true. He writes: "In spite of great obscurity of expression, Kant's thought here is profoundly true . . ." And Ross talks about the possibility of convincing the morally blind that "there is a duty to treat every man not as a mere means . . . *but as a being in whom good will can and should be promoted.*"[2]

[1] Abbott's translation is ". . . for such a will cannot without contradiction be *postponed* to any other object": the German runs: ". . . *denn dieser kann ohne widerspruch keinem andern Gegenstand nachgesetzt werden.*" *C.* p. 296. "Postponed" is a very odd translation for "*nachgesetzt*".

[2] Ross is using "good will" here in an unanalysed and ambiguous sense: in so far as he is following Kant this is of course inevitable. See below, Chapter II, Section A.4, pp. 322 ff.

Now it seems not only possible but essential, to draw a firm distinction here. We must insist on a distinction between (i) the undoubted truth of the proposition that "There is a duty to treat men as Ends" (i.e. negatively to limit our own end-seeking by the absolute value of their persons, and positively to "advance humanity"), and (ii) the supposed truth of any proposition which suggested that the ground of this duty lies in any man's potential possession of the "*absolute*" value of good will, in the actual or potential possession of an *end* or *ends*.

As the first thing, *i* is true so the second, *ii*, is false.

Further, the second position is pharisaical—as well as being false—in so far as it derives man's value ultimately and specifically from his possible keeping of the sabbath.

I must save Jones the burglar from drowning not because I think that he pursues the ineluctable worth of a worthy will, or because I share the optimism of the local Salvationist Captain, who believes that the presently incontinent Jones can be brought to righteousness some day; I must save Jones simply because he is a person.[1] Kant obscures this fact with his talk of "a will that may be *absolutely* good".

As well as being pharisaical, the view that my duty to treat a man as an End depends on his putative ability to pursue *ends* is indeed conceptually confused. It is confused, as we have already indicated, because it relies on an untenable and eccentric notion of the absolute goodness of *ends*. The "absolute worth of mere will" is, as we have already seen, *absolute* only in a rather vacuous sense: axiologically this absoluteness is of no real importance at all. But it can obscure our view of something that is important.

It seems self-evidently pharisaical and self-evidently a confusion to base the absolute value of a man on the "absolute" value of his possible good will, but I do not know what I

[1] I must seek to rescue Jones the Jemmy; but if Hitler were floundering in the river, the place Germany, and the year were 1945, I would consider it my duty not to save him, but to let him drown, even to run for a Rabbi so that we could both pelt him with stones, to make sure that he did not crawl up the bank by himself. This would not be because I conceived Hitler as incapable of the pursuit of *ends* (which he was), but because I knew that he no longer respected Ends. Such men, if they cannot be locked up, are to be put down.

would say to someone who did not see it in this light. Recourse to self-evidence is either utterly conclusive, or very inconclusive indeed. One may perhaps attempt to bring the evident to light.

Even conceding that good will has an "*absolute*" worth in the sense which it has, that is the sense of *Groundwork* Chapter I, paragraph 3, it is preposterous to have the value of the person depend on the possible "*absolute*" value of his righteousness. It seems necessary to say this, and in a sense otiose to try to prove it further, but clarifications are possible here, and are indeed very much needed.

It is preposterous to suggest, as Kant seems to be suggesting, that what I must do is respect the *ends* of others. What I must respect is, surely, Others; that is I must respect Ends, and sometimes, as a consequence, their ends. Other Persons' *ends*, unless these other persons are my children, or persons for whose moral welfare I am somehow responsible, are not my business at all but entirely their own.

It is not because you are capable of generating the ineluctable, "absolute" goodness of good will that I must behave in a moral fashion towards you: it is because you are a person and an End. Your ineluctable "good will" is between yourself and God or yourself and your self-respect: it is not what comes between the two of us in our dealings with each other.

What stands between you and me in all our relationships is our End-ships: and these turn, not on good will 2, but if on good will at all, then on good will 1. We must treat each other as "beings in whom good will can and should be promoted" in so far, simply, as this *comes to* treating one another as rational agents. Each inter-personal relationship is, in the first instance, an encounter of rational persons; and the decent management of such encounters is the essence of morality. Mutual improvement is altogether a secondary matter; and it would, often enough, be quite simply impertinent for me to be concerned with your "good will" in any pious or elevated sense.

Your good will as "moral worth" and the rest of it is between yourself and God, as we have said, or between yourself and your own Autonomy. You, not I, are the keeper of your conscience.

The sense in which good will I may be the crux of Endship is explored below in Chapter II. At this present point in our argument it will be useful to analyse, in some detail, the passages in Kant which seem to propound an incorrect doctrine of End-ship and of its relations with good will. This analysis will serve both as a survey of the present argument, and as a preface to a discussion of End-ship and good will I.

B. ANALYSIS OF KANT'S TEXT

In the section of Chapter II of the *Groundwork* labelled by Professor Paton "Review of the whole Argument", there is a long paragraph (p. 105: p. 67: A. p. 56), which sets out Kant's ontology of personal value. Crucial to this passage is a notion of **end.** This notion is highly ambiguous and very general. And it is extremely hospitable, sheltering under it certain quite disparate notions, and giving them the semblance of a mutual relevance and of a mutual dependence which they do not in fact have. The expression/notion "end"/**end** behaves with a high, aesthetic ambiguity which recalls the behaviour of "unconditioned" in Chapter I of the *Groundwork.*

The crucial paragraph of Chapter II of the *Groundwork* can be divided into six sections. Each occurrence of "end" can be assigned to one of the four senses of the expression which occur in the passage.

In the analysis which follows, the passage has been set out in sections ¶1 to ¶6. In the passages from Kant each occurrence of "end" or of some synonym has been numbered.

In the comments on the ¶¶ the typographical conventions for the interpretation of the sense of "end" which have been followed so far will be made use of. That is to say we shall print **end,** where the notion is being used in a large general, and as we have suggested, aesthetically inclusive sense; we shall print *end*, where what is in issue is the immanent, ineluctable, end of the righteous will, i.e. the "absolute worth of mere will"; we shall print end, where it is a matter of ends in the most ordinary sense of things-to-be-willed-or-obtained; and finally we shall put End, where this is a Kantian synonym for "*Person*". The sections ¶1 to ¶6 are from the *Groundwork*, p. 105: 67: A. p. 56.

1. *Ends and* **ends**

> ¶1. Rational nature [i.e. End-ship] separates itself out from all other things by the fact that it sets itself an 1 end. An 2 end would thus be the matter of every good will.

Here "1 end" = **end** or *end*, or both. The expression "*an* end" would seem to cut off at once the ordinary notion of end, since rational nature sets itself, to the ordinary way of thinking, not "*an* end" but "ends": here "end" read as **end** may allude to the ordinary sense of end, but in effect it paves the way for *end*. The strategy of this paragraph is, like the strategy of the *Groundwork* as a whole, contrived in such a way as to suggest the Rationalist scheme: *one faculty*, *one end*. And the "end" of rational nature is for rationalists, as we have seen, *end*: i.e. the ineluctable and unfailing *end* of immanent, "*absolute*" worth This *end* takes priority even over End-ship.

And "2 end" is ambiguous: perhaps "2 end" = **end,** perhaps *end*: it even alludes, by hindsight when one has scanned the whole paragraph, to End.

"Good will" here could be construed, minimally, as *Good will 1*.

The importance of the paragraph lies not in the precise analysis that one can give of the logical grammar of the expression "end", but in the example which it gives of the extreme and subtle ambiguities of these usages of "end", which come together as **end.**

> ¶2. But in the Idea of a will which is absolutely good—good without any qualifying condition (*namely*, *that it should attain this or that 1 end*)—there must be complete abstraction from every 2 end that has to be produced (as something which would make every will only relatively good).

In this section "end" on both occasions means end in the ordinary sense: nevertheless the key notion of the section is *end* adverted to, if obliquely, in the first parenthesis. In this parenthesis, and indeed in the passage taken as a whole, we are in the presence of *good will 2*: "a will which is *absolutely good*, *good without any qualifying condition*, namely [without the condition] that it *should attain* this or that end". And the "end" which rational nature is said in ¶1 to set itself is actually this *end* in ¶2, namely a good will which prescinds from the attainment of ends in the ordinary sense. "The absolute worth of mere will", as Kant has called it, is the *end* of will. And as a condition of its absoluteness, this worthy will 'abstracts from every end that has to be produced': (the second parenthesis in this passage belongs, in effect, to the next ¶, q.v.)

¶3. Hence the 1 end must here be conceived, not as an 2 end to be produced, *but as a 3 self-existent end.* It must therefore be conceived only negatively—that is, as an 4 End against which we should never act, and consequently as one which in all our willing we must never rate *merely* as a means, but always at the same time as an 5 End.

This is all highly complex; "end" is used in this passage with extreme ambiguity and each "end" tends to be **end** as well as end or End. The talk about self-existence in 3 "a self-existent end", connects up with the remark in ¶2 about an 'end that has to be produced'. This talk, and the contrast which it puts up between the self-existent and that-which-needs-to-be-produced does very little real work.[1] Such work as it does do will have to be examined in Section B.2 of the present chapter when we consider another and earlier formulation of the doctrine of Ends. Here it is sufficient to note (*a*) "self-existence's" juxtaposition with (*b*) its affinities to, *end*. That is, we must notice the resemblance which the idea of self-existence bears to the notion of the good which, while not "self-existent", is "absolute" and which enjoys as much ontological necessity as anything sublunary can. Notice too the contrast between *absolute* good in ¶2, discussed above, and "relatively good" in the second parenthesis of the same section, and see how it fits into the self-existence talk of the present extract, ¶3. "Self-existence" and *end*-ish-ness cohere here under the hospitable umbrella of **end.** Here in ¶3 "1 end" = **end** rather than end; "2 end" = end; "3 end", "4 end" and "5 end" = End, with "3 end" highly ambiguous and paronomastic, hovering between End and a notion of self-existence which Kant never fully worked out. Kant has, or thinks he has, an argument which

[1] The notion of self-existent-end takes on moral sense and significance if it is considered as an "End", i.e. Person-existing-as-a-Self: cf. below, pp. 328 ff.

establishes the sense of End on the basis of a notion of 'something that has not to be produced' (a notion which has the strongest aesthetic affinities of course, with *end*), and this will have to be gone into further on in the present essay.[1] For the moment one can see how "end" here = **end,** an aesthetic idea, which then unpacks into: end ("2 end"); *end*, as at least *suggested* by the notion of "self-existence" in "3 end"; and finally into End, 4 "an End against which we should never act"; itself an End which "we must never rate *merely* as a means, but always at the same time as an 5 End".

¶4. Now this 1 End can be nothing other than the Subject of all possible 2 ends himself, because this subject is also the Subject of 3 *a will that may be absolutely good*; for such a will cannot without contradiction be subordinated to any other object.

This section is, as Ross has pointed out, crucial. It is here that Kant points up the sense of his ontology of personal value, and suggests a derivation of End from *end* (of occurrence 1 from occurrence 3). That is, it is here that Kant suggests a metaphysic of morals which would ground the value of Persons, the value of "Subjects", on the capacity which they have for producing "the *absolute* worth of mere will".

Here "1 end" = End; "2 end" = ends [?]; and "3 a will which may be absolutely good" is synonymous with *end*. *This synonymity is central to the whole passage.*

Kant is quite explicit here. The Person or End is the "Subject of all possible ends himself", "*because* this Subject is also the Subject of a *will that may be absolutely good*". The possible production, by Ends, of *good will* i.e. of *ends*, is made the ground of the value of Ends; "*for such a will*[*end*] cannot *without contradiction*[2] *be subordinated to any other object*".

[1] See above, Part II, Chapter III, Section C.3, p. 272; see below, [Part III] present chapter, Section B.2, pp. 304 ff.

[2] The sense of "contradiction" here is essentially axiological, and has nothing very much to do with such obvious notions as a *contradiction* in the false-promise case. What Kant means is of course obvious enough: if something is of a value higher than, or incommensurably higher than, another, then to prefer the lower to the higher is absurd: it is *as irrational* as uttering, or acting, a contradiction. If one examined the text of the

Kant's doctrine here is clear enough: but it is not argued for, and it is by no means obviously true. On the contrary, it is plain false.

Without the legerdemain of: **end** = End; *end*; and sometimes end, the statement of the doctrine would be, as it is in Ross's transliteration, so bald as to invite as bald a rejection. Once we have a transliteration, we must simply ask ourselves, "Do we treat persons as Ends because they are the potential generators of the *end*, the 'absolute' goodness of good will, or for some other reason?" And we shall be forced to answer, "For some other reason". What this other reason may be we shall discuss further in our next chapter: but it is simply obvious that I treat you as a person, as an End, for reasons quite other than your ability so to will that you may generate, immanently, "the *absolute* worth of mere will".

Your personal value, the *necessity* to treat you as an End, owes nothing at all to the rationalistically defined *absolute* of the "absolute worth of mere will". Kant seems to be resting a categorical imperative on a category mistake.

Here, in ¶4 above all, is that "high flown fantasticality" against which Kant sought, so inadequately, to defend himself. We no longer merely suspect, but actually detect, the "*hochfliegende Phantaserei*", which began its painful migration in the third and fourth paragraphs of the first Chapter of the *Groundwork*, and which comes home to roost here.

¶5. The principle 'So act in relation to every rational being (both to yourself and to others) that he may at the same time count in your maxim as an End-in-himself' is thus at bottom the same as the principle 'Act on a maxim which at the same time contains in itself its own universal validity for every rational being'.

Here "end" = End; and Kant is himself making the point which might be made against his (apparent) claim that the principle of universalizability is a matter essentially of logic and of 'contradiction avoided'. Here Kant acknowledges that what

Groundwork carefully one could no doubt find traces of an aesthetic paronomastic notion of *contradiction*, which held a number of disparate notions in complex play.

is crucial is not systematic coherence simply, but coherence and chaos as bearing down upon Ends.

¶6. For to say that in using means to every 1 end I ought to restrict my maxim by the *condition* that it should also be universally valid as a law for every subject is just the same as to say this—that a subject of 2 ends,[1] namely, a rational being himself, must be made the ground for all maxims of action, never *merely* as a means, but as a *supreme condition* restricting the use of every means—that is, always also as an 3 End.

In this section "1 end" = end, "2 end" = end; "a rational being himself" = End; and "3 end" = End.

The doctrine of this section, with the 'universal validity' of the lawful maxim qualified only as it is by ¶5, is unexceptionable. Persons-as-Ends are the conditions or should we say "Conditions", of all maxims. They set up the *Achtung* which warns us off selfishly profitable but anti-personalistic enterprises, and which compels us to social and to charitable ones. This is all clear, and clearly right. This sense of "condition" gives, too, the inner sense of the conditionality-*d* of happiness. The person is the Condition of the Categorical Imperative.

One does not quarrel at all with ¶¶5 and 6 of this crucially important paragraph from the *Groundwork*: but one must quarrel with ¶4 and with any suggestion that ¶¶5 and 6 in any sense derive from ¶4.

The doctrine in ¶4 is pure metaphysics, and whatever it is a metaphysic of, it is not of a personalist morals. Kant's ontology of personal value as we have it in ¶4 is 'metaphysics' in the pejorative sense. It is nonsense.

We value personality, personhood, for its own sake, not for the sake of the possible "*absolute*" worth which a personal will may generate ineluctably in the very act of righteous willing. The worth of the person "conditions [that is *conditions-d*], the use of every means": but this conditioning has nothing to do, at all, with the personal will as the generator and locus of the

[1] The phrase "subject of ends" marks "rational nature" as something which *has* ends: each Person has his own purposes, and must not have the purposes of Others simply thrust on him. See below, Part III, Chapter II, pp. 331 ff.

Rationalistically *unconditioned* worth of "the absolute worth of mere will".

2. *The End-in-himself, and Self-existence*

We have said that the notion of 'self-existence' as used by Kant in his talk about Ends-in-themselves does no work. It has affinities with End and under the cover of **end** it forms a composite but aesthetic notion with *end*: but beyond this it is lax and useless.

This needs to be shown; and it can be shown, perhaps, from an earlier account which Kant gives of Ends. In the part of Chapter II which Professor Paton heads "The Formula of the End in Itself", Kant sets up a 'hypothetical' statement about Ends:

> Suppose, however, there were something *whose existence* has *in itself* an **absolute value** something which as *an End in itself* could be a ground of determinate laws; then in it, and in it alone, would there be the ground of a possible categorical imperative—that is, of a practical law. (*G*., p. 95: p. 55: A. p. 46. Italics and bold mine.)

Now we are all quite prepared to make this "supposition". Why? Because either it is true, or there is no morality; and the second proposition is absurd. In granting Kant his supposition we also, *inter alia*, grant him his technical terms, and while there is a sense in which we must agree that there is "something whose *existence* has in itself **absolute value**", we would be wise to question the kind of capital that Kant makes of the terms which we have italicized. The notion of the absolute value of mere will, which haunts Chapter I of the *Groundwork*, and which reappears in the Second Chapter in the passages we have already examined, ¶¶1–6 may even, under cover of Kant's technical expressions, intrude itself into our present passage from pages 95: 55: A. 46.

There is not much point, however, in plotting this intrusion here; and we may with more profit direct our attention to the expression "existence". This expression, taken in an ordinary sense, does all the work we need: while taken in a technical Kantian one, it does more than anyone would need, and that by no means successfully.

Kant states his argument at length, taking up at once from the passage which we have just quoted:

> Now I say that man, and in general every rational being, **exists** as an end in himself, *not merely as a means* for arbitrary use by this or that will: he must in all his actions, whether they are directed to himself or to other rational beings, always be viewed *at the same time as an End*. All the objects of inclination have *only a conditioned value*; for if there were not these inclinations and the needs grounded on them, their object would be valueless. Inclinations themselves, as sources of needs, are so far from having an *absolute value* to make them desirable for their own sake that it must rather be the universal wish of every rational being to be wholly free from them.[1] Thus the value of all objects that *can be produced* by our action *is always conditioned*. Beings whose **existence** depends, not on our will, but on nature, have none the less, if they are non-rational beings, only a relative value as means and are consequently called *things*. Rational beings, on the other hand, are called *persons* because their nature already marks them out as Ends in themselves—that is, as something which ought not to be used merely as a means—and consequently imposes to that extent a limit on all arbitrary treatment of them (and is an object of reverence). (*G.*, pp. 95–6: 55: A. p. 46. Italics and bold mine.)

Kant is flirting, here, with an argument that he never, perhaps, quite embraces: the argument that being-of-conditioned-value is a consequence of needing-to-be-produced, or of being-able-to-be-produced-by-and-externally-to-a-will.

The suggestion that this is the drift of his argument is reinforced by related talk about *existence*, in the paragraph above the one quoted, and ten pages on by talk of "*a self existent end*". Needing-to-be-produced, and even being-able-to-be-produced, is, in an ordinary enough sense, being *conditional;* that is, it is being-conditional-upon-the-object's-conditions-of-being. But that this 'conditionality' has any immediate axiological implications is far from clear to anyone not enamoured of a Kantian

[1] See *C.Pr.R.* A. p. 215: *C.J.* §29, M. pp. 124–5: B. p. 113, and above p 283*n*.

metaphysic of morals. What is so significant about not-needing-to-be-produced?

Clearly, for the rationalist, not-needing-to-be-produced is, like being-ineluctably-produced, a way of escaping the sublunary condition: and such an escape constitutes, obscurely, a kind of value.

The trouble is, as Kant himself realizes, that there are a number of things not-needing-to-be-produced which are of no very high value. "Beings whose **existence** depends, not on our will, but on nature, have none the less, if they are non-rational beings, only a *relative value* as means and are consequently called '*things*'." Kant has recalled, suddenly, that lots of things other than men are self-existent, i.e. exist independently of our individual and contingent wills; and self-existence, not-needing-to-be-produced-because-already-existing, ceases to be, as it bid fair to become, a ground of absolute value and Endship.

The argument never quite gets going, but the technical language does: and all that is saved from Kant's second thoughts is an aesthetic notion, one which gets self-existence and ineluctability into the curious relationship which they have in the paragraph on p. 105: p. 67: A. p. 56 of the *Groundwork*, ten pages on from the paragraph we are presently analysing.

Though it never gets going, one can see how the argument would run. And it is an argument that is at once, less than one would need since it clearly will not work, and more than one would need since it embarrasses with a metaphysic the evident truth that persons are Ends, that persons are those-against-whom-one-must-not-act. Any metaphysic *might* be an embarrassment: one which collapses cannot fail to be exquisitely embarrassing.

Kant hastily reforms his forces and goes on, dropping the idea of self-existence and settling for an evident truth:

> Rational beings, on the other hand, are called *Persons because their nature already marks them out as Ends-in-themselves*—that is, as something which *ought not to be used merely as a means*—and consequently imposes to that extent a limit on all arbitrary treatment of them (and is an object of reverence). [Abbott, an object of respect.] (*G.*, p. 96: p. 55: A. p. 46.)

Self-existence in a plain sense, and self-existence in the less plain sense with which it gets mixed up, drops out of sight. The "self-existence" of ineluctable worth makes its exit, unobtrusively, from the argument, and the "nature" of persons, presumably rationality as such, becomes the ground of the value of Ends. Persons are persons, and valuable, reverenceable, because they are rational: and they are Ends, because they can rationally set themselves ends. We may usefully forget, at this point, that for Kant reason's *end* is good will 2, and simply concentrate on rationality-in-itself as a ground for the acknowledged absolute value of the person.

Will this do? Talk about the "nature" of persons is clearly preferable to the other stories; it is better than the half-formed argument about self-existence, and it is immensely better than the metaphysical tale about the rational agent's possible possession of the absolute worth of mere will. But is it enough?

CHAPTER II

RATIONALITY AS VALUE: TOWARDS A HUMANISTIC ONTOLOGY

> It was the slavery of the primitive Hebrew nations, allowed by Scripture and practised by the patriarchs, but which refinement and Christianity, the well-being of society, and the respect which man owes his fellow, alike forbid.
>
> W. R. Wilde on the Slave Market, Cairo. *Narrative of a Voyage to Madeira, Teneriffe, and Along the Shores of the Mediterranean*

A. RATIONALITY AS VALUE

Kant writes, in the second Chapter of the *Groundwork*:

> If then there is to be a supreme practical principle and—so far as the human will is concerned—a Categorical Imperative it must be such that from the idea of something which is necessarily an **end** for every one because it is an *end in itself*[1] it forms an *objective* principle of the will and consequently can serve as a practical law. The ground of this principle is: *Rational nature exists as an End in itself.* This is the way in which a man necessarily conceives his own existence: it is therefore so far a *subjective* principle of human actions. But it is also the way in which every other rational being conceives his existence on the same rational ground which is valid also for me; hence it is at the same time an *objective* principle, from which, as a supreme practical ground, it must be possible to derive all laws for the will. The practical imperative will therefore be as follows: Act in such a way that you always treat humanity, whether in your own person or in the person of any other, never simply as a means, but always at the same time as an End. We will now consider

[1] This particular occurrence of the expression "an end in itself" uses "end" in the pregnant, aesthetic, **end** sense. That is, there is an ambiguity, a pun, on "end" and on "End" which serves, usefully here, to establish Ends as the end of every will. This is not, of course, to say that Kant produces an argument: but at least, here, his curious "end" talk brings out the truth. It usually manages to obscure it.

whether this can be carried out in practice. (*G.*, p. 96: p. 56: A. pp. 46–7. Italics and bold mine.)

Here, rather than in any universalizability conceived of in terms of contradiction avoided, is the formal principle, the formal-practical-principle, of action. Any maxim whatever must at least avoid being such that it is incompatible with the proto-obligation "*always* [*to*] *treat humanity . . . never simply as a means but always at the same time as an End*". We must allow Ends and the ends of Ends to burden our own subjectivity, because "the way in which a man necessarily conceives his own existence" is as an End, having his own ends. So, he must conceive the existences of others in a similar way; and his conception must be practical, not merely theoretical or imaginative. Here we have an account of morality which has the authentic feel, and the bite of reality.

In this new second chapter context, Kant re-works his promise example, the example which in its first chapter form stands at the root of a great deal of contentious talk about universalizability as the mark or as the essence of moral maxims. What Kant says, here, in Chapter II tends to bring out the important point that what is wicked in false-promising is the "intending to make use of another man *merely as a means to an end which he does not share*", (*Groundwork*, p. 97) [Abbott: ". . . he would be using another man *merely as a mean* [sic], without the latter containing at the same time the end in himself", p. 57: A. pp. 47–8].[1]

Universalizability conceived after the model of Chapter I of the *Groundwork* is indeed the mark rather than the essence of moral maxims. The trouble about universalizability *qua* universalizability is that it does not distinguish moral from non-moral contexts. That I can universalize "Let one help the poor and

[1] Abbott is giving a very literal construe of the German: ". . . *dass er sich eines andern Menschen bloss als Mittels bedienen will, ohne dass dieser zugleich den Zweck in sich enthalte.*" *C.* p. 288. The last five words of the German happen to have, it should be noticed, a nice existentialist tone, see below A. 5, pp. 331–32 and p. 333.

In the *C.Pr. R.* Kant insists that not even God can use a rational being 'merely as a means': A. p. 229. This principle would provide the basis for a profound critique of traditional theology, and of its Kierkegaardian restatements.

needy" marks it as a right maxim; but the moral content is not distinguished, as moral content, by the mere universalizability of a maxim. I can equally "universalize" "Let things like *x* be called stones", and indeed must do so, since to specify *x*'s qualities and structures, and to use a generic term of this *x* is to commit myself to 'universalizing' the verbal activity: that is, it is to commit myself to calling all *x*-similars "stones" too. All that this example shows, of course, is that things other than maxims with moral content can be universalized. Even when I do use the universalizability test in a moral context, what is at issue is (i) the morally relevant aspects of the situation which universalizably turns up ("utility"), and (ii) the principle of equity. Morals are never concerned with universalizability itself: they are concerned with what is moral and what is immoral. A banal remark, but true.

Certain contemporary moral philosophers seem to overlook the fact that even if all lawful maxims of action are universalizable, it does not follow that all universalizable things are *eo ipso* maxims of moral action. It is true that no non-universalizable maxims of action are moral, i.e. no such maxims are compatible with the obligation to treat persons as Ends. It is not true that all universalizable 'maxims' are moral in intension: not all such have morally relevant matter.

Nothing that bears on Ends can fail to be concerned with morals: and, if this is a tautology, it is so only because it states a rule. And the rule which it states is inescapable, and one not liable to revision.

Kant was not as much preoccupied as are some contemporary philosophers with pure possible-universalizability: what he was concerned with was our avoiding action on maxims that are *not* universalizable. And he had two stories, often run together, but notionally separate at least, about non-universalizability: one was the story about the systematic contradiction that issued from the wishing (or willing and following) of a bad maxim—and the Chapter I version of the promise example is the classic case in point; the other was the story which we get in Chapter II. This is the Chapter II account:

> ... so far as necessary or strict duty to others is concerned, the man who has a mind to make a false promise to others

will see at once that he is intending to make use of another man *merely as a means to an end he does not share*. For the man whom I seek to use for my own purposes by such a promise *cannot possibly agree with my way of behaving to him, and so cannot himself share the end of the action*. This incompatibility with the principle of duty to others leaps to the eye more obviously when we bring in examples of attempts on the freedom and property of others. For then it is manifest that *a violator of the rights of man intends to use the person of others merely as a means* without taking into consideration that, as rational beings, they ought always at the same time to be rated as Ends—that is, only *as beings who must themselves be able to share in the end of the very same action*. (*G*., p. 97: p. 57: A. pp. 47–8. Italics mine.)

Now the real principle of morality emerges: an act is immoral if it is anti-personal: "the man whom I seek to use for my own purpose . . . cannot possibly agree with my way of behaving to him . . .". Equity forbids that I do to NM what imagination or the 'utility reflection' shows me to be something to which NM would not agree: no end may be sought by any agent which is not *allgemeinzweckmässig*.[1] And an end that cannot be 'shared' or agreed to by another, must be forgone, if it would bear on him. Likewise, as a moral rule, *all such* acts must be left undone: I do not need to be able to name a specific Other who sets up an *Achtung!*: Others-in-general will do. Morality can become anonymous while remaining personalistic.

Kant wants, to put it a little misleadingly perhaps, to have,

[1] The collectivity in question in the case of things that are *allgemeinzweckmässig* need not, of course, be the whole public, or the collectivity of all rational Ends: it is and need be only parties to the situation.

Even so, the ends of a collectivity *de facto* small must not be other than the ends of the collectivity which is *de jure* the whole of the Kingdom of Ends. Even when the whole Kingdom is not actually involved, the righteous will must will as if it were.

One can of course construct the usual curious cases: "Can it be morally correct for me to stand in the bus shelter if it would be dangerous or impossible for *all* the citizens of the town to do so *at once*?" Such cases, however, seem to be concocted only when one is being deliberately naive and fundamentalist about the sense of "universalizability". What one needs, here, is not an anguished analysis of "universalizable" but a consideration of the concept of, and the logistics of, bus shelters.

at once the benefits both of rule and of act utilitarianism. I must avoid *any act* which would involve "The use of the person of others simply as means", and I must avoid *all acts* of that same class.

As we have said above (Part II, Chapter III, Section B.1), what 'universalizability' tests is the quality of the action: "Is my proposed action *such that any person could agree to it* as done to him?" And what the universalizability test forbids, seen as a categorical command, is *my* doing what *he* could not agree to: or *my* doing what *one* could not agree to. Equity rules that *I* and *he* shall, to borrow a phrase, "each count for one and no more than one". Utility and disutility mark out how the One, with a vote equal to mine, who is to be the patient of the act, will judge of that act as sufferable or insufferable. What is "categorical" or "necessary" is my strict obligation to abide by the rule, 'You shall not *do* what you would find intolerable done' where this rule puts the agent into the shoes of the patient of his own act. 'I' become 'One': morality is *im*-personal in that it respects no person no more than any other: agent and patient are equal. Morality is personalistic in that it respects persons.

The crux of morality lies in the reference of maxims to states of affairs where these states of affairs are seen as affecting persons in terms both (*a*) of utility (is the act approvable, sufferable, insufferable to the patient?) and (*b*) of equity, where patient and agent, both as Ends, each limit the action of the other.

Kant's morals are, here, *au fond* political in the loose sense in which all morals are so: that is in the sense of politics which turns on 'living together' whether 'in cities' or not. Kant brings out the polity of morals and of politeness in paragraphs like this one: ". . . rational beings ought always . . . to be rated as Ends—that is, only as beings who must themselves be able to share in the end of the very same maxim". *Individual* ends must be adjusted to *universal* ends, and even if the *collectivity* involved be two persons and no more, the maxim must be *allgemeinzweckmässig*.

Some things can be "universally" agreed to: some cannot. And it is because the status of potential-dissidents-as-Ends sets up the absolute *Achtung!* that the disagreeable is apt to become the immoral. And it is because the Sovereign Ends will agree to the agreeable that the agreeable, i.e. the non-disagreeable, is morally permissible. Each End says "*placet*", considering himself, of course, as he says it, in terms of his own End-ship, and not merely as an object. Ends say "*placet*" only to things which it is proper for Ends to suffer and to do.[1] Each End is 'part of the sovereign' of a Kingdom of Ends.

1. *Rational Nature and Good Will*

What characterizes rational nature, apart that is from this proto-moral quality which it has of being-an-End? And, if

[1] As Ross puts it ". . . in all our action we must treat neither ourselves nor others as mere possible enjoyers of pleasure . . ."; op. cit., p. 52. From this we may conclude that an orgy would not be a "universal end" in Kant's sense, however agreeable to it the participants might be. What an End *may in fact agree to* and what he *can morally agree to* may be different. [See Boswell's reflections on "The dignity of human nature" and the consequences of these: e.g. *Boswell in Holland*, ed. Frederick Pottle, London (Heinemann), 1950/1952, pp. *119*, 35, 59, 207.] The dignity of Ends binds Ends in their possible agreement to a piece of conduct: and the actually-willing-will in any particular case of the application of the universalizability test *may* be erroneous. Even when people, slaves included, accepted slavery, it was, presumably, still inconsistent with the respect due to Ends, but nobody realized this. Kant's touchstone for maxims cannot work *any better* than the moral consciousness of an epoch or a particular agent will let it work. Morally insensitive persons can be subjected to pressures. So, of course, can epochs and cultures: as witness the great, and successful, efforts of the seventh Earl of Shaftesbury. A way of bringing pressure to bear is to insist that all maxims be universalized: but there is nothing infallible even about the categorical imperative test.

One can see how a logico-rationalist could be driven to talk of 'real wills' and 'merely phenomenal wills', just as Rousseau was driven to the postulation of an actual will in every citizen which willed what the General Will willed, even if this actual will did not know *what* it was that it willed. What one may happen to will when one tries to will universally, and what one might more properly Will (and 'ought to' will), can differ: and this is a very unfortunate fact indeed.

In the 1970s we tend to talk of men willing in accord with the images that they have of themselves. Different images will produce what are, in effect, different wills, even, alas, when the categorical imperative itself is being invoked. Kant's formulation in terms of a law of nature is useful here, since nature is supposed to be the norm: reality, and the reality principle face and out-face images.

anything else should qualify rational nature, besides this being-an-End, what is, or would, be the relationship of this something else to the proto-moral quality?

The answer to the first of these questions is obvious to any reader of Kant: rational nature is characterized by good will. That is to say, it is characteristic of rational nature, of persons, that they have good will in the first of the senses suggested in the *Groundwork*. Persons have in them that which enables them to manage their own gifts of character and of fortune, and to adjust the maxims of their individual actions to universal ends.

This, surely, is the ground, or at least one of the grounds, for treating them as Ends, namely that they can treat others as Ends. So "good will" is the ground of personal value?

"Good will" in the sense of good will 1 is the, or one of the, grounds of personal value; and if this were *all* that Kant were saying, then one would have no quarrel with him. But there is, as has been argued at length in Part I of the essay, all the difference between good will 1 and good will 2. Furthermore, as we have argued in the present Part, it seems to be good will 2 that is selected by Kant as the basis of personal value.

"'Good will' is the basis of personal value" is true or false, depending on what you mean by "good will". Kant, for rationalistic reasons, seems to mean by "good will" good will 2 rather than good will 1, and his is the alternative which makes the whole slogan false.

But what of the alternative that makes the slogan true? Has one given the whole ground of personal value when one has derived the value of person N from his ability in principle to treat person M as an equal value or sovereign End? Is the power to act in accord with good will 1 and good will 3 the root of one's absolute value an as End? This is a complex question: and in a historical sense it requires the answer "No". In another, philosophical, sense, it may require "Yes".

Historically, personal value is something in which we have come to believe. Even so, it was and a-temporally is, always, something worthy of belief.

There are, or for some people were, theological reasons for valuing rational nature. Rational nature depended upon the possession of a soul, the soul is immortal, and it has been redeemed by the Son of God Himself. All men in a general sense, and all Christians in a specific and particular sense, are then sons of God, and as "co-heirs with Christ", equal in value each to each: "There shall be no slave, no bond man. . . ." For Christians these theological considerations still hold, in some form or other; and if they do, then personal value can be seen to be grounded on something else. Not on something metaphysical in the rationalist sense, but on something metaphysical only in the positivists' sense.

It is pointless, in the end, to ascribe a mere metaphysic of value to the Christian: his view is, for better or worse, more than metaphysical. That is, it is more than the result of a systematic intellectual construction, and it puts its cash value in alleged theological-transcendental facts. That these facts are not verifiable here below is an unfortunate characteristic of them: but the Christian can always trump the positivist in the way in which a rationalist cannot, by being himself an eschatological positivist: "You must wait and see."

It is important, however, to see how personal value is grounded, for the Christian on the Christian's sonship of God. We are not valuable, simply, as Coleridge seems in effect to be saying in the passage which we cite at the end of Part I, because we are immortal and have eternal destinies. Such a destiny is valuable *to* the person, but it does not follow that it is the ground of the value *of* the person.[1]

We are valuable in a theological sense, even, not because we are being saved for such eternal destinies: we must be valuable because God thought it worth sending his Son to save *us*.

Our value, in the eyes of God, is witnessed not so much by what we are saved for, as by our being redeemed, simply. God so valued us as Ends that he sent his Son to save these Ends from frustration in their eternal ends. And though it is our eternal end that we have been saved for, it is, one must stress, *we* and not the ends that have been redeemed. Value, even for God, lies first in the person, and then in the person's ends.

Traditional theology, especially in its popular forms, has not been very clear on this: and it is a matter for regret that it should have been so. The Christian notion of personal value

[1] See *C.Pr.R.* A. pp. 260 ff., and compare with Coleridge, above, Appendix to Part I, pp. 159 ff.

needs to be saved from certain damaging vulgarizations: but this would be the matter for another essay: we cannot pursue the subject any further here.

Vulgarized or not, it is the Christian notion of the person which stands, historically, behind the purely humanistic one.

For a large number of people the Christian account of human value will not do at all, in either its vulgar or its non-vulgar form, and the particular transcendent support which Christianity may offer to the notion of personal value will be less than useless. How can personal value be grounded, for non-believers?

One is inclined to say that it cannot be grounded, but that, nonetheless, or even for that reason, it must be accepted in itself. If nothing else is offered as a premise for the notion that persons are Ends, then that notion must be accepted as evident. And it must be accepted as categorical: that is, as formal and as regulative with regard to conduct.

In effect, the notion of personal value itself becomes the object of a simple but absolutely necessary belief or commitment;[1] its being a condition of all humane conduct is seen to be its only "support". To see that there are Ends, and that all rational beings (*a*) are Ends, (*b*) can see that others are Ends too, is to see the first principles of morality as such.

Now this may very well be enough: yet even as we agree that it may be enough, we may be hankering after a 'transcendental deduction' of personal value.

2. *Rational Nature: What Is It?*

Clearly, we act in the ordinary way as though N's being of a rational nature were in itself enough to set up a moral claim on N's behalf and a moral liability on all his neighbours. All humans are the objects of moral regard as human, whether they themselves are capable, or for some occasional reason are incapable, of moral action. And from the majority of human

[1] Such a commitment would be rather different in intension from Kant's "faith of pure practical reason" *C.Pr.R.* A. p. 244: but it might be as much a 'faith'. It would be less transcendent than the Christian's since its object would not be other-worldly, and less transcendental than Kant's, since its object would be absolutely non-noumenal.

beings, that is from all who are not incapacitated by age or mental infirmity, moral action is expected, where "expected" means "required".

Readers of science fiction, an unjustly neglected source of *gedanken experimenten*, are familiar with the problem of aliens as it presents itself in the *genre*: are the things from outer space persons? That is, must they be treated, and can they treat, morally?

There are good S–F stories dealing with this problem and bad ones. But the form of the solution of the problem turns out to be the same, virtually, in all of them: if communication can be established between us and them, then they are like us, and like us in the moral sense, and are Ends.

The contents of the first communications tend, in S–F stories, to be simple mathematical or geometrical formulae: and perhaps the content of a communication might have some bearing on the rational nature of the being communicating. But having something to communicate, and being able to do so by means of a set of symbols, a code of sounds or of gestures seems, in fiction at least to be, and might yet just in fact be, the earnest of "rational nature". And rational nature is *moral nature*, for both Kantians and for S–F writers.

Inter-galactic utilitarianism would present problems not faced, or not faced by any means as acutely, by terrestrial utilitarianism. We all agree that boiling in oil is insufferable, and is therefore immoral. Venusians might agree to boiling in oil, for Venusians, but agree that it was insufferable for humans. An ice-cream sundae might be poison to a Martian but a treat for a young human. Utility would have to be re-worked, but not End-ship. Equity would hold, though what would be considered as satisfactory as content for right acts would need to be discussed in terms of the nature and structure of the beings concerned.

Any creature which can see himself and another equally as an End, and can fill in the cash value of treatment-for-Ends in both cases, is in a moral relationship with other Ends *eo ipso*. Now in all the stories, and in at least one odd live case, the test for End-being and End-recognizing is less than the actual present performance of both of these.

Since then, an Entity might be-an-End to itself, and recognize-that-Another-is an End, while not quite knowing what to *do* about the Other, we settle, in fiction, and sometimes in fact, for the prior condition of End-recognition, and do not wait for actual examples of End-recognition itself. That is, we settle for the rule, "If it can talk or communicate, then it is an End".

The Russians, who as dialectical materialists reject all theological or God-related transcendent grounding for personal value[1] have found themselves in a curious position with regard to dolphins. Since there is some evidence that dolphins may communicate with each other, and might therefore just possibly communicate with us some day, it seems that they are, or may be, persons. And the following news item is not without philosophical, and moral, interest:

> The Soviet Union has banned the catching and killing of dolphins—because their brains are strikingly close to those of humans.
>
> Fisheries Minister Alexander Ishkov said the decision was taken after extensive research showed the dolphin's brain made it a marine brother of man.
>
> He accepted theories that dolphins could talk and might eventually be able to teach their languages to man.
>
> "We hope other countries will follow our example," Mr Ishkov said. "Dolphins are selfless and brave, and have been known to save drowning people or play with children."[2]

If one wants to object to calling a dolphin "brother", "comrade" or "citizen" at some future date, or if one baulks at recognizing this mammal's altruism now, then it will have to be shown that the usual test for rational nature, or person-hood, is mistaken and can be annulled: or it will have to be shown that it has been somehow misapplied by the Russians in the case of dolphins. Or, one can regard the Russian case as speculatively interesting, but as not yet proven. Life is coming rather closer to science fiction than we may like: but the point of the example remains, one which must be taken.

It may be a matter of empirical fact that the evidence for

[1] They would, too, have to reject all theological limitations to value. If NM is *not* the child of God, because there is no God, then he must still be treated as a person. 'If there is no God, all is *not* permitted.'

[2] *The West Australian*, Monday, March 14, 1966.

dolphin rationality has all been grossly over-interpreted, and it may be the case that dolphins are really quite unlike us. Yet, if the facts were to be as alleged by Comrade Ishkov, then his moral position would be consistent: consistent not only with dialectical materialism, but with certain rule-of-thumb tests which are applied often in fiction, and occasionally, if rather unexpectedly, in real life. We shall come to a real life case a little later on: it is at once curious and poignant and should be put at the end, where it can speak for itself.

From the point of view of ordinary life the criteria of Endship are hardly problematic—that they may be so in philosophy, or might become so in Soviet marine biology, is of less concern than one might think to everyday morality. Unless one is committed to accounting for actual and actually practised slavery in terms of there being "natural slaves", or unless one is involved in some rather nasty *apartheid* situation, one has no difficulty at all in recognizing the proper objects of one's moral concern. There is no master race: there is simply the race: and one has dealings with its members.

Loving them, tolerating them, meeting one's barest obligations to them, these things may present the most acute practical problems: but we have no difficulty in recognizing Ends.

3. *Kant's Rationalism, a threat to the worth of End-ship*

Kant is, surely, right when he says:

> *Now morality is the only condition under which a rational being can be an End in himself*; for only through this is it possible to be a law-making member in a Kingdom of Ends. *Therefore morality, and humanity so far as it is capable of morality, is the only thing which has dignity.* Skill and diligence in work have a market price: wit, lively imagination, and humour have a fancy price; **but** fidelity to promises and kindness based on principle (not on instinct) have an intrinsic worth. (*G.*, p. 102. 64: A. p. 53. Italics and bold mine).

Or, he is right up until the **"but"** which opens his final clause. After that, Kant is less conscious than he might be that his "intrinsic worth" here is a kind of metonomy. He goes on to shift the locus of value, not very subtly, but quite inexorably, *from* the rational being as End (to whom morality itself is a kind of public utility as a condition of the practical working out of his End-ship), *on to* attitudes of mind, and on to the usual immanences:

> In default of [fidelity and kindness] nature and art alike contain nothing to put in their place; *for their worth consists, not in the effects which result from them*, not in the advantage or profit they produce, *but in the attitudes of mind*—that is, *in the maxims of the will*—which are ready in this way to manifest themselves in action *even if they are not favoured by success*. (*G.*, p. 102: p. 64: A. p. 53. Italics mine.)

Smoothly, and predictably enough, an empty 'intrinsic' good usurps the place of a real one: immanent, "absolute" worth ousts the very worth of Ends from morality itself. Morality, of which fidelity and kindness are parts, has, one may concede, its own worth and end in being the practical condition of the recognition of the Endship of Ends. But it follows from this that the worth of fidelity and of kindness *does* indeed "consist in the effects which result from them": or it consists at least in the results that *may reasonably be expected to result* from them. Kant, having in principle acknowledged this, yet goes back, in the last line of the passage which we have cited, to harp again on the immanent-if-fruitless worth of mental attitudes (which mental attitudes, as before, he conflates with maxims): the locus of value lies " . . in the attitudes of mind, that is in the maxims of the will".[1] Succeed or fail, the will has the absolute, the final worth. Such a doctrine is altogether false.

If morality is the condition of a Kingdom of Ends, then even morality itself may be held in this sense to have a conditional value: it serves Ends. And if, *per impossibile*, it could cease so to serve Ends, then morality would decay, like the constitution of a historical kingdom.

Morality which does not serve Ends is pointless; and though morality as such cannot lapse, and though morality in general is indestructible, we do indeed drop moral rules which seem to us no longer to serve their purpose.

[1] The phrase, "attitudes of mind, that is maxims of the will" makes synonymous expressions which refer to two quite different sorts of things: see Section 4 immediately below, and see above, Part II, Chapter III, Section C.1 ff.

The concept of moral revolution is never total: but it is never quite empty.

The value of Ends sets the point, the value, of morality itself.

Kant, however, moves from the absolute value of Ends, and the conditional value of morality, back to the fatal absoluteness of "attitudes of mind", that is "maxims of the will" which remain absolutely worthy "... even if they are not favoured by success". And the absoluteness of their worth is completely accounted for when one rehearses, again, the phrase "even if not favoured by success". Kant goes on:

> Such actions too need no recommendation from any subjective disposition or taste in order to meet with immediate favour and approval; they need no immediate propensity or feeling for themselves; **they exhibit the will which performs them as an object of immediate reverence;** nor is anything other than reason required to *impose* them upon the will, not to *coax* them from the will—which last would anyhow be a contradiction in the case of duties. This assessment reveals **as dignity the value of such a mental attitude** and puts it **infinitely above all price,** with which it cannot be brought into reckoning or comparison without, as it were, a profanation of its sanctity. (*G.*, pp. 102–3: p. 64: A. pp. 53–4. Italics and bold mine.)

The spotlight has swung quite away from personal value, from the value of Ends, and back to mental attitudes. Kant's attention moves away from the person back to the rationalist "absolute value of mere will".

We may simply protest that what Kant says here in this passage is not true.

We may, and do, justify any high opinion which we may have of "mental attitudes" by a humanist-utilitarian argument. We revere a righteous disposition because it is a disposition-to-do-right: and right is how Ends deserve to be done by. It is Ends, not "mental attitudes" which are "infinitely above price".

Of course we revere "fidelity to promises and kindness based on principle", and the reasons why we do are obvious enough: but our reverence for persons goes even deeper. I must 'revere' you as a moral agent, that is treat you as an End, without any present evidence of your kindness and fidelity: it is not your accomplished virtue, either overt or immanent in your faultless but fruitless rectitude, which, being reverenceable, extends its *mana* to you. It is your End-ship which limits my behaviour, simply as End-ship, quite apart from any actual moral qualities that you may display. It is you, not your "mental attitude", which commands my respect.

I must respect the person, not his moral qualities: respect is due to anyone who can be presumed capable of playing the moral game—that is to any rational creature. Respect is not something which we accord, simply, to fine moral performances or to good will 2 as "absolutely good": we 'respect' these too but in a less primitive sense: a much less primitive sense.

Moral capacity may be—indeed it is—a mark, and a ground of End-ship: moral accomplishment, the generation of the ineluctable goodness of good willing, is an admirable thing and it is "absolutely" valuable: but the "absoluteness" of its value is infinitely less than the *absoluteness* of the value of mere, moral capacity. In respecting you it may be, in part at least, moral capacity which I am respecting: after all, moral capacity makes up a great segment of "rational nature". But it is certainly not your "mental attitude" which binds my actions unconditionally. You, and not your inner rectitude, place me under moral restraints.

If "mental attitude" is indeed "infinitely above price" its value, even so, is derived from and depends ultimately on, the value of Ends: the primordial axiological value is the End, and not the *end*.

Rational nature is the axiological absolute, and the *absoluteness* of the value of "mere will" is an illusion if it blinds us to this central, moral fact: Ends matter before, and condition, *ends*. You cannot be high-minded and virtuous without something to be high-minded and virtuous about: and the only thing that is worth the moral effort, is persons.

4. *Mental Attitude or Moral Competence?*

It is not the person but "a mental attitude" which is for Kant "infinitely above all price". What does this mean?

The "mental attitude" which expresses itself in kindness and in fidelity to promises is beyond valuation and, as Kant writes:

> ... with [such a value as price] it cannot be brought into reckoning or comparison without, as it were, a profanation of its sanctity ... (*G.*, p. 103: 64: A. p. 54.)

It would be difficult to write an encomium, for mental attitude or for anything else, which was more lavish than this one of Kant's. But what precisely *is* "mental attitude" that it should be esteemed so highly: what is it indeed that has such "sanctity"? This question is crucial.

The expression "mental attitude" has for Kant the same ambiguity as has his "good will". The ambiguities are, furthermore, isomorphic. The phrase "mental attitude" can swing, without warning from a sense which makes "mental attitude" equivalent to good will 2, over to a sense which makes it equivalent to good will 1.

There is all the difference in the world between the two notions of "mental attitude", but Kant oscillates from one to the other, with nothing more to mark the change of sense than the ending of one paragraph and the beginning of another. Kant begins his new paragraph:

> What is it then that entitles a morally good attitude of mind—or virtue—to make claims so high? It is nothing less than the *share* which it affords to a rational being *in the making of universal law*, and which therefore fits him to be a member in a possible kingdom of Ends. (*G.*, p. 103: pp. 64–5: A. p. 54.)

The phrase "a morally good attitude of mind" is no longer, as it was in the previous paragraph, to be taken as a kind of synonym for "good will 2"; it is no longer, that is, equivalent to "attitudes of the mind" unconditionally good even "if they are not favoured by success". What Kant now seems to be saying is that the respect due to persons is due to them as morally competent and autonomous agents. The person is valuable as 'a member of the Sovereign' in a Kingdom of Ends. This is altogether a more convincing doctrine than the one which would have the person valuable because of the "absolute" worth of his will.[1] "Virtue" now means something like practical reason: it has ceased to be the mere precipitate of rectitude that may remain *after*, and be all that remains *of*, a right but fruitless act.

The new paragraph, expounding the new doctrine, continues:

> For this [membership of a Kingdom of Ends man] was already marked out in virtue of his own proper nature as an end in himself and consequently as *a maker of laws in the Kingdom of Ends*—as free in respect of all laws of nature, obeying only those laws which he makes himself and in virtue of which his maxims can have their part in the making of universal law (to which he at the same time subjects himself). For nothing can have a value other than that determined for it by the law. But the *law-making* which determines all value must for this reason have a *dignity*—that is, *an unconditioned and incomparable worth*—for the appreciation of which, as necessarily given by a rational being, the word '*reverence*' is the only expression. *Autonomy* is therefore the ground of the dignity of human nature and of every rational nature. (*G.*, p. 103: pp. 64–5: A. p. 54. Italics mine.)

The full sense of this passage can be taken only if we analyse "autonomy" at length, and such an analysis is beyond the scope of the present essay. Nevertheless, the outlines of the doctrine are clear enough. The "*unconditioned and incomparable worth*" of "*law-making*" is a very different thing indeed from the "absolute [and unconditioned] worth of mere will", as this worth is defined in the third paragraph of Kant's First Chapter.

The expression "a morally good attitude of mind" is, in Kant's second chapter, as systematically confused as are the expressions "inner worth" and "moral content" in the first.[2] The phrase "a morally good attitude of mind" swings violently between two meanings. Sometimes "*attitude* of mind" dominates, and we are in the presence of sound, inevitably-worthy-even-if-possibly-fruitless good will. Sometimes "attitude of

[1] Kant's talk of "my worth as an *intelligence*", *C.Pr.R.* A. p. 260, is happier than much of his doctrine in the *G.* But the official metaphysics of *C.Pr.R.* is as much a stumbling block as is the more occasional and domestic one of *G.*

[2] See above, Part II, Chapter III, Section C.1 (i) and (ii), pp. 253–65.

mind" dominates; and *mind* = *practical reason*. The worth of the person is now a matter of his moral competence, and not a matter of the "absolute worth of his *mere* will" where the "mere" is defined by the reflection that will may fail to effect even a right act, but still, itself, remain for ever righteous.

Indeed, the ambiguity of the expression "a morally good attitude of mind" as we find it in the passage under scrutiny, is simply a projection into the second part of the *Groundwork* of the initial ambiguity of "good will" which is set up in the first paragraphs of the book. From the very beginning of the *Groundwork* the notion of "good will" is fatally split: and Kant is consistent, meticulously if disastrously, in his mistakes.

Kant's use of the expressions "good will", "moral content" and "mental attitude" is so ambivalent that he can, in effect, offer us two doctrines at once, running them in tandem either side of the shaft. We are free to choose either doctrine; and it is by no means evident that we have any need of both.

Looking at what we have called the "second doctrine" of Chapter II of the *Groundwork*, the doctrine which places the value of man in good-will-as-moral-competence, we can see that it is extremely attractive. The "proper nature of man" is to-be-autonomous (in a number of senses of "autonomous"), and it is to-be-morally-competent. It is evident, if anything in morals can be evident, that *dignity* and *worth* lie in such a nature. Dignity lies in being able to entertain the concept of one's own dignity, and in being able to recognize the dignity of others: worth lies in being able 'to love one's own being'. The humanistic part of the law and of the prophets is "To love thy neighbour *as thyself*": my worth-to-me must be the model of my neighbour's worth to me.

Man transcends[1] nature: as Kant writes, he is "free in respect of all laws of nature", and he is, as far as we can tell, the only animal who regards himself as a self with self-determined ends. This is simple rational nature. And, man transcends himself

[1] The existentialists' senses of *transcendence* are, some of them, very much to the point here: any full examination of their relevance is beyond the scope of this essay, but see below, Section A.5.

again, in transcending his self-conscious subjectivity: this is rational nature as moral. M. Maritain writes:

> . . . The paradox of consciousness and personality is that each of us is situated precisely *at the centre* of [the] world. Each is at the centre of infinity. And this privileged subject, the thinking self, is to itself not object but subject; in the midst of all the subjects which it knows only as objects, it alone is subject as subject.[1]

Morality, the treatment of Ends or Others as Ends, is an overcoming of this epistemic isolation; it is a transcendence of the subjectivity of the subject, itself a transcendence of the world. The Christian obligation *to love our neighbour as ourselves* is no more than a restatement in a new context of the moral, humane, imperative, to treat the subjectivity of another not as one treats an object, but as one treats self, as one treats an "I".[2] What is 'known' as an object must be treated as a subject.

The "I" and the "Thou" are the proper actors in the moral sphere: and their essence, their worth and their dignity lie in their own power of transcendence and of double-transcendence. Man transcends nature: and his transcendent subjectivity can transcend itself.

At the very least, one can say of the doctrine that worth-is-autonomy-autonomy-is-worth, that it bears further exploration. It has dimensions both theological and existentialist which might well be developed by moral philosophers. The same cannot be said of the rationalist doctrine that virtue-is-worth where "virtue" has the sense, predominantly, of good will 2.

[1] Jacques Maritain, *Existence and the Existent*, New York (Doubleday, Image Books), 1957, pp. 75–6.

[2] The moral obligation may, one suggests, pre-exist the Christian obligation 'logically': in fact, it is the Christian notion which, historically, has given us the notion of the person and of respect. This will be acknowledged, one supposes, by most people, and even by non-Christian humanists.

A man may be able to obey the second of the two great commandments, without believing that obedience to the first is possible. The moral essence of man is defined by his possible relation to the second great commandment, at least as this commandment may be read in an a-theological sense. "Love thy neighbour" may command only respect, which is humanistic and moral: or it may command charity, which is a religious as well as a humane virtue.

We are not to be treated as objects, *because we are not objects*. If morality must have reasons, then this is a good reason for morality.

And morality must have reasons, if we are not to slip into Kant's error of supposing that "nothing can have a value other than that determined for it by the Law"[1] (*Groundwork*, p. 103: p. 65, A. p.54). That is to say, we must insist that the reason for the value of the person lies in something other than the *fiat* of the Law. The Law itself is valuable only, as even Kant himself sometimes seems to acknowledge, because it is the condition of the practical recognition of the Endship of Ends. The Law cannot give value: it can only order it, where "order" means "put in order" simply.

The material point on which we must stand firm in the face of Kant's rationalism is this: Endship is *given*, prior to the Law; it is given "by nature", that is, it is given by the nature of man, doubly transcendent.

That Endship should, by nature, involve the power to apprehend Endship in the Self and in Others is only fitting. The pattern is as neat as any rationalist one. Indeed it is neater: and it is, as far as one can see, the ultimate pattern in morals.

The ontology of personal value is, indeed, an ontology of autonomy, of transcendence and of transcendence-of-transcendence: it is not a mere ontology of the worth of righteous will. The ultimate value is not righteousness, nor even 'self-existence', conceived as self-subsistence or an ineluctable-immanence: the ultimate value is existence-as-a-Self. Perhaps it is this truth that Kant was grasping for in his obscure but oddly pregnant talk of self-subsistence?

Though his rationalistic Stoicism led him into the cul-de-sac of a sterile ontology of value Kant remains, essentially, open to a richer, more existentialist, and more humanist axiology. He

[1] Kant does not acknowledge this to be an error, but in *C.Pr.R.* he does allow it to be a "paradox", A. pp. 154–5. When Kant says, A. p. 155, ". . . it is the moral law that first determines the good" we may counter with, "And what would determine the practical effect of the law, viz, the universalizability or otherwise of maxims, if not good?" Such a reply can at least stalemate Kant. He would fight back, as *C.Pr.R.*, A. pp. 155–8 shows, because of his commitment to a doctrine of *a priori* and non empirical determination of the will. Such a doctrine is, of course, metaphysical, and not essentially moral at all.

began to map the two paths; but he chose the wrong one for himself.

5. *The Transcendental Deduction that We Might Have Had, and May Still Need*

What Kant might have done in the *Groundwork* is in principle the thing that some people believe him to have done in the great *Critiques*: namely, exhibit the *a priori* structure of experience.

He might have shown that reason, which is needful both for prudence and for morality, is thus necessary, and so Categorical, and capable of imposing categorical commands on us: he might have shown that reason and morality are "one".

Or: Kant might have shown that since men are Selves, exist-as-Selves, have-ends-and-are-Ends, so all conduct must structure itself to these facts.

Such a Transcendental Deduction,[1] or such Deductions, would have been immensely useful. But, in so far as he allowed his rationalistic absolute, the "absolute worth of mere will", to dominate his argument, Kant spoilt the argument and flawed his Deduction, if indeed the *Groundwork* is such a deduction.

The present essay's aim is to show how far Kant went down the wrong fork of the two paths that he sketched: and the conclusion of this essay is that we must begin again, though not without some immensely valuable suggestions from Kant, the task that he failed to bring to a satisfactory conclusion either in the *Groundwork* or in the *Critique of Practical Reason*.

The *Groundwork* itself may, as an attempt, exhibit "the absolute value of good will". But it does not succeed in its Deductive aim: and here we would have preferred success to mere virtue.

[1] In the text, above, the expression "transcendence" has already been used, with very minimal specifications of sense. Now "transcendental" is used, as in "Transcendental Deduction", and shortly, we shall quote a use of "transcendental" from Wittgenstein.

Clearly, we have here a set of notions which all come together under one expression, or under a set of near-synonyms and cognates: "transcendental" can become as confused and as confusing as Kant's "unconditioned". Exploring a tract of ideas, swiftly and speculatively, one sometimes has to walk into ambiguities with one's eyes open. The analytical machete must be wielded in another essay.

We may still need a Transcendental Deduction of personal value. Or: we may simply assert such a value.

How far is such assertion the substance of the matter that a Deduction would investigate? Clearly, a great deal that Kant wrote in the *Groundwork* and in the *Critique of Practical Reason* bears importantly on all this. But there may be a great deal that needs to be clarified further. Conceptual and phenomenological analyses have a wide scope here. And, as we have said, we may need them. The enigmatic remarks on ethics which Wittgenstein put at the end of the *Tractatus* highlight both the need, and, in some sense, the terms of the discussions that might meet it.

Wittgenstein's remark in the *Tractatus*, that:

> 6.41 The sense of the world must lie outside the world. In the world everything is as it is and happens as it does happen. *In* it there is no value—and if there were, it would be of no value . . .[1]

might be taken up by a Christian apologist; it plays into the hands of those who give life a transcendent, other-worldly, point or sense which, 'must lie outside the world'. And, indeed, when it is a question of the *sense* of the world, the Christian account supplies a sense which atheism simply has to do without. The choice may be: God, or the absurd.

However transcendental in this sense the "sense" of the world may be, we may, even so, reject Wittgenstein's consequential remarks about ethics:

> 6.42 . . . there can be no ethical propositions.
> 6.421 It is clear that ethics cannot be expressed.

and we may reject them simply by giving an existentialist reading to his other two aphorisms under 6.421:

> Ethics are transcendental.
> (Ethics and aesthetics are one.)

Ethics may be "transcendental", but not be so in the sense in which God is, or in the way in which the sense of the world is.

One is not sure that this is, by any means, Wittgenstein's

[1] *Tractatus* 6.41, Ogden's translation, London (Routledge), fifth impression: all the citations of Wittgenstein are from this edition.

point: but it is a point that can be made. The ego, consciousness, is transcendent, in that it lies on the limit of the world, on the edge of all *mere* "happening and being so",[1] and even if all human being is, as Heidegger insists, "being-in-the-world" and all consciousness is, as Sartre insists, "consciousness-of", it remains true that, as Sartre also says:

Consciousness knows itself only as absolute inwardness.[2] This inwardness is where the limit, and the transcendence, of the world both lie. And it is in inwardness that happiness is felt, and anguish, and irritation and loathing—and all the other feelings and emotions for which we have, or for which we lack, conventional names. It is in this inwardness, outside and transcending the very world of "care" which binds him, that the person, the End, exists as consciousness. In this 'inwardness' he formulates those ends and those intentions that the world, or others, may thwart: it is in this inwardness that he feels the success of his intentions carried out, or the pang of their frustration.

It is against certain intolerable and avoidable frustrations of his ends and intentions, manifestable in the world but felt by End NM in his inwardness, that the Moral Law should protect him: if the world which is "quite another",[3] is indifferent to him, other people can be kinder than the world: they are, after all, of his kind.

When one sets Sartre's "consciousness knows itself only as absolute inwardness" against the stated thesis of *The Transcendence of the Ego*, this produces a sense of paradox, if not the appearance of contradiction. Sartre writes at the beginning of the book:

> We should like to show here that the ego is neither formally nor materially *in* consciousness: it is outside, *in the world*. It is a being of the world, like the ego of another.[4]

Consciousness and the world confront one another as limits of, and paradigms of, what *is*. The ego is an ego because it is

[1] See *Tractatus* 6.41, §2.

[2] J. P. Sartre, *The Transcendence of the Ego*, trans. F. Williams and R. Kirkpatrick, New York (Noonday), 1957, p. 41.

[3] See *Tractatus* 6.43.

[4] *Sartre*, p. 31.

conscious; but where it *is*, where it *acts*, is in the world, and the world gets taken up into consciousness. The paradox solves itself, and being-in-the-world is seen to be a function of consciousness, even if consciousness transcends the world. On the 'inside' we are necessarily alone, and 'alone' now means something different from what it means in circumstances in which we could be 'not alone' too. Even so, though 'inside' we are alone, most of our living is done 'on the outside': it is on the inside that action is suffered as much as done. On the outside we encounter Others, and they us: they must be brought in, and they must bring us in, to consciousness.

An ethical or moral deduction of a more or less Kantian sort, a kind of "Transcendental Deduction", could be made simply by reversing the charge of Sartre's thesis. Just as the ego is in-the-world, like the ego of another, the Other must be treated with the consideration that he would be treated with, were he the ego of that privileged consciousness which stands at the centre of [one's own] experience.

If the ego, though a function of 'transcendent' consciousness, is, even so, in-the-world like any Other; yet, or for this reason, the Other must be 'brought into consciousness', as far as this is possible. Now it is not possible, as an actual 'bringing in': but this bringing in can be approximated in love; and its least mode is simple *respect* for others.

"Love thy neighbour as *thyself*!" can be given an existentialist and phenomenological expression: and so it should be given one. Morals are not a matter of keeping universal rules for the rules' sake; they are a making universal of the consideration which the ego-in-the-world feels to be its due 'on the inside', in consciousness.

What is 'on the inside' gives point to morality itself. The first aspect of Endship is not so much social, moral competence as rational, autonomous, sentience. This is the essence, it would seem, of self-hood: to be self-conscious, to feel and to will. And the rational self is the central value, the categorical condition of values. To feel and to know that you feel is to set the conditions of value itself.

A rational being is, for Kant, "a subject of ends" (see above, Part III, Chapter I, under ¶6, p. 303). A rational being is this, even before he participates in the policies of morality. A being who has the power to order the economy of his own affairs—and by extension any member of a species which has this power—is a Self and he determines value, in the sense of being an End-in-himself.[1]

The notion of the rational being as "a subject of ends" is important; and it is more important than Kant allows it to become in the second chapter of the *Groundwork*, where he lets himself get side-tracked from what one would like to think of as his chief purpose, a Deduction of personal value. Kant is side-tracked: by his rationalism in the first place; and in the second, if not by misanthropy, at least by a certain innate and immoderate prejudice against eudaemonics.

Happiness is given too small a part in Kant's general scheme, as we have already said. Happiness is central for moral theory since it is, as Kant himself acknowledges, the end which each subject of ends sees as pointful for himself; hence to underrate the end which existence itself sets Ends is, necessarily, to distort the picture of the human situation.

Nevertheless, though Kant is guilty of this kind of distortion, he sees in the subjectivity of the subject-of-ends, a ground of the subject's Endship. And perhaps Kant's new perspective on the existential situation, here, is useful.

The new, odd, perspective may be useful since it draws our attention away from the end of eudaimonia, and focuses it on the Subject of that end, the End. This Subject is, now, the point of that happiness which is, for him, the point of his being. Kant may be redressing the balance here, talking less about man's end than his predecessors did: and suggesting, if only obliquely, that we might consider man at least as much as we have been accustomed to considering his end.

[1] The "species of creatures . . . which though rational, were possessed of such inferior strength, both of body and mind that they . . . could never . . . make us feel the effects of their resentment", which Hume invents in the *Enquiry*, in order to illustrate the artificiality of justice, would have to be used with 'humanity', as he says. According to Kant, as Subjects-of-ends they would have clear moral claims upon us. The claims would be 'politically' sanctionless, but none the less moral. See: *Enquiry*, Section III, Part I, §152, Selby-Bigge edition, p. 190. Kant would, were he now alive, see as "sick" the magazine cartoon which shows Mickey Mouse, dead, in a common mousetrap.

Kant writes, *apropos* of the possibility of my getting out of an embarrassing situation by means of a false promise,

> The man whom I seek to use for my own purposes by such a promise cannot possibly agree with my way of behaving to him, and so cannot himself share the end of the action. (*G.*, p. 97, 57: A. p. 48. See above pp. 309 and 311.)

Here Kant puts precisely the wickedness of the wicked, the anti-personal act, I use a person for my ends, ignoring *his* ends. But each person, End or Subject has his own ends: the end of happiness which is *given*; and the ends which seem to him necessary to the attainment of this overriding purpose, eudaimonia. His eudaimonia, and his contingent ends, are for each self his concern: and he is right to be concerned with these things, and has *a* right to be concerned with these things. Who am I to force my ends on a person who can have his own ends? His self, to himself, is self-regarding, and self-directing. Who am I unreasonably to intrude on him?

Being the subject of ends is not simply being able to play the 'political' moral game. Subjectivity as a rational, internal economy is, in a real sense, prior even to morality; and good will 1 may itself be split, notionally at least, into two moieties. One clear purpose of practical reason is, as Kant himself seems to acknowledge in the first page of the *Groundwork*, to manage the goods of fortune and of character to the best advantage of the possessor of these goods. One end, that is to say, of practical reason, is the prudential management of the Subject's own affairs in the interest of his own happiness. The other purpose of it, of course, is to merge the economic and eudaemonic strategy of each action into the system of universal ends. Moral competence has two aspects answering very roughly to the ancient and the modern notions of the moral: it can look to the agent's eudaimonia; and it can look to the claims of others on his action.

To be the subject of ends is, essentially, to be able to make up one's own mind about one's own affairs: and the integrity of the management of one's own affairs is one of the things that the Kingdom of Ends is supposed to guarantee. This integrity is not only a condition of morality, it is also an end of it. The Self is an End-in-itSelf, and a Condition of ends.

Like a real kingdom or a real republic, the Kingdom of Ends must guarantee "life, liberty and pursuit of Happiness". Happiness is the end which the Subject of ends finds already set for him; but it is the rational autonomous self which, finding such an end 'set as a task', goes reasonably about the interesting business of fulfilling the task. And to-be-fulfilling this given *telos* is to be being-a-Self. *C'est vivre sa vie.*

It is autonomy, or the rational autonomous nature, however, rather than this nature's end, that Kant would have us respect, at least when this end is happiness. Coleridge seems, in his hurried note in the *Vermichte Schriften,* to have valued man only in the last resort because man has a valuable, and an eternally valuable, end. Kant makes no reference in the *Groundwork* at least to such an end; he values man as and because he is the *Subject of* ends, and of earthly ones at that.

The rationalism of the talk of the "absolute value of good will" obscures Kant's real point by providing a false-eternal *end,* which, though it replaces eudaimonia, at the same time displaces the End, leaving us worse off than before. Kant's real notion seems, when one reads him carefully, and with existentialist hindsight, to have been to fix the locus of value in the Subject or the End and not in the Subject's ends. Value lies in the Subject, not in the end, even though it is as being a subject of ends that this subject exhibits his true nature, and true value.

What we must respect is "good will" as rational Selfhood; we must treat all beings who are under the burden of rational consciousness and rational autonomy as we treat ourselves—or we ought so to do, and this is the first obligation of all. The object of respect is not, by any means, the accomplished "good will" of attempted virtue, the *end* good will 2: it is the mode-of-being in Another which precisely matches the mode which we enjoy, or possess without enjoying,[1] in ourselves; the mode of being-a-Subject-of-ends.

Behind the ultimately irrelevant and tedious rationalism of the *Groundwork* there is a valuable piece of conceptual analysis

[1] Thomistic and other Christian optimisms which make being *eo ipso* good, and theological arguments, against self-destruction when being seems not to be, any longer, good are subject nowadays, equally to an existentialist critique.

at least begun: Kant is attempting to refine, and to provide a humanistic and a-theological translation of, the commandment to "Love they neighbour as thyself". Out of a phenomenological and reflexive analysis of *thy-self*, comes, or might come, the Deduction of practical love, and of its being obligatory.

Each End who is an end to himself, must respect the Endship of the others whom he meets: he encounters them as objects but must realize them to himself as persons. The view of the Other as person must overrule the view of the other as object: I must 'do as *I* would be done by', because the one to whom *I* do is his "I", and is done *to*. The *I* would *do*, rather than be *done to*: or it would censor, first, what is done to it. This censorship and choice of "passion" is, to some degree yet to be specified, its moral right as an I. This basic right derives from the *mere* fact of what an *I* is: rational, self-aware, capable of joy, of resentment, and of all the rest of the emotions of a self-conscious being-in-the-world.

The *I* is aesthetic in Kant's sense before it is so in Baumgarten's;[1] and if "ethics and aesthetics are one", this is why they are. In its aesthetic capacity, its capacity to feel self-consciously, lies the first ground of the I's moral value. The second ground lies in its rational or practical transcendence of its own world-transcendence; this second ground lies in its having a specific concept of itSelf, and in its being able to act on this concept of Self, and on a practical concept of any Other as a self too.

And here we can see how our test for *prima facie* personhood, "Can the being communicate with us?" turns out to be—in part at least—a test for the full capacities of personhood.

It is certainly possible to construct a science-fiction story in which the beings from outer space are rational and can communicate with us, but still lack moral responsibility. But the possibility of writing this story must not obscure for us a very material connection which may hold between reason and

[1] See the footnote in *Critique of Pure Reason*, B.36, p. 66 of Kemp-Smith's translation. There is a possible Transcendental Aesthetic Deduction of the Tolerable and the Intolerable: the obligation to abstain from the second, and to advance the first, arises from the possession of reason and the 'aesthetic' faculty together.

practical reason, between intelligence and speech and morality and concern. Austin Farrer sketches this connection, brilliantly and sharply:

> Man, once endowed with speech, starts making an inventory of the universe. The speaker, having labelled everything else, labels himself, and becomes an item on his own list. He is now no more than a pebble on the beach, a part of the description he constructs; he falls under the net of an impartial rule, an equal justice binding on himself as much as on his neighbour. That justice is the child of speech, is evident; . . .[1]

To be rational and capable of speech is already to be capable of the distancing of oneself, of a self-transcendence which is both a condition of and part of the substance of, morality. It would be easy to describe the intelligent beings from outer space as having no moral concern for us: it would be difficult to describe them, consistently, as having none for anyone.

Ethics can be "transcendental", if not in Wittgenstein's sense, then in other senses, without going beyond the world to eternity and God.[2] The "transcendence" that lies within gives

[1] *Love Almighty and Ills Unlimited* by Austin Farrer, London, Collins [1962], Fontana, 1966, p. 109.

[2] Wittgenstein is correct when in his *Lecture on Ethics* [*Philosophical Review*, Vol. LXXIV, 1965, pp. 3–16] he treats "pain & rage" in his "world-book" as mere facts and not as "Ethics". That is, he is right to avoid Hume's simple-mindedness. But when he writes about the man who grows a lion's head ". . . if it were not for hurting him I would have him vivisected" (p. 10), he *evinces* the very Ethical, which he calls 'running against the walls of our cage', etc. That we can suffer and cause suffering, is a function of our first transcendence of the world, consciousness. That we can respond to this pair of possibilities by censoring action by the rules *Universalize!*, *Bring-into-consciousness!*, *Do as you would be done by!*, is the substance of our 'second transcendence'. Transcendence is a fact, i.e. is the case. But not everything that is the case is—merely—the world. Our transcendences are the *ratios*, the forms of our being-in-the-world. They obtain, as facts: but as ratios they are better than mere facts. Consciousness and moral capacity are more than *der Fall*: and respect is at once a possibility, and so a necessity, a fact and so a form, of man's life. Transcendence is not, as Wittgenstein has it, simply towards God: it is (1) away from the mere world, (ii) towards Others. I don't 'take my hat off' (loc. cit., p. 16) to the world: I do to other persons—and to humanity in its characteristic manifestations (including that of philosophizing).

a *ratio* to my needing to be treated in a way which I do not find intolerable: and the capacity so to treat others in a rational, reciprocal, manner is the *ratio* of morality.

The value which transcends the world may lie, as Kant seems to have thought, *within* us. But it does not lie in the will as "absolutely good". It lies in the man as man: and man-as-man has, in sharp contrast to the "absolute good of mere will", an indefinite and not a tight and precisely-circumscribed definition. We are always finding out about "man", about ourselves and others. And what man is transcends the world, and gives it value.

Man gives the world value not wilfully, but really. We make values by being-in-the-world: but we do not 'make values up'. There is all the difference in the world—and out of it—between these two things, 'making' and 'making up'.

The End, the conscious-ego, is a value because he is the categorical, the necessary, condition of all values: where things are valued is in consciousness, and consciousness is a value to itself. Even without God, man can be-to-himself and be-to-others self-like but unselfish: and so he can make values. If there is no God, then we are alone in the universe. But we are all alone, together.

In these facts about man—and not in the inevitable-value of his will willing in rectitude—lie the forms of all values. Values transcend 'facts', 'mere facts', "all happening and being so": values relate to man, essentially, for he alone transcends all happening and being so. Even if materialism of the crassest sort were true, we would still be, as being-to-ourselves, transcendent. We could still value: we could still be value-able.[1]

[1] The curious thing about materialism is that were it true we would not be, as Kant has us, "free in respect of all the laws of nature" (*G.* p. 103: 64–5: A. p. 54); but that it can be true seems ruled out by our taking freedom—already and before we are "scientifically" sure—as a category of experience. Materialism and the unfreedom of the will would, if they were to obtain, mean *so* much to us that we cannot begin to say what they *would* mean. When Dr Johnson said, "Sir, we *know* our will is free, and there's an end on't" [Boswell's *Life* 16 October 1769] he was being, perhaps, unphilosophical: but where he started from, so might a philosopher—on a Deduction. What makes one uneasy about Kant's noumenon-phenomenon talk is that it looks too much like double-talk, and talk bound to involve us in a double mystery: in (1) the appearance of determinism in the phenomena of inner sense, an appearance which, (*a*) does not appear, and

In Heidegger and the existentialists, we find something of the Transcendental Deduction of value that Kant might have given us in the *Groundwork*. "Existentialism is a humanism": or it is, at any rate, more like one than is Kantian rationalism.

The sense of the world lies rather in rational sensibility than in any rationalistic absolute; the rational, not the rationalistic, defines such absolutes as we may have without invoking the Deity.

The inexorable goodness of a will willing in righteousness overcomes the 'accidental' and all "happening and being so",[1] where this might stand for 'chance': but rational nature, the person, transcends it, where it stands for "the world".

6. *Rational Nature, Communication and Morality*

The communication test may be used to establish the presence of rational nature: rational nature given, then selfhood and moral competence are, and presumably must be, assumed. And, if Austin Farrer's sketch is accurate, rationality and moral competence and capacity for discourse are all aspects of a common ground.

If any being is rational, then it can regard itself and any other rational being as an End: and capacity for the moral game implies that this game is already being played. Admit capacity, or even the most minimal Self-hood, and commitment follows at once: there are no reserves on the moral team.

Rational nature then, is or comes to, "good will" in the senses 1 and 1.1 of good will, which we have examined in Part I, Chapter III, Sections C, 1–5, and in the proto-sense, where "good will" marks the possibility of an autonomous economy of Self. The worth of the person has nothing to do with the "inner worth" about which Kant is already so concerned on the first page of the *Groundwork*. And the value of character itself—of which he also talks on his first page—is relative simply to the actual disposition of any agent to use the practical

(*b*) could not as we 'now' conceive conceivably be coped with if it did: in (2) a freedom that is noumenal, in a noumenal realm of which we can *know* nothing. By lumping freedom in with God and immortality as unknowable, Kant seems to have made the worst of both his possible worlds [See *C.Pr.R.* A. pp. 232–3 and 241].

[1] *Tractatus*, 6.41, §2 and §3 q.v.

reason which he has in accordance with principles of universal adjustment. Character has use, that is, rather than value, when it is seen from the point of view of Ends.[1]

Nor is there any other point of view.

We can give a public or quasi-utilitarian account of the value of character: good men are to be relied on to do right acts, bad ones are only to be expected to do wrong ones. Character is the subject of judgments which are—apart from the allowance which we must make for false conscience[2] —essentially judgments of public utility.

What we value in a man is not, at the rock bottom of morality, his character, but what character is a disposition towards—that is, rational action, action governed by practical moral reason. Character bears on our moral responsibility towards the possessor of it only negatively: we do not have to treat as Ends only those of good character, but everyone. And bad character excuses us from treating the bearer of it as an End only when it is so bad that the bearer is to-be-outlawed. A thorough scoundrel may abrogate the moral 'contract' and turn every man against him; he may 'willingly run mad' and give up all rational obligation, and he must be treated severely, if only to protect the reasonable. Nevertheless, the ordinary sinner must, in humanistic as much as in religious contexts, be treated as an End, and as a monad of absolute value, weak though his *character* may be.

The judgment of character is 'politic' and utilitarian, and to that degree relative: the judgment of personal value as Endship is absolute. That is to say, we do not decide whether a

[1] Why my character as one made pleasing to God by my righteousness matters, even to me, is that I must take care of the End-who-is-me, and do as well by him as I can. If there is no God, then the Self-respect of my self must be served: I am obliged not to let myself be lost, and not to let myself become so that I hate myself.

The paradox of selfishness is that it can make the self intolerable to itself. In this lies the '*real*' contradiction of wickedness.

[2] We may admire, even reverence, the motives by which a man is prompted to act, though deplore the act. But such allowances for 'false conscience', 'conscientious wrong-headedness' and the rest are parasitic upon valuing actions done upon "truly" universalizable maxims.

person is to-be-valued, in terms of public policies. We may decide in terms of public policy how useful a man is, how edifying, how praiseworthy or how contemptible, but personal value as such is not judged on criteria of this sort. *It* is given, as value, with person-being.

The criteria for personal value are the same as the criteria for personality, in the sense of person-being or person-hood, and what we are looking for is not good will in any elevated sense, or any pietistic or metaphysical one. What we are looking for is selfhood and practical reason. It happens, as we have said some pages above, in fiction and sometimes if rather rarely in fact, that the specific and occasional test which we use for selfhood and for reason is the test of communication.

If a being can communicate, has things to say and can say them in a way analogous to the way in which those of us who are already in the moral game have things to say and say them, then he too must be included in this game, and he must be treated as an End: he shows an initial capacity for morality in being able to talk at all.

The following story is an account of something that happened about 130 years ago, some ten miles from the place where this essay is being written. Since the persons concerned were Christians—Christians of a sort, some of them—and since the author was a Quaker, the "Golden Rule" is cited explicitly. Had the historical circumstances been different, the story might have been cast in purely Kantian terms:

> At one time, it was intimated, in a Swan River paper, that the language of the Aborigines was a mere jargon! but an intelligent individual acquired so much knowledge of it, as to prove its power of communicating ideas. Hostile views against these people, at one period proceeded so far, as to meditate a war of extermination against them, but the same individual made so powerful an appeal against the injustice and iniquity of such a measure that the settlers, convened at Guildford, on the occasion, inquired what they should do in the case. To this, the friend of the Aborigines replied, "Do, my dear Sirs, what our Lord and Saviour Jesus Christ has commanded." And to the further question, "What is that?" he answered, "Whatsoever ye would that men should do to

> you, do ye even so to them". The conviction produced, was so strong, that the war of extermination was abandoned.[1]

The possession of reason, evinced in the possession of a language which has the "power of communicating ideas", implies the possession, as well, of practical reason: and this sets up moral obligations towards the possessors. Capacity for membership of a Kingdom of Ends makes anyone actually a member.

This is as little metaphysical as may be: but then, so, in the end, is morality itself.

B. CODA: THE PERSON AS A LIMIT

The notions of an End and of *the person as a limit* have an interesting analogue in an observation which Havelock Ellis makes, in the course of an extremely speculative analysis of the nature of religion and of art. It would seem that even an aesthetic, symbolical, or poetic-cum-mystical appropriation of the world, the sort of thing that may occur when we are alone in a landscape and full 'on the inside', of the appropriate feelings, can be *limited* by the presence of another person. Havelock Ellis writes:

> Perhaps no modern man has better expressed the religious aspects of nature than Thoreau. Of the American wood-thrush Thoreau can rarely speak without using the language of religion. 'All that was ripest and fairest in the wilderness and the wild man is preserved and transmitted to us in the strain of the wood-thrush . . . Whenever a man hears it, he is young, and Nature is in her spring. Wherever he hears it, there is a new world and a free country, and the gates of heaven are not shut against him. Most other birds sing, from the level of my ordinary cheerful hours, a carol, but this bird never fails to speak to me out of an ether purer than that I breathe of immortal vigour and beauty.' Generally, however, this emotion appears to be associated, not so much with isolated beautiful objects, as with great vistas in which beauty may scarcely inhere—

[1] James Backhouse, *A Narrative of a visit to the Australian Colonies*, London (Hamilton, Adams & Co.), 1843, p. 547.

> 'all waste
> And solitary places; where we taste
> The pleasure of believing what we see
> Is boundless, as we wish our souls to be.'
>
> It is indeed myself that I unconsciously project into the large and silent world around me; the exhilaration I feel is a glad sense of the vast new bounds of my nature. *That is why, at the appearance of another human being, I sink back immediately into the limits of my own normal individuality. I am no longer conterminous with the world around me; I cannot absorb or control another individuality like my own. I become a self-conscious human being in the presence of another self-conscious human being.*[1]

If what Ellis maintains is indeed the case, phenomenologically, then the fact may have some significance for the existentialist notions of the person and of the value of the person, and for that matter, for the most ordinary view of morality. Any other person is for me a limit, and a *limit* even to my merely imaginative or empathetic possession of the world. He prevents me both from un-selving myself, and from occupying the whole landscape. This double effect is of the first importance for morality: a single man might 'be the world': two men establish each for the other a limit, and each for the other, establishes a positive Selfhood.

[1] Havelock Ellis, *The New Spirit*, London (Walter Scott), 1892, Third edition: "Conclusion", pp. 242–4 (Italics mine).

INDEX

Date Due